EEC Anti-Trust Law
Principles and Practice

EEC Anti-Trust Law

Principles and Practice

by

D. BAROUNOS

Solicitor

D. F. HALL

Solicitor

J. RAYNER JAMES

Barrister

LONDON
BUTTERWORTHS
1975

ENGLAND: BUTTERWORTH & CO. (PUBLISHERS) LTD.
LONDON: 88 Kingsway, WC2B 6AB

AUSTRALIA: BUTTERWORTHS PTY. LTD.
SYDNEY: 586 Pacific Highway, Chatswood, NSW 2067
MELBOURNE: 343 Little Collins Street, 3000
BRISBANE: 240 Queen Street, 4000

CANADA: BUTTERWORTH & CO. (CANADA) LTD.
TORONTO: 2265 Midland Avenue, Scarborough, M1P 4S1

NEW ZEALAND: BUTTERWORTHS OF NEW ZEALAND LTD.
WELLINGTON: 26/28 Waring Taylor Street, 1

SOUTH AFRICA: BUTTERWORTH & CO. (SOUTH AFRICA) (PTY.)
LTD.
DURBAN: 152/154 Gale Street

©

BUTTERWORTH & CO. (PUBLISHERS) LTD.
1975

ISBN: 0 406 11440 4

Preface

Chapter 1 of Title I in Part III of the Treaty of Rome entitled "Rules on Competition" is divided into three sections of which the first deals with the "Rules applying to undertakings". It is this limited, but very important, aspect of the EEC competition rules with which this book is concerned; no attempt is made in these pages to deal with those of the rules on competition which are to be observed at the level of the member states.

The term "anti-trust", as referring to a body of principles, legislation, case law and practice concerned with the control of restraints on competition and of monopoly, has, we think, received sufficiently wide acceptance in this country to justify its use as a convenient abbreviation to identify our subject, without at the same time defining it too restrictively having regard to the need to discuss certain subjects peripheral to the main theme.

The anti-trust law of the EEC, as is generally now well-known, is grounded in arts. 85 and 86 of the Treaty of Rome prohibiting (subject to the possibility of exemptions) restrictive agreements between, and the abuse of a dominant position by, undertakings where trade between member states may be affected. These and other related articles contained in Section 1 referred to above are commented on extensively in the pages that follow. In addition we have felt justified in including in this book, under the general umbrella of anti-trust, discussion of other aspects of the defence of competition by the European Commission, either under other provisions of the Treaty, e.g., under art. 36 to prevent the unilateral exercise (in the absence of agreement or market dominance) of industrial property rights to isolate national markets (which in turn raises the problem of the proposed Convention for a Community patent); or by extension of the Commission's powers, e.g., under the Regulation for the control of mergers proposed by the Commission in view of the limited effect of the principle established by the *Continental Can* Case whereby certain mergers are brought within the scope of art. 86, but only when instigated by a dominant undertaking.

We have sought to identify the principles or policy involved in the development and application of EEC anti-trust law, wherever possible, by reference to the actual decisions of the European Commission and the judgments of the European Court of Justice, summaries of the most important of which are given in the book in their context. Further, it is hoped that the more detailed of such summaries will help to give the reader a general idea of the kind of analysis of the relevant economic factors which must be made when considering whether, and if so how, the competition rules may apply to a particular agreement or practice. The authors have also endeavoured by certain of the summaries to convey to the reader some idea of the enormous economic significance of action by the Commission under the competition rules; certain of the Commission's decisions have had the effect of modifying the structures of whole industries by breaking up cartels and other forms of co-operatives, which in many cases had subsisted since the years of depression in the thirties, or even earlier. Conversely other decisions of the Commission have sanctioned extensive restrictions of competition and have allowed substantial co-operation in the interest of improved production, distribution or technology, and summaries of such decisions are given to show how the Commission has used its powers to exempt otherwise prohibited agreements.

We have not hesitated, where appropriate, to quote American opinion or precedent having regard to the vast experience gained in America in the field of anti-trust since the passing of the Sherman Act in 1890. For while there are many differences between the American and the EEC systems, certain problems seem to us to be common to both, e.g., the need to define the relevant market as a preliminary to determining whether the Sherman or Clayton Acts, or the EEC competition rules, as the case may be, apply to an agreement or practice. We are, of course, aware that competition law and practice in other countries, particularly in Germany gives valuable leads to solutions to anti-trust problems arising under the EEC's own anti-trust regulations but it has been regretfully necessary, within the modest framework of this book, to ignore these sources.

However, EEC competition law presents problems of its own for the solution of which no outside help is available; these arise mostly from the legal effects of art. 85 and Regulation 17 (adopted in implementation of arts. 85 and 86) as interpreted from time to time by the Commission and the Court of Justice. We have in mind particularly such extremely difficult problems as those related to the possible retroactive nullity of accession agreements, i.e., agreements in force before the accession of the United Kingdom, Denmark and Ireland to the EEC on 1 January 1973 and to which the EEC anti-trust rules had no application before such date, in so far as they may be enforceable pending a finding by the Commission that they infringe art. 85 (1); or to the effects *inter partes* where an agreement held to be unenforceable by a national court as infringing the article is subsequently granted exemption by the Commission under art. 85 (3), and generally questions of conflict between Community law and national law. A further question discussed, which must interest all parties to agreements found to infringe art. 85 (1), is that of any possible liability to compensate third parties.

We have discussed some of these problems on the basis that merely to know that a problem exists is of value; in relation to certain of them we have not hesitated to give our own opinion. Regretfully, here again, within the scope of this book, it has not been possible to consider solutions discussed with regard to the same problems in the context of the legal systems of other member states.

We have discussed at some length the investigation procedure of the Commission and we hope to have brought out the following points:

(a) The considerable differences between the Commission's procedures and the procedures under the Restrictive Trade Practices Acts in the United Kingdom, due to the very different structures of the relevant legislations resulting in a largely administrative procedure in Brussels as compared to a judicial procedure in this country.

(b) The opportunities available under the EEC system for "dialogue" between the parties to agreements and the Commission permitting the amendment of the agreements so that they conform with the EEC anti-trust rules.

We hope that our description of the Commission's procedures will be helpful to the reader, and particularly to the practitioner, in giving him a general idea of what is involved in proceedings before the Commission and the Court of Justice in relation to art. 85 or 86.

We are aware that in parts of this book, as lawyers, we have trespassed into the field of economics, and it is hoped that shortcomings in any discussion of economic matters will be forgiven us by the experts. Nevertheless in the field of anti-trust the legal and economic aspects of a problem are inter-related, and it is therefore necessary for the lawyer at least to know to what economic questions an answer must be sought to enable him to arrive at a correct legal answer from the point of view of EEC competition law.

The task of writing this book was begun shortly after the signature of the Treaty of Accession by the United Kingdom; these final paragraphs are being written when our continued membership of the EEC depends on the result of the forthcoming Referendum. Although this book follows on a number of others published for the benefit of the public in Britain since our accession to the Communities, we venture to hope, if for no other reason than that it has the advantage of later publication, that it will add something to the understanding of a difficult and continually evolving subject, which, we are sure, will remain of considerable importance to lawyers and businessmen in the United Kingdom and elsewhere whatever the future may hold for the relations between the United Kingdom and the EEC.

During this three year gestation period, we have been fortunate in receiving constant help and encouragement from friends and colleagues, for which we are sincerely grateful. We would like in particular to record our thanks to Professor Michel Waelbroeck for reading the completed manuscript; we are indebted to him not only for pointing out inaccuracies and inconsistencies, but also for his many constructive suggestions, which in one way or another have helped us to improve on our task. It must not, however, be taken that the text represents his views in every particular, for there are several matters upon which he would doubtless adopt a different attitude.

We are similarly indebted to W. J. Sandars and R. C. Clemens for reading the completed manuscript and for their valuable comments which have prevented us from committing errors both of style and of substance. We are grateful to Jochen Thiesing for sparing us the time to read the manuscript and for his general encouragement, and also to R. Z. Swift for reading and commenting on the first draft of the chapter on Industrial Property Rights; and to Jacques Delmoly for the guidance given to us in Brussels and his unstinting help in thrashing out in discussions numerous aspects of the subject.

We would like also to thank certain staff members of the EC Commission, and in particular Bastiaan Van der Esch, Madame F. E. Espion, Sergio Benini, Antonio Camia Marchini, Jean Pierre Dubois and Kurt Spormann, who have generously given us their valuable time; needless to say, the responsibility for the views expressed in this book remains the authors' alone.

We are very grateful to David Oliver, David di Mambro and Basil James who have at one stage or another valiantly proof read and checked the entire manuscript—here again, any responsibility for residual errors is our own. Very special thanks are due to Valerie Sullivan for her really splendid work in typing the manuscript in its many "final" versions, and also to Dalice Woodford and Mark Barounos who gave similar help in the early stages of the manuscript. Our publishers have given us the greatest co-operation and have shown much patience in adapting their schedules to keep pace with the developments of the subject: we are grateful to them.

Last, but not least, our thanks are due to those at home for their unfailing encouragement and support.

This book purports to set out the law as at 1 January 1975, except for certain more recent references incorporated at the proof stage.

DFH	DB	JRJ
Barrington House, 59–67 Gresham Street, London, EC2	25 Avenue de Tervueren Brussels 1040	5 New Square, Lincoln's Inn, London, WC1

1 *April* 1975

ERRATUM

Page 278   **Commission's powers of investigation**

Second paragraph:

Delete the words "Before carrying out any investigation"
and substitute:

> "The investigation is carried out by officials of the Commission or of the national authorities. As regards investigation by officials of the Commission, they must be authorised in writing by the Commission, and the national authorities of the members states concerned must be informed.[3a] Should the undertaking refuse to co-operate in such investigation" . . .
>
> "3a Reg. 17, art. 14 (2)."

Fourth paragraph:

Delete the whole paragraph and substitute:

> "Accordingly the Commission is precluded from mounting an investigation without notice to the national authority in whose territory it is to be carried out; but there is no obligation on the Commission to give advance notice of a proposed investigation to the undertaking concerned which may, however, refuse to submit to the proposed investigation until a formal decision is taken by the Commission."

Table of Contents

Table of Statutes

References in this Table to "*Statutes*" are to Halsbury's Statutes of England (Third Edition) showing the volume and page at which the annotated text of the Act will be found.

Table of European Communities Legislation

Page numbers in **bold** type indicate where a Treaty or Regulation is set out in part or in full.

TREATIES

SECONDARY LEGISLATION

Table of Cases

XXV

Bibliography

including works referred to in the text

W. ALEXANDER: The EEC Rules of Competition, Kluwer Harrap
Handbooks, London 1973
Brevets d'inventions et règles de concurrence du Traité CEE,
Bruylant, Brussels 1971
C. BELLAMY and G. CHILD: Common Market law of Competi-
tion, Sweet & Maxwell, London 1973
A. CAMPBELL: Common Market Law, 3 vols. with supplements,
Longmans Oceana 1969
J. P. CUNNINGHAM: Competition law of the EEC: a practical
guide, Kogan Page, 1973
A. DERINGER: Competition Law of the European Economic
Community, Commerce Clearing House Inc., Chicago 1968
J.-P. DUBOIS: La Position Dominante et son Abus dans l'Article 86
du Traité de la CEE, Librairies Techniques
W. VAN GERVEN and F. L. LUHOFF: Commercial agency and
distribution agreements and related problems of licensing in
the law of the EEC countries and European Communities,
Université de Louvain, Louvain 1970
GIDE-LOYRETTE-NOUEL: Le droit de la concurrence des
communautés européennes, by X. de Roux and D. Villemot,
Dictionnaires André Joly, Paris
Dictionnaire du Marché Commun, Dictionnaires André Joly,
Paris
B. GOLDMAN: Précis de droit commercial européen, 2nd Edn.,
Dalloz, Paris 1971
Also available as: European Commercial Law, Stevens,
London 1973
J. GUYENOT: Régime juridique des ententes économiques et des
concentrations d'entreprises dans le Marché Commun, Librairie
Générale de Droit et de Jurisprudence, Paris 1971
F. G. JACOBS and A. DURAND: References to the European
Court: Practice and Procedure, Butterworths, London 1975
K. LIPSTEIN: The Law of the European Economic Community,
Butterworths, London 1974

J. MEGRET: Le droit de la Communauté économique européenne, vol. iv: Concurrence, by J. Mégret, J.-V. Louis, D. Vignes and M. Waelbroeck, Editions de l'université de Bruxelles, Brussels 1972

A. D. NEALE: The Antitrust Laws of the USA, Cambridge University Press 1970

LES NOVELLES: Corpus juris belgici: Droit des Communautés européennes, Larcier, Brussels 1969

C. W. OBERDORFER, A. GLEISS and M. HIRSCH: Common Market Cartel Law, 2nd Edn. Commerce Clearing House Inc., Chicago 1971

J. A. RAHL (Editor): Common Market and American Antitrust, Overlap and Conflict, McGraw-Hill Book Company, 1970

D. SWANN and D. L. McLACHLAN: Competition Policy in the European Community, MacMillan

OTHER SOURCES

Cahiers de droit européen, Larcier, Brussels, 1965–
Commission Publications:

   Bulletin of the European Communities, issued monthly
   General Reports on the Activities of the Communities, issued annually
   Practical Guide to Articles 85 and 86 of the Treaty of Rome, unofficially translated in the Board of Trade Journal, 9 October 1962, and reprinted in A. Campbell, Common Market Law, vol. II, para. 2605.
   Reports on Competition: 1st – April 1972
                           2nd – April 1973
                           3rd – May 1974

Common Market Law Review, 1963–
Common Market Reporter, Commerce Clearing House Inc., Chicago
Revue trimestrielle de droit européen, 1965–
Treaties establishing the European Communities, Office for Official Publications of the European Communities, 1973

List of Abbreviations

Bulletin – Bulletin of the European Communities (Commission)
CMLR – Common Market Law Reports
CMLRev – Common Market Law Review
ECR – European Court Reports
ECSC – European Coal and Steel Community
EEC – European Economic Community
IP – Informations de presse (Commission)
JO – Journal Official des Communautés (French)
OJ – Official Journal of the Communities (English); where a pre-1973 reference is to the OJ, the English text will be found in the Special Edition 1952–1972 (authentic translation)
Rec.-Recueil de la Jurisprudence de la Cour
RTPA – Restrictive Trade Practices Acts, i.e. Restrictive Trade Practices Act 1956, Resale Prices Act 1964 and Restrictive Trace Practices Act 1968, as amended by Fair Trading Act 1973

Chapter 1

General Introduction

SECTION 1 PRELIMINARY COMMENTS

It was primarily by the creation of a common market that the six nations who signed the Treaty of Rome[1] (the Treaty) envisaged the way forward to the wider objectives of the European Economic Community (the EEC). According to the conception of the authors of the Treaty the inter-penetration of the economies of the member states implicit in the concept of a common market (as distinct from a mere customs union), coupled with the operation of undistorted competition within the common market, would lead to the more efficient use of resources and this in turn would lead to the wider goals of the Community, outlined in art. 2 of the Treaty.

The removal of customs duties and the elimination of quantitative restrictions on trade are only a first step towards the creation of a common market. That much was achieved in the Europe of the six as far back as 1 July 1968 and is to be achieved in the Europe of the nine by 1 July 1977, the end of the transitional period under the Treaty of Accession by which the United Kingdom, Denmark and Ireland joined the EEC on 1 January 1973. The full realisation of a common market requires, in addition to the elimination of customs duties and quantitative restrictions, the removal of all other artificial impediments and distortions to trade across the boundaries of the States comprising a common market. Such impediments and distortions can result from the actions of Governments, for example subsidies, special incentives, differential taxation or the maintenance of differing technical standards, or from the actions of undertakings through restrictive trade practices and the abuse of market power. It is the object of this book to introduce the reader to the provisions of the Rome Treaty concerned with such impediments to intra-Community trade brought about by the actions of undertakings.

---

1 The Treaty establishing the European Economic Community signed at Rome on 25 March 1957 by the representatives of Belgium, the Federal Republic of Germany, France, Italy, Luxumbourg and the Netherlands.

The Treaty begins by setting out certain basic principles of which the following are relevant:

"Article 1

By this Treaty, the High Contracting Parties establish among themselves a EUROPEAN ECONOMIC COMMUNITY.

Article 2

The Community shall have as its task, by establishing a common market and progressively approximating the economic policies of Member States, to promote throughout the Community a harmonious development of economic activities, a continuous and balanced expansion, an increase in stability, an accelerated raising of the standard of living and closer relations between the States belonging to it.

Article 3

For the purposes set out in Article 2, the activities of the Community shall include, as provided in this Treaty and in accordance with the timetable set out therein:

. . .

(f) The institution of a system ensuring that competition in the Common Market is not distorted".

This last obligation is purely of a general nature, and is followed up by implementing articles in Part III, Title I, of the Treaty.

It is seen therefore that it is a fundamental principle of the EEC as envisaged by the Treaty that the Common Market should be based upon a market economy – that is, that the direction and strength of the currents of trade between member states should normally be determined by the operation of the laws of supply and demand under conditions of competition – by which is meant workable competition.[1] It was conceived that these laws, when allowed to operate without distortion, would provide a self-regulating economic system ensuring the most efficient use of resources. This economic concept was adopted not only as being in harmony with the economic systems of the member states, then as now primarily based on private enterprise, but moreover as one which, being self-regulatory, did not involve politically unacceptable direct intervention by the institutions of the Community in the internal economic affairs of the member states.

But whereas in the framework of a single state the protection of competition can be ensured by adequate anti-trust legislation,[2] at the

---

1 See p. 36, below.
2 By which American term is meant a body of law and practice directed against or controlling restrictive trade practices and the acquisition and exercise of monopoly power.

level of international trade where the undertakings involved are subject to differing taxation, to different legal systems and may be recipients of varying degrees of state aid in differing forms, any legislation against restrictive practices must be supplemented by provisions for the elimination of such inequalities, if fair conditions of competition are to be created. It is not surprising therefore to find included under Part III, Title I, together with articles concerned with anti-trust policy, provisions aimed at bringing about some equality in the trading conditions in the several countries of the EEC. These are art. 91 dealing with the practice of dumping; arts. 92 to 94 concerned with aids granted by states (subsidies); arts. 95 to 99 dealing with tax advantages; and arts. 100 to 102 relating to the approximation of laws.

In this book we shall deal only with those articles in Part III, Title I, of the Treaty which relate to distortion of competition by undertakings resulting either from restrictive trade tractices, whether by agreement or concertation, between undertakings (art. 85) or from the abuse of market power by dominant undertakings (art. 86). We shall also consider the distortion of competition even in the absence of agreement or market dominance by the use of industrial property or other legal rights in a manner considered improper by the EEC authorities in the light of competition policy – when art. 36 may be relevant.

Further, as the European Court of Justice has ruled that a merger can in certain circumstances constitute an infringement of art. 86 we include some discussion of the EEC's policy in relation to mergers.

In concluding these opening remarks it should be said that while arts. 85 and 86 take effect by prohibiting certain types of agreements and practices, the Community's anti-trust policy is also applied in a positive manner by the Commission. The EEC must necessarily be strong technically, economically – and, consequently, politically – if it is to be effective, particularly in meeting the industrial challenge of America and Japan. If Europe was backward in its technology (particularly in the new technologies) and in management techniques in 1958, and to the extent that it still is, the reason is attributable in many instances to the fragmented nature and small scale of European undertakings, which resulted or result from their being geared to national markets of small or medium-sized European states.

It will be seen therefore that it is the policy of the Community to encourage co-operation between undertakings, where the co-operation is designed to strengthen them at the technical, managerial, production and marketing levels.[1]

---

1 For the Commission's approach to co-operation and concentration between undertakings, see Ch. 7, p. 177, below.

By way of introduction to the main subject matter, it is thought useful:

(a) to sketch out the legal basis on which the EEC anti-trust rules are binding on undertakings in the United Kingdom;
(b) to compare the main provisions of arts. 85 and 86 with corresponding legislation in the United Kingdom; and
(c) to draw attention to what may be considered the overriding purpose of EEC competition policy, namely to ensure that the free movement of goods within the Common Market is not prejudiced by practices condemned under arts. 85, 86 or 36 of the Treaty.

SECTION 2 THE LEGAL BASIS OF THE EEC ANTI-TRUST RULES IN THE UNITED KINGDOM

1. Articles 85 and 86 are directly applicable Treaty provisions, in the sense that once the Treaty has been incorporated as part of the law of each member state such articles are to be given legal effect in the member state and create both rights and obligations enforceable by individuals before its national courts, without further enactment being necessary.[2] The incorporation of the Treaty into United Kingdom law is achieved by s. 2 (1) of the European Communities Act 1972, which states that such directly applicable provisions "shall be recognised and available in law, and be enforced, allowed and followed accordingly".

2. In addition to the provisions of the Treaty itself, certain instruments issuing from certain of the institutions of the Community[3] may also be directly applicable; namely, regulations of the Council of Ministers and of the Commission (acting in the competition sector under authority given by a Council regulation) which under art. 189 "shall be binding in [their] entirety and directly applicable in all Member States"; and decisions of the Commission which also under art. 189 "shall be binding in [their] entirety upon those to whom [they are] addressed".

---

2 See generally on Community law and domestic law, K. Lipstein: The Law of the European Economic Community, Butterworths London, 1974, pp. 21–45.
3 The four institutions of the Community are: the Assembly (or European Parliament), the Council of Ministers, the Commission and the Court of Justice.

3. The implementation of the competition rules is entrusted to the Commission under art. 89 of the Treaty.[1] The Commission fulfils its duties in this respect by virtue of Regulation 17 of the Council of Ministers adopted in 1962.[2] Nevertheless, arts. 85 and 86 may be enforced within limits by national anti-trust authorities under art. 9 (3) of Regulation 17 "for so long as the Commission has not instituted any proceedings".[3]

4. Rulings of the Commission on agreements and practices within arts. 85 and 86 or otherwise relating to the EEC's competition policy may be given by decision binding on the undertakings to whom the decision is addressed. Such a decision may be the subject of appeal to the Court of Justice under art. 173.[4]

5. In addition to regulations and decisions, the Commission may issue certain other instruments in implementation, or explanation, of the competition rules of the Treaty. These instruments include recommendations and opinions, which have no binding force,[5] and communications, a procedural stage in the Commission's decision-taking process in the anti-trust field.[6] Further the Commission has from time to time set out its views on the application of the competition rules to certain types of agreements or practices; somewhat confusingly these announcements are also officially referred to as communications, but they are without legal force and should be treated with some caution, since the Commission itself has not, in certain cases, followed its communications;[7] in any event the Communications are always expressed to be without prejudice to any subsequent interpretation of the Court of Justice.

6. In addition to its role as an appellate court with jurisdiction to review the decisions of the Commission the Court of Justice has jurisdiction under art. 177[8] of the Treaty to give rulings as to the interpretation of the Treaty and regulations at the request of national courts: indeed, a national court from which there is no appeal must refer to the Court of Justice any such question of interpretation. It will be seen that interpretative rulings of the court under art. 177 play a considerable role in the development of the EEC anti-trust rules.

7. It follows from the incorporation of the Treaty into domestic

---

1 The text is set out in Appendix I, p. 315, below.
2 OJ 1962 13,204; set out in Appendix II, p. 318, below.
3 This is discussed further in Ch. 11, Section 5, p. 290, below.
4 Set out in Appendix I, p. 316, below; and see Ch. 12, Section 1, p. 302, below.
5 Art. 189 of the Treaty. For an example of the use made in the anti-trust field of the power to issue a recommendation see p. 288, below.
6 See p. 285, below.
7 See, e.g. p. 229, below, and cases there cited in relation to the Communication on Patent Licensing Agreements.
8 Set out in Appendix I, p. 316, below; and see Ch. 12, Section 2, p. 307, below.

law that a national court of a member state is required to apply Community law together with its national law. Community law comprises not only the provisions of the Treaty and regulations thereunder, but also the body of case law of the Court of Justice interpreting these provisions.

The Treaty having been incorporated into United Kingdom law,[1] the courts of the United Kingdom are therefore required to take account of the judgments of the Court of Justice. This is reflected in the European Communities Act 1972, s. 3 (1), which also specifies that a question of Community law is to be treated as a question of law, meaning that Community law is, in the same way as English law, within the cognizance of the court and is not, as in the case of a foreign law, a matter of fact to be proved by expert evidence; the section provides:

> "For the purposes of all legal proceedings any question as to the meaning or effect of any of the Treaties, or as to the validity, meaning or effect of any Community instrument,[2] shall be treated as a question of law (and, if not referred to the European Court, be for determination as such in accordance with the principles laid down by and any relevant decision of the European Court."[3]

8. Technically there is no corresponding obligation to take account of principles established by decisions of the Commission, (which are binding only on the persons to whom they are addressed)[4] unless and until the principles are confirmed by a judgment of the Court of Justice. Nevertheless, any principles of general application enunciated by the Commission in its decisions must necessarily have considerable persuasive authority as statements of the enforcement authority of the Community's competition policy, especially in view of the fact that the Commission's general interpretation of the articles has usually been endorsed by the Court of Justice on appeal.

9. The Court of Justice has established the concept of the primacy of Community law over conflicting national legislation;[5] it is left

---

1 See para. 1, above.
2 A Community instrument is defined as any instrument issued by any Community Institution: European Communities Act 1972, Sch. 1, Part II.
3 The use of the term "judgment" would have been more appropriate, since in the context of Community competition law it is the Commission, not the Court of Justice, which issues decisions in the technical sense referred to in art. 189 of the Treaty.
4 See para. 4, above.
5 *Van Gend en Loos* v. *Nederlandse Administratie der Belastingen,* 5 February 1963, [1963] ECR 1; [1963] CMLR 105; *Costa* v. *ENEL,* 15 July 1964, [1964] ECR 585; [1964] CMLR 425; *Lutticke GmbH* v. *Hauptzollamt Sarrelouis,* 16 June 1966, XII Rec. 293; [1971] CMLR 674; *Molkerei Zentrale Westfalen-Lippe* v. *Hauptzollamt Paderborn,* 3 April 1968, XIV Rec. 211; [1968] CMLR 187; *Walt Wilhelm* v. *Bundeskartellamt,* 13 February 1969, XV Rec. 1; [1969] CMLR 100.

for the national courts of each member state to apply this principle as best they can under their constitutions.[1]

10. The Treaty is not in many important respects closely drafted in the same way as an English statute; and is to be regarded as a framework law within which there is room for development "on a case to case basis" having regard to the general objectives of the Treaty.[2] Accordingly, undue attention to actual wording may lead to incorrect interpretation. Indeed, in the first case in which a question of Community law was raised before the Court of Appeal, Lord Denning, M.R., stated, in relation to arts. 85 and 86:

> "Those provisions are framed in a style very different from an English statute. They state general principles. They lay down broad policies. But they do not go into detail. The words and phrases are not defined. There is no interpretation clause. Much is left unsaid. So much, indeed, that a great deal has to be filled in by the courts of law. If you read through the *Common Market Law Reports*, you will find that case after case is referred to the European Court of Luxembourg so as to find out the meaning of those Articles. The European Court interprets them according to the "wording and spirit of the Treaty". Every one of these cases is of importance to commercial men. That court is moulding the law of Europe into a single whole which every country of the nine must obey."[3]

11. Decisions of the Commission are published in the Official Journal of the Community (OJ), issued in all the official working languages of the institutions of the Community.[4] Judgments of the Court of Justice are published in the Reports of Cases before the Court (ECR).[5]

SECTION 3 EEC AND UNITED KINGDOM ANTI-TRUST LEGISLATION: A COMPARISON

Article 85[6] has the effect of prohibiting and declaring void agreements, decisions and concerted practices (collectively referred to throughout this book as "agreements", unless the context otherwise

---

1 See K. Lipstein, *op. cit.*, pp. 39–45.
2 For a particularly striking instance of this "teleological" approach, see the *Continental Can* Case, pp. 162, 163, below.
3 *Application des Gaz* v. *Veritas Ltd.,* [1974] 3 All ER 5q, at p. 56; [1974] 3 WLR 235.
4 These are Danish, German, English, French, Italian and Dutch; Council Reg. 1, OJ 1958 17385, art. 1, as amended by the Treaty of Accession.
5 Decisions and judgments issued after 1 January 1973 will be found in English in these official publications of the Community. Decisions and judgments prior to that date are as yet only in the original four official languages of the Community (German, French, Italian and Dutch) though usually may be found unofficially translated into English in Common Market Law Reports.
6 The text in the authentic English version is set out in Appendix I, p. 313, below.

requires)[1] which may affect trade between member states and the object or effect of which is to prevent, restrict or distort competition in the Common Market.

Article 86[2] has the effect of prohibiting the abuse of a dominant position by one or more undertakings in the Common Market (or a substantial part of the Common Market) insofar as trade between member states may be affected.

It is seen then that the two articles broadly reflect the division in the United Kingdom between legislation dealing with restrictive trade practices resulting from agreement or arrangement between undertakings (the Restrictive Trade Practices Acts – RTPA)[3] and legislation dealing with the control of monopolies and mergers, (the Fair Trading Act 1973, Parts IV and V) – a merger in certain circumstances being within the scope of the abuse mentioned in art. 86.

It is revealing therefore to draw a number of comparisons (by no means exhaustive) between certain provisions of the RTPA and the Fair Trading Act, Parts IV and V, with corresponding provisions (or their absence) in arts. 85 and 86. From the comparison it is hoped that there will emerge an approximate picture of EEC anti-trust legislation and practice as a preliminary to detailed treatment.

Article 85

1. Although both art. 85 and the RTPA are concerned with the control of restrictive practices there is a basic difference in the approach of the two systems to the problem. While art. 85 has as its object the protection of competition as such by prohibiting agreements which tend to restrict competition, the RTPA provide that agreements containing certain restrictions[4] are registrable with the Director General of Fair Trading[5] and as such are presumed to be against the public interest.[6]

2. It is irrelevant to the application of art. 85 whether the place of business, the residence or the domicile of the parties to an agreement is within or outside the EEC; the test is whether the agreement has

---

1 The distinctions between agreements, decisions and concerted practices are discussed at pp. 16–22, below.
2 The text in the authentic English version is set out in Appendix I, p. 313, below.
3 Restrictive Trade Practices Act 1956, Resale Prices Act 1964 and Restrictive Trade Practices Act 1968, as amended by Fair Trading Act 1973.
4 Listed in RTPA 1968, s. 6, with the exceptions provided for in ss. 7 and 8.
5 RTPA 1956, s. 9; the functions of the office of Registrar of Restrictive Trading Agreements have been transferred to the Director General of Fair Trading: Fair Trading Act 1973, s. 94.
6 RTPA 1956, s. 21, as amended by RTPA 1968, s. 10.

effect in the Common Market.[1] This contrasts with the RTPA which do not apply to an agreement unless two or more parties carry on business in the United Kingdom.[2]

3. Article 85 applies to the whole spectrum of economic activity including, in theory, shipping and aviation but excepting activities covered by the ECSC Treaty – although special provisions apply to agriculture, and to road, rail and inland waterway transport.[3] Assuming the extension of the RTPA to services, as contemplated by the Fair Trading Act 1973,[4] the scope of the United Kingdom restrictive practices legislation is broadly similar, although rather more activities are to be excluded.[5]

4. Information agreements are not, as under the RTPA,[6] subject to special provisions under art. 85. Insofar as an agreement of this type operates so as to restrict competition it falls within the general provisions of the article as an agreement which has as its object or effect the restriction of competition.[7]

5. Article 85 may apply whenever the commercial freedom of any person is restricted by an agreement (whether or not he is a party to it). This is in contrast to the RTPA which are concerned with the acceptance of restrictions by two or more parties.[8]

6. The concept of agreement under both systems is very much the same. Under neither system is an agreement limited to a legally binding agreement, the RTPA defining "agreement" as including an "arrangement",[9] whether or not enforceable or intended to be enforceable at law, and art. 85 specifically referring to concerted practices.

7. The effect of both the RTPA and art. 85 is to prohibit (subject to exemption) agreements which are within their respective provisions, but while restrictive provisions in a registered agreement under the RTPA are valid until prohibited by Court Order – nullity attaches (in principle) to an agreement within art. 85 from its commencement[10].

8. An agreement which is within art. 85 is prohibited and void.[11]

---

1 See p. 44, below.
2 RTPA 1956, s. 6.
3 See Ch. 9, Sections 1 and 2, pp. 238, 242, below.
4 S. 107.
5 See the exceptions provided for in the Fair Trading Act 1973, s. 109 and Sch. 4, and the Notice by the Secretary of State for Prices and Consumer Protection on the proposed scope of the Order under s. 107.
6 RTPA 1968, s. 5, and FTA 1973, s. 108, for information agreements relating to services.
7 See, for examples, p. 49, below.
8 RTPA 1956, s. 6.
9 RTPA 1956, s. 6 (3).
10 See further Ch. 4, Section 1, p. 116, below.
11 Art. 85 (2).

Third parties may accordingly have claims against the parties to the agreement for damage suffered by reason of the agreement. Whether in fact such third party claims are sustainable will depend on the national law of the forum where it is sought to bring the claims.[1] No such claims are sustainable in respect of agreements condemned under the RTPA, although claims for breach of statutory duty can arise in the case of a registrable agreement which has not been registered.[2]

9. To determine whether or not the agreement is within art. 85 it is necessary to make an appreciation of its effect on competition by considering the agreement in its real economic context. The test is not simply whether the parties accept restrictions on their commercial freedom but whether a consequence of the restrictions is to bring about a perceptible change in market conditions, by reference to what they would have been in the absence of the agreement, affecting third parties (whether other traders in their capacities of suppliers or buyers, or consumers). Such appreciation of an agreement for the purposes of art. 85 contrasts with the mere existence of relevant restrictions which is sufficient to bring an agreement within the scope of the RTPA, though the Director General of Fair Trading may, in certain circumstances, be discharged from taking proceedings before the Restrictive Practices Court with respect to an agreement which, though registered, contains no restrictions of "such significance as to call for investigation".[3]

10. Both under the RTPA[4] and under art. 85[5] there are requirements as to registration (or notification in EEC terminology) of restrictive agreements (with the Director General of Fair Trading in the former case and with the EC Commission in the latter), Such registration or notification (subject to certain prescribed exceptions in the latter case)[6] are prerequisites to obtaining, with respect to the restrictions in the agreement, favourable rulings (referred to in the next paragraph) under s. 21 of the RTPA or under art. 85, para. 3, as the case may be.

11. Provisions preventing, restricting or distorting competition in an agreement which are within art. 85 (1) may nevertheless be allowed if falling within the exempting provisions under para. 3 of art. 85, in the same way that restrictions in a registered agreement

---

1 In relation to such claims in England, see pp. 131ff, below.
2 RTPA 1968, s. 7 (2).
3 RTPA 1968, s. 9 (4).
4 RTPA 1956, s. 9. The particulars required are listed in s. 10.
5 Under Regulation 17, art. 4 (1), see Ch. 10, Sections 3 and 4, pp. 255, 267, below.
6 Under Regulation 17, art. 4 (2), see pp. 257ff., below.

under the RTPA may be held by the Court not to be against the public interest. The grounds for exemption under each system differ, but there is involved in each case a process of balancing detriments against benefits expected to accrue under the agreement. In particular, while under the RTPA an agreement may be upheld on grounds of public policy, e.g. the avoidance of adverse effects on employment, such considerations are completely outside the scope of art. 85 (3) which is limited to restrictive agreements which bring about improvements in the production or distribution of goods or the promotion of technical or economic progress. The EEC is not indifferent to the public interest but except to the limited extent indicated, it is not the direct concern of art. 85.

12. Where an agreement is found to be within art. 85 (1) and is not exempted under art. 85 (3) the parties to it may be liable to substantial fines which the EC Commission has power to impose.[1] There is no corresponding power to fine under the RTPA.

Article 86

1. Article 86 involves at the Community level a prohibition of certain practices which in a monopoly situation in the United Kingdom could be held to operate against the public interest under the provisions of the Fair Trading Act 1973. Much in the same way as under the Fair Trading Act the public interest is not specifically defined (except by the enumeration in s. 84 of certain specific matters, among all others which may be relevant, to be taken into account by the Monopolies and Merger Commission), art. 86 also refrains from limiting the notion of abuse by definition and merely gives a non-exhaustive list of practices which may constitute abuse, such as unfair pricing, employing unfair trading conditions, limiting production, outlets and technical developments, discriminating practices and tying arrangements.

2. Nor does art. 86 define what is meant by dominant position. This must be determined in each individual case on the basis of general criteria such as the extent to which the firm in question is responsive to the forces of competition in the relevant market within the Common Market. It will therefore be more difficult to ascertain whether art. 86 applies to any particular situation than whether a "monopoly situation" exists under the Fair Trading Act, where it is quantitatively defined by reference to the market shares of the undertaking concerned.[2]

3. Under the Fair Trading Act there is control of mergers in so

---

1 See further pp. 296ff., below.
2 Ss. 6–9.

far as the consequence of the merger is the creation or enlargement of a
monopoly situation. In contrast to the Paris Treaty[1] (establishing
the European Coal and Steel Community) the Rome Treaty includes
no specific provision for control of mergers whether or not resulting
in the creation of a dominant undertaking, although in certain circumstances a merger involving such an undertaking could be within art. 86
as an abuse of a dominant position – the relevant abuse being the
elimination as a consequence of the merger of competition in a substantial part of the Common Market. However the EEC is moving
towards the institution of a system of merger control.[2]

4. As in the case of art. 85, breach of art. 86 can result in substantial
fines imposed by the EC Commission. There is no corresponding
power of fining under the Fair Trading Act. On the other hand under
the latter Act there is substantial power for "dismantling" a monopoly
and "unscrambling" a merger. The EC Commission does not have
corresponding powers but by the imposition of fines and penalties,
failing compliance by the undertaking(s) with its requirements, the
Commission can in fact enforce rulings to the same effect.

It may be seen from these comparative notes that arts. 85 and 86
bring into the law of the United Kingdom notions which are not
entirely foreign in spite of many differences. These articles, as Community law, together with accompanying implementing regulations,
take their place as part of our national law. The respective areas of
application of the domestic United Kingdom law and Community
law are sometimes different, sometimes the same: even if the same, the
two systems may coincide as regards their substantive effects or they
may conflict. Thus arts. 85 and 86 apply only where the relevant
agreement or abuse of a dominant position may affect trade between
member states. It follows that agreements and abusive practices with
local effect *only* are outside their scope. On the other hand an agreement which escapes the application of the RTPA in spite of restrictions
on trade within the United Kingdom, e.g. by reason of only one party
to the agreement carrying on business in the United Kingdom, may
be within art. 85; and varying the example slightly, by postulating
that two parties to the agreement carry on business in the United
Kingdom, the agreement can then be both within art. 85 and the
RTPA with the consequence that it may be found lawful under the
one and forbidden under the other. However, under the European
Communities Act, s. 10, both the Director General of Fair Trading

---

1 Art. 66.
2 See further pp. 199 ff., below.

and the Restrictive Practices Court have wide discretions which should enable, in practice, conflict in this situation to be avoided.[1]

SECTION 4 THE FREE MOVEMENT OF GOODS WITHIN THE EEC

The free movement of goods across the borders of states the territories of which constitute a common market, unimpeded by artificial trade barriers, is of the very essence of such a market. Such freedom is not only the goal of the EEC's competition policy in relation to restrictive practices, in the sense that the object of that policy is to prevent impediments to such movements by restrictive practices, but also the tool of that policy in that it is by the free movement across borders that restrictive practices practised in a member state can be neutralised. For example, if the wholesale price of a product in country A is higher than the corresponding price in country B, a retailer, by importing the cheaper product from B to A (such imports generally referred to in EEC terminology as parallel imports), may force the wholesaler in A to reduce his price if he wishes to remain competitive; and to the extent that the higher price in country A is due to a restrictive practice, e.g. a resale price imposed by the manufacturer, or by agreement with other wholesalers, the maintenance of the restriction will be rendered ineffective as a consequence of cheaper parallel imports from country B.

It is not surprising, then, to find that the EC Commission, in its implementation of the EEC's competition policy, is above all concerned with the removal of impediments to the free movement of goods across the borders of the member states of the EEC. Where this is impeded by agreement, the Commission can invoke art. 85 to re-establish the normal pattern of trading. But artificial impediments of trade can result otherwise than from agreement, or not only from agreement, as, for example, from the use of industrial property rights, such as a trade mark or a patent, Thus, in the example given, trade from country B to country A could be prevented by a trade mark or patent infringement action – that is, by the holder of a legitimate monopoly in country A exercising rights relating to that monopoly – and it is a measure of the importance attached to the free movement of goods that EEC law now limits the exercise of industrial property rights in so far as they may be used as a weapon against the free circulation of goods and, accordingly, as a means of preventing competition within the EEC.

---

1 See further Ch. 4, Section 3, p. 137, below.

This question will be dealt with more fully in Chapter 8, but it will be useful to give here an account of possibly the most famous of the EC Commission's decisions to date, the *Grundig* Decision,[1] as a vivid illustration of the importance the Community attaches to the principle of the free movement of goods in the establishment of a common market.

The Consten-Grundig Case

The facts, in so far as they are relevant, are that Grundig (a German manufacturer of recording appliances) appointed Consten, a French company, to be its exclusive distributor in France; Grundig intended that Consten should enjoy absolute territorial protection there, i.e. protection from imports into France by other dealers of Grundig machines acquired otherwise than directly from Grundig. In order to support the exclusivity, Consten was registered in France as the licensee of Grundig's trade mark "GINT" so that Consten could bring trade mark infringement proceedings against parallel importers of Grundig apparatus, all of which carried the same "GINT" trade mark. UNEF, another dealer in electrical appliances, imported into France Grundig products purchased from German wholesalers and proceeded to under-cut Consten. Consten claimed that UNEF's action constituted unfair competition, a cause of action allowed under French law, and at the same time brought proceedings for the infringement of the "GINT" trade mark.

The Commission decided that the agreement between Consten and Grundig violated art. 85 (1), and that Consten's rights under its trade mark licence must be limited in so far as the exercise of those rights would enable Consten to prevent parallel imports of the products from other member states. The Commission's Decision was upheld by the Court of Justice in all material respects.[2]

The *Consten and Grundig* Case related to the use of a trade mark in connection with an exclusive distribution agreement, but the principle involved has since then been extended to the use of other types of industrial property rights.

These and related questions will be discussed further in Chapter 8, but it must already be clear that the importance of EEC law in this regard can hardly be exaggerated for those engaged in international trade.

---

1 *Re Agreement of Grundig Verkaufs-GmbH*, 23 September 1964, JO 1964 161/2545; [1964] CMLR 489.
2 *Etablissements Consten SA and Grundig Verkaufs-GmbH* v. *EEC Commission*; 13 July 1966, XII Rec. 429; [1966] CMLR 418.

Chapter 2

Article 85 (1)—Prohibition

SECTION 1   INTRODUCTION

Article 85 comprises three short paragraphs:

para. (1) prohibiting certain restrictive agreements, decisions and concerted practices;

para. (2) declaring the prohibited agreements and decisions to be automatically void;

para. (3) providing for an agreement or category of agreements which would otherwise be prohibited under para. (1) to be nevertheless exempted from prohibition if certain conditions are satisfied.

This chapter is concerned with para. (1), the following two chapters dealing respectively with paras. (3) and (2), in that order, since it is more convenient to deal with the consequences of the prohibition of an agreement under para. (2) after discussing the possibility of its exemption from prohibition under para. (3).

The authentic[1] English text of art. 85 (1) states:

"1. The following shall be prohibited as incompatible with the common market: all agreements between undertakings, decisions by associations of undertakings and concerted practices which may affect trade between Member States and which have as their object or effect the prevention, restriction or distortion of competition within the common market, and in particular those which:

(a) directly or indirectly fix purchase or selling prices or any other trading conditions;

(b) limit or control production, markets, technical development, or investment;

(c) share markets or sources of supply;

(d) apply dissimilar conditions to equivalent transactions with other trading parties, thereby placing them at a competitive disadvantage;

---

1 This term is used by the Community to indicate the authoritative text of a Community provision in one of the official languages of the Community.

(e) make the conclusion of contracts subject to acceptance by the other parties of supplementary obligations which, by their nature or according to commercial usage, have no connection with the subject of such contracts."

The paragraph begins with a general prohibition, as incompatible with the Common Market, of certain agreements. The general prohibition is followed by a non-exhaustive list of examples of agreements and practices prohibited under the article, provided that they are otherwise within the general prohibition, and in particular satisfy the two conditions that they may affect inter-state trade *and* prevent, restrict or distort competition within the Common Market.

SECTION 2 AGREEMENTS, DECISIONS AND CONCERTED PRACTICES BETWEEN UNDERTAKINGS

"All agreements between undertakings, decisions by associations of undertakings and concerted practices"

Agreements

In considering whether a transaction is an agreement within art. 85 (1), the Commission will look at its substance to ascertain whether it involves the acceptance of an obligation (even if not legally binding[1]) on at least one of the parties.[2] If so, it is immaterial what the transaction is called by the parties. Thus in the *Quinine Cartel* Case,[3] where manufacturers of quinine entered into binding obligations with regard to those of their arrangements relating to the EEC and chose to designate their understanding a "gentleman's agreement", taking the additional precaution of not signing it, the Commission nevertheless held that there was an agreement within art. 85 (1), finding that:

> "in spite of their insufficiently precise name of gentlemen's agreements they expressly [laid] down, in writing, binding provisions to which the parties could be held through arbitration proceedings."[4]

Similarly, binding obligations accepted by members of a trade association did not escape condemnation as an agreement within art. 85 (1) notwithstanding their designation as "Fair Trading Rules".[5]

---

1 *Re Franco-Japanese Ballbearings Agreement*, 29 November 1974, OJ 1974 L343/19, at p. 24; [1975] 1 CMLR D8.
2 Compare under RTPA 1956, s. 6, where the acceptance of the restrictions must be by at least two persons for the agreement to be within RTPA.
3 *Re Cartel in Quinine*, 16 July 1969, JO 1969 L192/5; [1969] CMLR D41.
4 [1969] CMLR D41, at p. D58, para. 19 (b).
5 *Re Agreements between Manufacturers of Glass Containers*, 15 May 1974, OJ 1974 L160/1; [1974] CMLR D50.

Moreover, in the framwork of the rules of a trade association, non-binding provisions of the rules may be held to be "agreements" within art. 85, where such provisions are intended to support the binding obligations of the rules.[1] However, many transactions which might escape art. 85 (1) through not being agreements may nevertheless be within the net of the article as a concerted practice (see below), of which documents not constituting agreements could be evidence.

A conveyance or other transfer of property is treated as an agreement between the transferor and transferee, as in the *Sirena* Case[2] where the assignment of a trade mark in 1937 was held to constitute an agreement between undertakings on which a breach of art. 85, occurring after the entry into force of the Treaty of Rome, was based.

Agreements may be horizontal (i.e. between parties of the same trading level, such as a market sharing agreement between manufacturers or between distributors) or vertical (i.e. between parties at different trading levels, such as an agreement between a manufacturer and his distributor or between a patentee and his licensee) or partly horizontal and partly vertical.

For the purposes of art. 85 there is considered to be no agreement in the absence of economic independence between the parties; thus there is no agreement between a parent company and its subsidiary (or between subsidiaries of the same parent) when the subsidiary, by reason of the degree of control exercised by the parent, is not capable of acting independently.[3]

In certain groups of companies, however, the subsidiaries may have substantial financial and managerial independence and in such cases an agreement, e.g. an exclusive distribution agreement between two companies in the same group, could constitute an agreement for the purposes of art. 85.[4]

Numerous decisions of the Commission show that in considering whether or not there subsists between parties an agreement infringing art. 85 (1) the whole complex of agreements and understandings between the parties in relation to the subject matter under investigation will be taken into account. Furthermore, an agreement may be considered from the point of view of its effects on competition and inter-

---

1 *Re Agreements between Manufacturers of Glass Containers,* 15 May 1974, OJ 1974 L160/1, para. 37; [1974] 2 CMLR D50.

2 *Sirena SRL* v. *Eda SRL,* 18 February 1971, XVII Rec. 69; [1971] CMLR 260; see also *Remington Rand,* Bulletin 1969 No. 3, p. 40, and *Re Advocaat,* 24 July 1974, OJ 1974 L237/12; [1974] 2 CMLR D79; and see pp. 208, 209 and 212, below.

3 *Re Kodak,* 30 June 1970, JO 1970 L147/24; [1970] CMLR D19; see also *Centrafarm and Adriaan de Peijper* v. *Winthrop,* 31 October 1974; [1974] 2 CMLR 480; and p. 215, below.

4 See p. 67, below, for a discussion of the application of art. 85 to groups of companies.

state trade not only by itself but together with other agreements entered into by one or more of the parties. This is instanced by the *Brasserie de Haecht (No.* 1) Case.[1] The facts of the case are that in an action before a Belgian court, brought by a Belgian brewery against its tied tenant for breach of agreement, the tenant claimed the nullity of the agreement as infringing art. 85 on the ground that the provision in the agreement preventing him from selling other beers restricted competition within the Common Market and affected trade between member states, in so far as the tie limited outlets in Belgium for foreign brewers. These effects would obviously be negligible in the case of a single agreement affecting one tied house, but the Court of Justice, on reference for a preliminary ruling under art. 177, held that the effects of a tying agreement must not be considered in isolation, but together with other like agreements.

In other words, all tying agreements which form part of a distribution system can be taken into account for determining whether one of them infringes art. 85 – and it may follow that if one infringes they all infringe.

Following the *Brasserie de Haecht (No.* 1) Case the Commission carried out an investigation into the brewery sector under powers conferred by Regulation 17,[2] but no decision implementing art. 85 (1) was eventually taken. Nevertheless, the implications of the Case must obviously be kept in mind by large undertakings operating through tied outlets.

Decisions by associations of undertakings

Article 85 mentions these specifically so as to leave no doubt that they are within the article, having regard to a possible argument that such decisions do not strictly constitute an *agreement* between undertakings. Much the same idea underlies s. 6 of the RTPA 1956 in relation to agreements by trade associations, whereby the members of the associations are in effect deemed to have agreed to be bound by such agreements.

Article 85 does not refer to decisions by associations of associations of undertakings; but the Commission clearly considers that such decisions are within the article – *Re Cematex*.[3] Nor does art. 85 (1) refer to recommendations by trade associations, in contrast to the

---

1 *Brasserie de Haecht* v. *Wilkin-Janssen (No.* 1*)*, 12 December 1967, XIII Rec. 525; [1968] CMLR 26; and see also *Brauerei Bilger Söhne GmbH* v. *Heinrich and Marta Jehle*, 18 March 1970, XVI Rec. 127, para. 5; [1974] 1 CMLR 382; and *Béguelin Import Co.* v. *GL Import-Export SA*, 25 November 1971, XVII Rec. 949; [1972] CMLR 81.
2 Under art. 12 (1), see p. 277, below.
3 *Re Cematex*, 24 September 1971, JO 1971 L227/26; [1973] CMLR D135.

RTPA.[1] Nevertheless, where the effects of the recommendation are to impose a uniform and co-ordinated conduct on the part of the association's members the Commission may find the elements of an agreement.[2]

Concerted practices

In its judgments[3] on appeal from the Decision of the Commission in *Re Dyestuffs*[4] the Court of Justice defined "concerted practices" in these terms:[5]

"If Article 85 distinguishes the concept of 'concerted practice' from that of 'agreements between enterprises', or 'decisions by associations of enterprises', this is done with the object of bringing under the prohibitions of this Article a form of co-ordination between enterprises which, without going so far as to amount to an agreement properly so called, knowingly substitutes a practical co-operation between them for the risks of competition.

"By its very nature, then, the concerted practice does not combine all the elements of an agreement, but may, *inter alia*, result from a coordination which becomes apparent from the behaviour of the participants."

What is involved therefore is the type of practice which under RTPA terminology is covered by the term "arrangement".[6] The concept is illustrated by the following cases.

THE SUGAR CARTEL DECISION[7]

In the *Sugar Cartel* Decision four distinct concerted practices were found by the Commission between, on the one hand, national undertakings in importing countries – Italy, Holland, the western part of the Federal German Republic and the southern part of the FGR – and on the other, Belgian, French and German firms selling to those markets. Such practices were held to have had as their object and effect the protection of the respective national markets of the importing countries, thereby infringing art. 85.

---

1 RTPA 1956, s. 6 (7).
2 As in *Re Vereeniging van Cementhandelaren*, 16 December 1971, JO 1972 L13/34; [1973] CMLR D16; and see p. 49, below, on recommendations as to prices.
3 *ICI Ltd.* v. *EC Commission*, 14 July 1972, XVIII Rec. 619; [1972] CMLR 557.
4 *Re Cartel in Aniline Dyes*, 24 July 1969, JO 1969 L195/11; [1969] CMLR D23.
5 [1972] CMLR 557, at p. 622.
6 RTPA 1956, s. 6 (3), and *Re British Basic Slag Ltd.'s Agreements*, [1963] 2 All ER 807; [1963] 1 WLR 727.
7 *Re European Sugar Cartel*, 2 January 1973, OJ 1973 L140/17; [1973] CMLR D65; and see further pp. 58–60 and 164, 165, below.

In the case of deliveries of sugar to the Italian market the Commission referred to a concerted practice consisting of "Italian producers agreeing together to buy sugar directly from French, Belgian and German producers" and referred to various meetings, in particular one held in September 1969 "for a general settlement of the problems arising in connection with the export of sugar to Italy [when] the basic principles governing deliveries to Italy were laid down . . .". No doubt the agreement arrived at fell short of what the Court of Justice termed an "agreement properly so called" with the result that this infringement of art. 85 was held to derive from a concerted practice rather than from an agreement between undertakings.

The special problem which arises in relation to concerted practices is that of bringing them within the scope of art. 85 in the absence of concrete evidence of actual agreement "properly so called" or otherwise. In the other three concerted practices in the Sugar Cartel it was from the whole pattern of the conduct of the parties that the Commission was able to deduce the existence of concerted practice as opposed to market conduct freely decided upon by the various producers of sugar concerned.

It must be borne in mind that concerted practices arise normally between sophisticated firms which, sensitive to restrictive trade practice legislation, do everything to ensure that as far as possible there is no trace of any "arrangement" which might be within the legislation; with the result that faced with market behaviour suggestive of concertation it is natural that enforcement authorities should wish to be able to imply concertation from such behaviour. Certainly a trend in this direction developed in the United States but was frustrated by the Supreme Court holding that while market behaviour could be admissible evidence of concertation it was not necessarily conclusive.[1] It is interesting then to see how the Court of Justice has responded to the same situation in the appeals[2] from the *Dyestuffs* Decision.[3]

THE DYESTUFFS CASE

The facts were that between 1964 and 1967 there occurred within the Common Market three general and uniform increases in the price of dyestuffs. The member firms concerned claimed that their parallel behaviour was the natural consequence in an oligopolistic market of a rise in prices effected by a price leader, and it was this fact of economic life and not consultation which explained the parallelism. The Commission replied, by adducing evidence that the market structure was

1 *Theatre Enterprises, Inc.* v. *Paramount Film Distributing Corporation*, 346 US 537 (1954).
2 *ICI Ltd.* v. *EC Commission*, 14 July 1972, XVIII Rec. 619; [1972] CMLR 557.
3 *Re Cartel in Aniline Dyes*, 24 July 1969, JO 1969 L195,11; [1969] CMLR D23.

not such that it necessarily explained the firms' parallel price increases – a view with which the Court concurred. This left the door open to the firms to say that they could even so have independently and spontaneously decided to raise their prices; the Commission accordingly further alleged that such uniform and general increases could not be explained otherwise than on the basis that the firms concerted; and the Commission claimed moreover to have adduced positive evidence of such concertation. But apart from such positive evidence, the question from the legal point of view is whether, generally speaking, an allegation against undertakings of concerted practices can properly be proved by circumstantial evidence, or even maybe by the mere fact of the parallel behaviour. The Court's answer was:[1]

> "Although a parallelism of behaviour cannot by itself be identified with a concerted practice, it is nevertheless liable to constitute a strong indication of such a practice when it leads to conditions of competition which do not correspond to the normal conditions of the market, having regard to the nature of the products, the importance and number of the enterprises and the volume of the said market. Such is the case especially where the parallel behaviour is such as to permit the parties to seek price equilibrium at a different level from that which would have resulted from competition, and to crystallise the status quo to the detriment of effective freedom of movement of the products in the Common Market and free choice by consumers of their suppliers."

In other words, parallel behaviour is strong but not conclusive evidence of concerted practice, the existence of which must be assessed in the context of all the relevant circumstances. In the event, the Court proceeded first to analyse the dyestuff market which was at that time characterised by few undertakings, a large number of different products, the substitutability of some but not of others, a tendency to oligopoly where certain products were concerned, small flexibility of demand, increasing demand – the most characteristic feature being, however, the compartmentalisation of the market into separate national markets of the member states, each under the influence of a price leader. It is in the context of such analysis that the Court reviewed the other circumstances of the case which revealed, *inter alia*, the following:

(1) While the increases in 1964, 1965 and 1967 were in principle uniform there were nevertheless discrepancies and the adjustments made for them showed the increases in each year not to be isolated but revealing a progressive co-operation.

---

1 [1972] CMLR 557, at pp. 622 ff., para. 66.

(2) Evidence of co-operation in the manner and timing of the increases; in particular by advance notice given by the price leader of the intention to increase prices, which allowed the other firms and the price leader to adjust their attitudes, so that the undertakings in question temporarily eliminated as regards price a risk otherwise inherent in the situation, i.e. that the price leader would increase the price and the others would not follow.

The Court enumerated further facts[1] to show that the uniform parallel behaviour was not spontaneous, referring in particular to the "compartmentalisation" of the Common Market, and to the fact that while independent differentiated price increases were conceivable, the uniform price increases put into effect on all the national markets were not.

In any event, whatever the position as regards price, in the words of the judgment, "a spontaneous attainment of such parallelism as regards the moment, the national markets and the assortment of products concerned, is difficult to conceive".[2] And after reviewing increases in co-operation in 1965 and 1967 between the firms concerned which eliminated a large number of the risks involved in autonomous behaviour, the Court concluded "that the general and uniform increase is only explicable by the convergent intention of those enterprises".[2]

Undertakings

The agreements and concerted practices must be between undertakings and the decision must be that of an association of undertakings. The term "undertakings" is not however defined in the Treaty.[3] It is ambiguous in that it can refer both to the business being carried on and to its owner; and since at least two persons are involved in an agreement, a concerted practice or a decision by an association of undertakings, questions were raised as to whether the necessary plurality of persons existed, for example, where a single business is owned by several persons or conversely a single person owns several businesses. Thus where the business is operated by a holding company through subsidiaries, is there only one undertaking, so that whatever

---

1 [1972] CMLR 557, at pp. 623 ff.
2 *Ibid.*, at p. 627.
3 It should be noted that the term undertaking is that of the authentic English version of the Treaty, corresponding to the French "entreprise", for which the term enterprise will be found in many translations made before the accession of the United Kingdom to the EEC.

restrictions are practised between the members of the group there can be no question of the application of art. 85, or is each subsidiary to be treated as a separate undertaking so that, on the contrary, art. 85 does apply? Since, however, in order to enter into an agreement an undertaking must have the capacity in law to do so, for the purpose of art. 85 the undertaking is identified with the legal entity owning it – with the result that in the case of a group of companies there can be as many undertakings as there are members of the group; and conversely where several businesses are operated by a single company, e.g. when the company operates through divisions which are not legal entities, there is only one undertaking and art. 85 has no application in relation to restrictive practices within the company.

It follows, theoretically at least, that the legal framework within which a company chooses to run its business (through subsidiaries or divisions) would govern whether or not the company's activities infringed art. 85. In fact this anomalous result is mitigated by two Decisions of the Commission, *Christiani and Nielsen*,[1] and *Kodak*,[2] the effect of which is, as will be seen,[3] that where one legal entity has, and exercises, a substantial measure of control over another, those two legal entities constitute a single undertaking for the purposes of the application of art. 85 (1).

From the identification of an undertaking with its legal owner it follows that an individual is subject to the provisions of art. 85 in relation to a business carried on by him personally; and it seems to follow that a partnership (when each partner is a part owner of the partnership business) will necessarily be within art. 85 if the other conditions of the application of the article are satisfied. There is in art. 85 no provision corresponding to RTPA 1956, s. 6 (8), which excludes partnerships between individuals from the scope of the Act. Businesses are however usually carried on by corporations, whether publicly or privately owned or state enterprises, and all such corporations are undertakings for the purposes of art. 85.[4]

NON-EEC UNDERTAKINGS

An undertaking for the purposes of art. 85 does not have to be established within the Common Market. Thus the exclusive distribution agreements between a Japanese firm and its French and Belgian distributors are agreements between undertakings for the purposes of

1 *Re Christiani and Nielsen NV*, 18 June 1969, JO 1969 L165/12; [1969] CMLR D36.
2 *Re Kodak*, 30 June 1970, OJ 1970 L147/24; [1970] CMLR D19.
3 See further p. 17, above, and pp. 67 ff., below; and see now *Centrafarm and Adriaan de Peijper* v. *Winthrop*, 31 October 1974, [1974] 2 CMLR 480; discussed at p. 215, below.
4 The application of EEC anti-trust law to public undertakings, in so far as they are the subject of special rules, is discussed in Ch. 9, Section 3, p. 245, below.

art. 85;[1] and in the case of a concerted practice before Britain's entry into the EEC involving a United Kingdom company, Imperial Chemical Industries Ltd (ICI), not itself directly present or trading within the EEC (although it had a subsidiary within the EEC), the United Kingdom company was treated as an *undertaking* for the purposes of art. 85 and fined for infringement of the article.[2] On ICI's appeal from the Commission's Decision the Court of Justice confirmed the Commission's finding that there had been concerted practices between various *undertakings*, including ICI.[3] ICI contended that since it was not directly present in the EEC, the assumption of extra-territorial jurisdiction by the Commission in relation to breach of anti-trust legislation was unjustified on various grounds including that it was contrary to generally accepted principles of both public international law and the domestic laws of individual states with "reasonably developed legal systems". The Commission claimed on the other hand that although ICI was not itself within the Common Market it took action within the Common Market in furtherance of the concerted practices by causing its wholly owned subsidiary (acting as distributor of the relevant products purchased from ICI) to give effect to concerted price increases; as an additional argument the Commission claimed that whether or not ICI could in the circumstances be said to have acted within the Common Market in relation to giving effect to the concerted practices, the concerted practices produced their effects within the Common Market.

The Commission's pleas therefore gave rise to the question whether, in order that a non-EEC undertaking (a foreign undertaking) should be subject to the Commission's jurisdiction under art. 85, there had to be a direct causal connection between the action of a foreign undertaking and the consequences of the action within the Common Market; or whether it was sufficient that there was a reaction of some kind within the EEC. The Court said the following:[4]

> "In a case of concerted practice, it is first necessary to ascertain whether the behaviour of the applicant manifested itself in the Common Market. It follows from what has been said that the increases in question took effect in the Common Market and concerned competition between manufacturers operating therein. Hence, the actions for which the fine in question has been imposed constitute practices carried on directly within the Common Market."

---

1 *Béguelin Import Co.* v. *GL Import-Export SA*, 25 November 1971, XVII Rec. 949; [1972] CMLR 81. See also, e.g., *Re Franco-Japanese Ballbearings Agreement,* 29 November 1974, OJ 1974 L343/19; [1975] 1 CMLR D8.
2 *Re Cartel in Aniline Dyes,* 24 July 1969, JO 1969 L195/11; [1969] CMLR D23.
3 *ICI Ltd* v. *EC Commission,* 14 July 1972, XVIII Rec. 619; [1972] CMLR 557.
4 *ICI Ltd* v. *EC Commission,* 14 July 1972, XVIII Rec. 619; [1972] CMLR 557, at p. 628.

The Court proceeded in effect to identify ICI with its subsidiary within the EEC as one economic unit (over-riding their separate legal entities) by reason of the measure of control exercised over the latter, thus justifying the expression "manufacturers operating therein" as including ICI, on the basis of the logic that the subsidiary is not a manufacturer but is within the Common Market, and ICI is not within the Common Market but is a manufacturer and that since they are to be deemed the same person, ICI is a manufacturer operating within the Common Market.

However, it will not in all cases be possible to show such identity. The foreign company might not be operating in the Common Market through a subsidiary but through an exclusive independent distributor; or even that link with the Common Market might be lacking; for example, the concerted practice between the undertakings could be simply to respect each other's national territories or to observe certain production quotas. If such practices were to have effects within the Common Market the Commission would wish to take action – can it do so? As in the *Dyestuffs* Case the Commission might claim that the foreign company concerned acted within the EEC – on the basis that purposeful inaction in furtherance of a concerted practice directed at the EEC was equivalent to action. And again failing acceptance of this argument the Commission might claim that the undertakings' action produced its effect within the Common Market and as such the Commission had jurisdiction. But some correlation must be established between the action and its effects. The Commission itself admitted in its submissions that it would not do for jurisdiction to be claimed on the basis of "any relationship whatever, however vague or uncertain" with the economy of the place where the effects manifested themselves. At the other end of the spectrum there could be the requirement that the relevant action had actually occurred in the place where its effects became apparent. A line has to be drawn somewhere between the two extremes and the Advocate General submitted that the effects of an action must be (1) direct and immediate, (2) reasonably foreseeable, (3) substantial.[1]

The Commission itself submitted that regard must be had to direct effects and to the principle of protection "since the maintenance of the economic order of a country and the preservation of the freedom of action of traders constitute for each state a major legitimate interest".

It is a pity that in view of its particular facts the *Dyestuffs* Case did not provide the Court of Justice with the opportunity of specifying

---

1 *ICI Ltd* v. *EC Commission*, 14 July 1972, XVIII Rec. 619; [1972] CMLR 557, at pp. 603 ff.

the necessary criteria. With the finding that ICI and its subsidiary within the EEC were one and the same economic person, answers to these questions became unnecessary to the resolution of the issues before the Court.

SECTION 3   EFFECT ON INTRA-COMMUNITY TRADE

"Which may affect trade between Member States"

Unless an agreement "may affect trade between Member States" it is not within art. 85. This is the first of the two essential conditions which an agreement must fulfil for the article to apply (the second being that the agreement should also have as its object or effect the restriction of competition within the Common Market).[1]

The first condition was included in art. 85 as a test enabling the segregation of those restrictive agreements which are within the sole jurisdiction of national authorities from those which are subject to the overriding jurisdiction of the EEC because of their incompatibility with the Common Market – namely those agreements which because they affect trade between member states render more difficult, or prevent, the economic integration which is the aim of the EEC. Thus the Commission's decisions invariably relate a finding of effect on trade between member states, with its undesirable consequences from the point of view of the creation of a Common Market, and spell out the manner in which such undesirable consequences are brought about.

If there is no effect on trade between member states, and if there is no reasonable probability of any such effect, the agreement is harmless from the point of view of the EEC and in so far as it may contain restrictive provisions these will be solely within the provisions of national law.

Indeed, the Court of Justice stated in the *Consten and Grundig* Case:[2]

> "The condition . . . aims at determining, as regards the regulation of agreements, the pre-eminence of Community law over that of the States. It is to the extent to which the agreement may affect trade between member-States that the alteration in competition provoked by the agreement relates to the prohibition in Community law of Article 85, whereas in the contrary it escapes."

As a result, legal doctrine became accustomed to treat the condition as purely jurisdictional in scope (i.e. merely as a criterion for deter-

---

1 See further Section 4, p. 35, below.
2 *Etablissements Consten SA and Grundig Verkaufs-GmbH* v. *EEC Commission,* 13 July 1966, XII Rec. 429; [1966] CMLR 418, at p. 472.

mining whether the EEC had jurisdiction over the relevant agreement), and accordingly to argue that the extent of the effect on trade was irrelevant, as long as there was some effect – the economic evaluation of the effect of the agreement being relevant only in connection with the applicability or otherwise of the second condition. This required, as a matter of legal logic, that in order to decide whether art. 85 applied to an agreement it should first be determined whether or not the restrictions in the agreement affected or might affect intra-Community trade and that only upon reaching such a finding should the decision deal with the applicability or otherwise of the second condition.

This logic must, however, have proved to be difficult to apply in practice as effect on trade presupposes the existence of a restriction of competition causing it, with the result that in the majority of its decisions the Commission follows economic rather than legal logic and considers first whether there is a restriction of competition and only in the case of such a finding considers the question of any resulting effect on intra-Community trade.[1] In other words the two conditions are now treated in practice as equal and, in so far as restriction of competition must be perceptible for art. 85 to apply,[2] so must the effect on trade also be perceptible, the Court of Justice stating in the *Béguelin* Case:[3]

> "The agreement must affect noticeably the trade between Member States and competition."[4]

Trade

This term is not defined in the Treaty or any regulation thereunder, but it is evident from the interpretation given to it by the Commission that in the context of art. 85 (and art. 86) trade embraces commercial intercourse in its widest sense, covering both the supply and processing of goods and the provision of services.[5] Trade relating to products covered by Annex I of the ECSC Treaty (i.e. coal and steel products) is subject to the special competition rules contained in that Treaty and to this extent is excluded from the EEC competition rules.[6] The term

---

1 See in particular the Commission's approach in issuing a negative clearance, p. 254, below.
2 See pp. 39 ff., below.
3 *Béguelin Import Co.* v. *GL Import-Export SA*, 25 November 1971, XVII Rec. 949; [1972] CMLR 81, at p. 96, para. 16.
4 The term perceptible renders the French expression *"sensible"*, for which the English word "noticeable" is often used; no distinction is intended between the two adjectives "noticeable" and "perceptible".
5 Though there is a general exclusion of the application of the competition rules to arms, munitions and war material intended for specifically military purposes; see art. 223 of the Treaty.
6 See art. 232 of the Treaty.

goods includes agricultural products,[1] though the Treaty contains special rules with regard to them,[2] and the supply of gas and electricity by public undertakings;[3] the term services does not include civil aviation and maritime transport,[4] and special rules exist with regard to transport by road, rail and inland waterway.[5] Services which have been considered by the Commission and by the Court include services provided by authors' rights societies,[6] by organisers of trade fairs[7] and by suppliers of television services,[8] and insurance[9] and banking[10] services.

The term trade includes not only actual but also potential trade.[11]

Between member states

The present member states of the Common Market comprise the original Six – Belgium, the Federal Republic of Germany, France, Italy, Luxembourg and the Netherlands, and the three states which acceded to the EEC on 1 January 1973 – Denmark,[12] Ireland and the United Kingdom of Great Britain and Northern Ireland.[13]

The trade which an agreement must be liable to affect, therefore, before the first condition of application of art. 85 is met, will be that between the national territories of any two or more of these nine

---

1 *Re European Sugar Cartel,* 2 January 1973, OJ 1973 L140/17; [1973] CMLR D65; *Re FRUBO,* 25 July 1974, OJ 1974 L237/16; [1974] 2 CMLR D89, and see Commission's 2nd Report on Competition Policy, April 1973, secs. 74ff.
2 Arts. 38 to 47 of the Treaty and Regulation 26, OJ 1962 30/993; see Ch. 9, Section 2, p. 242, below.
3 See Commission's 2nd Report on Competition Policy, April 1973, secs. 58ff. and 65ff, and see Ch. 9, Section 3, p. 245, below.
4 But see Ch. 9, Section 1, p. 238, below. It is an open question whether the services provided by the professions are included.
5 Arts. 74 to 84 of the Treaty and Reg. 1017. See Commission's 2nd Report on Competition Policy, April 1973, secs. 70ff., and Ch. 9, Section 1, p. 238, below.
6 *Re GEMA,* 2 June 1971, JO 1971 L134/15; [1971] CMLR D35; on appeal *sub. nom. GEMA* v. *EC Commission,* 18 August 1971, XVII Rec. 791; [1972] CMLR 694; *Belgische Radio en Televisie* v. *SV SABAM and NV Fonior,* 30 January 1974, [1974] ECR 313; [1974] 2 CMLR 238.
7 *Re Cematex,* 24 September 1971, JO 1971 L227/26; [1973] CMLR D135; *Re CECIMO,* 13 March 1969, JO 1969 L69/13; [1969] CMLR D1.
8 *Guiseppe Sacchi,* 30 April 1974, [1974] ECR 409; [1974] 2 CMLR 177.
9 Bulletin 1969 No. 5, p. 35, and see p. 49, below; see also Commission's 2nd Report on Competition Policy, April 1973, secs. 54ff.
10 *Ibid.,* secs. 51ff.
11 *Zoja* v. *Commercial Solvents Corporation,* 14 December 1972, JO 1973 L299/51; [1973] CMLR D50, at p. D59; and see *Re Advocaat,* 24 July 1974, OJ 1974 L237/12; [1974] 2 CMLR D79.
12 Including Greenland.
13 EEC Treaty, art. 227 (1), as amended by Act of Accession, art. 26 (1), as modified by Adaptation Decision, art. 15 (1).

states.[1] As to the extent of the respective national territories, it is to be noted that the competition rules of the EEC Treaty also apply to *Land* Berlin[2] and to French Guyana, Reunion, Guadeloupe and Martinique.[3] Thus an agreement which affects trade, for example, between *Land* Berlin and France, or between Martinique and Belgium may fall under the prohibition of art. 85. Presumably agreements affecting trade *only* between *Land* Berlin and the Federal Republic of Germany, or between Martinique and France, are not agreements affecting trade between member states, and are therefore outside the scope of the Treaty provisions.

With regard to the Channel Islands and the Isle of Man,[4] only those provisions of the EEC Treaty apply as are necessary to ensure implementation of the rules relating to customs matters and quantitative restrictions "under the same conditions" as in the United Kingdom.[5] It is submitted that the rules of competition contained in arts. 85 to 90 of the EEC Treaty, which are common rules designed and applied to ensure the free movement of goods between member states, should be regarded as applying in principle to these territories, so that trading arrangements between them and any member state other than the United Kingdom may be within art. 85 (1).[6]

Whilst Gibraltar is subject in principle to the Treaty[7] except with regard to rules relating to the common agricultural policy and certain tax provisions, since it has been excluded from the definition of the common customs territory[8] it is therefore doubtful that the provisions of arts. 85 to 90 apply to it. The EEC Treaty does not apply to the

---

1 The Commission considers that the continental shelf can be assimilated, with regard to the applicability of the Treaty, to the territories of the signatory States over which they exercise sovereign rights (Memorandum concerning the applicability of the EEC Treaty to the Continental Shelf, Brussels, 18 September 1970).

2 Declaration of the Government of the Federal Republic of Germany on the application of the Treaties to Berlin.

3 Art. 227 (2), which extends the provisions of the EEC Treaty relating, *inter alia*, to competition to the French overseas departments; it is not thought that such rules continue to apply to Algeria following the independence it gained from France on 1 July 1962.

4 Which are included in the definition of the customs territory of the Community: Council Reg. 1496/68, art. 1, OJ 1968 L238/1, as amended by Act of Accession, art. 29 and Annex 1.

5 Art. 227 (5) (c); Protocol No. 3, art. 1 (1), attached to the Treaty of Accession.

6 See also the provisions of the European Communities (Isle of Man) Act 1973; the European Communities (Bailiwick) Law 1973 and the European Communities (Jersey) Law 1973 which recognise, in relation to those provisions of the Treaty and of secondary legislation which apply to the Islands by virtue of Protocol No. 3, attached to the Act of Accession, the concept of direct applicability.

7 See art. 227 (3), para. 2, of the Treaty, added by art. 26 (2) of the Act of Accession.

8 Reg. 1496/68, OJ 1968 L238/1, as amended by Act of Accession, Annex I.

Faroe Islands,[1] nor to the Vatican, San Marino, Monaco and Andorra, which are independent states and were not signatories to the EEC Treaty.[2] Agreements affecting trade only between these territories and that of a member state will not therefore come within the scope of the EEC Treaty competition provisions.

A number of the Association Agreements also contain competition rules: for instance, the Agreements signed between the EEC and Greece in 1961[3] and Turkey in 1963[4] provide that arts. 85 and 86 should apply in these territories; however, in the absence of any implementing regulation such as Regulation 17, it is extremely doubtful that they have any present application.[5] There are also rules contained in the Association Agreements signed between the EEC and the non-candidate EFTA countries, Austria, Iceland, Portugal, Sweden and Switzerland, and also the Agreements signed with Norway and Finland[6]. These state that certain arrangements which affect trade between the Community and the Associated Territory are incompatible with the respective Agreements, and provide for an administrative procedure to secure compliance with the rules in the event of complaint by either Contracting Party.

Which may affect

The use of the permissive "may" in the authentic English text perhaps does not fully reflect the French "susceptible d'affecter", which indicates a probability rather than the mere possibility conveyed by the single English word "may". Indeed the Court of Justice has defined the scope of the first condition in these terms:

> "To fulfill this condition, the agreement in question should, on the basis of a collection of objective legal or factual elements, allow one to expect, with *a sufficient degree of probability*, that it would exercise a direct

---

1 In the absence of a notice given by the Government of Denmark declaring that the Treaty shall apply to the Faroe Islands, in accordance with art. 227 (5) (a) of the Treaty.
2 Nor are they included by virtue of art. 227 (4) of the Treaty (cf. in relation to San Marino and Monaco, Mégret, *op. cit.*, Vol. 1, p. 142, para. 13). However, San Marino and Monaco enjoy a *de facto* relationship with the Community by reason of commercial arrangements which exist between them and Italy and France respectively, and for this purpose are referred to as part of the customs territory of the Community: Reg. 1496/68, art. 2 and Annex, OJ 1968 L238/1.
3 JO 1963 26/294, arts. 51, 52.
4 JO 1964 217/3687, arts. 16, 22.
5 See Mégret, *op. cit.*, p. 109, para. 18.
6 In force 1 January 1973: Austria, JO 1972 L300/2, arts. 23, 27.
                                Sweden, JO 1972 L300/97, arts. 23, 27.
                                Switzerland, JO 1972 L300/189, arts. 23, 27.
                                Portugal, JO 1972 L301/165, arts. 26, 30.
            1 April 1973:   Iceland, JO 1972 L301/2, arts. 24, 28.
            1 July 1973:   Norway, OJ 1973 L171/2, arts. 23, 27.
            1 January 1974: Finland, OJ 1973 L328/2, arts. 23, 27.

or indirect, actual or potential, effect on the eddies of trade between member-States."[1]

Trade is affected when by reason of a restriction of competition trade between member states develops otherwise than it would do in the absence of the restrictions – so that there is an effect on trade even when trade increases in a certain direction. It is true in this connection that in certain of the official languages in which the Treaty of Rome is published (all these languages having equal validity) terms are used which superficially seem to suggest that the condition applies only in cases of reduction of trade; thus the use of the word "prejudiciare" in the Italian version. The effect of the *Consten-Grundig* Case[2] is however that the prejudice must be implied from the mere change of direction in trade. The policy of the EEC is that trade between member states should flow along natural channels resulting from the interplay of the laws of supply and demand across national borders of member states in the same way as it does across the sub-divisions of a single state and to the extent that this does not occur such trade has been prejudiced or affected. Or in the words of the judgment:[3]

> "In this respect, it is necessary in particular to know whether the agreement is capable of endangering, either directly or indirectly, in fact or potentially, freedom of trade between member-States in a direction which could harm the attainment of the objects of a single market between States. So the fact that an agreement favours an increase, even a large one, in the volume of trade between States is not sufficient to exclude the ability of the agreement to 'affect' the trade in the above-mentioned direction."

The following are instances where trade between member states has been affected:

In *Re CFA*[4] the case of a joint sales agency operated by a trade association (CFA) on behalf of its members who received the same average price whether the products were sold in France or were exported to other EEC countries where prices were lower, the Commission stated with respect to the condition of trade being affected:[5]

> "In that connection, examination should be made of whether the agreement is capable of [prejudicing] freedom of trade between Member-

---

1 *La Technique Minière* v. *Maschinenbau Ulm GmbH*, 30 June 1966, XII Rec. 337; [1966] CMLR 357, at p. 375.
2 *Etablissements Consten SA and Grundig Verkaufs-GmbH*, 13 July 1966, XII Rec. 429; [1966] CMLR 418.
3 [1966] CMLR 418, at p. 472.
4 *Re Comptoir Français de l'Azote*, 6 November 1968, JO 1968 L276/29; [1968] CMLR D57.
5 *Ibid.*, [1968] CMLR, D57, at p. D64.

States in a way which could injure the good functioning of the Common
Market. In the present case, one should therefore examine whether the
provisions of the agreement and those taken for its application are capable
of impeding the freedom of importation and exportation of the parties or
of third parties within the Common Market."

As a result of its consideration of the terms of the agreement as originally notified, the Commission informed the parties[1] that the members
of the association had no incentive individually to seek export outlets
in other EEC countries since by selling through CFA they received a
price which though lower than the ruling price on the home market
was higher than the export price to EEC countries and that trade
between member states was thereby affected. In the event the agreement was altered so that the disincentives to export within the EEC
were eliminated and the Commission was able to issue a negative
clearance.[2]

In *German Ceramic Tiles*[3] an aggregate rebate system operating
through a trade association of German producers of tiles was held by
the Commission to affect trade between member states. Customers
were given rebates based on their total purchases from members of the
association thus discouraging purchases from producers in other EEC
countries. But an aggregate rebate system was found also to affect
trade between member states where, under the rules of a trade association of suppliers of gas water heaters to the Belgian market, the
rebate had to be given to all purchasers of such apparatus, even on
purchases from non-members of the association. The consequence was
to make the penetration of the Belgian market unduly onerous for
suppliers who did not belong to the association, including suppliers
from other member states.[4]

A further example of trade between member states being affected
is found in the *VCH* Case[5] – concerning a trade association of Dutch
dealers in cement between whom there were restrictions on competition. The association's members controlled two thirds of the Dutch
market on which they sold considerable quantities of cement imported
from other Common Market countries. The restriction on competition
necessarily influenced the currents of trade within the Common
Market; in particular fixed prices for small quantities limited sales

---

1 In a statement of objections pursuant to Reg. 99/63, art. 2 (1), see p. 281, below.
2 As to negative clearance, see Ch. 10, Section 2, p. 257, below.
3 *Re German Ceramic Tiles Discount Agreement*, 29 December 1970, JO 1971 L10/15;
   [1971] CMLR D6.
4 *Re Gas Water Heaters*, 3 July 1973, OJ 1973 L217/34; [1973] CMLR D231.
5 *Re Vereeniging van Cementhandelaren*, 16 December 1971, JO 1972 L13/34; [1973]
   CMLR D16; on appeal *sub. nom. Vereeniging van Cementhandelaren* v. *EC Commission*,
   17 October 1972, XVIII Rec. 977; [1973] CMLR 7.

(including sales from other EEC countries) and the demand for cheaper Belgian and German cement was reduced in view of fixed selling prices agreed between the association's members. Further the restrictions inhibited growth and therefore imports from other EEC countries. The Commission held that the agreement infringed art. 85 (1) and did not grant exemption under art. 85 (3). The Decision was upheld on appeal to the Court of Justice; the *VCH* Case is discussed further at p. 60, below.

The Commission's Decision in *Re Cematex*[1] is an example of the applicability of the first condition in relation to the provision of services. Cematex was a trade association concerned with the organisation of industrial fairs (ITMA fairs) for the exhibition of textile machinery manufactured by the association's members, who by reason of their membership were restricted from exhibiting at fairs other than ITMA fairs; so that on the one hand the sales promotion activities of the members were limited and conversely organisers of other fairs were deprived of business through the abstention of the Cematex members. The Commission decided that "these restrictions on the provision of services by organisers of fairs and exhibitions and on transactions in textile machinery between countries in the European Economic Community can jeopardise the freedom of trade between member-States directly and in a manner capable of impairing the achievement of the objectives of a single market between those States."[2]

Obviously all prohibitions on exports and imports between EEC countries affect trade between member states. Such an effect, however, may also result from prohibitions on exports to or reimports from non-EEC countries, since if prices are lower on an export market the exported product might profitably be imported back into the Common Market; such source of supply is eliminated by an export or import prohibition. In *Re Omega*[3] the Commission held that in the circumstances of the case it was unlikely that products exported outside the EEC could surmount tariffs on re-entry into the Common Market; and even more unlikely for such re-imports to an EEC country to be followed by a further re-export within the Common Market – and without such re-export no trade *between* member states is involved. Nevertheless the principle remains applicable in such cases, and had the external tariff not been considered prohibitive the Commission

1 *Re Cematex*, 24 September 1971, JO 1971 L227/26; [1973] CMLR D135.
2 *Re Cematex*, [1973] CMLR D135, at p. D141, para. 26.
3 *Re Omega Watches*, 28 October 1970, JO 1970 L242/22; [1970] CMLR D49.

could have found the condition of effect on intra-Community trade satisfied.[1]

Trade between member states is necessarily affected by an exclusive distribution agreement between a distributor in an EEC country and a supplier in another EEC country since the trade flow in the relevant goods will be channelled through the distributor.[2]

Specialisation agreements (i.e. agreements by which undertakings in the interest of greater efficiency agree to limit their production of certain ranges of goods to be manufactured by the other party to the agreement), even where they are between undertakings in a single member state, may affect trade between member states by reason of a narrowing of the choices open to buyers in other member states[3].

An exclusive patents or knowhow licence granted in the Common Market can affect trade between member states. This is because the exclusivity prevents production by other licensees in the territory of the exclusive licensee, and the reduction in production possibilities causes a reduction in potential exports to other EEC countries.[4]

The above are some instances of how trade between member states may be affected by restrictive agreements. It would serve no useful purpose to continue the list of illustrations as each case depends on its own facts and it is not possible to draw any general principles from the cases; all that can be said is that once a restriction of competition is established the Commission appears to have little difficulty in finding a consequential effect on trade, whether actual or potential,[5] between member states. For example it might not at first glance be evident how an agreement between the respective trade associations of importers and wholesalers of fruit in the Netherlands, whereby the wholesalers were required to purchase their supplies only at certain auctions at Rotterdam, at which the Dutch importers' products were sold, could affect trade between member states. The Commission held that the restriction of competition, due to such limitation on the

---

1 Other factors to be considered include transport costs and accumulated profit margins: *Re Omega*, above; and see p. 94, below, and *Re Goodyear Italian-Euram*, 19 December 1974, OJ 1975 L38/10.
2 Exclusive distribution agreements are dealt with at pp. 55ff. and 97ff., below.
3 *Re Papeteries Bollore SA*, 26 July 1972, JO 1972 L182/24; [1972] CMLR D94; and see further, on specialisation agreements, p. 54ff. and 108ff.
4 *Re Agreement of the Davidson Rubber Co.*, 9 June 1972, JO 1972 L143/31; [1972] CMLR D52; and see further, under patent licensing agreements, p. 227, below.
5 *Zoja v. Commercial Solvents Corporation*, 14 December 1972, JO 1972 L299/51; [1973] CMLR D50; and see *Re Advocaat*, 24 July 1974, OJ 1974 L237/12.

wholesalers' source of supply, weakened the competitive structure of a sector of the Common Market, this weakening of a sector being capable of affecting the flow of trade between member states.[1]

SECTION 4   RESTRICTION ON COMPETITION

"Which have as their object or effect the prevention, restriction or distortion of competition within the Common Market"

We are here concerned with the second of the two conditions which agreements must satisfy to be within art. 85 (1).

Prevention, restriction or distortion

These three terms describe, with reference to competition, objects or effects of an agreement which bring it within the second criterion.

Prevention and restriction would appear to be self-explanatory. For an example of distortion see *Re German Ceramic Tiles*[2] where an aggregate rebate system operated to deflect trade away from non-German suppliers – although admittedly it could equally be said in such a case that competition was restricted. Another example of distortion is to be found in the price-fixing agreement operated between Dutch dealers of sanitary ware through their trade association GISA;[3] the members of GISA were required to apply a substantial surcharge over the manufacturer's selling prices according to whether the goods were classed by GISA as luxury goods or not. As a result (apart from the higher prices payable by certain classes of consumer) competition between manufacturers was arbitrarily distorted to the disadvantage of manufacturers producing better quality goods.[4]

It may be thought that the three terms constitute distinctions without differences, but be that as it may, the use of the three terms ensures that all relevant ways in which competition may be affected are

---

1 *Re FRUBO*, 25 July 1974, OJ 1974 L237/16; [1974] 2 CMLR D89.
2 *Re German Ceramic Tiles Discount Agreement*, 29 December 1970, JO 1971 L10/15; [1971] CMLR D6.
3 *Re Vereniging van Groothandelaren in Sanitaire Artikelen (GISA)*, 22 December 1972, JO 1972 L303/45; [1973] CMLR D125.
4 See also *Re Gas Water Heaters*, 3 July 1973, OJ 1973 L217/34; [1973] CMLR D231.

covered. In practice the Commission has found that most agreements are within art. 85 (1) by reason of "restriction" on competition, and for brevity's sake this term will be used below to include the two others, unless the context otherwise requires.[1]

Competition

While art. 3 of the Rome Treaty mentions "the institution of a system ensuring that competition in the Common Market is not distorted" as one of the activities of the Community for attaining its main objectives described in art. 2,[2] the Treaty does not define competition. The task of delimiting the concept therefore fell to the Commission as the authority entrusted with the enforcement of competition policy.

With perfect competition (in the economist's sense of a market structure comprising a sufficient number of participants on each side of the market such that the transactions of no single participant can affect the market price) at one end of the scale, and monopoly at the other (where, within limits, the price can be set by the monopolist) and with various degrees of imperfect competition in between, it is by reference to the notion of workable competition that the Commission has chosen to judge the application of art. 85 to any particular case. Thus, M. von der Groeben, a former member of the Commission responsible for Competition, writing on the Commission's competition policy[3] has described the competition which is to be protected by that policy as competition which is effective in practice. "What is needed" he continues, "is to ensure access to the markets in question, for changes in supply and demand to be reflected in prices, for production and sales not to be artificially restricted and for the freedom of action and choice of suppliers, buyers and consumers not to be compromised".

Such a concept of competition is consistent with the existence of a highly concentrated market and does not aim at the perfectly competitive market described above. In the latter case, owing to the insignificant market share of each supplier, the market price is determined by overall supply and demand and at that price each supplier can sell as much or as little as he wants; he is therefore indifferent to

---

1 For an early judgment in which the Court of Justice examined an agreement with reference to each of the three terms, see *Etablissements Consten SA and Grundig Verkaufs-GmbH* v. *EEC Commission,* 13 July 1966, XII Rec. 429; [1966] CMLR 418, at pp. 473 and 474.

2 These Treaty articles are set out at pp. 311, 212, below.

3 Droit des Communantés européenes, Les Novelles, Brussels 1969, No. 1994; authors' translation.

the action on the market of other suppliers. In fact, in a perfectly competitive market there is between suppliers no individual competition.

In a highly concentrated market, however, where there are a few suppliers in a market or where an important portion of the market is in the hands of a few suppliers – an oligopolistic market – each supplier is directly affected by the market behaviour of his competitors to which he must react positively or negatively – using the term "competitor" in its more usually accepted and common sense meaning.

It is this exposure of each market participant (whether he is one of many or of a few, or indeed the only one) to the competitive action of existing or potential competitors which is the essence of the "competition" that it is the object of the Treaty to protect.

Effective competition requires that there should be in a given market a degree of self-interested rivalry such that no one undertaking or group of undertakings acting in concert should have the power to choose its level of profits by giving less and charging more.

Whether or not there is such rivalry in a market will be a question of economic analysis having regard to the size of the market, the number of undertakings involved, their relative sizes and efficiencies and various other factors which it is beyond the scope of this book to discuss and, above all, the opportunity for entry into the market of new rivals.

Clearly, the effective competitiveness of a market can be affected to a smaller or greater degree by mergers between undertakings (concentrations) reducing the number of competitors. The control of mergers is not however within the scope of art. 85 (although art. 86 may have very limited application).[1]

If a market is found not to be effectively competitive the reason may be merely a market structure such that one or more undertakings operating in the market have a dominant position – a situation which the Treaty permits provided there is no abuse by the dominant undertaking or undertakings such as to constitute an infringement of art. 86. Here we are concerned with art. 85 which applies when a market is not effectively competitive or is less so or competition in the market is distorted as a result of agreement or concertation between undertakings.

It is important to note in this connection that the requirement is that the agreement be between undertakings and not between competitors. Indeed, many agreements which have been considered by the Commission in relation to art. 85 have been vertical agreements

---

1 See pp. 195, 199, below.

between non-competitors, i.e. where the parties to the agreements are engaged at different trading levels, as in the cases of exclusive distribution agreements between manufacturers and their wholesale distributors and other exclusive dealing agreements made for the purpose of effecting vertical market sharing[1], which distort competition in the sense that the commercial freedom of other traders and the choice of goods available to consumers are thereby restricted.

To determine whether effective competition is restricted by agreement it is necessary to take into account both actual and potential competition. There can be no restriction of competition if no competition subsists either actually or potentially. Thus in *Re Cement Makers*[2] manufacturers of artificial cement invoked art. 85 to avoid obligations to make certain payments to the producers of natural cement in return for the latter agreeing not to produce artificial cement and to accept certain limitations on sales. The Commission found, in view of technical developments since the agreement was entered into, that natural cement was no longer competitive with artificial cement, and that production of the former had shrunk to an insignificant proportion of the latter. Thus in the light of circumstances when the case was heard by the Commission the agreement did not have as its object or effect the restriction of competition – since there was no longer effective competition between the producers of natural and artificial cement. The Commission also considered whether the producers of natural cement could convert to production of artificial cement, but for economic reasons this was not considered realistic.[3] Consequently neither actual nor potential competition between the parties was found to be restricted by the agreement.

There was however restriction of potential competition in *Re Clima-Buderus*.[4] Here, Clima and Buderus each manufactured ventilating apparatus, but of different kinds; and they agreed to restrict their future production to the types of apparatus produced at the time of the agreement. Contrary to the situation in *Re Cement Makers* where the natural cement producers were found to be economically incapable of converting to artificial cement, both Clima and Buderus were financially and otherwise capable of extending their production ranges and, in so far as they had agreed not to do this, there was a restriction of potential competition, in that consumers' choice of alternative products was limited by the agreement.

---

1 See p. 60, below.
2 *Re Cement Makers' Agreement*, 5 May 1969, JO 1969 L122/8; [1969] CMLR D15.
3 The reality of potential competition was also considered in *Re Rank-Sopelem*, 20 December 1974, OJ 1974 L29/20, para. II, 1.
4 *Re Agreement of Clima Chappée S.A*, 22 July 1969, JO 1969 L195/1; [1970] CMLR D7.

Competition must subsist at all trading levels or, in other words, in each relevant market.[1] A restriction on competition between whole-salers is not therefore acceptable merely because of the adequacy of competition among producers. Thus in the *Consten and Grundig* Case[2] the Court did not accept the plea that because of competition subsisting between the *manufacturers* of recording instruments of different makes, no restriction of competition resulted from the absolute territorial protection given to Consten as Grundig's exclusive distributor in France.[3]

Further, in the case of branded products such as those in point in the *Consten-Grundig* Case (recording equipment), the Commission argued that it was not possible, in view of the differing technical characteristics of the products of the same type made by different manufacturers, for purchasers to make realistic price comparisons. If manufacturer A's tape recorder in a particular country costs more than B's corresponding product – is this because the former is a superior product or on account of excessive distribution costs? It is therefore necessary, in the view of the Commission, that A and B's products should be available on the same geographic market[4] through different distribution channels so that better standards of comparison are afforded to the consumer as a result of inter-brand competition which will show up any price difference attributable to excessive profit at the distribution level. This, according to the Commission, is all the more important where the distribution costs are high in relation to the actual cost of the product; the Commission's views were upheld on appeal by the Court of Justice.[5]

Object or effect

In the *LTM-MBU* Case[6] the Court of Justice stated the principles involved in testing whether an agreement had as its object or effect the restriction of competition; these may be summarised as follows:

(a) It is first necessary to ascertain the object of the agreement from its actual provisions, considered against the real economic background of the agreement;

---

1 See, for full discussion of relevant market, Ch. 6, below.
2 *Etablissements Consten SA and Grundig Verkaufs-GmbH* v. *EEC Commission,* 13 July 1966, XII Rec. 429; [1966] CMLR 418.
3 See also *Parfums Christian Dior and Lancôme,* 20 December 1974, 1 P (74) 239; Bulletin 1974, No. 12, point 2123: an obligation on retailers to sell only to final consumers infringes art. 85 (1) by preventing trade between retailers, thus insulating EEC markets at the distribution level.
4 The geographic market is discussed in Ch. 6, Section 3, p. 175, below.
5 *Etablissements Consten SA and Grundig Verkaufs-GmbH* v. *EEC Commission,* 13 July 1966, XII Rec. 429; [1966] CMLR 418, at p. 474. See, however, for criticism on this aspect of the Decision and Judgment, A. Deringer, *op. cit.,* para. 170 and footnotes thereto.
6 *La Technique Minière* v. *Maschinenbau Ulm GmbH,* 30 June 1966, XII Rec. 337; [1966] CMLR 357.

(b) If the preceding test by reference to its object should not reveal the agreement to be harmful to any real extent from the point of view of competition, the effects of the agreement must be considered – and the second condition will be satisfied if it is shown that the agreement in fact restricts competition *perceptibly* by reference to the competition which would exist in the absence of the agreement – here again the agreement being considered against its real economic background.

The provisions of the agreement must reveal as its object the restriction of competition and such restriction must be of sufficient importance to be perceptible – that is to participants on the relevant market other than the parties to the agreement, and to consumers. In its judgment in the *Costen and Grundig* Case[1] the Court of Justice held that if the object of the agreement was to restrict competition the second condition of art. 85 was ipso facto satisfied, the degree of restriction of competition being irrelevant.

But in the *Völk* Case[2] the Court of Justice in effect reversed its judgment in the *Consten and Grundig* Case on this point. In an action before a Munich court the defendant, the exclusive distributor in Belgium and Luxembourg for washing machines manufactured by the plaintiff, on being sued for breach of the distribution agreement, pleaded its nullity as infringing art. 85 by its provisions to secure absolute territorial protection for the distributor's territory. The plaintiff's goods had only an insignificant share of the market for washing machines in Germany (where the plaintiff carries on business) and in Belgium and Luxembourg. The Munich Court under art. 177 of the Treaty asked the Court of Justice for a ruling as to whether for the purpose of the application of art. 85 regard must be had to the fraction of the market which the plaintiff has in fact won or has sought to win in the member states of the EEC, in the particular case in Belgium and Luxembourg, where the defendant has absolute territorial protection. The Court's answer was that an agreement is not within art. 85 (1) where it only affects the market insignificantly, account being taken of the weak market position held by the parties in the products which are the subject of the agreement.

The *Völk* Case confirms the view of the Commission in its Communication of 23 July 1968[3] (dealing with permitted co-operation between undertakings) which states that art. 85 does not apply when the overall market strength of the co-operating undertakings is too

---

1 *Etablissements Consten SA and Grundig Verkaufs-GmbH* v. *EEC Commission*, 13 July 1966, XII Rec. 429; [1966] CMLR 418, at p. 473.
2 *Franz Völk* v. *Etablissements Vervaecke*, 9 July 1969, XV Rec. 295; [1969] CMLR 273.
3 JO 1968 C75/3; [1968] CMLR D5; set out in Appendix IV, p. 407, below.

small for the co-operation to result in a perceptible restriction of competition.[1] The principle that only perceptible restrictions of competition are relevant in considering the applicability of art. 85 to an agreement is further reflected in the Communication of the Commission dated 27 May 1970,[2] in which there are set out criteria as to the size and market shares of undertakings, agreements between which will not normally fall within art. 85, in that they will not usually restrict competition appreciably.

If, however, a perceptible effect on competition *may* be the consequence of an agreement the *object* of which is to restrict competition, it is not necessary that the agreement should actually have had such effect.[3] Thus in proceedings for infringement of art. 85 against a supplier of records (WEA-Filipacchi Music SA (Filipacchi)[4]) which had entered into agreements with its retailers requiring them to observe certain prohibitions on exports, the Commission (which found that Filipacchi's market strength was such that the resulting restriction on competition would be perceptible) did not accept the defence that Filipacchi would not have been able to enforce the prohibitions at law and that in consequence they were without effect – this being relevant only to any fines to be imposed. Further, Filipacchi argued that in the absence of actual effects to the agreements, no infringement of art. 85 was involved but only an attempt to infringe. The Commission held, however, that the infringement was completed when the agreement was entered into.

Where an agreement cannot be shown to have as its object the restriction of competition it has to be tested by reference to whether *in fact* it perceptibly restricts competition (which includes as we have seen potential competition).

An agreement as such may be neutral from the point of view of the restriction of competition – what matters is the use to which it is put. If rights under the agreement are used to restrict competition, the restriction will be treated as an effect of the agreement.

Thus in the *Sirena* Case,[5] the Court of Justice was asked by the Italian trial court on a referral under art. 177 of the Treaty, whether art. 85 prevented an Italian company (Sirena) from asserting the trade

---

1 See Section I, 4th para. p. 408, below. The Communication applies to the permitted forms of co-operation, irrespective of the size of the undertakings; the statement to which this note refers applies to other forms of co-operation not covered by the Communication.
2 See pp. 74 ff., below.
3 For an application of this principle, see *Re Franco-Japanese Ballbearings Agreement,* 29 November 1974, OJ 1974 L343/19; [1975] 1 CMLR D8.
4 *Re WEA-Filipacchi Music,* 22 December 1972, JO 1972 L303/52; [1973] CMLR D43.
5 *Sirena SRL* v. *Eda SRL,* 18 February 1971, XVII Rec. 69; [1971] CMLR 260.

mark "Prep" of which it was the registered owner in Italy to prevent the sale in Italy of similar products made by a German manufacturer under the same trade mark registered in Germany, the rights under both registrations of the mark having been originally acquired from the same American company, in the case of Sirena by transfer as far back as 1937.

In so far as the transfer to Sirena constituted an agreement,[1] its object could not have been the prevention of competition within the Common Market which did not exist in 1937. Whether or not an infringement of art. 85 was involved depended on its effect, i.e. the use to which the trade mark rights acquired under the transfer were in fact put. They could, no doubt, without infringement of art. 85 be used to prevent the use of the mark by a person with no claim to it. But the products imported from Germany were not mere counterfeit products. The German manufacturer had, as stated, acquired his right to the use of the German registered mark from its true owner, the same American company which had transferred the Italian registered mark to Sirena. The Court of Justice declared in answer to the question raised by the Italian Court that, in such circumstances, the use of a trade mark to prevent imports of products bearing the same mark from another member state would infringe art. 85.

Further, the Court declared that whereas in the *Sirena* Case agreements were entered into before the date when the Rome Treaty came into force, it was sufficient that their effects should be manifest after such date for art. 85 to apply.

The Court's judgment in *Sirena* implies a causal link between the agreement or agreements by which the American owner of the trade mark assigned it or licensed its use and its effect as manifested by the specific use to which, in the event, the trade mark right was put, i.e. the prevention of imports, which prevention would have been impossible but for the agreement(s), since it was by virtue of the agreement(s) that Sirena acquired its right to the use of the Italian trade mark.[2]

An agreement may however affect competition quite fortuitously, e.g. A and B enter into a co-operation agreement under which no restrictions are accepted but which is so successful that C is eliminated as a valid competitor. The agreement between A and B will have had as its effect the restriction of competition in the Common Market. It could not be, it is submitted, that in such circumstances the agreement would be within art. 85 (1). And certain authorities[3] have argued that

---

1 As to which, see discussion at p. 17, above.
2 See also *Re Advocaat*, 24 July 1974, OJ 1974 L237/12, discussed at p. 212, below.
3 See Mégret, *op. cit.*, p. 31 and authorities there quoted.

the agreement must be a sufficient cause of the restriction or, in other words, that it must tend to restrict competition. In this connection Mégret writes:

> "It is to be emphasised that this tendency to restrict competition must be assessed objectively. It is not necessary that the aim of the parties should have been the restriction of competition for in such a case, this would have been the object of the agreement; nor is it necessary that they had or should have foreseen its restrictive effects; in each such case the agreement is already forbidden by reason of its object and there is no occasion to consider its effects.
>
> "It is sufficient that objectively the agreement should be of a kind capable of restricting competition. But regard must not be had only to effects attributable directly to the provisions of the agreement. If as the result of the performance of the agreement there ensues a factual or legal situation such that the parties are able to restrict competition, the agreement could be forbidden if the parties in fact profit from this situation to restrict competition. It is not necessary to prove that the restrictions are the result of concerted practice. It is enough that they should have been made possible by the agreement."[1]

The test that the relevant agreements must have a tendency to restrict competition could be said to have been satisfied in the *Sirena* Case, since it is a classical method of market sharing to create "frontiers" through the licensing of trade marks and other industrial property rights by taking advantage of the exclusivity conferred by such rights in the territories of the states conferring them.

An exclusive distribution agreement has by its very nature a tendency to restrict competition, so that where French legislation against unfair trading was invoked to prevent parallel imports into the distributor's territory, the exercise of such legal rights to restrain competition was treated by the Court of Justice as an effect of the agreement; the agreement itself being thus void under art. 85 (1) it could not form the basis of such an action.[2]

Competition cannot be restricted in the abstract, but only on a particular market – the relevant market, for a discussion of which the reader is referred to Chapter 6, below. Suffice it to say here that to define the relevant market in which an agreement has its effects is an essential prerequisite to any consideration of whether or not art. 85 applies to the agreement.

---

1 Mégret, *op. cit.*, p. 31; authors' translation.
2 *Béguelin Import Co.* v. *GL Import-Export SA*, 25 November 1971, XVII Rec. 949; [1972] CMLR 81.

Within the Common Market

The Common Market is a geographical area comprising the territories of the nine member states with the extensions referred to above under the heading "Between Member States".[1] Article 85 applies to an agreement where all or part of the geographical component of the relevant market[2] in which an agreement has its effect is situated within the Common Market.

If there is restriction of competition within the Common Market it is immaterial whether or not the parties to the agreement are domiciled, resident, or otherwise present in the Common Market. Conversely if the agreement has effect only outside the Common Market, art. 85 is not applicable to the agreement. Thus in *Re DECA*[3] relating to an agreement in which Dutch and other civil contractors specified the basis of tendering for orders from outside the EEC, a negative clearance[4] was granted on the ground that by its terms the agreement did not restrict competition in the Common Market and that the Commission was not aware that the co-operation had in fact restrictive effects on such competition.

Similarly in *Re Supexie*[5] a joint marketing agreement for the export of phosphate fertilisers through a trade association was granted negative clearance on the ground that competition was not restricted in the Common Market, but only after modification so that the agreement related only to exports to non-EEC countries.

In *Re Rieckermann*[6] the Commission held that in so far as a manufacturer in the Common Market (AEG) agreed not to sell in Japan otherwise than to its exclusive distributor (Rieckermann) there was no restriction of competition within the Common Market; but that there was such restriction (though on the facts held not to be perceptible) in relation to certain resale and other prohibitions imposed within the Common Market to support the distributor's exclusivity in Japan.

As regards agreements by parties outside the Common Market having effects within the Common Market see comments on the *Dyestuffs* Case at pp. 23 ff., above.

---

1 See pp. 28 ff., above.
2 See Ch. 6, below.
3 *Re Rules of Dutch Engineers and Contractors Association,* 22 October 1964, JO 1964 173/2761; [1965] CMLR 50.
4 This term is explained in Ch. 10, Section 2, p. 251, below.
5 *Re Agreement of Supexie,* 23 December 1970, JO 1971 L10/12; [1971] CMLR D1.
6 *Re Agreement of Johs. Rieckermann KG and AEG-Elotherm GmbH,* 6 November 1968, JO 1968 L276/25; [1968] CMLR D78.

Restriction on competition must be perceptible: an example – Re Rieckermann

It may at this stage be useful to look more closely at the *Rieckermann* Decision.[1] It is a good example of the Commission's attitude to practices which though restrictive do not restrict competition significantly. The decision, dealing with the appointment of an exclusive distributor in Japan under an agreement having also repercussions within the Common Market, is also interesting as an example of the principle that art. 85 is limited in its application to restrictions of competition in the Common Market and more generally the case is a good illustration of the kind of analysis the Commission engages in when considering whether the second essential condition of application of art. 85 is satisfied.

Rieckermann (R) was appointed AEG's exclusive distributor in Japan for the sale of certain plant and equipment made by AEG, generally on the basis of individual orders varying considerably from customer to customer to meet local conditions. By the agreement AEG undertook (i) not to export to or sell in Japan except to R; (ii) to prevent its customers from reselling to Japan.

R undertook (a) not to re-export AEG equipment imported into Japan; (b) not to sell in Japan competing equipment.

These restrictions were analysed in the following manner in the Commission's Decision:

AS REGARDS AEG'S OBLIGATIONS

Under (i) AEG is restricted with regard to its direct sales to Japan. This is without repercussion on the level of supply and demand in the Common Market, and consequently no restriction of competition in the Common Market is involved.

Under (ii) AEG is, in effect, restricted from selling to exporters in the Common Market except on terms that they do not export to Japan. These restrictions taking effect in the Common Market do not however have a perceptible effect on the levels of supply and demand in view of the fairly large number of manufacturers of the relevant equipment within the EEC. The effect of the agreement is only to eliminate AEG from among the suppliers of the relevant equipment to exporters selling to Japan – a market which AEG in all probability would in any event wish to supply only through an exclusive distributor, in view of the technical complications of the product.

AS REGARDS R'S OBLIGATIONS

R's obligation under (a) not to re-export AEG equipment implies

---

1 *Re Agreement of Rieckermann KG and AEG-Elotherm GmbH*, 6 November 1968, JO 1968 L276/25; [1968] CMLR D78.

that it cannot be re-exported to the Common Market. This could be restrictive of competition by reducing the level of supply in the Common Market. It could, that is, theoretically but not in fact: R is not equipped to sell in the Common Market, and the equipment being for the most part tailor-made to the needs of specific customers in Japan, is not readily marketable in the Common Market. For these and certain other reasons specified in the Decision the prohibition on R against re-export to the Common Market does not constitute a perceptible restriction on competition.

The prohibition on R under (b) not to sell other manufacturers' equipment in Japan also involves in theory a restriction of competition in the Common Market in so far as R is restricted as to his sources of supply in the Common Market; he can buy only from AEG and the level of demand in the Common Market is reduced. But the elimination of R as a buyer does not in fact materially reduce the other manufacturers' outlets as regards their exports to Japan. On the facts, therefore, competition in the Common Market is not perceptibly reduced.

The *Rieckermann* Decision therefore brings out two points:

(a) While the acceptance of a direct restriction on export to a non-EEC country such as that accepted by a supplier who has appointed an exclusive distributor for that country does not normally restrict competition in the Common Market, it must not be assumed that every restriction on exports to non-EEC countries (or for that matter any other restriction relating to a market outside the EEC) is in all circumstances outside the scope of art. 85 (see AEG's restriction (ii)) – since there may be repercussions within the EEC;

(b) Nor must it be assumed that restrictions on imports into the EEC will necessarily be within art. 85 (see R's prohibition (a)) – since in the light of market conditions these may have no perceptible repercussions on competition within the EEC (see also in this latter connection *Re Grosfillex*[1] and *Re Kodak*[2]).

SECTION 5   EXAMPLES OF PROHIBITED PRACTICES

"and in particular those which:"

After specifying the conditions subject to which it is applicable, art. 85 (1) proceeds by enumerating "in particular" – that is by way of example – certain types of agreement (or types of clauses in agreements) which art. 85 (1) is intended to catch, provided of course that they

---

1 *Re Agreement of Grosfillex SARL,* 11 March 1964, JO 1964 58/915; [1964] CMLR 237.
2 *Re Kodak,* 30 June 1970, JO 1970 L147/24; [1970] CMLR D19.

restrict competition and affect trade between member states. The enumeration is therefore by no means exhaustive either in theory or in practice. Nevertheless most types of agreement caught by art. 85 (1) come within one or more of the types of agreement listed in sub-paragraphs (a) to (e) and it is useful to look at some of the actual agreements which have been considered by the Commission during the years 1962 to date under the various headings.

Fixing of prices and other trading conditions

> "(a) directly or indirectly fix purchase or selling prices or any other trading conditions;"

AGREEMENTS RELATING TO PRICES

Horizontal price fixing – Horizontal price fixing by agreement between competitors in different EEC countries is obviously one of the most serious forms of restrictive practice in view of its direct and immediate effect on the flow of goods between Common Market countries. In the *Dyestuffs* Case[1] the Commission found ten major producers of dyes in various countries both within and without the EEC involved in concerted practices leading to simultaneous and equal price increases by the companies concerned over a number of years. While the firms concerned remained competitors as to quality and service they had "contracted out" of price competition to the detriment of consumers, and this both restricted competition within the Common Market and affected trade between member states.

Direct horizontal price fixing was also involved in the *Quinine Cartel* Case[2] where prices and discounts were agreed between the members of the cartel comprising the leading producers in Europe. The Commission found this particularly serious as in this industry price competition was the only effective form of competition.

The *Dyestuffs*[1] and *Quinine Cartel*[2] Cases are extreme examples of direct horizontal price fixing across national borders and in both cases the Commission imposed fines[3]. A recent interesting example of direct price fixing is *Re Franco-Japanese Ballbearings Agreement*,[4] where Japanese producers agreed, on pressure from their French competitors, to increase the price of their exports to France.

Price fixing may be indirect. Thus Cimbel,[5] a trade association of Belgian cement manufacturers, fixed its members' prices for sales to

1 *Re Cartel in Aniline Dyes,* 24 July 1969, JO 1969 195/11; *ICI Ltd v. EC Commission,* 14 July 1972, XVIII Rec. 619; [1972] CMLR 557.
2 *Re Cartel in Quinine,* 16 July 1969, JO 1969 L192/5; [1969] CMLR D41.
3 As to power to impose fines, see Ch. 10, Section 6, p. 293, below.
4 29 November 1974, OJ 1974 L343/19.
5 *Re Cimbel,* 22 December 1972, JO 1972 L303/24; [1973] CMLR D167.

Belgium but not for sales to other EEC countries. In the absence of repercussions outside Belgium, price fixing in Belgium would not be within art. 85. But Cimbel's members, through the association, operated a compensation system for equalising the proceeds of home and foreign sales. The Commission held that this necessarily influenced the export prices and the conditions of sale of each manufacturer. The Commission went on to hold that the system generally distorted competition in the Common Market by subsidising Belgian exports out of the higher prices obtainable on the home market, to the prejudice of non-Belgian manufacturers and of the Belgian consumer who was overcharged to provide the funds to operate the compensation scheme.

Indeed price fixing in the sense of withdrawal from price competition by undertakings in the same country has generally been found in the context of the activities of trade associations of various kinds. The expression "trade association" is used here in the sense of its definition under the RTPA[1] – that is a body of persons, whether incorporated or not, formed to further the trade interests of its members.

Thus joint marketing through a trade association at prices and on terms fixed by the association has been common in the six EEC countries. As a result of action by the Commission many such arrangements have either been brought to an end or modified so as to relate only to exports to non-EEC countries and to trade within the country of the trade association only.[2]

Restrictions relating to prices have also been condemned by the Commission where a trade association fixes its members' selling or minimum selling prices or precludes them from engaging in indirect forms of price competition such as by the grant of rebates or of favourable payment terms, or by loans of plant, or generally from engaging in any practice resulting in the buyer being enabled to acquire goods on better terms than those allowed by the association. In the *VCH* Case[3] the trade association concerned fixed its members'

---

1 RTPA 1956, s. 6 (8).
2 For decisions of the Commission in relation to joint marketing arrangements, see:
    Re Agreement of Comptoir Belge de l'Azote (Cobelaz) (No. 1), 6 November 1968, JO 1968 L276/13; [1968] CMLR D45; *Re Agreement of Comptoir Belge de l'Azote (Cobelaz) (No. 2)*, 6 November 1968, JO 1968 L276/19; [1968] CMLR D68; *Re SEIFA*, 30 June 1969, JO 1969 L173/8; *Re Comptoir Français de l'Azote (CFA)*, 6 November 1968, JO 1968 L276/29; [1968] CMLR D57; *Re Nederlandse Cement-Handelmaatschappij NV*, 23 December 1971, JO 1972 L22/16; [1973] CMLR D257; *Re Agreement of Supexie*, 23 December 1970, JO 1971 L10/12; [1971] CMLR D1.
3 *Re Vereeniging van Cementhandelaren*, 16 December 1971, JO 1972 L13/34; [1973] CMLR D16; and *Vereeniging van Cementhandelaren* v. *EC Commission*, 17 October 1972, XVIII Rec. 977, [1973] CMLR 7.

selling prices for quantities below a certain level and also, in relation to sales above that level, required them to make a provable profit, thus in effect fixing a minimum selling price for these quantities.

Where selling or minimum selling prices are not fixed by a trade association but purport to be recommended, art. 85 may still apply to the recommendations. While by definition a recommendation can be accepted or not, in practice recommendations may lead to what the Commission termed in *VCH* "a uniform and co-ordinated conduct"[1] resulting in a restriction of competition. In upholding the Commission's Decision condemning the VCH agreement, the Court of Justice stated:[2] "[a recommended price] affects competition by the fact that it permits all the participants to foresee with a reasonable degree of certainty what the price policy of their competitors will be".

This reasoning, though formulated with regard to agreements recommending prices, would seem equally applicable to agreements relating simply to the exchange of information, whether directly between competing undertakings, or through a trade association, since such agreements may well be a means of equivalent pricing between competitors. This is especially true of "open price system" agreements, by which competitors simply inform each other, through a trade association or otherwise, of their prices. While under the "open price system" agreements competitors are free to charge what they wish, the practical effect of such agreements is to bring about a levelling of prices between competitors, each competitor knowing that any alteration in his own prices will be matched by his competitors. These agreements clearly restrict competition.[3]

Indeed the Commission has investigated an agreement between national associations of undertakings of four member states operating in a specialised insurance branch. The agreement provided for the extensive exchange of information where cover was transferred from one country to another: the insurer approached to provide cover was obliged to request, and the previous insurer obliged to provide, information as to the rate of premium charged, the actual premium received and the financial background of the contract taken over. The Commission considered that this information normally constituted business secrets not exchanged between genuine competitors and that its exchange was liable to curtail the scope for competitive action between insurers in this specialised branch, jeopardising the freedom of intra-Community trade with regard to offers and supplies of insurance

---

1 [1973] CMLR D16, at p. D28, para. 47.
2 [1973] CMLR 7, at p. 22, para. 21.
3 See *Cartridge Manufacturers' Agreement*, which was voluntarily ended after intervention by the Commission; Bulletin 1973 No. 7/8, point 2111.

services. On the Commission's intervention the agreement was terminated without the need for a decision to be adopted.[1]

Vertical price fixing: resale price maintenance – Price fixing is involved in agreements imposing on a buyer a fixed or minimum resale price (resale price maintenance – or RPM). The practice is however generally either forbidden or controlled under the national laws of member states and therefore has not presented a serious problem from the point of view of EEC competition policy. Moreover, it is virtually impossible to maintain prices on a market open to imports of the same or similar products; and it is primarily indirectly, through its action against impediments to the free movement of goods within the Common Market, that the Commission seeks to ensure that RPM allowed under national law does not affect trade between member states. Thus in Germany, until the law was changed in 1973, RPM was allowed provided a watertight system ensured the effective enforcement of the system to secure fair trading. Nevertheless the *Deutsche Grammophon* Judgment of the Court of Justice[2] frustrated that company's attempt to safeguard its RPM system by the use of industrial property rights to prevent imports of records for resale at less than the maintained price.

If an RPM system cannot be protected by the exercise of otherwise perfectly valid industrial property rights, a fortiori clauses in agreements such as export prohibitions imposed on distributors in other countries or re-import prohibitions, to ensure that there is no undercutting of the specified resale price are equally unacceptable,[3] and in two cases the Commission has forbidden direct RPM across the borders of member states. Thus in one case[4] German retailers of certain products of N.V. Philips Gloeinlampen were obliged by the distributor in Germany, Deutsche Philips (the German subsidiary of N.V. Philips), to sell at prices fixed by the latter, irrespective of whether the sales were made in Germany or in other EEC countries; and the retailers were to be bound by the fixed price even in the case of re-imports – "re-import price-fixing". The Commission held the extension of the

---

1 Under the "informal procedure" (as to which see p. 273, below); Bulletin 1969 No. 5 p. 35. For further comments by the Commission regarding agreements for the exchange of information see the Commission's Communication on Co-operation Agreements, set out in Appendix IV, p. 407, below; see also the Commission's decision in *Re Agreements between Manufacturers of Glass Containers*, 15 May 1974, OJ 1974 L160/1, at para. 43; [1974] 2 CMLR D50.

2 *Deutsche Grammophon Gesellschaft-mbH* v. *Metro SB-Grossmärkte GmbH & Co. KG*, 8 June 1971, XVII Rec. 487; [1971] CMLR 631; and see p. 216, below.

3 As the Commission made clear in the statement of objections (as to which see p. 281, below) to the Agfa-Gevaert Group with regard to the group's distribution arrangements for colour film; Bulletin 1970 No. 2, p. 63.

4 *Re Deutsche Philips GmbH*, 5 October 1973, OJ 1973 L293/40; [1973] CMLR D241.

German fixed prices to other member states was purely and simply a restriction of competition within art. 85 (1) and in condemning re-import price fixing the Commission stated[1]:

> "This reimport price-fixing cannot be justified by the fact that it serves to protect the price-fixing which is legally permitted in Germany by preventing the sale of imported goods below the prices fixed in Germany and thus makes it possible to maintain the price-fixing. The fact that vertical price-fixing is allowed in a given Member-State is not sufficient justification for exempting measures designed to preserve this price-fixing from the scope of Article 85 (1). A market-sharing policy conflicting with the objectives of the Common Market cannot be considered to comply with the competition rules in the EEC Treaty simply because the national legislature has permitted the fixing of consumer prices for certain goods.
>
> "Clearly it should not be overlooked that retailers in Germany did not, as a result of the reimport price-fixing, lose the possibility of purchasing products in other EEC countries on more favourable terms, notably at lower purchase prices. However, the only advantage to be gained from this would be an increase in dealers' trading margins without the dealers being able to pass this advantage on to consumers in the form of lower prices, and thereby increase sales and obtain new customers. At any rate the competitive position at the retail stage – as regards the prices which were decisive for the consumer – would be the same as in the case of protection by means of export or reimport bans."

In *Re Du Pont de Nemours (Deutschland)*[2] the Commission held certain resale price maintenance obligations, imposed by German manufacturers of photographic materials on dealers, to infringe art. 85 (1) to the extent that the RPM obligation related to re-imports from other EEC countries.

But in any event there will be a direct prohibition under art. 85 in the case of collective (as opposed to individual) resale price maintenance, as where members of a trade association are bound to impose resale prices and to support each others' maintained prices by an embargo and other measures against infringers. Thus in *Re ASPA*[3] the Commission granted a negative clearance only after the removal from the relevant agreement of all provisions relating to the support of resale prices.

It is to be noted that while price fixing has been touched on above in the context of example (a) as an isolated phenomenon, it is but one

---

1 [1973] CMLR D241, at p. D245.
2 14 June 1973, OJ 1973 L194/27; [1973] CMLR D226.
3 *Re Association Syndicate Belge de la Parfumerie*, 30 June 1970, JO 1970 L148/9; [1970] CMLR D25.

of several devices employed in relation to market sharing or the control of outlets – see further discussion below under examples (b) and (c).

AGREEMENTS RELATING TO ANY OTHER TRADING CONDITIONS

Price is only one of the elements in a commercial transaction, so that it is natural that any other restrictions on the commercial freedom of undertakings should be mentioned in the same example as the fixing of prices. Mention is made below of various terms and conditions of trade which have been considered by the Commission.

Export and import prohibitions – Terms involving prohibitions on exports and imports above all others restrict the freedom of movement of goods and constitute the most direct method of isolating national markets within the EEC, and naturally it is only in the case of insignificant agreements (as in the *Völk* Case[1]) that export or import prohibitions would be tolerated. *Re Kodak*[2] is an example of export prohibitions being incorporated into the conditions of sale. That company established a distribution system under which sales by distributing subsidiaries in various EEC countries were on terms that trade purchasers at retail level in the country of the distributing subsidiary should not export Kodak products. Kodak's standard conditions of sale to the retailer were only accorded negative clearance by the Commission after removal of the export prohibitions and with them the impediment to parallel imports from an EEC country where prices were low to another such country where higher price levels might prevail.

Tantamount to a direct prohibition on export or import would be a term inhibiting these activities. Thus the direct prohibition on export referred to above in *Re Kodak* was reinforced by a provision that if there were exports the sale had to be at the price prevailing in the country of destination.[3] Parallel imports being impossible in these conditions the elimination of the provision was required by the Commission before it would issue a negative clearance. Similarly the practice of a supplier who charged his customer extra if he exported the goods sold to him was not approved by the Commission.[4]

Personal qualifications required of trading parties – Competition can be restricted where undertakings agree to trade only with persons who

---

1 *Franz Völk* v. *Ets. Vervaecke SPRL*, 9 July 1969, XV Rec. 295; [1969] CMLR 273; and see p. 40, above.
2 *Re Kodak*, 30 June 1970, JO 1970 L147/24; [1970] CMLR D19.
3 See also *Re Agreements between Manufacturers of Glass Containers*, 15 May 1974, OJ 1974, L160/1; [1974] 2 CMLR D50.
4 See Mégret, *op. cit.*, p. 46, and the Commission's Press Communication of 22 May 1967 there discussed; for a further example see *Christian Dior and Lancôme*, noted at p. 39, n. 3, above.

have certain qualifications – whether personal, financial, or technical or that they are members of an association, such requirements being a means of restricting market access. An example is found in the *VCH* Case (a trade association of Dutch dealers in cement) where members were not allowed to sell to or buy from other traders in cement unless "recognised" as such.[1]

Where however technical qualifications are needed of a purchaser buying for resale to ensure the proper distribution and servicing of the manufacturer's goods, such purchaser can be required to have the necessary qualifications. Thus Omega's goods can only be sold to qualified jewellers and watchrepairers for retailing, and similarly in relation to Kodak's products, which must be sold for resale only to qualified persons with properly equipped premises. (See also under "Exclusive Distribution", p. 55, below.)

Trade marks – An agreement that goods must be sold only under a certain trade mark restricts competition; for example in *Re Transocean Marine Paint*[2] members of a trade association were required to sell their production of paints of a certain quality under the name "Transocean". For the optional use of a quality mark see *Re ASBL*[3] concerning a trade association for the promotion of electrically soldered tubes.

Publicity – Publicity is an important competitive weapon so that an undertaking's freedom to conduct such publicity as it thinks fit must not be restricted by agreement. No such restriction is, however, involved where general publicity is conducted by a trade association provided that its members can also conduct their own individual publicity.[4]

Description of goods – An obligation on the members of an association to sell under descriptions designated by the association goods satisfying minimum quality requirements was held to be restrictive of competition by the Commission but negative clearance was granted on the basis of a "watered-down version" of the obligation, such that the minimum quality requirements were to be reasonably determined, having regard to various factors, including the description of the goods.[5]

---

1 *Re Vereeniging van Cementhandelaren*, 16 December 1971, JO 1972 L13/34; [1973] CMLR D16; and p. 60, below.
2 *Re Transocean Marine Paint Association*, 27 June 1967, JO 1967 163/10; [1967] CMLR D9. See p. 87, below, for comment on this decision.
3 *Re Association pour la Promotion du Tube d'Acier Soudé Electriquement*, 29 June 1970, JO 1970 L153/14; [1970] CMLR D31.
4 Commission's 1st Report on Competition Policy, April 1972, sec. 36, and the Communication on Co-operation Agreements, set out in Appendix IV, p. 407, below.
5 *Re Vereeniging van Vernis- en Verffabrikanten in Nederland*, 25 June 1969, JO 1969 L168/22; [1970] CMLR D1.

Limitation of production, markets and investment

> *"(b) Limit or control production, markets, technical development or investment;"*

Included under this heading are agreements relating to: quotas; specialisation; exclusive distribution; joint selling and purchasing and limitation of investment.

Quotas – Quota agreements which have come before the Commission have usually been associated with schemes for the sharing of markets on a geographical basis or for securing a national market to local manufacturers and/or distribution channels (see also below under "Market Sharing", p. 57). Thus the *Quinine Cartel* Case[1] involved in relation to quinine the acceptance of sales quotas by all the parties and the acceptance of a total prohibition on the manufacture of quinidine, a derived product, by two of the firms involved. The quotas and prohibitions had as their object the maintenance at the same level of the relative market strengths of the undertakings concerned, which if upset might lead to the excess production by one national producer being imported into another producer's reserved territory.

In *Re NCH*[2] a company jointly owned by German cement manufacturers was employed to act as the distributor of such manufacturers in the Benelux countries. Both the total amount to be marketed and proportions in which it was to be supplied by each manufacturer were the subject of quotas established to give effect to a market sharing agreement (the NCA agreement) between Dutch, German and Belgian cement manufacturers by which German sales in Holland were to be limited to a certain tonnage.[3]

Specialisation – Specialisation agreements are those whereby firms agree to refrain from the production of certain ranges of goods on the basis that they can be more efficiently produced by the other party to the agreement. Thus, in *Re Jaz-Peter*[4] there was an agreement between Jaz, a French manufacturer of clocks, and Peter, a German manufacturer of clocks, whereby Jaz was to produce a range of electrical clocks to the exclusion of Peter and Peter was to produce a range of mechanical clocks to the exclusion of Jaz. The agreement involved a limitation or control of production and also limited and controlled

---

1 *Re Cartel in Quinine*, 16 July 1969, JO 1969 L192/5; [1969] CMLR D41.
2 *Re Nederlandse Cement-Handelmaatschappij NV*, 23 December 1971, JO 1972 L22/16, [1973] CMLR D257.
3 For a further discussion of the agreements affecting the Dutch cement industry, see p. 60, below.
4 *Re Agreement of Jaz SA*, 22 July 1969, JO 1969 L195/5; [1970] CMLR 129.

outlets, each party being appointed the other's exclusive distributor in their respective territories (see further below).

Specialisation agreements often provide for co-operation in research and development thereby limiting the parties' freedom with respect to technical development and investment. Nevertheless, specialisation agreements generally qualify for exemption under art. 85 (3).[1]

Exclusive distribution – By the appointment of an exclusive distributor for all or part of the Common Market a manufacturer or other supplier foregoes the right to sell his products directly in the distributor's territory. He is therefore limited by the exclusive distribution agreement as to the markets he can supply, which may also involve a limitation with respect to sources of supply since a distributor will normally be precluded from acquiring competing goods. But as in the case of specialisation agreements, exclusive distribution agreements are, subject to certain safeguards, looked upon favourably and qualify for art. 85 (3) exemption.[2]

Of special interest in this connection are selective distribution agreements, i.e. agreements whereby in order to ensure the efficient distribution throughout the Common Market of goods of high quality and technicity,[3] restrictions are imposed by a manufacturer on his exclusive distributors within the Common Market limiting their outlets qualitatively (by requiring retailers appointed by the distributors to satisfy certain technical or personal qualifications) and/or quantitatively (by restricting the number of the distributor's retail outlets). Such agreements, provided they do not result in the isolation of national markets, may be exempted by the Commission under art. 85 (3).[4] It is important, however, that the criteria for selecting distributors are applied in a uniform and non-discriminatory manner to all potential distributors.[5]

Joint Selling – Joint selling particularly of uniform products such as cement and fertilisers has been a common feature of the marketing of such products in Europe. Agreements relating to joint selling have often provided for goods to be supplied exclusively and in agreed

---

1 See pp. 108, 184, below.

2 See p. 81, below, for individual exemption, and p. 97, below, for group exemption.

3 Luxury goods not requiring technical maintenance do not justify a selective distribution system: *per* M. Borschetta, Commissioner for Competition, Statement to European Parliament, 18 October 1974, Bulletin 1974, No. 10, point 1304, referring to *Parfums Christian Dior and Lancôme,* 20 December 1974 1 P (74) 239; Bulletin 1974, No. 12, point 2123.

4 *Re Omega,* 28 October 1970, JO 1970 L242/22; [1970] CMLR D49; for a detailed analysis of which, see p. 92, below. See also *Re Bayerische Motoren Werke AG,* noted at p. 94, n. 2, below.

5 See Commission's 3rd Report on Competition Policy, May 1974, sec. 10.

proportions to a common sales agency (a trade association) which sells at prices and on terms which it determines, the association accounting to the firms concerned for the proceeds of sale, usually after adjustment to ensure that all the firms receive the same price per unit sold. The effect of this type of arrangement on the market is that exclusive selling through the sales agency and supply quotas at fixed prices prevent all competition between those participating in the market, suppliers having neither the incentive nor the ability to undertake the sales of their products at prices, in quantities and on markets freely decided, and purchasers are deprived of choice between offers and the benefit of price competition between suppliers. Nevertheless such arrangements may suit the needs of particular national markets and have been cleared by the Commission, but only after amendment so as (a) to limit the joint selling to one EEC country only and to sales outside the EEC; (b) to remove all restrictions on the freedom of buyers with regard to exporting and importing; (c) to remove restrictions on direct sales by the firms concerned to other EEC countries; and (d) to remove provisions for averaging prices realised by the sales agency as between home sales and sales to non-EEC countries (which at certain price levels discourage individual sales by the firms concerned to other EEC countries). By these means the permeability of the market within the EEC is ensured. For cases dealing with joint sales agencies see *Re Cobelaz-Usine de Synthese*,[1] *Re Cobelaz-Cokeries*,[2] *Re CFA*,[3] *Re SEIFA*.[4] However in relation to such decisions generally the Commission has stated:[5] "The Commission is at present making enquiries and undertaking investigations in order to see that, independently of the removal of the explicit restrictions on exports to other Member States, the maintenance of *national*[6] joint selling agencies does not lead to a de facto protection of internal markets incompatible with the competition rules of the Treaty."

Joint Purchasing – The corollary of joint selling is joint purchasing. By this means suppliers contract out of competition in acquiring goods for trade or processing and competition as between the sellers is dis-

---

1 *Re Agreement of Comptoir Belge de l'Azote (Cobelaz) (No. 1)*, 6 November 1968, JO 1968 L276/13; [1968] CMLR D45.
2 *Re Agreement of Cobelaz (No. 2)*, 6 November 1968, JO 1968 L276/19; [1968] CMLR D68.
3 *Re Comptoir Français de L'Azote (CFA)*, 6 November 1968, JO 1968 L276/29; [1968] CMLR D57.
4 *Re SEIFA*, 30 June 1969, JO 1969 L173/8.
5 Commission's 1st Report on Competition Policy, April 1972, sec. 13.
6 Authors' emphasis.

torted. Joint purchasing however usually results in lower costs to the benefit of the ultimate consumer and it is not surprising that few such agreements have come before the Commission for decision; one example is *Re SOCEMAS*[1] concerning a trade association formed by medium-sized French multiple food stores to prospect foreign sources of supply. The association in fact only agreed terms with foreign sellers, the members of the association being free to place or not to place the order, and the Commission accordingly granted a negative clearance.[2]

Limitation of investment – Belgian cement manufacturers, members of the trade association Cimbel, undertook, under the rules of the association, not to create new industries except with the consent of all interested parties. The Commission held competition to be restricted[3] in that (1) Belgian manufacturers were prohibited from setting up new plants within their foreign competitors' trade areas, and (2) there ensued a lack of demand from the Belgian cement industry for capital goods and services requisite for the establishment of new production facilities.

Market sharing

"(c) share markets or sources of supply;"

Market sharing, whether in relation to outlets or sources of supply, can be horizontal, i.e. where the relevant agreement affects the position of parties at the same trading level, such as a quota arrangement between manufacturers, or vertical, i.e. where the relevant agreement affects the position of parties at different trading levels, such as a distribution agreement between manufacturers and wholesalers. The effect of horizontal market sharing will normally be the allocation of supply or demand quotas between the parties to the agreement, while the usual effect of vertical market sharing will be the exclusion of third parties from access or full access to a particular geographic or product market. As will be seen below market sharing arrangements are often implemented through the operation of two or more connected agreements with both vertical and horizontal effects.

Horizontal market sharing – The geographic allocation of markets is considered by the EC Commission as particularly restrictive of

---

1 *Re Société Commerciale et d'Etudes des Maisons d'Alimentation*, 17 July 1968, JO 1968 L201/4; [1968] CMLR D28.
2 As to negative clearance, see Ch. 10, Section 2, p. 251, below.
3 *Re Cimbel*, 22 December 1972, JO 1972 L303/24; [1973] CMLR D167. For further discussion of this case, see p. 83, below.

competition and contrary to the realisation of a single market. In the words of the Commission:[1]

> "Agreements or concerted practices for the purpose of market sharing are generally based on the principle of mutual respect of the national markets of each Member State for the benefit of producers resident there. The direct object and result of their implementation is to eliminate the exchange of goods between the Member States concerned. The protection of their home market allows producers to pursue a commercial policy – particularly a pricing policy – in that market which is insulated from the competition of other parties to the agreement in other Member States, and which can sometimes only be maintained because they have no fear of competition from that direction. The fixing of delivery quotas in relation to total sales, combined in some cases with a compensation scheme to ensure that the quotas are respected, means that the members of the group give up any possibility of obtaining an advantage over their competitors by applying an individual sales policy."

An extreme example of horizontal market sharing is found in *Re Julien-Van Katwijk*,[2] where Julien (a Belgian firm) agreed to limit its exports of tubing to the Dutch market and Van Katwijk (a Dutch firm) agreed not to export at all to the Belgian market. In the absence of any redeeming features qualifying it for exemption under art. 85 (3) the agreement was condemned.

The *Quinine Cartel* Case[3] is a more complex example. A number of producers of quinine agreed to reserve to themselves certain territories, primarily their own national markets. To ensure the success of this agreement they also agreed upon prices and quotas (coupled with provision for adjustment if they were exceeded) – the purpose of the quotas and price fixing being to eliminate incentives which could lead a participant to "invade" the reserved territory of another producer. As a result each participant was enabled to trade under conditions of monopoly in his reserved market.

A more recent decision is *Re Sugar Cartel*,[4] where the main producers of sugar in France, Belgium, Holland, Germany and Italy, against a background of excess production in France and Belgium, deficiencies in Italy and Holland, and of approximately balanced production and consumption in Germany, concerted so as to reserve to each national group of producers its own national market by one or more of the following methods, according to the characteristics of the particular

---

1 Commission's 1st Report on Competition Policy, April 1972, sec. 2.
2 *Re Agreement of Van Katwijks Industrieën*, 28 October 1970, JO 1970 L242/18; [1970] CMLR D43.
3 *Re Cartel in Quinine*, 16 July 1969, JO 1969 L192/5; [1969] CMLR D41.
4 2 January 1973, OJ 1973 L140/17; [1973] CMLR D65.

market: selling directly or indirectly only to *competitors*, i.e. other producers, in another national market; or not without the latter's consent; or at an increased price aligned on that of the national producer; and by compelling *dealers* to co-operate in such isolation of national markets.

The effect of sales between producers is (in the words of the Commission[1]) that "without these sales between producers . . . the sugar producers in the surplus countries . . . would sell their sugar individually on the [market of a deficiency country, e.g. Holland] fixing the quantities, prices and conditions themselves and using their own trade marks. In respect of the quantities sold to their competitors the producers have thus given up independent commercial activity on the Dutch market"; and further "normally it is not to a producer's advantage to sell large quantities of his product to one or more competitors. He can obtain higher profits by supplying dealers and consumers direct. Deliveries from one producer to another are thus to be explained by the fact they were an effective means of restricting competition between the [producers] concerned and preventing . . . consumers from obtaining the sugar they need freely from foreign suppliers." Since "foreign suppliers" include, in addition to producers, independent dealers, it is necessary for the restriction of competition between suppliers to be supplemented by measures to prevent cheaper sugar traded by dealers finding its way on to the market of the deficiency country, if the isolation of that market is to be effective. Thus, dealing with sales of the Belgian producer, Raffinerie Tirlemontoise (RT), to Holland, the Commission states "with the exception of its own deliveries direct to the Dutch producers, RT gave the exclusive handling of its sales in the Netherlands to two firms, Export and Hotlett, on condition that they should only deliver to buyers or final users approved by the Dutch sugar producers CSM and SU" and Export and Hotlett were also prohibited from selling to the Netherlands sugar produced by the Belgian producers other than the RT group. The circle was closed in the trading years 1970/71 by Dutch dealers being made party to the market sharing agreement between Dutch producers and RT so that thereafter deliveries of Belgian sugar to the Netherlands were made through Belgian and Dutch dealers in agreement with the Dutch producers; and when Dutch dealers had in the trading years 1968/69 entered into an agreement with French producers for the purchase of large quantities of sugar to be delivered over several years, the dealers had to agree with Dutch producers that the sugar would not be sold at too competitive a price in relation to Dutch produced sugar. In the

---

1 OJ 1973 L140/33.

western part of the German market sales of Belgian sugar were made by dealers of whom it had been required that, in the case of sales for human consumption, the consent of Pfeifer & Langen, a German producer, was to be obtained, or the dealers' selling price increased by a specified amount.

As regards the supply of sugar for the Italian market sales were made by a suppliers' group of Belgian, French and German producers to an importing group of Italian producers – it being understood that other sales to the Italian market would only be made by the suppliers' group *at a higher price.*

Enough has been said to indicate the general nature of the practices of the sugar cartel. The full facts are however complex relating as they do to practices of producers in France, Belgium and Germany over several years regarding sales to the Italian, Dutch and German markets, and the interested reader must refer to the actual Decision.

Vertical market sharing – While exclusive distribution agreements between two parties generally qualify for exemption under art. 85 (3)[1] – exclusive dealing involving more than two parties may be a means of excluding non-participants from a market and as such is unlikely to be exempted under art. 85 (3).

Thus a group of suppliers may agree between themselves the proportions in which they will supply a particular EEC national market and to supply on that market only such traders as agree to buy exclusively from them. The result of such an arrangement is that instead of a single national market there are two markets, one comprising the suppliers participating in the arrangement and their tied customers, and the other comprising the non-participating suppliers and their customers who are not tied. This has the double consequence that suppliers from other EEC countries will not have access to the whole of the market and customers in the country concerned are deprived of certain sources of supply. Such arrangements can isolate a particular national market from the rest of the Common Market and reinforce horizontal market sharing.

A large section of the Dutch cement market was tied up in this way by two main agreements which have been the subject of Decisions or action by the Commission: (a) the "Noordwijks-Cement-Accoord" (NCA) agreement between Dutch, Belgian and German cement manufacturers fixing quotas and uniform prices and conditions for sales to Holland and imposing various other restrictions; (b) the "Vereeniging van Cementhandelaren" (VCH) contract, by which members of VCH, a trade association of Dutch wholesale cement

---

1 See p. 97, below.

dealers and the manufacturers participating in the NCA agreement agreed on mutual exclusive dealing, and that cement purchased by members of VCH would be resold at prices fixed or recommended by VCH, which also required its members to impose on their customers various restrictive conditions including prohibitions on resale.

The VCH contract was voluntarily ended in 1967 but since the marketing of considerable quantities of cement continued to be effected to a large extent through members of VCH who remained bound by the terms of their membership of VCH, no great benefit to consumers ensued and the next step was therefore the condemnation by the Commission[1] of the restrictive practices of VCH itself – the Commission deciding that as a result of the price fixing consumers were deprived of the benefits of competition between manufacturers after 1967 when the VCH contract was ended, a deprivation by no means compensated by certain advantages claimed for the system as regards saving of costs and efficiency, which, in the opinion of the Commission, would be secured by price competition in any event.

The NCA agreement was ended voluntarily on 31 December 1970. However it was immediately revived in a very diluted form – under the name of the "Cementregeling voor Nederland 1971" (CRN) – only to be finally condemned by the Commission who refused to grant exemption under art. 85 (3).[2]

Two further agreements which related to the vertical market sharing of the Dutch cement market were (i) the "Nederlands Cement-Handelmaatschappij NV" (NCH) agreement, by which the German manufacturers participating in the NCA agreement fixed, as between themselves, the proportions in which they would meet the German quota under the NCA agreement; and (ii) the "Co-ordination 1966" agreement by which Belgian cement manufacturers, through their trade association Cimbel, fixed delivery quotas which included quotas for meeting the Belgian quotas under the NCA agreement. Both these agreements were the subject of unfavourable Decisions of the Commission in 1972.[3]

---

1 *Re Vereeniging van Cementhandelaren*, 16 December 1971, JO 1972 L13/34; [1973] CMLR D16; and *Vereeniging van Cementhandelaren* v. *EC Commission*, 17 October 1972, XVIII Rec. 977; [1973] CMLR 7, in which the Court of Justice upheld the Commission's Decision.
2 *Re Cementregeling voor Nederland*, 18 December 1972, JO 1972 L303/7; [1973] CMLR D149; and for a discussion of the refusal of exemption, see p. 86, below.
3 *Re Nederlandse Cement-Handelmaatschappij NV*, 23 December 1971, JO 1972 L22/16; [1973] CMLR D257; *Re Cimbel*, 22 December 1972, JO 1972 L303/24; [1973] CMLR D167; and see p. 83, below.

There are of course many variants to schemes such as that established for cement marketing in Holland. For example, the dealer's obligation to purchase exclusively from the manufacturer concerned might be dispensed with (as in the *Pottery Convention*[1]), but this does not improve matters as regards opening a market to foreign competitors if artificial technical standards are imposed which competitors cannot reasonably comply with.[2]

An interesting "device" adopted in relation to a vertical market sharing scheme in an attempt to circumvent the prohibition of art. 85 appears in *Re Central Heating*.[3] In this case a trade association representing Belgian manufacturers of heating equipment (CSM) and the trade association representing undertakings installing such equipment in Belgium (UBIC) agreed that such undertakings would only purchase equipment "certified" by a committee of representatives from each association; but while the certification of the equipment manufactured by members of CSM was automatic that of the equipment of other manufacturers, whether Belgian or foreign, was subject to extensive enquiry and delay. This device, among others, restricted competition and since there was an effect on trade between member states the agreement fell within art. 85 (1), exemption under art. 85 (3) being refused.

Enough may already have been said to indicate to the reader that art. 85 is indeed an effective instrument in the hands of the Commission for bringing to an end market sharing cartels under the protection of which major industries survived the years of depression between the wars and went on to prosper in post-war years, as in the case of the cement industry in the Benelux countries. For a discussion of *Re Cimbel*[4] (the Belgian cement industry cartel, very similar to that operating in Holland by virtue of the NCA/VCH agreements men-

---

1 Bulletin 1964 No. 5, p. 49.
2 For further cases relating to market sharing arrangements which were voluntarily ended, see:

> Building Materials: 8th General Report on the Activities of the Community, p. 70;
> Sanitary Ware: *Ibid.*, p. 71;
> Building materials (natural sand): 9th General Report on the Activities of the Community, p. 71;
> Cement and Clinker: *Ibid.*, p. 72;
> Camping Material: 1st General Report on the Activities of the Community, p. 66;
> Timber from the North: Bulletin 1968, No. 4, p. 31;
> Sanitary Installations: Bulletin 1970, No. 8, p. 65.

3 *Re Belgian Central Heating Agreement*, 20 October 1972, JO 1972 L264/22; [1972] CMLR D130.
4 22 December 1972, JO 1972 L303/24; [1973] CMLR D167.

tioned above) and why notwithstanding apparent benefits exemption under art. 85 (3) was not granted, the reader is referred to p. 83, below.

Discrimination

> "(d) apply dissimilar conditions to equivalent transactions with other trading parties, thereby placing them at a competitive disadvantage;"

Under this heading discriminatory practices as a consequence of agreement or concerted practice are covered.

An example clearly within the heading would be the case where A and B agree to discriminate in favour of C as against D, or vice versa. This would be so, for instance, where suppliers at a certain level of trading, e.g. manufacturers, agree to supply a certain class of consumers, e.g. those belonging to a certain trade association, on more advantageous terms than those not belonging to the association.[1] The latter would, in such circumstances, suffer a competitive disadvantage in comparison to the members of the association.

But even where discrimination does not result in competitive disadvantage to other trading parties the Commission condemns under art. 85 discrimination where it is a method of isolating national markets within the EEC, whether the discrimination is collective (by agreement between A and B in the example in the preceding paragraph) or individual (i.e. discrimination practised by A or B without agreement or concertation between them).

Thus in *Re Pittsburg Corning*[2] the Commission found a concerted practice between Pittsburg Corning Europe (PCE) and its distributors in Belgium (Formica) and likewise between PCE and its Dutch distributor (Hertel), whereby (with a view to the prevention of parallel imports into Germany where higher prices prevailed than in Belgium and Holland for PCE's products) a pricing system was practised such that goods for export to Germany were priced by the distributors higher than goods for sale in their own country. There was thus discrimination against exporters to Germany. The distributor did not benefit from a discount if the goods were resold for export to Germany with the necessary result that sales to that country were priced higher than goods sold in the distributor's own country.

---

1 For an example of a trade association practising such discrimination, see *Re Cimbel*, 22 December 1972, JO 1972 L303/24; [1973] CMLR D167; and p. 83, below.
2 *Re Pittsburgh Corning Europe*, 23 November 1972, JO 1972 L272/35; [1973] CMLR D2.

In *Re Kodak*[1] that company's distribution system was only approved by the Commission after removal from the conditions of sale operated by Kodak's marketing subsidiaries in various European countries of a condition that goods purchased from a subsidiary for export were to be paid for not at the selling subsidiary's normal price but at the price charged by Kodak's subsidiary in the country to which the goods were to be exported. Here again (with a view to the prevention of parallel imports) there was discrimination against certain buyers, i.e. buyers purchasing for export out of the distributor's country.

While in *Pittsburg Corning* the discrimination was practised as a consequence of the agreement between PCE and each of its distributors, in *Kodak* the discrimination was individual i.e. the group consisting of Kodak and its selling subsidiaries, who as we have seen[2] were treated as a single undertaking, entered into agreements involving the discriminatory conditions of sale independently of agreement with any third party.

It is interesting to consider in these circumstances where the agreement between undertakings necessary for the application of art. 85 is to be found. The only agreement upon which the application of the article can be based is the actual sales contract relating to the goods sold on a discriminatory basis and the traditional, and perhaps majority, opinion[3] is that such a sales contract was never intended by the authors of the Treaty (notwithstanding the wording which on a literal reading would support an opposite and therefore wider interpretation) to constitute an agreement restrictive of competition by the mere fact that it fixes the selling price of goods. By extension such view also excludes from the scope of art. 85 an individual purchase and sale contract which is discriminatory as regards the buyer or which imposes on him obligations of the kind referred to in example (e) below, art. 85 applying only to contracts which limit one or several parties in their freedom to determine prices or trading conditions *in other contracts*. This conclusion may be compared with the position under United Kingdom law whereby, subject to qualifications, restrictions in a purchase and sale agreement relating exclusively to the goods which are the subject of the agreement are to be ignored in determining whether the agreement is registrable.[4] This conclusion is, however, contrary to the American solution of the question, in the

---

1 30 June 1970, JO 1970 L147/24; [1970] CMLR D19.
2 See p. 17, above, and p. 67, below.
3 E.g. Goldman, *op. cit.*, paras. 285, 286; and Conrad W. Oberdorfer, Alfred Gleiss and Martin Hirsch, *Common Market Cartel Law*, para. 66, CCH 1971.
4 RTPA 1956, s. 7.

Robinson-Patman Act of 1936 under which individual discrimination is generally forbidden.

However, whatever the theoretical justification for the views expressed by the authors referred to above, in practice the Commission (generally with the approval of the Court of Justice)[1] interprets arts. 85 and 86 in the light of the objectives of the Treaty's competition policy – and since a restrictive interpretation would seriously limit the possibilities under art. 85 of preventing individual discriminatory practices (such as those resulting from export prohibitions intended to isolate national markets within the EEC) it is not surprising that these views have not found the support of the Commission, as shown by the *Kodak* Decision.

It is to be noted that the example under the heading is concerned with the application of dissimilar conditions to equivalent transactions. A purchase and sale transaction involving large quantities of goods with the consequent saving of cost to the seller is not equivalent to a transaction involving smaller quantities. Quantity discounts or other price reductions related to cost saving do not therefore constitute discrimination. Similarly, sales on differing national markets may not be equivalent transactions in view of the differing conditions in each country and price differences merely reflecting these would be permitted. Indeed the Commission has stated:[2]

> "Within the context of Article 85, there can be no objection in principle to producers pursuing independent specific supply policies for each EEC member country and adapting their pricing systems to the market competitive conditions peculiar to each country. But they cannot be allowed to ensure for themselves through direct or indirect curtailment of the intermediaries' operations, entailing market fragmentation, scope for pursuing sales and pricing policies differing appreciably according to the part of the market in which they are implemented."

The Commission goes on to discuss its *Pittsburg Corning* Decision which makes it clear that while there was nothing wrong in higher prices being charged in Germany than in Belgium or Holland, the price differential could not be maintained by measures designed to prevent parallel imports.

Tying

> "(e) *make the conclusion of contracts subject to acceptance by the other parties of supplementary obligations which, by their nature or*

---

1 See, e.g., the *Continental Can* Case, pp. 162, 163, below.
2 Commission's 2nd Report of Competition Policy, April 1973, sec. 41.

according to commercial usage, have no connexion with the subject of such contracts."

What is aimed at are tying agreements, the most obvious example being an agreement by which the purchaser of a machine agrees to buy materials to be worked with the machine from a source specified by the seller, where this is not essential for the proper functioning of the machine. It is a clear restriction of competition if a buyer is not free to shop around for a product by reason of his being forced to buy it from the supplier who has sold him another product.

It may be asked whether an agreement which provides for benefits conditional on fulfilment of supplementary obligations is within the prohibition against tying, for example a provision that the life of a machine is guaranteed, or the machine will be serviced, for a certain period, provided that all spare parts, lubricants, etc. are bought from the supplier or persons nominated by him. The point has not been considered specifically by the Commission. A suggested solution could be that adopted in English law in relation to tying provisions in a patent licence: these are permitted provided that the licensee has been given the opportunity to contract on other reasonable terms which do not include the tying provision.[1]

As in the case of discriminatory practices and for similar reasons to those mentioned under (*d*) above, it has been argued that only agreements by which undertakings agree to tie third parties are within the example[2] – but it is thought that this view is wrong for the reasons previously given.

The *Glass Containers* Case[3] is an example of tying by horizontal agreement between producers. Some of the principal producers in the EEC of glass container products agreed among themselves to operate a delivered price system by which prices quoted to buyers automatically included an average freight charge which was the same irrespective of the actual cost of transport to the place of delivery, and no other price basis was available to the buyer. The Commission held that there was thereby imposed on the buyer a supplementary obligation – the obligation to accept the transportation of the goods to the place of delivery – which had no necessary connection with the sale of the goods. The effect of such a system is to nullify the competitive advantage which a producer might gain from the proximity of his customers.

---

1 Patents Act 1949, s. 57 (3) (a).
2 Oberdorfer, Gleiss and Hirsch, *Common Market Cartel Law*, para. 71.
3 *Re Agreements between Manufacturers of Glass Containers*, 15 May 1974, OJ 1974 L160/1; [1974] 2 CMLR D50.

SECTION 6   SPECIAL CONSIDERATIONS APPLYING TO CERTAIN TYPES OF AGREEMENT

Agreements between companies of the same group

An agreement between at least two undertakings is a pre-requisite to the application of art. 85 and it follows that a single undertaking by itself, unless it is dominant (when it will be subject to art. 86[1]), can conduct its business as it thinks fit notwithstanding resulting restrictions of competition.

If, however, a single undertaking for reasons of administrative convenience, carries on its business through subsidiary companies an action which in the case of a "unitary" company would be a matter of internal decision, could become the subject of an agreement between two or more companies in the group and therefore be within the scope of art. 85.

In fact this anomalous result is to a certain extent mitigated by such Decisions of the Commission as *Christiani and Nielsen*[2] and *Kodak*,[3] and by the Judgment of the Court of Justice in the *Béguelin* Case[4] but on the whole the Commission's approach to the question is extremely cautious[5] and it is only within narrow limits that art. 85 has been declared inapplicable in relation to intra-group transactions.[6]

In *Re Christiani and Nielsen*, art. 85 was held not to apply to a market sharing agreement between Christiani and Nielsen (Copenhagen) and its wholly owned subsidiary Christiani and Nielsen (The Hague) on the grounds of the absence in any event of competition between the parent company and its subsidiary which could be restricted by the agreement. The Commission stressed the need to ascertain whether a subsidiary is in fact capable of acting as an independent economic unit towards its parent company, and continued:[7]

"[10] The company Christiani & Nielsen (Copenhagen) created the company Christiani & Nielsen (The Hague) in order to carry out in optimum conditions on Dutch territory the work in which it specialised.

---

1 See Ch. 5, below.
2 *Re Christiani and Nielsen NV*, 18 June 1969, JO 1969 L165/2; [1969] CMLR D36.
3 *Re Kodak*, 30 June 1970, JO 1970 L147/24; [1970] CMLR D19.
4 *Béguelin Import Co.* v. *GL Import-Export SA*, 25 November 1971, XVII Rec. 949; [1972] CMLR 81.
5 Though endorsed by the Court of Justice; see *Centrafarm BV and Adriaan de Peijper* v. *Winthrop BV*, 31 October 1974, [1974] 2 CMLR 480; p. 215, below.
6 Compare the solution under English law; RTPA 1956, s. 6 (8), provides that two or more interconnected bodies corporate (i.e. members of the same group, as defined in s. 36 (1)) are to be treated as a single person for deciding whether there is an "agreement between two or more persons" under s. 6.
7 [1969] CMLR D36, at p. D39.

It was considerations of management which led this undertaking, the activity of which is international, to create subsidiaries in different countries rather than establishing there branches or agencies. That is a piece of market strategy which cannot have the effect of causing us to consider, in the present case, a wholly-owned subsidiary as an economic entity which can enter into competition with its parent company.

"[11] In addition, Christiani & Nielsen (Copenhagen) has the right to nominate directors of Christiani & Nielsen (The Hague) and to give directives to its subsidiary, which is obliged to carry them out. Christiani & Nielsen (The Hague) is therefore an integral part of the economic whole making up the Christiani & Nielsen group."

In fact the logic of the Commission's reasoning is suspect since it seems to be based on the need for competition to exist *between* undertakings which may be restricted by an agreement between them. As we have seen, however, competition may be restricted by an agreement between undertakings who are not competitors, i.e. in the case of vertical agreements.[1]

Be that as it may, the actual result of the Decision is essentially correct, having regard to the subservience in fact of the subsidiary to the parent, which has the consequence of equating the territorial division of the activities of the Danish company and the Dutch company with the position that would obtain if different departments of a single undertaking looked after the business originating in each country.

The requirement that one company should be subservient to the other before an agreement between them could be excluded from art. 85 was also emphasised by the Commission in *Re Kodak*, though in that case the non-application of art. 85 was based on the sounder ground that the effect of the subservience of the subsidiary companies to the parent was that there was not real agreement between them.[2]

The Commission stated:[3]

"When it is established, as is so in this case, that the subsidiary companies in question are exclusively and wholly subject to their parent company, and that the latter in fact exercises its power of control by issuing to them precise instructions, it is impossible for them to behave independently *inter se* in the areas governed by the parent company.

"Consequently the identical nature of the conditions of sale of the Kodak companies in the Common Market does not result from an agreement or concerted practice either between the parent company and its subsidiaries or between the subsidiaries *inter se*."

---

1 See pp. 38, 39, above.
2 See p. 17, above.
3 [1970] CMLR D19, at p. D21.

And in the *Béguelin* Case[1] the question which came before the Court of Justice for determination was whether the transfer of the benefit of an exclusive distribution agreement between a parent and its wholly owned subsidiary involved a breach of art. 85. The Court held that the article had no application as between two companies, one of which was not economically (as opposed to legally) independent of the other.

Whether one company is economically independent of another is a question of fact. Namely, whether the former's commercial decisions are reached by its governing body in full independence of the other company, irrespective of the latter's shareholding or other rights of control.

In its *Christiani and Nielsen* Decision the Commission considered that it was impossible for a wholly owned subsidiary to act autonomously – but it may be questioned whether the statement is necessarily true in all circumstances. Wholly owned subsidiaries in a group may be organised on the basis of the complete independence from their parent company – if only for taxation reasons where the parent and the subsidiary are in different countries. Further, if a wholly owned subsidiary cannot be independent, what lesser shareholding can a parent company hold in the subsidiary without the latter thereby becoming economically independent of the parent company?

In truth, it is not possible to answer the question asked in this form. However, in the *Dyestuffs*[2] and *Zoja*[3] Judgments (where in each case the question was whether a company outside, and a subsidiary within, the Common Market were to be treated as a single entity) the Court of Justice established the relevant criterion to be that one company has power of control over another, and actually exercises that power.

The same tests should, it is submitted, be equally applicable in determining the dependence or independence of related companies for the purposes of the application of art. 85 to an agreement between them.

Further, in the *Zoja* Case[4], it was sufficient that the parent company should have exercised its power only in relation to the transaction which was the subject of proceedings under art. 86, for the two undertakings to be treated as a single undertaking for the purposes of that transaction. We see no reason why the position should be different in relation to art. 85. If a parent company exercises its power of control

---

1 *Béguelin Import Co.* v. *GL Import-Export SA*, 25 November 1971, XVII Rec. 949; [1972] CMLR 81.
2 *ICI* v. *EC Commission*, 14 July 1972, XVIII Rec. 619; [1972] CMLR 557.
3 *ICI-CSC* v. *EC Commission*, 6 March 1974, [1974] ECR 223; [1974] CMLR 309; and see p. 158, below for the facts of the Case.
4 *Zoja* v. *Commercial Solvents Corporation*, 14 December 1972, JO 1972 L299/51; [1973] CMLR D50; and on appeal *sub. nom. ICI-CSC* v. *EC Commission*, above.

over a subsidiary to secure that the latter enters into an agreement with the parent company, even though the subsidiary enjoys in other respects complete independence, it does not seem to us that in such circumstances there can be any agreement between undertakings for the purposes of the application of art. 85 thereto.

For the application of the above tests it is not necessary for the companies concerned to be parent and subsidiary in the legal sense. It suffices that one company should in fact be able to exercise control over the other company – e.g. by virtue of a relatively small shareholding where the balance of the shares is held widely, or by virtue of other rights deriving otherwise than from any shareholding.[1] It is then a question of fact whether the power of control is actively exercised.

Exclusive agency agreements

The Commission issued a Communication on 24 December 1962[2] to the effect that exclusive agency agreements were not within the scope of art. 85 (1) where, on behalf of another undertaking acting as principal, an agent is appointed to transact business in a part of the Common Market exclusively on behalf of the principal.

In the case of such an agent, that is to say an agent in the real sense of the term, acting for and on behalf of a principal without acceptance of any commercial risk (other than the *del credere* risk) the Commission's view is that the agency agreement escapes art. 85 on the basis that it does not restrict competition within the Common Market. Where the transactions involve any element of risk for the agent he is to be considered as an independent trader rather than an agent and his so-called exclusive agency agreement will be an exclusive distribution agreement, which will be within art. 85 (1) but subject to exemption under art. 85 (3).[3]

The real agent acts only in an auxiliary capacity, on the instructions and in the interest of his principal. The principal therefore remains a competitor on the market for the goods in question to the same extent as before the appointment of the agent and in this respect no prevention, restriction or distortion of competition is involved. However the Commission points out that a limitation of supply on a particular market results from an agent's obligation to deal only in the goods of a particular supplier – but for that obligation the agent could also supply in his territory the products of other suppliers: and the supplier's

---

1 See, e.g., the list of rights which may constitute control for the purposes of the draft Regulation on Control of Concentrations, pp. 201, 202, below.
2 JO 1962 139/2921; set out in Appendix IV, at p. 405, below.
3 See p. 97, below.

obligation to sell only through one agent results in a limitation of demand from the agent's territory – but for the obligation the supplier could receive orders from other agents in that market. These limitations involve a restriction of competition by reason of sources of supply being denied to consumers and outlets being denied to suppliers. But the Commission "views these restrictions as a result of the special obligation between the commercial agent and his principal to protect each other's interests" and concludes that therefore "they involve no restriction of competition."[1]

It is difficult to follow the logic of this conclusion for while the fiduciary relationship between agent and principal may justify the restriction of competition, which in the opinion of the Commission exists by reason of the limitation of supply and demand mentioned above, it can hardly eliminate the restriction.

It might have been better for the Commission to have based the argument for the exclusion of the agency agreements in question from the scope of art. 85 on the ground of a degree of subservience (when it is the case) on the part of the agent to his principal, such that he is to be assimilated to an employee – in which event, the arrangement would no more constitute an agreement between undertakings (the necessary precondition for art. 85 to apply) than an employment contract.

In fact, since the date of the Communication, the Court of Justice has stated[2] that art. 85 does not apply to an agreement by which the distribution of a product (e.g. through an agent) is "integrated" with the undertaking of the manufacturer; and the Commission in the *Sugar Cartel* Case[3] rejecting the contention of German sugar producers that certain commission contracts and trade representation contracts were within the Communication, stated:[4]

> "[The Communication] defined the role of a commercial agent as that of a temporary employee integrated into the principal's undertaking."

In fact there is no such definition in the Communication, identifying an agent with a temporary employee but, be that as it may, after reviewing the actual activities of the agents in question, the Commission concluded "under these circumstances the agents of WZV and Pfeifer & Langen are not employees. They are not integrated into the

---

1 See the Communication, at p. 407, below.
2 *Etablissements Consten SA and Grundig Verkaufs-GmbH* v. *EEC Commission,* 13 July 1966, XII Rec. 429; [1966] CMLR 418.
3 *Re European Sugar Cartel,* 2 January 1973, OJ 1973 L140/17; [1973] CMLR D65.
4 OJ 1973 L140/41.

undertaking of the principal, which would have been a reason for not applying Article 85."[1]

The Communication sets out the following non-exhaustive list of criteria which will result in the exclusion of an agency agreement from the benefit of the Communication, namely where the agent:

—is required to keep or does in fact keep, as his own property, a considerable stock of the products covered by the contract, or

—is required to organise maintain or ensure at his own expense a substantial service to customers free of charge, or does in fact organise, maintain or ensure such a service, or

—can determine or does in fact determine prices or terms of business.

In the *Sugar Cartel* Case, the fact that the agents did not work exclusively for their respective principals was held to exclude the application of the Communication, the Commission stating:[2]

"The peculiarity of this case lies in the fact that the agents described as commission or commercial representatives do not work for one principal alone. They provide clients not only for WZV but also for some of its members and for the NWZV.

"In so far as [their principals are] agreeable they can also market sugar in their sales territory as agents for other producers. Their activity as dealers in sugar for denaturing and more especially in sugar intended for third countries is definitely more important.

"Consequently the agents do not work exclusively for one employer, but act on their own to a considerable extent, as independent dealers, particularly as regards sales to third countries. Even on the national market they work for several undertakings at the same time with their agreement."

Curiously, the Commission in this context again mis-quotes its own Communication referring to an agent's obligation to work exclusively for a certain time for one employer as a consequence of the special obligation of a mutual defence of interest as between commercial agent and principal. What the Communication does in fact say is that the obligation to work only for one principal restricts competition – a restriction however which is then said not to exist in view of the fiduciary relationship between the principal and the agent.

It may be queried therefore whether the agent's employment by one principal only should in all circumstances be essential for an agency agreement to be within the Communication. Undoubtedly from the

---

1 *Ibid.*, OJ 1973 L140/41.
2 *Ibid.*

quotation given above in relation to the activities of the agents of the German sugar producers it is clear that, where the agent acts for several principals in relation to the same product, particularly with the degree of independence described, the Communication does not apply. But it is submitted that much in the same way as an employee could have a part-time employment, an agent should be able to represent principals marketing different lines of non-competing goods, without thereby losing the benefit of the Communication provided that in relation to each line he satisfies the criteria of the Communication.

The practical implication of what precedes is, of course, that if art. 85 does not apply to an agency agreement, it is possible to impose on the agent restrictions (e.g. on exports to other EEC countries), which would be out of the question if the agent is in fact an independent trader. If the agent is "integrated" with his principal to the requisite degree, so that the Communication applies such a prohibition in the agreement would not be different to a prohibition contained in a directive issued, for example, by a company to its sales staff and as such unobjectionable, since independent action by an undertaking in the absence of any agreement or concerted practice, is outside the scope of art. 85. Abuse of a dominant position may however be involved if the undertaking is dominant in which case art. 86 would apply to this prohibition.[1]

Attempts, however, to camouflage what are essentially distribution agreements as agency agreements will normally fail as the Commission examines the real economic significance of each agreement and the designation of the relevant agreement as an exclusive agency agreement will be ineffective if on the facts it is shown to be a distribution agreement. Thus in *Re Pittsburgh Corning*[2] the Commission rejected Pittsburgh's contention that certain discriminatory practices by its Belgian agents were covered by the Communication, stating:[3]

"... the Commission, while trying to indicate to undertakings some criteria to allow them to assess their own situation with regard to Article 85, in no way said that it intended to accept appearances and abandon the right to re-establish the true character of legal acts, relations between undertakings and economic situations. On the contrary, it stated 'that it did not link its judgment to the description applied' and 'that it was

---

1 See Ch. 5, below.
2 *Re Pittsburgh Corning Europe*, 23 November 1972, JO 1972 L272/35; [1973] CMLR D2.
3 [1973] CMLR D2, at D6, para. 7.

absolutely necessary that the contracting party described as agent should in fact be so'."

Agreements of minor importance

It has been seen that art. 85 (1) is not applicable to an agreement unless the possible effect on trade between member states and the restriction of competition which may be the object or effect of the agreement, is in each case perceptible.

But firms, particularly small and medium-sized firms, will often not be able to gauge the effect of their agreement because of the lack of statistics or other information. The resulting uncertainty is detrimental in that legitimate co-operation which the Commission wishes to encourage may not take place through fear of infringing art. 85 (1).

The Commission accordingly issued a Communication on the 27 May 1970[1] setting out quantitive criteria by reference to the market shares and turnovers of the parties to an agreement, stating that it did not consider agreements which satisfied these criteria to be within art. 85 (1), thus enabling the parties proposing to enter into agreement to judge for themselves on the basis of factual information which will normally be available to them whether or not art. 85 would be applicable to the agreement. If the parties conclude that art. 85 (1) is not applicable there is normally no need for them to notify[2] the agreement or to seek a negative clearance,[3] but in a case of doubt these steps should be taken.

If it appears that art. 85 (1) does not apply to the agreement, having regard to the provisions of the Communication, the agreement may include any restriction, even prohibition on export and other provisions to secure absolute territorial protection for a territory.[4] However, as will be seen from the comment to para. 3, below, there may be exceptional circumstances when although the criteria are satisfied the nature of the agreement is such that perceptible restrictions on competition and perceptible effect on trade between member states ensue in which case reliance cannot be placed on the Communication.

The Communication is now set out and commented on.

---

1 JO 1970 C64/1; [1970] CMLR D15 (no authentic translation is at present available).
2 As to notification, see Ch. 10, Section 3, p. 255, below.
3 As to negative clearance, see Ch. 10, Section 2, p. 251, below.
4 As in *Franz Völk* v. *Ets. Vervaecke Sprl*, 9 July 1969, XV Rec. 295; [1969] CMLR 273.

NOTICE OF THE COMMISSION OF THE
EUROPEAN COMMUNITIES[1]

27 May 1970

Concerning agreements of minor importance which are not covered by the provisions of Article 85 (1) of the Treaty instituting the European Economic Community.

I

[1] As it has already indicated on various occasions, the Commission considers it important to promote co-operation between undertakings in so far as it is economically desirable and gives rise to no objection as regards competition policy; in particular, it desires to facilitate co-operation between small- and medium-scale undertakings. In that light it published the Practice Direction of 23 July 1968[2] – a direction which sets out a series of agreements which, by their nature, do not restrict competition. With the present practice direction the Commission is continuing its effort to define the field of application of Article 85 (1) of the Treaty instituting the European Economic Community with the aim of promoting co-operation between small- and medium-scale undertakings.

[2] The Commission considers that the prohibition of agreements decreed in Article 85 (1) of the EEC Treaty does not cover agreements which affect trade between member-States and competition only to an insignificant degree. Only agreements which have noticeable effects on market conditions are forbidden, i.e. those which noticeably alter the position on the market of undertakings which are not parties to the agreement and also of the consumer, i.e. their outlets and their sources of supply.

The Commission refers without distinction, in the second paragraph, to the two conditions of application of art. 85, i.e. effect on intra-Community trade and restriction of competition within the Common Market. It should be remembered, however, that the conditions are conjunctive and that therefore art. 85 has no application where either one of the conditions is not satisfied.

[3] In the present practice direction the Commission gives to the term "noticeable" a sufficiently substantial content for the undertakings themselves to be able to assess whether their agreements with other undertakings fall outside the provisions of Article 85 (1) because of their minor importance. The quantitative definition of "noticeable", given by the Commission, is not, however, absolute: it is quite possible that in given instances

---

1 [1970] CMLR D15.
2 Communication on Co-operation Agreements, JO 1968 C75/3; [1968] CMLR D5; see p. 79, below, and Appendix IV, p. 407, below.

agreements concluded by undertakings which exceed the limits given below will affect trade between member-States and competition only to an insignificant degree and consequently will not fall under the provisions of Article 85 (1).

But conversely it is important to note that compliance with the terms of the Communication does not guarantee that the Commission will consider art. 85 (1) to be inapplicable in all circumstances. In the *Béguelin* Case[1] (before the Court of Justice) the Commission stated in its submissions:

"Article 85 (1) may be applicable even where the limits stated in the [Communication of 27 May 1970] are not reached; in such cases also the restriction of competition can be perceptible."

The Court did not comment on this submission, but it is clearly of importance to note that such is the view of the Commission as the enforcing authority.

[4] The present practice direction should dispense with the need to obtain a negative clearance within the meaning of Article 2 of Regulation 17 for the agreements covered by it.[2] Nor should it be necessary to want the legal position clarified by individual decisions of the Commission; there is, therefore, no need to notify such agreements for that purpose.[3] However, when there is doubt in a particular case as to whether an agreement does noticeably affect trade between Member-States or competition, undertakings may request negative clearance or notify the agreement.

[5] The present practice direction is without prejudice to any interpretation by the Court of Justice of the European Communities.

Regarding the legal status of a Communication by the Commission, see p. 5, above.

II

[6] The Commission considers that agreements between undertakings engaged in the production or distribution of goods are not governed by the prohibition in Article 85 (1) of the Treaty instituting the European Economic Community:

Although it is not very clear from the wording, it is understood that the Commission would consider a vertical agreement between an

---

1 *Béguelin Import Co.* v. *GL Import-Export SA*, 25 November 1971, XVII Rec. 949; [1972] CMLR 81; authors' translation.
2 As to which see Ch. 10, Section 2, p. 251, below.
3 As to which see Ch. 10, Section 3, p. 255, below.

undertaking engaged in production and another in distribution (e.g. an exclusive distribution agreement) to be covered.

"Production or distribution of goods" – Agreements for the provision of services are therefore not included in the Communication.

> —when the products covered by the agreement do not represent, in the part of the Common Market in which the agreement produces its effect, more than five per cent. of the amount of business done with identical products or with products considered by the consumer to be similar by reason of their properties, their price or their use, and

It is understood from the Commission that the word "or" where it appears above in two places should read "and". The turnover percentage must be applied to the total of identical products *and* substitute products; and a product will be treated as similar by the consumer only if it is so by reason of characteristics *and* price *and* use.[1]

"The part of the Common Market in which the agreement produces its effect." – The question here is to define the relevant market within the Common Market.[2]

> —when the total annual turnover of the undertakings taking part in the agreement does not exceed 15 million units of account or, in the case of commercial undertakings, 20 million units of account.[3]

This turnover test must be satisfied as well as the test relating to market shares in the preceding paragraph.

"Commercial undertakings" – By this expression the Commission is understood to be referring to undertakings which are distributors of goods as opposed to manufacturers.

In the case of an agreement involving both manufacturers and distributors the view has been expressed to the authors by an official of the Commission that the lower of the two figures must be taken.

The turnover to be taken into account is not only the turnover in the goods which are the subject of the agreement but the total turnover of goods and services of the parties and other undertakings referred to in the numbered sub-paras. 2 and 3 of para. 8, below.

> [7] The Commission also considers that the above-mentioned agreements are not governed by the prohibition in Article 85 (1) if, during two consecutive financial years, the shares of the market and the turnover thus determined show an excess of less than 10 per cent.

---

1 Compare criteria in Reg. 67/67, art. 6 (a), p. 167, below.
2 As to relevant market, see Ch. 6, below.
3 The value of the unit of account is explained at p. 294, below.

Market shares and turnovers can accordingly attain 5·5% and 16·5 million units of account for two consecutive years but the latter will be adjusted upwards if the higher turnover threshold limit is taken – see second sub-paragraph under para. 6 of the Communication.

If either of the threshold limits is exceeded for a third consecutive year the agreement ceases to have the benefit of the Communication.

[8] The total turnover is made up of the sum of the turnovers of the previous financial year covering all products and services and relating to:

1. the undertakings participating in the agreement;
2. the undertakings in which the participating undertakings hold:
   —at least 25 per cent. of the capital or working capital, either directly or indirectly,
   —or at least half the voting rights,
   —or the power to appoint at least half the members of the supervisory board or board of directors or of the organs representing the undertaking at law,
   —or the right to manage the affairs of the undertaking;
3. the undertakings which have in a participating undertaking:
   —at least 25 per cent. of the capital or working capital, either directly or indirectly,
   —or at least half the voting rights,
   —or the power to appoint at least half the members of the supervisory board or board of directors or of the organs representing the undertaking at law,
   —or the right to manage the affairs of the undertaking.

[9] The total turnover does not include transactions taking place *inter se* between the undertakings participating in the agreement.

While it is to the advantage of undertakings that these transactions should be excluded, the reason is not clear since transactions between the participating undertakings can contribute to the financial strength and market power of the undertakings, and the group, if any, to which they belong.

Undoubtedly the drafting of the Communication is far from precise and it will not be easy to interpret in many instances, and in a case of doubt the agreement should be notified.[1] It is however intended to cater for simple situations in relation to small and medium-sized undertakings and in the majority of these cases there should be no real problem in determining whether in the relevant agreement the criteria are satisfied and, if they are, whether there are nevertheless special

---

1 See under Part I, para. 4 of the Communication, above.

features which render relevant the caveat expressed by the Commission in the *Béguelin* Case (see under Part I, para. 3).

Co-operation agreements

Whereas some classes of agreements could be said not to satisfy the second condition of application of art. 85 because the competition which they restrict is either not substantial or else does not exist in real economic terms, there is the converse case of substantial competition which is not considered restricted by certain classes of agreement between undertakings. One such class of agreement is that of co-operation agreements.

It must be recalled that the protection of competition is not as such an object of the Treaty. Competition is but one of the means of achieving the closer integration of the economies of member states implied in the notion of the Common Market.[1] Closer co-operation between undertakings from different member states (in ways not incompatible with the rules of competition) is one of the manifestations of such closer integration. The very objects of competition policy would be defeated if fear of infringing its rules prevented such co-operation. The Commission therefore issued a Communication on 23 July 1968,[2] in order to make it clear that it is in favour of co-operation between undertakings, and in particular co-operation between small and medium-sized undertakings, when the result is more rational operation and increased productivity and competitiveness in the larger market constituted by the Common Market. The Communication thus specifies certain types of agreement which in the Commission's opinion do not, as a general rule, restrict competition and are not therefore within Article 85 (1). The aim is that, unless there are special circumstances or doubts, there is no need in respect of such agreements to apply for negative clearance[3] or to seek exemption under art. 85 (3).[4]

The Communication applies to agreements whose sole objects are those listed with respect to each of eight specified categories of agreement:[5]

(1) Agreements having as their sole object:

(a) An exchange of opinion or experience.

---

1 See Ch. 7, Section 2, p. 178, below.
2 JO 1968 C75/3; [1968] CMLR D5.
3 See Ch. 10, Section 2, p. 251, below.
4 See Ch. 10, Section 3, p. 255, below.
5 Where an agreement forms only one part of a series of agreements between the parties it is not enough when deciding whether the Communication applies to it to consider its object in isolation from those other agreements: *Re Agreements between Manufacturers of Glass Containers*, 15 May 1974, OJ 1974 L160/1; [1974] 2 CMLR D50; and see note to p. 410, below).

    (b) Joint market research.
    (c) The joint carrying out of comparative studies of enter-
        prises or industries.
    (d) The joint preparation of statistics and calculation models.

(2) Agreements having as their sole object:

    (a) Co-operation in accounting matters.
    (b) Joint provision of credit guarantees.
    (c) Joint debt-collecting associations.
    (d) Joint business or tax consultant agencies.

(3) Agreements having as their sole object:

    (a) The joint implementation of research and development
        projects.
    (b) The joint placing of research and development contracts.
    (c) The sharing out of research and development projects
        among the participating enterprises.

(4) Agreements which have as their only object the joint use of
production facilities and storing and transport.

(5) Agreements having as their sole object the setting up of
working partnerships for the common execution of orders,
where the participating enterprises do not compete with each
other as regards the work to be done or where each of them by
itself is unable to execute the orders.

(6) Agreements having as their sole object:

    (a) Joint selling arrangements.
    (b) Joint after-sales and repair service, provided the participa-
        ting enterprises are not competitors with regard to the
        products or services covered by the agreement.

(7) Agreements having as their sole object joint advertising.

(8) Agreements having as their sole object the use of a common label
to designate a certain quality, where the label is available to all
competitors on the same conditions.

It is only therefore to a limited number of agreements that the Communication can be applied as such, but the explanations it contains
provide valuable insight into the Commission's thinking, useful in
considering whether individual clauses in agreements of wider scope
are, in the context of such agreements, liable or not to be considered
by the Commission as restrictive of competition; the reader is
referred to Appendix IV for the full text of the Communication.[1]

---

1 At p. 407, below; see further Ch. 7, Section 2, p. 178, below, "Co-operation between
Undertakings".

Chapter 3

Article 85 (3)—Exemption

Where an agreement is within art. 85 (1) it is forbidden and, as will be seen, under art. 85 (2) it is automatically void.[1] Article 85 (3) provides, however, for the possibility of exemption from the prohibition for a particular agreement or category of agreements. This will be the case where the agreement or category of agreements satisfies the two positive and the two negative conditions set out in art. 85 (3).

The authentic English text of art. 85 (3) of the Treaty states:

"3. The provisions of paragraph 1 may, however, be declared inapplicable in the case of:
—any agreement or category of agreements between undertakings;
—any decision or category of decisions by associations of undertakings;
—any concerted practice or category of concerted practices;
which contributes to improving the production or distribution of goods or to promoting technical or economic progress, while allowing consumers a fair share of the resulting benefit, and which does not:
(a) impose on the undertakings concerned restrictions which are not indispensable to the attainment of these objectives;
(b) afford such undertakings the possibility of eliminating competition in respect of a substantial part of the products in question."

SECTION 1. INDIVIDUAL EXEMPTION

Council Regulation 17 of 1962[2] (which is the basic regulation setting out the powers and duties of the Commission in relation to the implementation of the competition rules of the Treaty – other than for transport[3]) provides that the Commission (and only the Commission[4]) has power to exempt agreements where, with certain exceptions,[5] they have been notified to the Commission.[6] In relation to

---

1 See Ch. 4, below.
2 OJ 1962 13/204; and see Ch. 10 and 11, below.
3 See Reg. 1017/68; OJ 1968 175/1; and Ch. 9, Section 1, p. 238, below.
4 Reg. 17, art. 9, and see further p. 291. below.
5 In the case of non-notifiable agreements, see pp. 257ff., below.
6 See generally Ch. 10, Section 3, p. 255, below.

particular individual agreements the exemption is given by decision, in which the date from which exemption is to operate will be stated. The Commission has the power to grant the exemption with retroactive effect back to the date of notification,[1] but not, again with certain exceptions,[2] to a date earlier than the date of notification.

The question of the grant of an exemption under art. 85 (3) need only be considered by the Commission if it first finds that the agreement is within art. 85 (1). As we have seen, whether or not an agreement is within art. 85 (1) depends, *inter alia*, on an appreciation of its consequences in relation to trade between member states and competition within the Common Market. For the purpose of such an appreciation, any countervailing advantages (such as those mentioned in para. (3) of the article) are irrelevant – in other words, there is no question of weighing the advantages of the agreement against its disadvantages for the purpose of the application of art. 85 (1).

But once the Commission finds that an agreement is within art. 85 (1) then, whether the restriction of competition and the effect on trade between member states are each great or small (it is enough that they are both perceptible), the agreement can only be exempted if specific benefits result, not any benefits, but the two positive benefits specified in para. (3), and if at the same time the two negative conditions in that paragraph are satisfied. However, it is important to note that exemption under art. 85 (3) will not be granted, even when the conditions are satisfied, unless the Commission is also satisfied that the beneficial effects claimed for the agreement are not capable of being achieved through competition. In *Re Cimbel* the Commission stated:[3]

> "In order to benefit from the exemption provided in Article 85 (3) the restrictions ... must objectively constitute an improvement compared with the situation that would exist without these restrictions. ... there can only be any question of "improvement" of the economic process or "promotion" of technical or economic progress within the meaning of Article 85 (3) in exceptional cases where competition could not produce the most favourable result economically."

The fact that art. 85 (3) exemption is only available once the agreement is found to be within art. 85 (1) is reflected in the form of the Commission's decisions, which follow the pattern first of setting out

---

1 Reg. 17, art. 6 (1).
2 See p. 264, below, as to "old" and "accession" agreements, and "non-notifiable" agreements.
3 *Re Cimbel*, 22 December 1972, JO 1972 L303/24; [1973] CMLR D167, at p. D189, para. [45].

the provisions of the agreement; secondly of establishing that these may affect trade between member states and restrict competition within the Common Market; and thirdly of applying to the agreement and its effects in turn each of the four tests of art. 85 (3): if they are all satisfied the exemption will then be granted (subject to the caveat mentioned in *Re Cimbel*, above), but not otherwise.

Decisions of the Commission in relation to particular agreements which it examines will therefore come within one of three categories:

(i) decisions relating to agreements found not to come within art. 85 (1) – as regards which the Commission will, if so requested, issue a negative clearance;[1]

(ii) decisions relating to agreements which are within art. 85 (1) but which do not qualify for exemption under art. 85 (3);

(iii) decisions relating to agreements which are within art. 85 (1) but which are granted exemption under art. 85 (3).

We are here concerned with the second and third categories of decisions, and by way of example of each category there are set out below summaries of certain of the principal Decisions of the Commission refusing exemption – *Re Cimbel*[2] and *Re NCA-CRN*,[3] and granting exemption – *Re Transocean Marine Paint*,[4] and *Re Omega*.[5]

Re Cimbel[2]

The agreement, designated Co-ordination 1966, was between the eight major Belgian manufacturers of cement, members of the trade association "Cimbel". The agreement provided for:

Delivery quotas applicable to the Common Market and the rest of the world.

Prices fixed by Cimbel for sales to the Belgian market discriminating in favour of certain classes of Belgian buyers "approved" by Cimbel.

Uniform conditions of sale, applicable to Belgian sales. A system of compensation of receipts as between Belgian and foreign sales.

No increase in members' production capacity unless other members were previously informed.

---

1 See Ch. 10, Section 2, p. 251, below.
2 *Re Cimbel*, 22 December 1972, JO 1972 L303/24; [1973] CMLR D167.
3 *Re Cementregeling voor Nederland*, 18 December 1972, JO 1972 L303/7; [1973] CMLR D149.
4 *Re Transocean Marine Paint Association*, 27 June 1967, JO 1967 163,10; [1967] CMLR D9.
5 *Re Omega*, 28 October 1970, JO 1970 L242,22; [1970] CMLR D49.

Sale or other transfer of production plant only to persons agreeing
   to comply with Co-ordination 1966.
Quality control by Cimbel.
Full information as to sales (including name of Belgian purchaser)
   to be supplied to Cimbel.
Power of enforcement conferred on Cimbel.

Having found on the above facts that Co-ordination 1966 was
within art. 85 (1), the Commission refused the participants' claim for
exemption under art. 85 (3) on the ground that it had not been shown
that the detriments resulting from the anti-competitive effects of the
agreement were outweighed by improvements in production or
technical or economic progress for reasons which appear from the
following paragraphs.

The participants maintained that with the high cost of cement
manufacturing plant unrestrained competition could lower prices
ruinously. In the Commission's opinion, however, judging from the
experience of other capital intensive industries, cut-throat competition
was not a necessary consequence of the absence of restrictive practices
in such industries; and it was not permissible to justify a present
restriction of competition by a theoretical and uncertain future con-
tingency. In any event, there was no present sign of crisis or the possibility of such competition either in Belgium or any other neighbouring
EEC country.

The Commission further remarked that the span of the useful life
of cement plants was greater than average in comparison with other
kinds of high cost equipment, and that while the industry undoubtedly
suffered between 1932 and 1935 it was not certain that the substantial
increase in prices resulting from previous restrictive agreements
between the participants was the only way to compensate the losses.
In any event the years referred to were exceptional.

A suggestion by the participants that competition between them
would necessarily result in a product of inferior quality was not
accepted. In the absence of quotas, competition ensured the maintenance of quality, since a producer selling inferior goods would lose his
market.

The participants claimed that the agreement did not restrict growth
but on the contrary would, while avoiding over-capacity, allow the
development of manufacturing units of a size and efficiency comparable
to any in the world. The Commission saw no merit in this contention.
To be exempted under art. 85 (3) an agreement must be such as to
show positively that it enhances rationalisation and modernisation
in a way that could not be expected under competitive conditions.

In the present case, on the contrary, the agreement helped to keep in being out-dated plant as a result of takeovers or acquisitions of failing undertakings for the purpose of acquiring their quota entitlements under the agreement. If as a result of payments made to acquire their quotas certain undertakings were enabled to branch off into more profitable lines of business, the cost was borne by the consumer of cement. This is not the right way to achieve the proper allocation of resources in a free economy where the norm is that unless an undertaking is viable it must be expected to go out of business. The reader will notice in this connection the absence of any considerations of a social nature, which are outside the scope of art. 85.

While the participants claimed for the agreement that it prevented over-capacity, the Commission found that there was in fact over-capacity and that Belgian capacity, for most of the time, was only 60–70% utilised. The Commission remarked that this state of affairs could only result from the absence of checks to the development of excessive capacity which would operate in competitive conditions, the over-capacity having been financed through the high level of prices fixed under the agreement. Far from preventing excess capacity, the agreement encouraged it since participants who had this capacity could, on the renegotiation of the agreement, claim higher quotas.

The Commission did not admit that the system of compensation of receipts as between foreign and Belgian sales improved production or distribution. While the system, amounting as it did to a private system of export subsidies, was such as to encourage Belgian exports, the exporters being compensated for the lower price obtainable on export sales, this was achieved at the expense of producers in other EEC countries. Such distortion of competition could not be considered as an improvement in production.

The Commission denied cost saving due, *inter alia*, to the more regular level of output resulting from the quota system, as alleged by the participants. At most there was a levelling of costs at an average level, to the detriment of the most efficient producers.

The participants' claim that the agreement ensured over a long period stable prices at a low level was not accepted. Credit for this might be attributable to plant modernisation and to price controls by the Belgian Government. The real question was whether prices would not have been even lower in the absence of the agreement.

The Commission did not find that any improvement of distribution resulted from favouring certain classes of "approved" buyers.

In conclusion the Commission held that since the agreement did not satisfy the two positive conditions for exemption under art. 85 (3) the exemption could not be granted and it was not necessary to consider the two negative conditions.

Re NCA-CRN[1]

The Noordwijks Cement-Accoord (NCA agreement) was entered into in 1956 between Dutch, Belgian and German cement manufacturers for regulating the Dutch cement market in the context of a chronic deficiency of Dutch manufacturing capacity to meet the particularly heavy demand in Holland for the product. The essential features of the agreement were supply quotas, uniform pricing and conditions of sale, restrictions on investments, and the exclusion from the Dutch market of other manufacturers by tying the distribution network in Holland to the manufacturers participating in the NCA agreement.[2]

Following the termination of the VCH agreement in 1967 various modifications were made to the NCA contract in an attempt to eliminate certain of its more glaring incompatibilities with art. 85 but the improvements were in the opinion of the Commission more apparent than real. The NCA contract was cancelled on 31 December 1970, and replaced by a new agreement for a transitional period of three years with provision for renewal – the Cementregeling voor Nederland 1971 (CRN), the restrictive effects of which were limited to a flexible system of quotas talking effect only with respect to supplies in excess of 550,000 tons – the quota constituting an obligation as well as a right to supply.

Having found that the system of quotas fell within art. 85 (1), the Commission went on to refuse the participants' claim for exemption under art. 85 (3) on the ground that in so far as it was claimed that improvements to production and distribution resulted from the agreement, the quota system was not indispensable for achieving these purposes.

The Commission doubted, however, whether such claims were in any event justified. The claimants based the justification for the quotas on the need to ensure production capacity commensurate with the demands of the Dutch cement market. This, according to the claimants, was difficult in the absence of quotas because of the economic and technical need for increasingly large production plant, and because of seasonal fluctuations of demand and low elasticity of demand in answer to price variations – all of which factors tend towards the creation of excess capacity. The Commission, however, thought that

---

1 *Re Cementregeling voor Nederland*, 18 December 1972, OJ 1972 L303/7; [1973] CMLR D149.
2 See discussion of the *VCH* Case at p. 60, above.

the problem had been exaggerated. In its opinion quotas do not prevent a tendency to construct increasingly large plants since undertakings tend to do so in any event – either to enable them to claim larger quotas on renewal of the quota agreement or to have maximum capacity at the end of the agreement. As regards seasonal fluctuations, these are less in Holland than elsewhere owing to the maritime climate – and in any event all use of cement is not seasonal and the problem could be mitigated by increasing storage capacity and the use of clinker; finally not all demand for cement is inelastic – this is true in relation to housebuilding but not in relation to other uses of cement.

The claimants also based the justification for the quotas on the need to guarantee deliveries to Holland by foreign manufacturers (because of the deficiency in production capacity of local manufacturers). The Commission, however, considered that quotas were unnecessary to achieve this, having regard to the excess capacity in both Belgium and Germany and maintained that security of delivery could be achieved by medium- or long-term supply contracts with foreign suppliers.

Re Transocean Marine Paint[1]

It is interesting to look at this case as exemplifying how art. 85 (3) can justify an agreement although it is riddled with restrictions on competition and affects trade between member states.

Eighteen medium-sized manufacturers of marine paint established both within and outside the EEC agreed to co-operate through a trade association which they established with a view to the standardisation of the quality of their marine paints and marketing throughout the world under the trade name "Transocean". By this means, the association's members hoped to be better able to compete with the major international producers supplying the shipping industry. The principal provisions of the agreement were to the following effect.

The association's members were required to promote the sales of marine paints in their own countries (their respective "reserved territories"); the paints were to be made to specified formulae and to be sold under the name "Transocean" coupled with the member's own name or mark; the members could only sell under their own name alone paint of superior or lesser quality; they were required to submit to quality controls and observe secrecy with regard to technical and

---

1 *Re Transocean Marine Paint Association,* 27 June 1967, JO 1967 163,10; [1967] *m*MLR D9; see also the renewal of the Decision: *Re Transocean Marine Paint Association* (*No.* 2), 21 December 1973, OJ 1974 L19,8; [1974] 1 CMLR D11; and p. 90, n. 1, below.

commercial information obtained as association members; they were required to give other members preference when granting patent licences.

The association's members were to have complete freedom as to pricing; but when sales were effected into another member's reserved territory, the other member was to be entitled to certain commissions; export of paint other than Transocean paint into another member's reserved territory was not permitted except with the latter's consent, which should not normally be refused; a member could require another member (but not any other person) to satisfy an order in the latter's territory, in which case a commission was due to the member from whom the order originated; and certain other contingencies were contemplated whereby compensating commissions became payable.

Provision was made for information as to sales to be given to the association. A member could not belong to other associations relating to marine paint or co-operate with any person in a reserved territory in relation to marine paint other than the member whose territory it was. A member was not to manufacture marine paint for another producer not belonging to the association except with the consent of any other member who might be principally concerned with the execution of the order, but the consent was normally to be given.

These facts were analysed by the Commission and found to involve the following restrictions on competition within the Common Market.

The requirement that exports of marine paints (other than Transocean paints) by a member to the reserved territory of another member could only be effected with the latter's consent restricted the former's commercial freedom; and even though consent was, in principle, required to be given the very fact that it had to be asked for led to complications and delays in export trade within the Common Market and to consultation and harmonisation of export policies.

The obligation of a member to pay commission in respect of exports into another member's reserved territory prejudiced the former's competitive position as regards sales in that territory.

The right of a member to require another member to execute an order in the latter's reserved territory, subject to payment of a commission by the latter to the former, enabled members to meet their customers' orders on another member's territory without competing in such territory: competition between members was therefore restricted and a preferential position was secured for the member in his own reserved territory.

The prohibition against manufacturing on behalf of a non-member, without the consent of the member primarily concerned, restricted the former member's competitive position.

An implied prohibition against a member himself manufacturing marine paint on another member's reserved territory, and the prohibition against having such paint manufactured there by a non-member, restricted the possibility of increased production in that territory, where the level of supply would consequently be reduced.

The preference to be granted to association members as regards patent licences involved restrictions on a member's freedom to grant licences and on the possibility of non-members being granted licences.

It is not surprising that in the circumstances the Commission found that, but for the agreement, there could have existed greater competition within the Common Market both between the association's members themselves and between the association's members and third parties; and that by the various restrictions trade between member states was prejudiced. The Commission, however, went on to examine the possibility of exempting the agreement under art. 85 (3), examining whether the answers to the following questions were such that the two positive and the two negative conditions of art. 85 (3) were satisfied:

(1) Does the agreement improve the production or the distribution of goods or promote technical or economic progress?

The Commission's finding was that the agreement resulted in improvement in distribution by enabling rationalisation and intensification of members' sales of paints as a result of the judicious allocation of reserved territories among members who knew their market and who, moreover, could deliver outside their territories. Buyers were therefore able to obtain their requirements of marine paint of uniform quality (indicated by their designation as "Transocean" paints) at all times and at all places. In the absence of the agreement members would be obliged to set up their own distribution networks in many countries at a cost and risk which would be excessive for medium-sized companies.

Moreover the medium-sized members of the association could, as a result of the agreement, compete with the major manufacturers represented in all important countries, with a consequent increase in the general level of supply.

(2) Does the agreement allow consumers a fair share of the resulting benefits?

The Commission found that benefits accrued to consumers through the increased level of supply and through buyers being able in a particular country to buy Transocean paints otherwise than from the local member of the association – for example if the latter's prices should be too high. The distribution network established through the operation of the agreement avoided the need for ships to carry the paint on board and the distribution system ensured the availability of technical advice from the representatives of members of the association in the various ports.

All these factors added up to a fair participation by consumers in the benefits of the agreement.

(3) Does the agreement include restrictions which are not indispensable?

The Commission found that to ensure the success of the scheme it was essential to confer on the local member in each territory a privileged position so that, unhindered by excessive competition from other members, he could build up his manufacturing and sales organisation by making the necessary investments to launch both existing and new products. This justified the prohibition against manufacturing marine paint or having it manufactured on another member's territory, and also those provisions regarding payment of commissions which tended to encourage purchase orders for delivery to another member's country to be passed to the local member.[1]

The use in common of the name "Transocean" (which in other circumstances could be restrictive of competition), was essential as a guarantee that the products of each member were interchangeable. Its registration in the name of each member in his country could not, however, be used to prevent imports in view of the principle established by the Commission and confirmed by the Court of Justice that it is an abuse of a trade mark to use it to restrict the free movement of goods in the Common Market.[2]

The limitation of the use of the name "Transocean" to sales of paints of specified qualities was again justified by the need to encourage the promotion of the name, and the liability of a member to pay commission in respect of exports to another member's territory of paints sold under the former's own trade name, coupled with the need to obtain the latter's consent for such exports, discouraged during the launching

---

1 On renewal of the exemption until 31 December 1978 (*Re Transocean Marine Paint Association (No. 2)*, 21 December 1973, OJ 1974 L19,18; [1974] 1 CMLR D11) the Commission required the deletion from the agreement of provisions requiring the consent of the "local" member to exports into his territory of other members' products sold under their own labels and for the payment of commissions to the local member in respect of Transocezn paint exported into his territory by other members. The Commission considered that these restrictions were justified only during the initial period of exemption to give the scheme time to become established.
2 See Ch. 8, Section 1, pp. 208–216, below.

period excessive concentration on such sales to the prejudice of the development of Transocean paints.

As regards the prohibition against members of the association manufacturing on behalf of non-members this was justified by the need not to support the business of firms which it was the very object of the association to compete against.

The secrecy and limitation on licensing provisions were justified for the same reason.

(4) Does the agreement afford the possibility of eliminating competition in respect of a substantial part of the products in question?

The exact market share of the members of the association was not stated but it was not large and consequently there was ample competition from non-members in relation to the supply of marine paints.

It is seen then that to obtain the exemption of an agreement under art. 85 (3) it is necessary first to show that it can improve distribution or production or technical or economic progress and that consumers benefit, and then that there are no unnecessary restrictions (for which purpose it is necessary to consider each restriction in turn) and that competition is not as a result eliminated in respect of a substantial part of the products in question. More often than not agreements notified to the Commission do include unacceptable restriction and in such circumstances the Commission will invite the parties to alter them. Thus in *Transocean* the agreement when originally notified contained certain restrictions which were much more stringent than those eventually appearing in the agreement, e.g. there was an absolute prohibition on export to other members' territories. This provision was altered to the one which has been examined above, namely a provision for the payment of *modest* compensating commission if such exports were made. In many cases the removal of the restriction will take the agreement out of the scope of art. 85 (1) altogether, the agreement will not then be exempted under art. 85 (3), but a negative clearance may issue in respect of it.[1]

If *Transocean* is typical of the dialectic of the Commission it is not typical of any particular type of agreement which has been considered by the Commission; it shows that art. 85 (3) can have quite wide and unconventional application. Indeed *prima facie* Transocean is no more than a blatant horizontal market sharing arrangement. Nevertheless the Commission found justification for it in the light of its special facts,

---

1 See further p. 266, below.

in particular that this was a case involving not powerful international companies but medium-sized undertakings concerned with making their products competitive in the face of the larger manufacturers. In fact *Transocean* is a good example of the Commission's flexibility in administering the competition rules.

Re Omega[1]

By its decision in this case the Commission granted exemption under art. 85 (3) to a selective distribution system and, as such, this case is of considerable practical interest as a model to undertakings concerned to limit selectively the distribution of their products internationally within the EEC[2].

Exclusive distributors (referred to as general agents) were appointed by the well-known Swiss watch manufacturing company, "Omega", for each of the Common Market countries of the original Six member states. Under the agreements by which they were appointed, the general agents were required to restrict their retail outlets to watch-maker-jewellers (referred to as concessionnaires) satisfying certain standards laid down by Omega; and moreover the number of such concessionnaires which the general agents could appoint was limited to the optimum number for best serving the particular town or region for which they were appointed, taking into account the size of the local population and its presumed purchasing power.

At the time when the relevant distribution agreements were first notified to the Commission, the general agents were forbidden to sell the products to concessionnaires outside their assigned area resulting in a watertight partitioning of the Common Market into sub-divisions allocated to each general agent. The Commission required that this prohibition should be relaxed to allow sales by general agents to other general agents and to concessionnaires in all Common Market countries. There was a continuing restriction, however, on the general agents from exporting products to non-member states. General agents were free to fix their resale prices to the retail trade.

In turn the general agents entered into standard form contracts with the retail concessionnaires appointed by them in the territory for which the general agent was distributor, by which contracts the con-cessionnaires were restricted as to their sources of supply of, and persons to whom they might sell, Omega products. Those concession-naires were entitled to obtain Omega products only from general agents or from other authorised concessionnaires, and while they

---

1 28 October 1970, JO 1970 L242/22; [1970] CMLR D49.
2 See also *Re Bayerische Motoren Werke AG*, 13 December 1974, OJ 1975 L29/1, a major Decision, confirming the principles first annunciated in *Re Omega*; see also p. 55, n. 3, above.

could sell to private customers wherever they might be, they could not sell to other watchmaker-jewellers unless they were other authorised Omega concessionnaires.

The concessionnaires were subject to obligations to publicise their appointment as Omega retailers, to display the goods in their shop, to keep a permanent minimum stock of articles in a good state, to operate Omega's international guarantee and to ensure the repair of such products either in their own or in the general agent's workshop.

The general agents on their part undertook to assist their concessionnaires with general and regular publicity and with the good turn-out of the concessionnaires' shops and in the management and maintenance of their stocks and to honour the international guarantee at their expense and to supply spare parts which might be required for repairs.

Under the standard contracts of certain of the general agents, provision was made for the concessionnaires to resell products purchased from the general agent by whom he was appointed at prices fixed by the latter.

In considering the application of art. 85 (1) the Commission analysed what sales of different Omega products were made in the EEC during a given period, and found that only a limited number of types were sold in all the member states; even then the same product did not represent the top selling line in each territory. Price was not a determining factor regarding the customer's choice; further, the same product was available at different prices in the EEC both with regard to the price charged by the general agent to his concessionnaires and by the latter to the consumers, the variations amounting to between 30% and 50% of the lowest prices for the twelve most popular Omega models sold in the EEC during the period in question. It was established that in the Common Market there were about 20,000 outlets for products competitive with those of Omega, of which 3,000 were authorised Omega concessionnaires.

The Commission held, in relation to the general agents' exclusive distribution agreements, that competition was restricted:

(1) by the appointment by Omega of exclusive general agents for different parts of the EEC which prevented other undertakings from purchasing Omega products direct from Omega, a restriction capable of leading to the division of the Common Market among such general agents;

(2) by the limitation on the number of Omega concessionnaires – not by reason of the qualifications required of them, but on account of the fixing by each general agent of a maximum quota of retailers for each town and each region.

The Commission did not consider that other obligations imposed upon the general agents had the object or effect of noticeably restricting competition within the Common Market, in particular the obligations to sell under the Omega trade mark and promote sales by maintaining stocks and organising a permanent servicing and repair organisation.[1]

The Commission also held that trade between member states was affected by the above agreements as a result of distortion of export trade within the EEC resulting from the prohibition on sales to retailers in other EEC countries who were not authorised concessionnaires. With regard to the prohibition imposed on the general agents from selling outside the EEC, however, the Commission did not think that it would have an effect on intra-Community trade, since further trade through re-import of products into the EEC was most unlikely because the accumulation of profit margins, transport costs and the Community's customs tariff, and the abolition of internal tariffs in the EEC should lead to other agents or concessionnaires importing the goods direct from authorised sources in other member states.

In considering an exemption under art. 85 (3) to the general agents' agreements with Omega, the Commission accepted that the restrictions imposed on the general agents with regard to the number of concessionnaires could be permitted because of the benefits with regard to rationalisation of distribution, maintenance of sales and after-sales service, better adaptation to local preference and improvement to the efficiency of the distribution system generally.[2] The Commission found the necessary condition satisfied that consumers should benefit by such improvements in that they could as a result obtain supplies more quickly and be assured of an effective guarantee and repair network. The Commission thought that this was particularly important because of the high price of the highly technical products.[3]

The agreements between Omega and the general agents involved no restrictions which were not indispensable. The general agents had accepted certain obligations similar to those contained in Regulation 67/67, art. 2 (2), under which such restrictions are acceptable from the point of view of the block exemption under art. 85 (3) by virtue of that Regulation,[4] i.e. obligations with regard to the sale of the products

---

1 See also *Re Bayerische Motoren Werke AG*, 13 December 1974, OJ 1975 L29/1, para. 21.
2 In *Re Bayerische Motoren Werke AG,* above, selective distribution was held to provide a better service to users of BMW vehicles than a system of free marketing. Need for special equipment and complex technology justified selectivity in choosing dealers and close co-operation between them and BMW, in the interests of safety, health and the protection of the environment.
3 See also p. 55, n. 3, above.
4 As to which, see further p. 103, below.

under the Omega trade mark and in the form laid down by Omega and the carrying out of certain sales promotion measures.

As regards the limitation on the permitted number of concessionnaires, which took the distribution agreements outside the scope of Regulation 67/67, the Commission considered such limitation justified because if there were too many concessionnaires in any particular area, the volume of business available to each would be too small to justify the concessionnaires' undertaking in relation to Omega products the necessary effort of sales promotion and customer assistance for achieving the improvement in distribution warranting the grant of exemption to the relevant agreements under art. 85 (3).

As regards the necessary condition for exemption under art. 85 (3) that the relevant agreement should not eliminate competition for a substantial part of the products in question, the Commission found that the general agents faced effective competition both within and outside the EEC from competing products and that the sole agency agreements contained no restrictions protecting Omega products from such competition. Further, the concessionnaires were free to obtain supplies from other member states, and could thus take advantage of the considerable price differences existing in different parts of the Common Market for the same models.

As regards the standard form of distribution contracts between the general agents and the concessionnaires, the Commission considered that they too qualified for exemption under art. 85 (3) since they are no more than "the transposition to the retail stage of the selective distribution system organised by agreement between Omega and its general agents." In particular the Commission found that the standard form contracts did not give the undertakings concerned the possibility of eliminating competition for a substantial part of the products in question, *inter alia*, because the concessionnaires were able to purchase Omega products from concessionnaires and general agents in other EEC countries – enabling them to obtain supplies wherever they might be cheapest. Moreover, the possibility available to concessionnaires of purchasing in other markets circumvented any competitive disadvantage to the concessionnaires resulting from the resale price maintenance obligation which under certain of the contracts general agents for certain countries could impose in relation to products sold by them to their concessionnaires.

The Commission granted exemption under art. 85 (3) with regard to the agreements, as amended, limiting the validity of its decision to ten years from the date of amendment of the sole agency agreements, and requiring notification each year of any withdrawal of the status of concessionnaire from any existing appointee.

Each case to be considered under art. 85 (3) depends so much on its special facts that no useful purpose is served in further analysing individual Decisions. Certain types of agreement are such, however, as by their very nature to be susceptible of exemption under art. 85 (3): these include specialisation agreements and exclusive distribution agreements. Such agreements, subject to satisfying certain conditions, are automatically exempted under para. (3) by special exempting Regulations issued by the Commission. These Regulations are discussed in the following section.

SECTION 2   EXEMPTION BY CATEGORY

The Commission had before it by the end of 1964 over thirty thousand notified agreements. To prevent the relevant departments being swamped by a continuing flood of agreements which for the greater part were harmless from the point of view of their anti-competitive effects, advantage was taken of the provision of art. 85 (3) allowing for art. 85 (1) to be declared inapplicable to *categories* of agreements between undertakings and correspondingly to categories of decisions by associations of undertakings and categories of concerted practices – thereby dispensing such agreements from the need to be notified in order to obtain an individual decision granting exemption. To this end, the Council under Regulation 19 of 1965[1] delegated power to the Commission to determine the conditions under which it would be prepared to grant exemptions by category in respect of two classes of agreements:

(a) exclusive bipartite distribution agreements;
(b) bipartite agreements which include limitations imposed in relation to the acquisition or use of industrial property rights or to the transfer or licensing of, in brief, know-how.

Council Regulation 19 of 1965 has been followed by Council Regulation 2821 of 1971[2] again delegating to the Commission authority to grant exemption by category this time in respect of the following three classes of agreements whose objects are:

(a) the application of standards or types;
(b) research and development of products or processes up to the stage of industrial application and exploitation of the results,

---

1 Council Reg. 19/65, OJ 1965 36/533; set out in Appendix II, p. 349, below.
2 Council Reg. 2821/71, OJ 1971 L285/46; set out in Appendix II, p. 380, below.

including provisions regarding industrial property rights and confidential technical knowledge;

(c) specialisation, including agreements necessary for achieving it.

Under the general powers conferred by the above Regulations the following specific Regulations have been adopted conferring exemption by category:

Regulation 67 of 1967[1] relating to bipartite exclusive distribution agreements;

Regulation 2779 of 1972[2] relating to specialisation agreements.

These Regulations are discussed in detail below. A regulation relating to patent licensing has been under consideration by the Commission for several years, but the difficulties attaching to the subject are such that to-date not only has no regulation been adopted, but no official draft has ever been published. Nor has the Commission's thinking been revealed by the publication of any draft[3] covering the remaining fields of possible exemption by category under the above-mentioned general powers, for bi-partite agreements relating to industrial property rights generally, and for agreements relating to the application of standards and types, and to research and development. Agreements within these categories can at present, therefore, only be exempted from the effects of the prohibition of art. 85 (1) by an individual decision of the Commission. It should be noted, however, that these types of agreement do already receive a measure of favourable treatment, as being exempt from the notification requirements of Regulation 17,[4] with the implication that "such agreements are generally less harmful to the smooth functioning of the Common Market"[5] and consequently are likely, if they come under examination, to be held not to infringe art. 85 (1).

Exclusive distribution agreements

Under an exclusive distribution agreement a supplier agrees, with respect to the marketing of certain products (the agreement products) in a territory, to sell only to the other party to the agreement (the distributor) who in turn resells as principal, the profit or loss being for

---

1 Commission Reg. 67/67, OJ 1967 57/849; set out in Appendix II, p. 354, below.
2 Commission Reg. 2779/72, OJ 1972 L292/23; set out in Appendix II, p. 384, below.
3 Such as is referred to in Reg. 19/65, art. 5.
4 See pp. 259–263, below.
5 *Brasserie de Haecht* v. *Wilkin* (*No.* 2) 6 February 1973; [1973] ECR 77; [1973] CMLR 287, at p. 302, para. 13; and see further on the scope and effect of exemption from notification, pp 257 ff, below.

his account. Conversely the distributor may agree to purchase the agreement products only from the other party to the agreement and not to deal in competing products.

The supplier therefore restricts himself as to his outlets in the distributor's territory, where competition is reduced, since dealers other than the distributor cannot purchase the agreement products directly from the supplier and thereby compete on equal terms with the distributor.

Further, where the distributor is precluded from purchasing the agreement products for resale otherwise than directly from the supplier or is precluded from dealing in competing goods, he cannot acquire the agreement products more cheaply, or goods of the same description, from other suppliers. The result is a distortion of competition by reference to the competitive position which would have existed in the absence of the agreement and trade between member states is affected in so far as alternative suppliers and the distributor are in different EEC countries.

Anti-competitive effects also result from exclusive dealing when it is sought to protect the distributor from parallel imports, i.e. imports by third parties of the supplier's products into the distributor's territory from other areas where they might be cheaper; and, which comes to the same thing, when it is sought to partition the Common Market for the benefit of the supplier – so that he may profit from high prices prevailing in one part of the Common Market without fear of competition from his own goods which, in another part of the Common Market, fetch lower prices. Methods of isolating markets in this way include, as has already been seen, prohibitions of all kinds on exports from one area of the Common Market to another, or correspondingly on imports, and the improper use of industrial property rights (patents, trade marks, etc.) and of other legal rights[1] – all of which can involve infringement of art. 85 or certain other provisions of the Treaty safeguarding the free movement of goods within the EEC[2].

While infringement of the Treaty would normally be avoided by distribution in a foreign country by the supplier himself, whether directly through a foreign branch, or indirectly through subsidiaries or agents, nevertheless the appointment of an exclusive distributor in that foreign country presents many commercial advantages and the Commission in accordance with the powers delegated to it by the

---

1 See p. 43, above, and *Béguelin Import Co.* v. *GL Import-Export SA*, 25 November 1971, XVII Rec. 949; [1972] CMLR 81.
2 See Ch. 8, Section 1, p. 205, below.

Council has adopted Regulation 67/67[1] granting exemption by category to such agreements satisfying certain criteria. The best expression of these commercial advantages is to be found in paragraphs (10) and (11)[2] of the recitals to the Regulations, which is now set out in full:

REGULATION No 67/67/EEC OF THE COMMISSION
of 22 March 1967

on the application of Article 85 (3) of the Treaty to certain categories of exclusive dealing agreements

THE COMMISSION OF THE EUROPEAN ECONOMIC COMMUNITY,

(1) Having regard to the Treaty establishing the European Economic Community, and in particular Articles 87 and 155 thereof;

(2) Having regard to Article 24 of Regulation No 17 of 6 February 1962;

(3) Having regard to Regulation No 19/65/EEC of 2 March 1965 on the application of Article 85 (3) of the Treaty to certain categories of agreements and concerted practices;

(4) Having regard to the Opinions delivered by the Advisory Committee on Restrictive Practices and Monopolies in accordance with Article 6 of Regulation No 19/65/EEC;

(5) Whereas under Regulation No 19/65/EEC the Commission has power to apply Article 85 (3) of the Treaty by regulation to certain categories of bilateral exclusive dealing agreements and concerted practices coming within Article 85;

(6) Whereas the experience gained up to now, on the basis of individual decisions, makes it possible to define a first category of agreements and concerted practices which can be accepted as normally satisfying the conditions laid down in Article 85 (3);

(7) Whereas, since adoption of such a regulation would not conflict with the application of Regulation No 17, the right of undertakings to request the Commission, on an individual basis, for a declaration under Article 85 (3) of the Treaty would not be affected;

(8) Whereas exclusive dealing agreements of the category defined in Article 1 of this Regulation may fall within the prohibition contained in Article 85 (1) of the Treaty; whereas since it is only in exceptional cases that exclusive dealing agreements concluded within a Member State affect trade between Member States, there is no need to include them in this Regulation;

1 OJ 1967 57/849.
2 The recitals have been numbered by the authors for convenience.

(9) Whereas it is not necessary expressly to exclude from the category as defined those agreements which do not fulfil the conditions of Article 85 (1) of the Treaty;

(10) Whereas in the present state of trade exclusive dealing agreements relating to international trade lead in general to an improvement in distribution because the entrepreneur is able to consolidate his sales activities; whereas he is not obliged to maintain numerous business contacts with a large number of dealers, and whereas the fact of maintaining contacts with only one dealer makes it easier to overcome sales difficulties resulting from linguistic, legal, and other differences; whereas exclusive dealing agreements facilitate the promotion of the sale of a product and make it possible to carry out more intensive marketing and to ensure continuity of supplies, while at the same time rationalising distribution; whereas, moreover, the appointment of an exclusive distributor or of an exclusive purchaser who will take over, in place of the manufacturer, sales promotion, after-sales service and carrying of stocks, is often the sole means whereby small and medium-size undertakings can compete in the market; whereas it should be left to the contracting parties to decide whether and to what extent they consider it desirable to incorporate in the agreements terms designed to promote sales; whereas there can only be an improvement in distribution if dealing is not entrusted to a competitor;

(11) Whereas as a rule such exclusive dealing agreements also help to give consumers a proper share of the resulting benefit as they gain directly from the improvement in distribution, and their economic or supply position is thereby improved as they can obtain products manufactured in other countries more quickly and more easily;

(12) Whereas this Regulation must determine the obligations restricting competition which may be included in an exclusive dealing agreement; whereas it may be left to the contracting parties to decide which of those obligations they include in exclusive dealing agreements in order to draw the maximum advantages from exclusive dealing;

(13) Whereas any exemption must be subject to certain conditions; whereas it is in particular advisable to ensure through the possibility of parallel imports that consumers obtain a proper share of the advantages resulting from exclusive dealing; whereas it is therefore not possible to allow industrial property rights and other rights to be exercised in an abusive manner in order to create absolute territorial protection; whereas these considerations do not prejudice the relationship between the law of competition and industrial property rights, since the sole object here is to determine the conditions for exemption of certain categories of agreements under this Regulation;

(14) Whereas competition at the distribution stage is ensured by the possibility of parallel imports, whereas, therefore, the exclusive dealing agreements covered by this Regulation will not normally afford any possibility of preventing competition in respect of a substantial part of the products in question;

(15) Whereas it is desirable to allow contracting parties a limited period of time within which they may, in accordance with Article 4 of Regulation No 19/65/EEC, modify their agreements and practices so as to satisfy the conditions laid down in this Regulation, without it being possible, under Article 4 (3) of Regulation No 19/65/EEC, to rely thereon in actions which are pending at the time of entry into force of this Regulation, or as grounds for claims for damages against third parties;

(16) Whereas agreements and concerted practices which satisfy the conditions set out in this Regulation need no longer be notified; whereas Article 4 (2) (a) of Regulation No. 27, as amended by Regulation No. 153, can be repealed, since agreements which it was possible to notify on Form B 1 would normally come within the scope of the exemption;

(17) Whereas agreements notified on Form B 1 and not amended so as to satisfy the conditions of this Regulation should be made subject to the normal notification procedure, in order that they may be examined individually;

HAS ADOPTED THIS REGULATION:

Article 1

1. Pursuant to Article 85 (3) of the Treaty and subject to the provisions of this Regulation it is hereby declared that until 31 December [1982][1] Article 85 (1) of the Treaty shall not apply to agreements to which only two undertakings are party and whereby:

(a) one party agrees with the other to supply only to that other certain goods for resale within a defined area of the common market; or

(b) one party agrees with the other to purchase only from that other certain goods for resale; or

(c) the two undertakings have entered into obligations, as in (a) and (b) above, with each other in respect of exclusive supply and purchase for resale.

Agreements (and concerted practices – see art. 8 below) which satisfy the provisions of the Regulation, as amended, are automatically taken out of the scope of art. 85 (1) until 31 December 1982.[1] Notification to the Commission of these agreements is not therefore necessary; but notification is advisable in all cases of doubt since if for any reason the agreement is held not to qualify for "exemption by category" under the Regulation it will not, in the absence of notification, be possible to claim an individual exemption in respect of it, unless the agreement falls within a limited class of non-notifiable agreements.[2]

---

1 Originally the 31 December 1972, extended to 31 December 1982 by Commission Reg. 2591/72, OJ 1972 L276/15.
2 I.e. under Reg. 17, art. 4 (2); see p. 242, below. As to notification generally see Ch. 10, Section 3, p. 255, below.

"*To which only two undertakings are party*"

It is immaterial that one of the parties is a foreign company – foreign that is by reference to the EEC.[1]

"*A defined area of the territory of the Common Market*"

This expression suggests that the Regulation applies only where the area in question covers less than the whole of the Common Market. The Commission has stated that in the case of exclusive dealing agreements for the whole of the Common Market "it is necessary to examine the extent to which such agreements are likely to restrict competition and affect trade between Member States, *taking into account the established flow of goods within the Common Market.* [In this field] systematic study of the existing notifications should enable test decisions to be made".[2] However, the Commission has now held that the Regulation does not apply to an exclusive dealing agreement covering the whole of the Common Market.[3]

> 2. Paragraph 1 shall not apply to agreements to which undertakings from one Member State only are party and which concern the resale of goods within that Member State.

This provision states that the exemption by category is not available in respect of an agreement of the kind described but such an agreement is unlikely to affect trade between member states; so that in any event it would be outside the scope of art. 85 (1).[4] If trade between member states were nevertheless to be affected the circumstances would be very special (e.g. under the *Brasserie de Haecht* (*No.* 1) principle[5]) and not suitable to be dealt with in the framework of an exemption by category.

Article 2

> 1. Apart from an obligation falling within Article 1, no restriction on competition shall be imposed on the exclusive dealer other than:
>   (a) the obligation not to manufacture or distribute, during the duration of the contract or until one year after its expiration, goods which compete with the goods to which the contract relates.

---

1 *Béguelin Import Co.* v. *GL Import-Export SA,* 25 November 1971, XVII Rec. 949; [1972] CMLR 81.
2 Commission's 1st Report on Competition Policy, April 1972, sec. 52, 3rd para.; authors' emphasis.
3 *Re Duro-Dyne/Europair,* 19 December 1974, OJ 1975 L29/11, at p. 12; but individual exemption was granted.
4 See recital 8, above, and now *Re Goodyear Italiana–Euram,* 19 December 1974, OJ 1975 L38/10, para. 11.
5 *Brasserie de Haecht* v. *Wilkin-Janssen* (*No.* 1), 12 December 1967, XIII Rec. 525; [1968] CMLR 26; and see p. 18, above.

"Goods which compete with the goods to which the contract relates"

While art. 2 does not define competing goods, art. 6, which is concerned with the maintenance of competition between goods, refers to goods "considered by the consumer as similar goods in view of their properties, price and intended use." It is submitted that these words can properly be read into art. 2, para. 1 (1), so that the distributor may be restricted as to manufacture or distribution not only of goods of the same description as those for which he is appointed distributor but also of substitute products.

> (b) the obligation to refrain, outside the territory covered by the contract, from seeking customers for the goods to which the contract relates, from establishing any branch, or from maintaining any distribution depot.

The restrictions which can be imposed on the exclusive dealer regarding solicitation of custom, establishing a branch or maintaining a distribution depot outside his territory do not imply a prohibition on sales outside the territory. On the contrary, while the exclusive dealer may be forbidden actually to promote sales outside his territory he cannot be prevented from meeting unsolicited orders from buyers in other EEC countries, the Court of Justice holding in the *Béguelin* Case[1] that the group exemption conferred by Regulation 67/67 does not apply where the agreement forbids the re-export by the distributor of the relevant products to other member states. An export prohibition could only be exempted, if at all, by an individual exemption under art. 85 (3). Where, however, the export prohibition is contained in an agreement of minor importance,[2] it may be acceptable on the basis that the agreement is not in any event within art. 85 (1) – and the question of exemption under art. 85 (3) does not then arise.

> 2. Article 1 (1) shall apply notwithstanding that the exclusive dealer undertakes all or any of the following obligations:
>
> (a) to purchase complete ranges of goods or minimum quantities;
> (b) to sell the goods to which the contract relates under trade marks or packed and presented as specified by the manufacturer;
> (c) to take measures for promotion of sales, in particular:
>
> > —to advertise;
> > —to maintain a sales network or stock of goods;
> > —to provide after-sale and guarantee services;
> > —to employ staff having specialised or technical training.

---

1 *Béguelin Import Co.* v. *GL Import-Export SA*, 25 November 1971, XVII Rec. 949; [1972] CMLR 81, at p. 97, para. 22.
2 See p. 74, above.

Article 3

Article 1 (1) of this Regulation shall not apply where:

(a) manufacturers of competing goods entrust each other with exclusive dealing in those goods;

Mutual exclusive dealing in competing goods can be a means of market sharing, since each party controls the other's outlets in his territory. If a manufacturer is concerned not only to sell his own goods but also the competing goods of a competitor, it is reasonable to assume that he will make only such effort in distributing the competing goods as is consistent with his own market position. If such an arrangement is reciprocal, it will be because each manufacturer wishes to be protected from unrestricted access by his competitor to his own market. It is not surprising then that automatic exemption under the Regulation is not available in these circumstances. There may be special cases justifying such an arrangement but relief must then be obtained on an individual basis.

(b) the contracting parties make it difficult for intermediaries or consumers to obtain the goods to which the contract relates from other dealers within the common market, in particular where the contracting parties:

(1) exercise industrial property rights to prevent dealers or consumers from obtaining from other parts of the common market or from selling in the territory covered by the contract goods to which the contract relates which are properly marked or otherwise properly placed on the market;

(2) exercise other rights or take other measures to prevent dealers or consumers from obtaining from elsewhere goods to which the contract relates or from selling them in the territory covered by the contract.

Whether or not an agreement benefits from Regulation 67/67 depends not only on the terms of the relevant agreement being within the provisions of arts. 1 and 2 but also on the subsequent conduct of the parties who will forfeit the benefit of the Regulation if, in order to partition the Common Market, they take steps to prevent the export or reimport of the agreement products from or into the distributor's territory, e.g. by the exercise of industrial property[1] or other rights[2] or by other measures taken for such purposes.

---

1 For industrial property rights, see Ch. 8, below.
2 For a case involving a right other than an industrial property right see *Béguelin Import Co.* v. *GL Import-Export SA*, 25 November 1971, XVII Rec. 949; [1972] CMLR 81; discussed at p. 43, above.

The principle involved is well expressed in para. 13 of the recital to the Regulation.

Article 4

1. As regards agreements which were in existence on 13 March 1962 and were notified before 1 February 1963, the declaration contained in Article 1 (1) of inapplicability of Article 85 (1) of the Treaty shall have retroactive effect from the time when the conditions of application of this Regulation were fulfilled.

2. As regards all other agreements notified before the entry into force of this Regulation, the declaration contained in Article 1 (1) of inapplicability of Article 85 (1) of the Treaty shall have retroactive effect from the time when the conditions of application of this Regulation were fulfilled, but not earlier than the day of notification.

Article 5

As regards agreements which were in existence on 13 March 1962, notified before 1 February 1963 and amended before 2 August 1967 so as to fulfil the conditions of application of this Regulation, the prohibition in Article 85 (1) of the Treaty shall not apply in respect of the period prior to the amendment, where such amendment is notified to the Commission before 3 October 1967. The notification shall take effect from the time of receipt thereof by the Commission. Where the notification is sent by registered post, it shall take effect from the date on the postmark of the place of dispatch.

Articles 4 and 5 of the original text deal with the application of Regulation 67/67 to agreements in force when the Regulation took effect on 1 May 1967.[1] These provisions are not irrelevant to United Kingdom undertakings in so far as they were on 1 August 1967 parties to exclusive distribution agreements with firms within the EEC of the Six. The articles deal with two different situations:

(a) Agreements in force on 13 March 1962 (when Regulation 17 came into force[2]) notified before 1 February 1963 (the extended date specified in Regulation 17 for notification of such agreements[3]). In these cases the exemption by category applies from the time "when the conditions of this Regulation were fulfilled", i.e. from the beginning of the agreement, if throughout its life it satisfied the conditions of Regulation 67/67 or from any point of time (whether before or after 1 May 1967 – the date of

---

1 See art. 9, below.
2 No date for entry into force was provided for in Reg. 17 itself, so that it entered into force on the twentieth day after its publication in the OJ on 21 February 1962: art. 191 of the Treaty.
3 Reg. 17, art. 5 (1), and see p. 356, below.

entry into force of Regulation 67/67) when the agreement was amended with the result that the conditions of the Regulation were satisfied. In the special case, however, of the amendment being made before 2 August 1967, and the Commission being advised of the amendment by 3 October 1967, art. 5 extends retroactively the exemption to the commencement of the agreement.

(b) Agreements which came into force after 13 March 1962 and were notified to the Commission before 1 May 1967. In these cases the exemption by category applies from the time when the conditions of this Regulation were fulfilled, *"but not earlier than the day of notification"*.[1]

By the Accession Treaty[2] "the following is inserted at the end of the first sentence of Article 5":[3]

> As regards agreements, decisions or concerted practices for exclusive dealing already in existence at the date of accession[4] to which Article 85 (1) applies by virtue of accession, the prohibition of Article 85 (1) of the Treaty shall not apply where they are modified within six months from the date of accession so as to fulfil the conditions contained in this Regulation.

The consequence of the Accession Treaty is that agreements which before 1 January 1973 were not within art. 85 (1), because they did not restrict competition within the EEC as constituted before that date, e.g. an agreement restricting competition in, and affecting trade between, the UK and Denmark or Ireland, will as from that date be brought within the scope of art. 85 (1) "by virtue of accession"; such agreements are hereafter referred to as accession agreements. But in so far as accession agreements relating to exclusive distribution are concerned, the above amendment to art. 5 provides that such agreements could be amended before 30 June 1973 so as to comply with Regulation 67/67, in which case art. 85 (1) will not apply to such agreements as from 1 January 1973 and for so long as the Regulation is in force – and as regards the period prior to that date, art. 85 (1) was not in any event applicable. If the agreement has not been appropriately amended by 30 June 1973 it is notifiable to the Commission –

---

1 Authors' emphasis.
2 See Act of Accession, Annex I, OJ 1972 L73/92, published in a Special English Edition, 27 March 1972.
3 The insertion after the first sentence is unfortunate in that the rest of the original article dealing with the communication of the amendment to the Commission has no application as regards agreements within art. 85 (1) "by virtue of accession".
4 1 January 1973.

so that it can thereafter only be exempted on an individual basis under art. 85 (3) – and any exemption granted will only relate to the period after the notification.[1]

Article 6

The Commission shall examine whether Article 7 of Regulation No 19/65/EEC applies in individual cases, in particular when there are grounds for believing that:

(a) the goods to which the contract relates are not subject, in the territory covered by the contract, to competition from goods considered by the consumer as similar goods in view of their properties, price and intended use;

(b) it is not possible for other manufacturers to sell, in the territory covered by the contract, similar goods at the same stage of distribution as that of the exclusive dealer;

(c) the exclusive dealer has abused the exemption:

   (1) by refusing, without objectively valid reasons, to supply in the territory covered by the contract categories of purchasers who cannot obtain supplies elsewhere, on suitable terms, of the goods to which the contract relates;

   (2) by selling the goods to which the contract relates at excessive prices.

As has been seen[2] Regulation 67/67 is a Regulation of the Commission issued under the general authority of Council Regulation 19/65, art. 7 of which requires the exemption by category to be withdrawn from an agreement which is found in practice not to satisfy the various conditions for obtaining an individual exemption under art. 85 (3).[3] Regulation 67/67, art. 6, implements Regulation 19/65, art. 7, which specifies that if exemption by category is withdrawn the agreement may nevertheless be justified on an individual basis under art. 85 (3), even though the agreement was not notified. The Commission might wish to make use of this provision and grant exemption by individual decision so as to be able to attach such conditions to the grant as it thinks fit under art. 8 (1) of Regulation 17.[4]

Article 7

1. Article 4 (2) (a) of Regulation No 27 of 3 May 1962, as amended by Regulation No 153, is hereby repealed.

2. Notification, on Form B 1, on an exclusive dealing agreement which does not fulfil the conditions contained in Articles 1 to 3 of this

---

1 See under "Effects of Notification", p. 274, below.
2 See p. 96, above.
3 The text of Reg. 19/65 is set out in Appendix II, p. 349, below.
4 See p. 289, below.

Regulation shall, if such agreement is not amended so as to satisfy those conditions, be effected before 3 October 1967, by submission of Form B, with annexes, in accordance with the provisions of Regulation No 27.

Article 8

Articles 1 to 7 of this Regulation shall apply by analogy to the category of concerted practices defined in Article 1 (1).

No reference is made here to decisions by associations of undertakings, which are outside the scope of the Regulation as involving more than two undertakings.

Article 9

This Regulation shall enter into force on 1 May 1967.

This Regulation shall be binding in its entirety and directly applicable in all Member States.

Specialisation agreements

The Commission has issued Regulation 2779/72[1] conferring exemption by category under art. 85 (3) on certain specialisation agreements, namely agreements by which the parties mutually renounce in favour of each other the right to manufacture certain products, having regard to the beneficial results referred to in recital (7)[2] normally to be expected from such agreements. The exemption applies where no restrictions other than those stated in art. 2 are accepted, the market share of the agreement products does not exceed a certain percentage of the relevant market and the aggregate turnover of the parties falls within certain limits.

The fact that an agreement is not or ceases to be within the criteria of the Regulation in no way prejudices its exemption under art. 85 (3) on an individual basis where it can be shown that the exempting conditions of art. 85 (3) are otherwise met. To obtain individual exemption it *may* be necessary to notify the agreement – (as to which see comment to art. 6, below). In all cases of doubt it is possible and advisable to notify the agreement. The Regulation is now set out with certain comments.

REGULATION (EEC) NO 2779/72 OF THE COMMISSION
of 21 December 1972

on the application of Article 85 (3) of the Treaty to categories of specialisation agreements

---

1 OJ 1972 L292/23.
2 The recitals have been numbered by the authors for convenience.

THE COMMISSION OF THE EUROPEAN COMMUNITIES,

(1) Having regard to the Treaty establishing the European Economic Community, and in particular Articles 87 and 155 thereof;

(2) Having regard to Council Regulation (EEC) No 2821/71 of 20 December 1971 on application of Article 85 (3) of the Treaty to categories of agreements, decisions and concerted practices;

(3) Having regard to the Opinions of the Advisory Committee on Restrictive Practices and Monopolies delivered pursuant to Article 6 of Regulation (EEC) No 2821/71;

(4) Whereas under Regulation (EEC) No 2821/71 the Commission has power to apply Article 85 (3) of the Treaty by regulation to certain categories of agreements, decisions and concerted practices relating to specialisation, including agreements necessary for achieving it, which fall within Article 85 (1);

(5) Whereas, since the adoption of such a Regulation would not conflict with the application of Regulation No 17, the right of undertakings to apply in individual cases to the Commission for a declaration under Article 85 (3) of the Treaty would not thereby be affected;

(6) Whereas agreements for the specialisation of production may fall within the prohibition contained in Article 85 (1);

(7) Whereas agreements for the specialisation of production lead in general to an improvement in the production or distribution of goods, because the undertakings can concentrate on the manufacture of certain products, thus operate on a more rational basis and offer these products at more favourable prices; whereas it is to be anticipated that, with effective competition, consumers will receive a fair share of the profit resulting therefrom;

(8) Whereas this Regulation must determine what restrictions on competition may be included in a specialisation agreement; whereas the restrictions on competition provided for in this Regulation are, in general, indispensable for the purpose of ensuring that the desired benefits accrue to undertakings and consumers; whereas it may be left to the contracting parties to decide which of these provisions they include in their agreements;

(9) Whereas in order to ensure that competition is not eliminated in respect of a substantial part of the goods in question, this Regulation applies only if the share of the market held by the participating undertakings and the size of the undertakings themselves do not exceed a specified limit;

(10) Whereas this Regulation should also apply to specialisation agreements made prior to its entry into force;

HAS ADOPTED THIS REGULATION:

Article 1

Pursuant to Article 85 (3) it is hereby declared that, subject as provided in this Regulation, until 31 December 1977 Article 85 (1) of the Treaty shall not apply to agreements whereby with the object of specialisation, undertakings mutually bind themselves for the duration of the agreements not to manufacture certain products or cause them to be manufactured by other undertakings, and to leave it to the other contracting parties to manufacture such products or cause them to be manufactured by other undertakings.

The *Jaz – Peter, F N – C F, MAN – SAVIEM, Clima – Buderus* Cases[1] are instances of the type of specialisation envisaged by the article; but not, it is submitted, the *ACEC – Berliet* and *Prym-Beka* Cases[2]. In the former case the parties agreed to co-operate in developing in common a new type of vehicle and each would contribute to the project according to its specialisation (ACEC the newly developed transmission system and Berliet the chassis, etc.); there was thus no renunciation by either party of any existing or future right to manufacture certain products. In the latter case the necessary mutuality in the restriction on manufacture would appear to be lacking.

Generally specialisation is a consequence of agreement, but for good measure art. 7 extends the scope of art. 1 to include specialisation as a consequence of decisions by associations of undertakings and concerted practices.

Article 2

1. Apart from the obligation referred to in Article 1, no other restriction on competition shall be imposed on the contracting parties save the following:

    (a) the obligation not to conclude with other undertakings specialisation agreements relating to identical products or to products considered by consumers to be similar by reason of their characteristics, price or use, except with the consent of the other contracting parties;

"Identical products or to products considered by consumers to be similar by reason of their characteristics price or use"

See comment to art. 3 (1) (a), below.

    (b) the obligation to supply the other contracting parties with the products which are the subject of specialisation, and in so doing to observe minimum standards of quality;

---

1 *Re Agreement of Jaz SA*, 22 July 1969, JO 1969 L195/5; [1970] CMLR 129; *Re Agreement of Fabrique Nationale d'armes de guerre and Cartoucherie française*, 28 Mary 1971, JO 1971 L134/6; *Re Agreement of MAN-SAVIEM*, 17 January 1972, JO 1972 L31/29; [1974] 2 CMLR D123; *Re Agreement of Clima Chappée SA*, 22 July 1969, JO 1969 L195/1; [1970] CMLR D7.
2 *Re Agreement of Ateliers de Constructions Electriques de Charleroi and Berliet*, 17 July 1968, JO 1968 L201/7; [1968] CMLR D35; *Re Agreement of William Prym-Werke KG and SA Manufacture Belge d'Aiguilles Beka*, 8 October 1973, OJ 1973 L296/24; [1973] CMLR D250; and see pp. 182, 193, below.

Provision can be included in the agreement to ensure that each party's requirements of the products made by the other are satisfied both as to quantity and quality, but a provision limiting the quantities which the other may make or sell would be outside the scope of this sub-paragraph, e.g. as in *ACEC – Berliet* where ACEC was restricted as to sales of its transmission systems to other vehicle manufacturers.

(c) the obligation to purchase products which are the subject of speciali-sation solely from the other contracting parties, except where more favourable terms of purchase are available elsewhere and the other contracting parties are not prepared to offer the same terms;

Care should be taken when drafting a specialisation agreement with a view to exemption by category to provide in positive terms for the qualification to the obligation.

(d) the obligation to grant to the other contracting parties the exclusive right to distribute the products which are the subject of specialisation so long as those parties do not – in particular by the exercise of industrial property rights or of other rights and measures – limit the opportunities, for intermediaries or consumers, of purchasing the products to which the agreement relates from other dealers within the common market.

While mutual exclusive dealing is generally suspect as a means of market sharing, it is necessary in the context of specialisation agreements for reasons given, for example, in *Re FN-CF* discussed at p. 185, below. By providing that the exclusive dealing must not be accom-panied by measures to prevent parallel imports the Commission once again emphasises the importance attached to the free movement of goods within the Common Market. It is understood that the Commission does not consider that the provisions of Regulation 67/67 can be imported into this Regulation. Accordingly the agreement will lose the benefit of the exemption by category by the imposition on the reciprocal distributor of ancillary obligations permitted under art. 2 of Regulation 67/67 in the case of a distributor where no reciprocity exists, except in so far as the obligations are also authorised under the specialisation Regulation.

2. Article 1 shall apply notwithstanding that the following obligations are imposed:

(a) the obligation to maintain minimum stocks of the products which are the subject of specialisation and of replacement parts for them;

(b) the obligation to provide after-sale and guarantee services for the products which are the subject of specialisation.

It is not clear whether the obligations which may be imposed are obligations on the manufacturer, or the other party acting as his distributor, or both. The Commission's view is understood to be that the obligations may only be imposed on the other party acting as such distributor for the specialised products. It remains to be seen whether this interpretation will be adopted in practice.

It will be noticed that the restrictions permitted by art. 2 are very limited and this considerably lessens the value of the Regulation. In particular, it is difficult to imagine a specialisation agreement which does not include a provision for a certain amount of joint research and development, yet an agreement containing such a provision cannot benefit from the Regulation, and such an agreement, not being exempt from notification by virtue of Regulation 17, art. 4 (2),[1] will have to be notified to the Commission. The practical utility of the Regulation as a means of avoiding the need to seek individual exemption is therefore to be doubted.

Article 3

1. Article 1 shall apply only:

    (a) if the products which are the subject of specialisation represent in any member country not more than 10 per cent of the volume of business done in identical products or in products considered by consumers to be similar by reason of their characteristics, price or use; and

The above formula is simple to apply where the respective specialised products of each manufacturer are part of the same product market in the sense that they are all considered by the consumer to be substitutes for one another by reason of their properties, price and use.[2] The total of each party's sales of the specialised products in each member state are compared to the total sales in that state of all products within the same product market (i.e. sales of the specialised products of the parties, of identical products of other manufacturers and of all products considered by the consumer to be substitutes). If in any member state the former is over 10% of the latter the Regulation will not apply, subject to the "marginal relief" referred to below in art. 3 (3).

The respective specialised products may not, however, form part of the same product market, in the sense that they are not considered substitutes by the consumer for the stated reasons. Thus where under

---

1 See p. 263, below.
2 It is understood from the Commission that the disjunctive "or" in the text of the Regulation should read "and", similarly in art. 2 (1) (a) above. For further discussion of product market, see pp. 167 ff., below.

an agreement between A and B, A specialises in the manufacture of electric mantelpiece clocks and B in mechanical watches, the relevant proportion in each member state for the purposes of the formula would appear to be established by taking A and B's aggregate sales of the specialised products and comparing the total to the aggregate of (i) A's sales of electric mantelpiece clocks plus sales of all other such clocks which are substitutes and (ii) B's sales of mechanical watches and all other mechanical watches which are substitutes.

It must be said, however, that the above interpretation of the text is not free from doubt.

[and] (b) if the aggregate annual turnover of the participating undertakings does not exceed 150 million units of account.

The paragraph refers to the turnover (computed in accordance with art. 4) in all products and services, not only those in which there is specialisation under the relevant agreement.

2. For purposes of applying paragraph 1 the unit of account shall be that adopted in drawing up the budget of the Community in accordance with Articles 207 and 209 of the Treaty.[1]

3. Article 1 of this Regulation shall continue to apply notwithstanding that in any two consecutive financial years the share of the market or the turnover is greater than as specified in paragraph 1, provided the excess is not more than 10%.

There may therefore be an 11% market share and/or a 165 million units of account turnover for two consecutive years. If in the third year the market share and total turnover have not reverted to the limits specified in para. 1 the agreement will no longer benefit from the exemption by category, but will continue to qualify for individual exemption subject to compliance with the notification requirements.[2]

Article 4

The aggregate turnover within the meaning of Article 3 (1) (b) shall be calculated by adding together the turnover achieved during the last financial year in respect of all products and services:

1. by the undertakings which are parties to the agreement;
2. by undertakings in respect of which the undertakings which are parties to the agreement hold:

—at least 25% of the capital or of the working capital whether directly or indirectly; or
—at least half the voting rights; or

---

1 The value of the unit of account is explained at p. 294, below.
2 As to which see Ch. 10, Section 3, p. 255, below.

         —the power to appoint at least half the members of the super-
           visory board, board of management or bodies legally repre-
           senting the undertaking; or
         —the right to manage the affairs of the undertaking;
    3. by undertakings which hold in an undertaking which is a party to the
        agreement:
         —at least 25% of the capital or of the working capital whether
           directly or indirectly; or
         —at least half the voting rights; or
         —the power to appoint at least half the members of the super-
           visory board, board of management or bodies legally repre-
           senting the undertaking; or
         —the right to manage the affairs of the undertaking.
    In calculating aggregate turnover no account shall be taken of
    dealings between the undertakings which are parties to the agreement.

When the undertakings have differing financial years it is understood that it is the results of each of the differing years which should
be aggregated.

Article 5

    The Commission shall examine whether Article 7 of Regulation (EEC)
No 2821/71 applies in any specific case, in particular where there is
reason to believe that rationalisation is not yielding significant results or
that consumers are not receiving a fair share of the resulting profit.

In the contemplated circumstances the Commission may, under
Regulation 2821/71, art. 7,[1] withdraw the exemption by category
and consider the agreement on an individual basis, the requirement
as to notification being dispensed with. This provision is similar to
that in Regulation 67/67, art. 6, and serves the same purpose; see the
comment to that article on p. 107, above.

Article 6

    The non-applicability of Article 85 (1) provided for in Article 1 of this
Regulation shall have retroactive effect from the time when the conditions
requisite for the application of this Regulation were satisfied. In the case
of agreements which, prior to 18 January 1972, were compulsorily
notifiable, the time aforesaid shall not be earlier than the day of notification.

The agreement may however be dispensed from notification under
Regulation 17, art. (4) (2) as amended by Regulation 2822/71.[2] Notification of the agreement will not in any event be necessary if it is

---

1 The text of Reg. 2821/71 is set out in Appendix II, p. 380, below.
2 See p. 263, below, and the amended text set out in Appendix II, p. 321, below.

within the terms of the Commission's Communication of 27 May 1970, relating to agreements of minor importance.[1]

Article 7

Articles 1 to 6 of this Regulation shall apply by analogy to decisions by associations of undertakings and to concerted practices.

Article 8

This Regulation shall enter into force on 1 January 1973.

---

1 See p. 74, above.

Chapter 4

Article 85 (2)—Effects of Prohibition

Agreements, decisions and concerted practices within art. 85, para. 1 (and which have not been exempted under para. 3) are prohibited. The consequence of the prohibition is spelt out in art. 85, para. 2, which provides that "agreements or decisions prohibited pursuant to this Article shall be automatically void". It is to be noted that no reference is here made to concerted practices; the explanation may be that concerted practice as a mere pattern of behaviour cannot be analysed in legal terms and therefore nullity as a legal concept can have no application to it.[1]

SECTION 1   AUTOMATICALLY VOID

These words in the authentic English version of the Treaty reflecting the term "*nul de plein droit*" in the French text (but which could possibly have been better rendered by an expression such as "void by operation of law"), imply that an agreement which infringes art. 85 (1) is void *ab initio* or at any rate as from when the Treaty of Rome came into force on 1 January 1958 (particularly as Regulation 17, art. 1, has added the additional gloss that such an agreement is prohibited without the need of a prior decision to this effect).

The present state of the law regarding the extent of the invalidity of agreements prohibited by art. 85 results from the combined effect of a number of judgments of the Court of Justice, the most recent of which was given in the *de Haecht* (No. 2) Case.[2] However, no area of the EEC's competition law has given rise to so many difficulties of interpretation, and the judgments handed down by the Court of Justice have not always been consistent, either with each other, or, in some instances, with the express wording of the Treaty. The *de Haecht* Judgment by no means resolved all the existing difficulties, and therefore before analysing the Judgment to see what changes it brought about, and the problems that it left unresolved, it is first

---

1 Goldman, *op. cit.*, para. 422, and cf. art. 86, p. 148, below.
2 *Brasserie de Haecht* v. *Wilkin* (No. 2), 6 February 1973, [1973] ECR 77; [1973] CMLR 287.

necessary to discuss what the position prior to the *de Haecht* Judgment is thought to have been. The discussion which follows is necessarily complex and to a certain extent speculative, and an attempt is made to summarise the present position at p. 123, below. Throughout the following discussion and in the summary certain expressions are used with particular meanings, viz:

"old agreement" – an agreement entered into before 13 March 1962 (the date when Regulation 17 came into force);

"accession agreement" – an agreement entered into before 1 January 1973 which was not then within art. 85 (1) and which was brought within the scope of the article by virtue of the accession of the new member states;[1]

"new agreement" – an agreement, not being an accession agreement, entered into on or after 13 March 1962.

Each of the above agreements may be either:

"notifiable" – i.e. required to be notified under Regulation 17, art. 4 (1) or 5 (1), in order to qualify for exemption under art. 85 (3);[2] or

"non-notifiable" – i.e. not required to be so notified by virtue of Regulation 17, art. 4 (2) or 5 (2).[2]

Position prior to the de Haecht (No. 2) Case

Prior to the *de Haecht* (*No.* 2) Case[3] in 1973, it was necessary to distinguish no fewer than six separate circumstances of nullity according to the type of agreement involved:

(1) As regards old agreements, if notifiable and duly notified, then nullity, upon the agreement being found to infringe art. 85 (1), was held to date only from 13 March 1962, on the ground that until the coming into force of Regulation 17 it was not possible to know the mechanism by which art. 85 would be applied in practice and the principle of legal security required that nullity should not attach to the agreement before the manner of the implementation of art. 85 was known. Such was the effect of the *Bosch* Case.[4] During the period from 13 March 1962 until its status from the point of view of art. 85 was decided, an old agreement was provisionally valid. If found to

---

1 The meaning of "accession agreements" has already been discussed in the context of the amendment to Reg. 67/67, art. 5, see p. 106, above.
2 As to which, see further, pp. 255 ff., below.
3 *Brasserie de Haecht* v. *Wilkin* (No. 2), 6 February 1973, [1973] ECR 77; [1973] CMLR 287.
4 *Kleding-Verkoopbedrijf de Geus en Uitdenbogerd* v. *Robert Bosch GmbH*, 6 April 1962, VIII Rec. 89; [1962] CMLR 1.

infringe the article and not to qualify for exemption, the resulting nullity was retroactive to 13 March 1962 but not earlier. If the exemption was granted the provisional validity ceased and the agreement became valid for the duration of the exemption.

However, in the *Portelange* Case[1] the Court of Justice said, in relation to an agreement notified in accordance with Regulation 17:

> "The question of whether such an agreement is effectively prohibited rests on the evaluation of economic and juridical elements which cannot be presumed to be acquired outside the express finding that the case in question, considered in its individuality, not only gathers together the elements set out in paragraph (1) of this Article, but also does not justify the exemption provided by paragraph (3). As long as no such finding has been arrived at, *any agreement duly notified must be regarded as valid*."[2]

The Court further said:[3]

> "it would be contrary to the general principle of certainty of law to draw, from the non-definitive character of the validity of notified agreements, the conclusion that, as long as the Commission has not ruled on them under Article 85 (3) of the Treaty, their effectiveness is not complete."

The expression "any notified agreement" in the first quotation includes a duly notified old agreement; so that as a result of *Portelange* an old agreement was avoided only after an unfavourable decision had been made with respect to it. To that extent *Portelange* is in line with *Bosch*,[4] but, in contrast to *Bosch*, there is nothing in the wording of *Portelange* to suggest that nullity is retroactive.

(2) In the case of non-notifiable old agreements the Court of Justice held in the *Bilger* Case[5] that, such agreements not being very likely to affect trade between member states, the principle of legal security required that they should not be treated less favourably than notified old agreements – i.e. on the basis of the prior *Portelange* Judgment they were to be valid until found to be void by the Commission, the resulting nullity being without retroactive effect.

(3) In the case of notifiable old agreements, not actually notified in accordance with Regulation 17, art. 5 (1), it must be assumed in the absence of contrary authority that the automatic nullity provided for in art. 85 (2) applies to them retroactively from the beginning of the agreement (or from 1 January 1958, if later).

---

1 *Portelange SA* v. *Smith Corona Marchant International SA*, 9 July 1969, XV Rec. 309; [1974] 1 CMLR 397, at p. 418, para. 13.
2 Authors' emphasis.
3 [1974] 1 CMLR 397, at p. 418, para. 15.
4 *Kleding-Verkoopbedrijf de Geus en Uitenbogerd* v. *Robert Bosch GmbH,* 6 April 1962, VIII Rec. 89; [1962] CMLR 1.
5 *Brauerei A. Bilger Söhne GmbH* v. *Jehle,* 18 March 1970, XVI Rec. 127; [1974] 1 CMLR 382.

(4) As regards new agreements, if notifiable and duly notified, the *Portelange* Judgment applied to them by reason of their inclusion in the class of "any notified agreement", and were therefore on the face of the Judgment to be treated as valid until a decision was taken that they did not benefit from art. 85 (3) exemption – failing which the agreement would be avoided with respect to the future, the Judgment making no mention of any possible retroactive nullity.

Considerable doubts were, however, expressed in competent circles as to whether such a radical departure from the apparently express intention of art. 85 was permissible and could really have been desired by the Court of Justice, involving as it did complete reversal from a legal situation where agreements caught by art. 85 were to be void unless exempted, to one where such agreements were valid until condemned—and while this might be justified in the case of old agreements it was difficult to see the justification where new agreements were concerned.

(5) Non-notifiable new agreements were to be treated under the *Bilger* Judgment in the same way as non-notifiable old agreements – i.e. valid until found void, when they became void with respect to the future only.

(6) Finally, there is the case of notifiable new agreements, which are not duly notified, to which the remarks made in para. (3), above, in relation to notifiable old agreements which have not been notified, apply.

The effect of the de Haecht (No. 2) Case

Considerable changes were brought to the situation described above by the *de Haecht (No. 2)* Case[1] of 1973. Before discussing these, it is important to know in relation to old agreements that while undertakings in the new member states will only exceptionally be concerned with them as such, understanding of their legal status as valid or void as the case may be is important in that under the Accession Treaty accession agreements are assimilated to old agreements. This appears to be the effect of the provisions of Regulation 17, art. 25,[2] which was added to the Regulation by the Accession Treaty,[3] and the Commission has endorsed this view.[4]

---

1 *Brasserie de Haecht* v. *Wilkin (No. 2)*, 6 February 1973, [1973] ECR 77; [1973] CMLR 287.
2 The full text of Reg. 17 is given in Appendix II, p. 318, below.
3 Act of Accession, Annex I, published in a special English Edition, 27 March 1972, OJ 1972 L73/92.
4 Commission's 3rd Report on Competition Policy, May 1974, sec 5, 3rd para.; for a contrary view, see Waelbroeck in *Cahiers de droit européen* (1974) Nos. 1–2, p. 165, at p. 178.

The *de Haecht* (*No.* 2) Case confirms in our opinion the *Portelange* and *Bilger* Cases in so far as they held that the nullity of old agreements was not retroactive upon such agreements being found to infringe art. 85, but it must be admitted that the position is not free from doubt for reasons which will appear below.

In the *de Haecht* Case new and old agreements are distinguished:

> "[9] as far as old agreements are concerned, certainty of law as regards contracts requires that a Court cannot, particularly where an agreement has been notified under Regulation 17, establish nullity until after the Commission has made a decision under this Regulation."

> "[10] as far as new agreements are concerned, it follows from the Regulation, on the assumption that so long as the Commission has made no pronouncement, the agreement can only be operated at the risk of the parties, that notifications under Article 4 (1) of Regulation 17 are without suspensory effect."[1]

It seems then that a notification has a "suspensory effect" in the case of old agreements whether non-notifiable, or notifiable and duly notified – para. 13 of the Judgment specifying that its remarks in relation to notifiable agreements apply equally to non-notifiable agreements.[2]

OLD AGREEMENTS

Old agreements having been entered into at a time when it had not been determined how and to what extent art. 85 would be given effect to (see as regards this the *Bosch* Judgment), it is necessary in the opinion of the Court in the *de Haecht* (*No.* 2) Judgment to ensure that they are dealt with with a degree of flexibility which it is within the power of the Commission, but not within that of a national court, to exercise[3] – hence, the suspension under para. 9 of the Judgment of a national court's powers deriving from the direct applicability of art. 85 (1) to hold an agreement void until the relevant agreement has been the subject of a decision by the Commission.

However, the national court might in the meantime have had to give effect to the agreement, in accordance with the *Portelange* Case, which held that until the Commission has given its decision on a duly notified agreement it is fully enforceable;[4] and the principle of legal security invoked by the Court of Justice requires, it is submitted, that there should be no "comeback" on the successful party in an action on the

---

1 [1973] ECR 27; [1973] CMLR 287, at p. 302.
2 For a contrary view that the suspensory effect applies only to duly notified, notifiable agreements, see Waelbroeck, *op. cit.*, pp. 175, 176.
3 [1973] ECR 27; [1973] CMLR 287, paras. 3, 4 and 5.
4 See p. 118, above; though it has been suggested that, as a result of para. 9 of the *de Haecht* (*No.* 2) Case, the national court may suspend civil proceedings with regard to an old agreement; see Waelbroeck, *op. cit.*, p. 175.

agreement if in due course the Commission should find the agreement to be void by reason of infringement of art. 85 (1). Any such nullity must therefore relate, it is submitted, to the future only, as indeed the Court of Justice held in the *Portelange* Case.

The old agreements referred to in the *de Haecht* (*No.* 2) Case are agreements in force on 13 March 1962, but, as stated above, accession agreements are to be assimilated to such agreements. Thus, a British company which has registered an accession agreement by 30 June 1973, as required by Regulation 17, art. 25 (2),[1] should be able to enforce and be bound by it until it has eventually been found to infringe art. 85 and not to qualify for exemption, in which case it is void as regards the future only.

This in no way operates to the prejudice of the EEC's competition policy having regard to the view of the Court in the *Portelange* Case that if a notified agreement infringes art. 85 it is always open to the Commission to take proceedings in respect of it.

It has been mentioned above that the legal basis of the *Portelange* Judgment has been criticised and if the Court of Justice has found it possible (as we submit it has) to reconfirm in the *de Haecht* (*No.* 2) Case that as far as duly notified old agreements or non-notifiable old agreements are concerned, they become void upon a finding that they infringe art. 85 only in relation to the period thereafter – this has been only on the basis that the Court has stepped in to fill a void left by the authors of art. 85 as regards essential transitional provisions to deal with agreements in force at the time of adoption of Regulation 17.

NEW AGREEMENTS

As far as new agreements are concerned, the Court of Justice has by the *de Haecht* (*No.* 2) Case reverted to a stricter interpretation of art. 85 (2) more in line with its text which states that agreements infringing art. 85 (1) are automatically void. If such is their status, the assumption expressed in para. 10 of the Judgment that the agreement can only be operated at the risk of the parties is a necessary consequence. There is no question of the agreement being provisionally valid as in the *Bosch* Case, and indeed the Court stated in the *de Haecht* (*No.* 2) Case that where the nullity of a new agreement is pleaded in an action before the national court,

> "it devolves on the court to judge, subject to the possible application of Article 177, whether there is cause to suspend proceedings in order to allow the parties to obtain the Commission's standpoint, unless it establishes either that the agreement does not have any perceptible effect on

---

1 Set out in Appendix II, p. 331, below.

competition or trade between Member States or that there is no doubt that the agreement is incompatible with Article 85."

The national judge, therefore, must either (a) determine himself whether or not the agreement infringes art. 85 (1), which he may do even where the agreement is the subject of proceedings before the Commission,[1] or (b) adjourn the proceedings to allow the parties to obtain the standpoint of the Commission, which will in effect mean obtaining a decision of the Commission, adjudicating one way or another upon the status of the agreement from the point of view of art. 85.

If in due course the Commission finds that a new agreement is contrary to art. 85 (1), it follows from the Court of Justice's ruling that a new agreement must be considered to have been operated at the risk of the parties that the resulting nullity will be retroactive to its commencement. The result will clearly be the same if the Commission's finding precedes the action before the national court.

The *de Haecht* (No. 2) Judgment was given in proceedings under art. 177 of the Treaty of Rome for a ruling, *inter alia*, on the question as to the date from which nullity took effect in the case of a non-notifiable agreement. The Court held such agreements to be void retroactively, thus reversing the *Bilger* Case in so far as that case decided that non-retroactive nullity was warranted by the relative harmlessness of such agreements; the Court now holds that dispensation from notification constitutes no more than an indication lacking any final authority that the agreements in question are generally less harmful to the proper working of the Common Market.

The following are the relevant extracts from the Judgment as regards the retroactive effect of non-notifiable agreements:

"[24] This question asks whether the nullity under Article 85 (2) of agreements dispensed from notification is to be taken to be established as from the date upon which one of the contracting parties has duly alleged it, or merely from the date of the judgment or Commission decision establishing such nullity.

"[25] It follows from what has been said above by way of general considerations that Article 85 (2) renders null and void agreements and decisions which are prohibited under this Article.

"[26] Such nullity is therefore likely to affect all the effects, past or future, of the agreement or decision.

"[27] Accordingly nullity under Article 85 (2) has retroactive effect."[2]

This appears to follow from *Belgische Radio en Televisie* v. *SV SABAM and NV Fonior,* 30 January 1974, [1974] ECR 51; [1974] 2 CMLR 238, paras. 20–22, though these paras. were dealing with the question in the context of art. 86.
[1973] CMLR 287, at p. 304.

It is to be noted that while para. 24 poses the question in relation to agreements dispensed from notification generally, the relevant agreement which gave rise to the reference from the national court was in fact a new agreement; and that paras. 25, 26 and 27 deduce nullity of non-notifiable agreements from "what has been said above by way of general considerations". It is submitted that the general considerations to which para. 25 refers are those dealing only with new agreements, having regard to the views put forward in our preceding paragraphs, particularly that to hold duly notified agreements and non-notifiable old agreements to be void retroactively after first being held fully enforceable, makes nonsense of the principles of legal security.

If this is wrong, the question arises as from what date an old agreement and/or an accession agreement is retroactively void, assuming in each case that if the agreement is notifiable it has been duly notified. As far as old agreements are concerned, presumably the *Bosch* Case is still authority so that nullity relates back only to 13 March 1962, and as to accession agreements to 1 January 1973, by reason of the assimilation of the two dates. The 1 January 1973 should, it is thought, also apply in the case of notifiable agreements which are not in fact notified on the basis that when they were entered into they were valid agreements without effect in the EEC of the Six. These non-notified agreements will not, however, qualify for art. 85 (3) exemption, contrary to the case of duly notified accession agreements.

SUMMARY OF PRESENT POSITION[1]

It is submitted that the correct interpretation of the *de Haecht* (No. 2) Case[2] is that old and accession agreements (whether non-notifiable, or notifiable and duly notified) are valid until avoided, nullity attaching to them only from the date of their being found by decision of the Commission or judgment of the national court to infringe art. 85.

In so far as this interpretation is not substantiated and the view that nullity attaches to such agreements only with respect to the future is wrong, the relevant old or accession agreement will be void retroactively to 13 March 1962 in the case of an old agreement and to 1 January 1973 in the case of an accession agreement.

Old agreements which are notifiable but not notified, if found to infringe art. 85, become void retroactively to 13 March 1962.

Accession agreements which are notifiable but not notified, if

---

1 The particular meaning of certain expressions used in the summary is given at p. 117, above.
2 *Brasserie de Haecht* v. *Wilkin* (No. 2), 6 February 1973, [1973] ECR 77; [1973] CMLR 287.

found to infringe art. 85, become void retroactively, but, it is submitted, not earlier than 1 January 1973.

Non-notifiable, and notifiable new agreements which are duly notified, are void retroactively to inception if found to infringe art. 85 (1).

Notifiable agreements which are not notified are likewise void retroactively to inception if found to infringe art. 85 (1) but, contrary to the case of non-notifiable and duly notified agreements, no exemption under art. 85 (3) is possible where there has been failure to notify a notifiable agreement.

SECTION 2   CONSEQUENCES OF NULLITY

While art. 85 (2) states that prohibited agreements under art. 85 (1) are void, it is silent as to the consequences. Until the Court of Justice decides otherwise, these consequences must therefore be determined by national law (as opposed to EEC law), including the private international law, of the forum. The civil consequences of an infringement of art. 85 (1) may therefore be different according to whether the forum before which the question of nullity is raised is in one country or another. Within the scope of this book it is not however possible to do more than offer a few comments on the consequences of an agreement being void under art. 85 (2) on the basis that the forum is English and that English law governs all aspects of the matter before the national court. These comments fall to be made as to the position between the parties and as between such parties and third parties.[1]

As between the parties

AN EXAMPLE IN THE CASE OF AN ACCESSION AGREEMENT

It will be helpful to consider a hypothetical example: In 1970 a Danish manufacturer, A, of a new product gave to B, an English company, an "exclusive licence" to manufacture the product in the United Kingdom in accordance with A's know-how, subject to a prohibition on direct or indirect sales by B or its customers to Denmark. On the accession of the United Kingdom and Denmark to the EEC,[2] the agreement being notifiable was duly notified on 30 June 1973, to the EC Commission in accordance with Regulation 17, art. 25.[3]

B, in breach of the licence, exported to Denmark and an action is brought in January 1975 by A in England for an injunction and

---

1 The question of the severability of illegal clauses is discussed at pp. 136, 137, below.
2 For a discussion of the general effects of accession. see p. 106, above.
3 For the procedural aspects, see p. 267, below; for the text of the amended Reg. 17, see Appendix II, p. 331. below.

damages. B's defence is the nullity of the agreement under art. 85 (1) while A pleads that art. 85 (1) is not applicable, e.g. on the general ground of the insignificance of the agreement and, in the alternative, that in the particular circumstances of the case (e.g. the need to protect, at any rate, temporarily, the new industry in Denmark from the competition of cheaper imports from the United Kingdom) exemption under art. 85 (3) may be expected when the agreement is considered by the Commission pursuant to the notification.

These facts give rise to the following considerations:

(A) The English court has power derived from the direct applicability of art. 85 (1)[1] to determine whether or not the agreement infringes art. 85 (1) but not to grant relief under art. 85 (3).

(B) The agreement being in force on 1 January 1973 it is an accession agreement which has the status of an old agreement in the terminology of the *de Haecht* (*No. 2*) Judgment.[2]

(C) The English court, therefore, under para. 9 of the above Judgment[3] cannot, in apparent derogation of its powers derived from the direct applicability of art. 85 (1), hold the agreement void until the Commission has adjudicated thereon.

(D) Pending the Commission's decision, the agreement, which *ex hypothesi* has been duly notified, is fully enforceable in accordance with the *Portelange* Case[4] by A who is therefore entitled to the injunction and damages claimed.

(E) The Commission may come to one of three conclusions in relation to the agreement:

(i) the agreement does not infringe art. 85 (1);
(ii) the agreement infringes art. 85 (1);
(iii) the agreement infringes art. 85 (1) but is exempt under art. 85 (3) with effect from a certain date.

(F) If the Commission finds that the agreement does not infringe art. 85 (1) it will have been valid from 1 January 1973 and will continue to be valid after the Commission's decision. Before 1 January 1973 the agreement was not subject to the Treaty and was therefore valid in any event. The Commission's decision will, therefore, have confirmed the English court's judgment in favour of A, and B will

---

1 *Belgische Radio en Televisie* v. *SV SABAM and NV Fonior,* 30 January 1974; [1974] ECR 51; [1974] 2 CMLR 238, para. 15.
2 See p. 119, above.
3 Cited on p. 120, above.
4 *Portelange SA* v. *Smith Corona Marchant International SA.*, 9 July 1969, XV Rec. 309; [1974] 1 CMLR 397; and see p. 118, above.

have no recourse except by way of an appeal to the Court of Justice against the Commission's decision.

(G) If the Commission finds that the agreement infringes art. 85 (1) it will certainly be void as from the date of the decision. It may also be void retroactively.[1]

In so far as the English court has already granted an injunction to A, this will obviously have to be discharged. As regards the award of damages, A will be entitled to retain these if the nullity dates only from the date of the Commission's decision. If the nullity is retroactive, can A be required to make restitution to B? While on the one hand it is obviously not right that B should have compensated A in respect of the breach of a contract which eventually is found to have been void, on the other hand, restitution is not consistent with the principle of legal security to which the Court of Justice attaches considerable importance.

In any event, the legal basis on which restitution would be made is not clear, the notion of an enforceable agreement followed by its retroactive nullity being unfamiliar to English law.[2] The concept has to be developed by Parliament or the courts, but, as argued previously,[1] the problem does not arise if nullity takes effect as regard the future only.

Whether the nullity consequent upon a finding of the Commission that an agreement infringes art. 85 is retroactive or not, will depend, pending clarification of the position by the Court of Justice, upon the view of the question taken by the national court (i.e. the English court in the example under consideration) which may always refer the matter for a ruling of the Court of Justice under art. 177 of the Treaty.[3]

If the agreement is held void retroactively, it may also be asked whether B can recover monies paid to A under the void contract, e.g. licence fees. In so far as agreements infringing art. 85 (1) are prohibited they are under English law not only void but also illegal and monies paid under illegal contracts are irrecoverable unless the parties are not *in pari delicto*. In the example under discussion both parties are clearly equally "guilty" in so far as they are guilty at all, bearing in mind that when the agreement was entered into before accession it was perfectly legal. Further, it will be difficult to justify recovery when the party making the repayment, e.g. B's royalty

---

1 See pp. 120, 121, above.
2 Cf. position under RTPA.
3 For this procedure, see Ch. 12, Section 2, p. 307, below.

payments in the example, has received value for them, e.g. rights under the licence.

If the agreement is held void as to the future only, it follows that it was valid until the Commission's decision, at which point of time it was avoided under art. 85 (2). It may be thought that in these circumstances the agreement is frustrated by supervening illegality, calling for adjustment of the rights of the parties under the Law Reform (Frustrated Contracts) Act 1943.

(H) If the Commission finds that the agreement infringes art. 85 (1) but benefits from exemption under art. 85 (3) from a certain date, the agreement will be valid during the period of exemption. In our example, the agreement was duly notified by 30 June 1973 and the exemption will therefore apply from 1 January 1973 (the period prior to that date being outside the scope of the Treaty in so far as the acceding states are concerned) and the benefit of the exemption will continue after the date of the Commission's decision for the period stated therein. Upon reference back to the English court A will therefore be entitled both to retain the benefit of any damages already awarded and to the continuance of any injunction.

If the agreement had not been notified by 30 June 1973 but at some later date, the exemption could not date back beyond the date of notification and the agreement will therefore have been void from 1 January 1973 to the date of commencement of exemption. Upon reference back to the English court any claim by A for damages in respect of that period would not be sustainable.[1]

AN EXAMPLE IN THE CASE OF A NEW AGREEMENT

Let it be assumed now that the agreement in the above example was made in 1974 instead of 1970 and being notifiable was notified to the Commission on signature. In these circumstances:

(AA) The English court has again the general power derived from the direct applicability of art. 85 (1) to determine whether or not the agreement infringes art. 85 (1).

(BB) The agreement is a new agreement in the terminology of the *de Haecht* (No. 2) Judgment.

(CC) There is no derogation of the court's powers under the Treaty (as in the case of an old agreement).[2] The English court under para. 12[3] of the *de Haecht* (No. 2) Judgment must therefore determine whether art. 85 (1) applies, unless it chooses to adjourn the proceedings to allow the parties to obtain the opinion of the Commission.

---

1 See remarks under 5th para. of (G), above.
2 See para. 10 of *de Haecht* Judgment, quoted on p. 120, above.
3 Quoted on pp. 121, 122, above.

(DD) A new agreement is under para. 10 of the *de Haecht* (*No. 2*) Judgment performed at the risk of the parties. It cannot therefore be fully enforceable during any period of adjournment as mentioned in (CC) above and the English court will presumably have to consider what interim relief should be ordered.

(EE) One of the following alternative conclusions may be reached by the English court or the Commission (or by the Commission alone in case (iii)):

 (i) the agreement does not infringe art. 85 (1);
 (ii) the agreement infringes art. 85 (1);
 (iii) the agreement infringes art. 85 (1) but is exempt under art. 85 (3) as from a certain date.

(FF) If the agreement does not infringe art. 85 (1) it will have been valid from the date of inception, and A in the example given will be entitled to the injunction and damages claimed in the action.

(GG) If the agreement is found to infringe art. 85 (1) it will be void from inception and, as in the case of an old agreement, the question arises as to the possible recovery of monies paid under the void contract. The remarks made under para. (G) above are relevant bearing in mind, however, that the notional guilt in the case of an old agreement is more real in the case of a new agreement which will have been entered into after art. 85 became law in the acceding states.

(HH) (a) If, upon the adjournment of the case by the English court for the parties to obtain the view of the Commission, the agreement is found to infringe art. 85 (1) but to be exempt under art. 85 (3), the agreement will be valid during the period of exemption, which period may be back-dated to the date of notification. If the agreement was notified on signature the exemption will, unless the Commission's decision otherwise provides, render the agreement valid for the whole of its duration to the date of the action and A will be entitled to the damages claimed relating to such period. A will also be entitled to an injunction as regards the future so long as the exemption remains in force. If the agreement was not notified on signature or if the Commission's exemption is not back-dated to cover the whole of the period from signature, the agreement will be void from the date of signature to the commencement of the exemption. With regard to such period, A will clearly not be entitled to damages.

 (b) If the English court determines that the agreement infringes art. 85 (1) and subsequently one of the parties, in our example

A, requires the Commission to deal with the notification and to determine whether exemption under art. 85 (3) is available and the Commission grants exemption for the whole of the period from notification, A should be entitled to institute a new action in the English court claiming damages for the breaches which have occurred from the beginning of the agreement to the date of judgment in the second action and an injunction as regards the future. If the exemption does not relate back to the date of signature of the agreement, there will be a period of invalidity from signature until commencement of the exemption. No claim in damages will obviously lie by A in respect of that period. As regards the question of recovery by B of money paid during that period, see para. (G) above.

It will be noted that in paragraph (EE) above reference was made to conclusions being reached in relation to the relevant agreement by the English court or by the Commission.

If the matter first comes before the English court, it is clear from both the *de Haecht* (*No.* 2)[1] and *SABAM*[2] Cases that the English court may adjourn proceedings to allow the parties to obtain the decision of the Commission, which, no doubt, it will treat as determinative of the applicability or non-applicability of art. 85 (1).

Equally, where the matter comes before the English court after the Commission has already reached a decision in relation to the same agreement, the English court would, no doubt, accept the decision of the Commission as to the applicability or otherwise of art. 85 (1).

However, where the facts of the case appear to present no particular problems, the English court is free to determine one way or another the question of the applicability of art. 85 (1); indeed the *SABAM* Case[3] would appear to encourage it to do so, and this is so even where the Commission has already initiated proceedings. The fact that an English court had concluded in civil proceedings before it that art. 85 (1) did or did not apply to an agreement, would not preclude proceedings in relation to the same agreement by the Commission, instigated either by the Commission itself, or by one of the parties to the agreement. This must be so, it is submitted, if for no other reason than that the English court would not have been able to assess the application of art. 85 (3) to the agreement.

---

1 *Brasserie de Haecht v. Wilkin* (*No.* 2), 6 February 1973, [1973] ECR 77; [1973] CMLR 287, para. 12.
2 *Belgische Radio en Televisie v. SV SABAM and NV Fonior,* 30 January 1974; [1974] ECR 51; [1974] 2 CMLR 238, para. 21.
3 *Ibid.,* para. 22.

Obviously extremely complex questions will arise if the Commission comes to a conclusion which conflicts with that of the English court, and one of the parties to the original dispute seeks to re-open the matter on the basis of the Commission's finding. Not least of these questions is whether the matter can be re-opened at all, or would the principle of *res judicata* apply in the interests of legal security?

If the matter can be re-opened problems will result;
(a) by reason of the agreement which the English court found to be valid as not infringing art. 85 (1) being avoided with retroactive effect by the Commission as infringing art. 85 (1);
(b) by reason of the agreement which the English court found to be invalid as infringing art. 85 (1) being validated with retroactive effect by the Commission as not infringing art. 85 (1) *simpliciter*, or as benefiting from exemption under art. 85 (3).

The problem referred to in (a) is the same as that discussed under para. (G) at p. 126, above, in relation to the provisional validity of old agreements, which led the present authors to submit that the avoidance of such agreements should be with respect to the future only. However, in the case of new agreements the *de Haecht* (*No.* 2) Case precludes an argument that the nullity of the agreement resulting from an unfavourable ruling of the Commission can be other than retroactive – with, in the present example, anomalous consequences similar to those already discussed in relation to old and accession agreements if the true interpretation of Community law were that such agreements are void retroactively if found to infringe art. 85.

The problem referred to in (b) gives rise to a corresponding problem which, by a similar process of reasoning, leads to the notion of provisional invalidity of the agreement pending a subsequent finding of the Commission validating it; the question then is whether subsequent validation with retroactive effect confers any rights to compensation on the party prejudiced by the initial decision of the national court. If so the position, it is submitted, could be equally anomalous, although it must be admitted that the circumstances envisaged are rather unlikely to occur in practice.

It is only possible to wait and see how the English courts, maybe with guidance from the Court of Justice under art. 177,[1] will cope with such intractable problems. In this connection it should be noted that although the *Walt Wilhelm* Case[2] establishes the principle of primacy of Community *law* over national law, this does not provide

---

1 As to which see Ch. 12, Section 2, p. 307, below.
2 *Walt Wilhelm and others* v. *Bundeskartellamt,* 13 February 1969, XV Rec. 1; [1969] CMLR 100; and see pp. 137ff., below.

an answer to the present questions, which involve a conflict between two jurisdictions applying the same, i.e. Community, law.

As between the parties to the agreement and third parties: breach of statutory duty

AS BETWEEN THE PARTIES TO THE AGREEMENT AND THIRD PARTIES

The question here is whether a third party suffering loss as a result of an agreement between undertakings which infringes art. 85 has a claim for damages against the parties to the agreement. In short does such infringement give rise to an action for breach of statutory duty, the prohibition of art. 85 being a provision of the Treaty directly incorporated into national law?

A similar question may arise where an individual or an undertaking has suffered loss as a result of an undertaking abusing its dominant position contrary to art. 86; the following discussion therefore relates equally to infringement of art. 85 and infringement of art. 86.

There is no provision of the Treaty dealing with this problem; and there is no decision of the Commission or judgment of the Court of Justice directly bearing thereon. The solution must therefore be sought in the national laws of the member state before whose courts such an action may be brought.

In this connection a group of European university professors, at the request of the Commission, made a study of the remedies available in each of the original six member states for breach of arts. 85 and 86.[1]

The study concludes that infringement of the competition rules of the Treaty does enable persons prejudiced to enforce through national courts such remedies as may be available under the respective national legal systems of the member states by way of damages or injunction. This general conclusion is however subject to the special rules of each member state and is subject to various exceptions.

THE POSITION IN THE UNITED KINGDOM[2]

Whether under English law the breach of the provisions of a statute (breach of statutory duty) gives rise to a civil remedy has been stated to depend on the consideration of the whole enactment and the circumstances (including pre-existing law) in which the statute was enacted.[3]

---

1 "La réparation des conséquences dommageables d'une violation des articles 85 et 86 du traité instituant la CEE", Série Concurrence, 1 Bruxelles 1966.
2 The reader is referred to an article by Paul Rew: "Actions for damages by third parties under English law for breach of Article 85 of the EEC Treaty" in VIII CMLRev. 462, to which the authors are indebted for the following discussion.
3 *Cutler* v. *Wandsworth Stadium Ltd.*, [1949] AC 398; [1949] 1 All ER 544.

In the framework of this general principle, four specific tests have been formulated which, if satisfied, should entitle a person suffering prejudice from a breach of statutory duty to claim compensation by way of damages. These are:

(A) that the plaintiff should have suffered the kind of prejudice contemplated by the legislation as a result of a breach of the duty;
(B) that the statute was intended to confer civil remedies in respect of the breach;
(C) that there has in fact been a breach of duty;
(D) that the prejudice was the direct consequence of the breach of duty.

It is not thought that tests (A) and (D) present special problems from the point of view of infringement of arts. 85 or 86. The kind of situation which would result in test (A) not being satisfied will not normally arise. If it is found that the other tests are satisfied, it is difficult to see how the plaintiff's cause of action can be other than the financial loss resulting from the restrictive practices or the abuse of a dominant position – and such a loss would necessarily have been a contemplated result of the infringement of the Treaty.

As regards test (D), admittedly there may be cases where the plaintiff will have difficulty in relating his loss to the defendant's infringement of the relevant articles – but this is a question of proof and does not go to the root of the matter.

Test (C) presents more problems for it raises the question of the nature of the duty which a party to a restrictive agreement or an undertaking in a dominant position owes in relation to the observance of arts. 85 and 86. Is a breach of the articles actionable in any event (i.e. is the duty to observe the articles absolute) or does a breach depend on fault?

It seems in this connection that English law would incline towards the view that fault is required. This, at any rate, results from the judgment of the Court of Appeal in *Ministry of Housing and Local Government* v. *Sharp*,[1] holding that "when a statutory duty is construed as absolute the statute (a) usually defines the duty with precision, (b) makes its breach punishable as a criminal offence, and sometimes (c) impliedly gives a right of action to the class of persons for whose protection the duty is created".

The question raised by condition (c) is also relevant in the more general context of test (B) – whether the statute was intended to

---

1 [1970] 2 QB 223, at p. 273, [1970] 1 All ER 1009, at p. 1022.

confer civil remedies for its breach and we revert to this question below.

With regard to condition (a) it is questionable whether an English court, comparing the broad sweep in arts. 85 and 86 with the detailed specification of what constitutes a registrable agreement under the RTPA, would find in arts. 85 and 86 the necessary degree of precision. But in any event condition (b) requiring the commission of a criminal offence cannot be satisfied since it seems that infringement of arts. 85 and 86 is not, according to Community law,[1] to be treated as a criminal offence.

However, in most cases infringement of arts. 85 and 86 will involve fault. Undertakings do not normally enter into restrictive agreements of sufficient importance to be capable of affecting trade between member states otherwise than deliberately; and normally they do not abuse a dominant position otherwise than knowingly although admittedly there may be an unintentional abuse when it consists of an undertaking increasing its market power otherwise than by eliminating all effective competition.[2]

But even where the infringement of arts. 85 and 86 is tainted by fault it is necessary to satisfy test (B) above, namely that the statute (i.e. the Treaty) was intended to confer civil remedies for the breach.

In considering this test the English court will take into account two factors:

(i) whether the statute provides for civil remedies or penal sanctions and, if the latter, whether the penal sanctions exclude civil remedies;

(ii) whether the thing enjoined or prohibited by the enactment is "for the benefit of a particular class of persons or for the public generally"?

As regards (i), it is true that the English courts have occasionally entertained civil claims for breach of statutory duty carrying penal sanctions, i.e. fines, as in *Groves* v. *Wimborne*[3] and *London Passenger Transport Board* v. *Upson*.[4] The fines involved in such cases were however insignificant in comparison to the fines which the Commission may impose. Thus in *Groves* v. *Wimborne* the Court found that the victim of an industrial accident through breach of statutory duty had a claim

---

1 As to which, see p. 300, below.
2 See the Judgment of Court of Justice in *Europemballage Corporation and Continental Can Company Incorporated* v. *EC Commission*, 21 February 1973, [1973] ECR 215; [1973] CMLR 199, quoted at p. 164, below, to the effect that the elimination of *all* effective competition is not essential for there to be an abuse.
3 [1898] 2 QB 402.
4 [1949] AC 155; [1949] 1 All ER 60.

in damages because the maximum fine (£100, payable at the discretion of the Secretary of State to the victim) could be inadequate compensation, so that it would be unreasonable to suppose that the legislature intended the penalty to be the only remedy for the injury; and in *LPTB* v. *Upson*, Lord Wright considered that a civil remedy is given by the common law to make effective for the benefit of the injured plaintiff his "right to performance by the defendant of the defendant's statutory duty".[1] Clearly, altogether different considerations must apply where fines of up to 1 million units of account[2] could be imposed under the Treaty (going up to 10% of turnover in certain circumstances).[3]

If, nevertheless, an English court were to find that the Commission's power of fining did not by itself exclude civil remedies for breach of statutory duty it would still have to consider the question in (ii) above. This question in the present context may be posed by asking whether the intention of arts. 85 and 86 in the context of the whole of the Treaty is (1) merely the preservation of a market economy, so that the breach of the articles is the concern only of the Commission as the authority responsible for the implementation of competition policy; or (2) whether, in addition, in such context they are *also* intended to protect consumers and competitors prejudiced by their breach, thereby enabling consumers and competitors to claim compensation (for breach of statutory duty, in English terminology) under the national law applied by the forum, irrespective of other rights or remedies which may flow from the supervening nullity of any agreement consequent upon it being found to infringe the articles in question or either of them.

It may be submitted that there is nothing in the preamble to the Treaty and the basic provisions set out in arts. 2, 3 and 5 or in the Rules on Competition in Part III of the Treaty, supporting the view that the protection of individual rights is an objective of the competition provisions of the Treaty. On the contrary, the whole emphasis of the basic arts. 2, 3 and 5 of the Treaty is on its economic objectives to be achieved through the establishment of the Common Market (art. 2) and by the specific measures of a public character to implement such objectives set out in art. 3, including that of the "institution of a system ensuring that competition in the Common Market is not distorted".

It is true that arts. 85 and 86 are directly applicable Treaty provisions

---

1 *Ibid.*, at p. 168 and p. 67, respectively.
2 The value of the unit of account is explained at p. 294, below.
3 As to fines, see Ch. 10, Section 6, p. 293, below.

and in the *SABAM* Case[1] the Court of Justice confirmed that these articles created individual rights which must be protected in the national courts. It is submitted, however, that the concept of direct applicability is intended only to enable individuals to enforce the observance of provisions of the Treaty in the national courts, such direct enforcement supplementing the powers of enforcement exerciseable by the Commission. Thus, in the context of arts. 85 and 86 the individual may seek in a national court a declaration that an agreement or practice is prohibited, and any consequential relief, but it is submitted that on the basis of the existing rulings of the Court of Justice it would be an unwarranted extension of the principle of direct applicability to suggest that it gives an individual a right, the infringement of which entitles him to monetary compensation.

Further, attention may be drawn to Regulation 17, art. 3, providing that persons who show a justified interest may request the Commission to terminate an infringement of art. 85.[2] This, however, also falls far short of a specific aim of the Treaty that such persons should have the right to claim damages in respect of the infringement.

As against this, in the Report of the professors referred to above,[3] as part of the discussion of the question whether civil claims for breach of arts. 85 and 86 are sustainable under German law, the following argument is put forward in favour of the admission of such claims:

> "Undoubtedly Articles 85 *et seq.* have as their primary object the protection of the Common Market in relation to agreements and dominant positions affecting such market. Nevertheless, the Common Market consists essentially in the total of all the possibilities which each individual has to exercise his activities as supplier or purchaser throughout the Common Market; accordingly impediments such as boycott, refusal to deal or other like measures intended to deny access to any part of the Common Market (in geographic or economic terms) must be considered as forbidden by Article 85 or 86 *in the interest of the person prejudiced.*"[4]

The report goes on to argue that third party claims could properly be admitted under German law when the prejudice suffered by the third party is his exclusion from a market within the EEC to which he would otherwise have access. In other words, third party claims would lie in respect of certain infringements of arts. 85 and 86, but not in respect of others.

---

1 *Belgische Radio en Televisie* v. *SV SABAM and NV Fonior,* 30 January 1974, [1974] ECR 51; [1974] 2 CMLR 238, para. 16.
2 See p. 274, below.
3 "La réparation des conséquences dommageables d'une violation des articles 85 et 86 du traité instituant la CEE", Série Concurrence, 1 Bruxelles 1966, p. 24 (authors' translation).
4 Authors' emphasis.

It is doubtful, however, whether an English court would allow such an argument (in which there is undoubtedly considerable force) to prevail over the view that the fines which the Commission can impose must have been intended as the only sanction for the breach of statutory duty having regard to the very substantial amount of the possible fines, particularly bearing in mind that an agreement infringing art. 85 may be void *ab initio*. If in such circumstance the principle of third party claims for breach of statutory duty were admitted, an undertaking which deliberately or negligently infringed art. 85 could be faced, in addition to the substantial fines mentioned above, with a civil claim based on loss of profit over several years as a consequence of the restrictive agreement. Similarly in the case of infringement of art. 86 the claims for breach of statutory duty could attain very high amounts in so far as the breach may have occurred over several years. Moreover, in the case of such claims both under arts. 85 and 86 there would be the possibility of a multiplicity of claims by different plaintiffs. With this in mind, the English court could with justification hold that an interpretation of the Treaty involving such drastic results should not be resorted to in the absence of specific legislative provisions or a ruling of the Court of Justice binding upon it.

In this connection it may be mentioned that in 1967 Lord Diplock stated emphatically[1] that actions for damages by third parties do not play a role in the enforcement of restrictive practices legislation in England. However, subsequently s. 7 of the RTPA 1968 has opened the way to such claims, but only in the event of a failure to register a registrable agreement. Maybe a similar approach should be followed in relation to infringement of art. 85 but it would be for the Community institutions or a national legislature and not for a national court to pave the way in that direction.

It is interesting to contrast the uncertain position under EEC law regarding third party claims and the negative attitude to such claims under English anti-trust law with the situation in the USA where the possibility of claims for penal triple damages at the suit of third parties prejudiced by breach of the anti-trust laws is perhaps the main deterrent against their infringement.

Severance

While art. 85 (2) states that agreements which are forbidden under the article are void, the effect of the Judgments of the Court of

---

1 The role of the judicial process in the regulation of competition, London 1967.

Justice in the *LTM – MBU*[1] and *Consten-Grundig* Cases[2] is that it is only those clauses which actually infringe the article which are avoided and that the rest of the agreement remains valid provided that the offending clauses can be severed. Moreover, the Court stated that it is not for Community law to determine the effect of the void clauses on the remaining clauses of the agreement. Where, therefore, a decision of the Commission holds that an agreement is within art. 85 (1) by reason of certain of its clauses, it will be for the national court trying an issue between the parties to determine to what extent those clauses are severable from the rest of the agreement. Severance is often possible under English law and it is beyond the scope of this book to discuss the principles involved.[3] The rules relating to severance are nevertheless complicated and as a matter of practice, in order to prevent the avoidance of an entire contract through one or more of its clauses infringing art. 85, it may be advisable for the parties to provide expressly for severance of such clauses from the rest of the contract, which is expressly to remain binding. To counter any suggestion that such a clause providing for severance might itself be avoided, it could be the subject of a collateral agreement.

SECTION 3 OVERLAP BETWEEN NATIONAL AND COMMUNITY LAW

The fields of application of the United Kingdom RTPA and art. 85 overlap. Indeed, whenever an agreement involves the acceptance by two or more persons carrying on business in the United Kingdom of any restrictions as defined in RTPA 1956, s. 6, there will almost invariably be involved a restriction of competition in the United Kingdom and therefore within the Common Market; and where firms from other EEC countries are parties to such agreements, trade between member states will more often than not be affected. This moreover can occur even in the case of agreements between United Kingdom companies only: for example, a mutual exclusive dealing arrangement between United Kingdom manufacturers and distributors preventing access to the United Kingdom market of products from other EEC countries.[4]

While an agreement may be contrary to the provisions of both

---

1 *La Technique Minière* v. *Maschinenbau Ulm GmbH,* 30 June 1966, XII Rec. 337; [1966] CMLR 357, at p. 376.
2 *Etablissement Consten and Grundig Verkaufs-GmbH* v. *EEC Commission,* 13 July 1966, XII Rec. 429; [1966] CMLR 418, at pp. 474–475.
3 Whether the illegality of an agreement infringing art. 85 prevents severance under English law is a matter which the English courts must determine.
4 See *Re Vereeniging van Cementhandelaren,* 16 December 1971, JO 1972 L13/34; on appeal 17 October 1972, XVIII Rec. 977; [1973] CMLR 7; at p. 48, above.

legislations in the first instance it may under each qualify for exemption. But the grounds for exemption under the RTPA 1956, s. 21, and art. 85 (3) are not the same and the exempting authorities are different, so that there is a possibility that the Restrictive Practices Court and the EC Commission may reach different conclusions as to the validity of the agreement.

Special provisions have therefore been included in the European Communities Act 1972, s. 10, to avoid conflict between the two jurisdictions, i.e. between the Restrictive Practices Court applying the RTPA and the Commission applying art. 85.[1] These provisions are:

"10. – (1) Part I of the Restrictive Trade Practices Act 1956 shall apply to an agreement notwithstanding that it is or may be void by reason of any directly applicable Community provision, or is expressly authorised by or under any such provision; but the Restrictive Practices Court may decline or postpone the exercise of its jurisdiction under section 20 of the Act, or may (notwithstanding section 22 (2)) exercise its jurisdiction under section 22, if and in so far as it appears to the court right so to do having regard to the operation of any such provision or to the purpose and effect of any authorisation or exemption granted in relation thereto, and the [Director][2] may refrain from taking proceedings before the court in respect of any agreement if and for so long as he thinks it appropriate so to do having regard to the operation of any such provision and to the purpose and effect of any such authorisation or exemption.

(2) Regulations under section 19 of the Restrictive Trade Practices Act 1956[2] may require that the [Director][3] shall be furnished in respect of an agreement with information as to any steps taken, or decision given, under or for the purpose of any directly applicable Community provision affecting the agreement, and that the information so given or such part, if any of it, as may be provided by the regulations shall be included in the particulars to be entered or filed in the register under section 11 (2); but an agreement shall be exempt from registration under the Act so long as there is in force in relation thereto any authorisation given for the purpose of any provision of the E.C.S.C.[4] Treaty relating to restrictive trade practices.[5]

---

1 This is a separate question both from that of the application of the effects of art. 85 (and art. 86) by the national courts to agreements in issue before them (see Ch. 4, above) and from that of the application of art. 85 (and art. 86) by the Restrictive Practices Court (see Ch. 11, Section 5, below).
2 The Registration of Restrictive Trading Agreements (EEC Documents) Regulations 1973 (S.I. 1973 No. 950) adopted under this subsection requires, in relation to "any agreement which is subject to registration under the Act of 1956", that details of steps taken with regard to registration with the Commission, and of any Decision of the Commission or Judgment of the Court of Justice must be delivered to the [Director] for entry on the register. The text of the Regulations is set out in Appendix V, p. 415, below.
3 Substituted by Fair Trading Act 1973, s. 139 and Sch. 12.
4 I.e. the Treaty establishing the European Coal and Steel Community, signed at Paris on 18 April 1951; and see further Fair Trading Act 1973, s. 99.
5 I.e. E.C.S.C. Treaty, arts. 60, 65 and 66.

(2A)[1] In this section 'the Director' means the Director General of Fair Trading."

[3][2]

In short, and in the words of the explanatory memorandum to the Bill which preceded the Act, s. 10 "provides for compatability between our Restrictive Trade Practices legislation and the provisions on Restrictive Trade Practices in and made under the EEC and the ECSC Treaties. The principal provision is to relieve the Registrar of Trading Agreements[3] of his duty to refer to the Restrictive Practices Court agreements rendered void or authorised in Community proceedings. The Restrictive Practices Court is given a similar discretion not to proceed with such agreements".

Sub-section (1) of s. 10 states in particular that the Restrictive Trade Practices Act applies to an agreement "notwithstanding that it may be void by reason of any directly applicable Community provision or is expressly authorised by or under any such provision".

As art. 85 is a directly applicable Community provision[4] an agreement is registrable under the RTPA even though automatically void as infringing art. 85 (1).

Equally an agreement is registrable even though authorised under art. 85 (3). This is so whether the authorisation is by means of exemption by category or by individual decision. In the former case the agreement is "expressly authorised *by* a directly applicable Community provision" in that exemption by category is conferred by regulation and art. 189 of the Treaty provides that regulations are directly applicable in all member states; in the latter case an individual decision of the Commission is made pursuant to its powers under Regulation 17, and therefore "*under* a directly applicable Community provision".

What then are the considerations which enforcement authorities in the United Kingdom will bear in mind in determining whether or not, in the exercise of their discretion under s. 10 of the European Communities Act 1972, to proceed against a registered agreement under the RTPA?

In exercising their discretion under s. 10, the Director General of Fair Trading or the Restrictive Practices Court, as the case may be,

---

1 This subsection was added by Fair Trading Act 1973, s. 139 and Sch. 12.
2 Subsection (3) has been repealed by Fair Trading Act 1973, s. 139 and Sch. 13 consequent on the repeal of Restrictive Trade Practices Act 1956, s. 33 (1) to which the subsection referred.
3 The office of Registrar of Restrictive Trading Agreements has been abolished and its functions transferred to the Director General of Fair Trading: Fair Trading Act 1973, s. 94 (1).
4 See p. 4, above.

must have regard to the provisions of Community law[1]. Thus any application of United Kingdom law with respect to an agreement within the RTPA which is also within art. 85 must not, according to the Court of Justice in the *Walt Wilhelm* Case,[2] prejudice the full and uniform application of Community law and of implementing regulations and decisions.

This Case brought to an end previous controversies arising out of the "single barrier" and "double barrier" theories as to the relationship between EEC law and national law. Under the first theory it was contended that an agreement affecting trade between member states should only be subject to EEC law; under the second that the validity of the agreement should also depend on compliance with national restrictive practices legislation. In the event, the Judgment of the Court of Justice is a compromise. The agreement must comply with the provisions of EEC law and also with national law, provided the application of the latter does not produce a result which is incompatible with the former by prejudicing its full and uniform application and implementation as mentioned above.

More specifically the *Walt Wilhelm* Case lays down the following specific guidelines for national authorities to follow:[3]

> "The E.E.C. Treaty instituted its own legal order, integrated into the legal systems of the member-States and which has priority before their courts. It would be contrary to the nature of such a system to accept that the member-States may take or maintain in force measures liable to compromise the useful effect of the Treaty. The imperative force of the Treaty and of the acts issued in implementation of it could not vary from State to State by the effect of internal acts, without the functioning of the Community system being obstructed and the attainment of the aims of the Treaty being placed in peril.
>
> Consequently, conflicts between the Community rule and the national rules on competition should be resolved by the application of the principle of the primacy of the Community rule.
>
> It follows from the foregoing that in the case where national decisions regarding an agreement would be incompatible with a decision adopted by the Commission at the end of the proceedings initiated by it, the national authorities are required to respect its effects.
>
> [7] In the cases in which, during national proceedings, it appears possible that the decision whereby the Commission will put an end to proceedings in progress concerning the same agreement may conflict with the effects of the decision of the national authorities, it is for the latter to take the appropriate measures.

---

1 See p. 5, para. 7, above.
2 *Walt Wilhelm and others* v. *Bundeskartellamt*, 13 February 1969, XV Rec. 1; [1969] CMLR 100.
3 *Ibid.*, at p. 119.

Consequently, and so long as no regulation adopted under Article 87 (2) (e)[1] of the Treaty has provided otherwise, the national authorities may intervene against an agreement, in application of their internal law, even when the examination of the position of that agreement with regard to the Community rules is pending before the Commission, *subject, however, to the proviso that such application of the national law may not prejudice the full and uniform application of the Community law or the effect of acts in implementation of it.*"[2]

It is clear from what precedes that an agreement may be proceeded against both under the national restrictive practices legislation and art. 85 with consequent exposure of the parties to penal provisions both under Regulation 17, art. 15,[3] and, if any, under the relevant national legislation,[4] and that the agreement can be held void both under art. 85 and national legislation with the civil consequences, if any, which may respectively attach under each system.[5]

Having regard to what is said in the above quoted passage from the *Wilhelm* Case to the effect that the objectives of the Community system and the aims of the Treaty must not be imperilled by variations in its implementation through the effects of "internal acts", it is thought that a national authority would feel precluded from exempting under its own law an agreement which is within art. 85, particularly as such exemption would be nugatory, since the parties could not operate their agreement notwithstanding exemption at national level, for so long as it remains prohibited under overriding Community law.

A more difficult question is whether it is open to a national authority to prohibit under its own restrictive practices legislation an agreement which at Community level has been authorised under art. 85 (3).

While the Judgment in the *Wilhelm* Case was not directly concerned with this specific question (the question referred to the Court of Justice under art. 177 being merely whether the German anti-trust authorities, the Bundeskartellamt, had jurisdiction in relation to certain concerted practices also subject to proceedings by the Commission) it contains the following passage:[6]

"Article 85 of the E.E.C. Treaty is addressed to all the undertakings of the Community whose behaviour it governs either by prohibitions or by means of the grant of exemptions given – subject to conditions which it defines – in favour of undertakings which contribute to improving the

---

1 Set out in Appendix I, p. 314, below.
2 Authors' emphasis.
3 See pp. 293ff., below.
4 But see p. 299, below, regarding double jeopardy to sanctions.
5 See Ch. 4, above.
6 [1969] CMLR 100, at p. 119.

production or distribution of products or to promoting technical or economic progress.

While the Treaty aims, in the first place, at eliminating thereby the obstacles to the free circulation of goods within the Common Market and at affirming and safeguarding the unity of that market, it also permits the Community authorities to carry out certain positive, albeit indirect, action with a view to promoting harmonious development of economic activities within the whole Community, in accordance with art. 2 of the Treaty."

Is then an art. 85 (3) exemption such a positive action, not to be frustrated by a conflicting decision of a national authority? Opinion is divided on this. Dr. K. Markert[1] mentions that most commentators consider that the positive action referred to does include exemption granted under art. 85 (3). Others consider that only certain exemptions under the article would be covered, whilst the view has also been expressed that the positive action has nothing to do with art. 85 (3).

With regard to the last interpretation, it is logical to argue that the consequence of exempting an agreement under art. 85 (3) is to take it out of the scope of art. 85 (1) – and that if art. 85 (1) does not apply no question of conflict with national law arises, so that whatever positive acts the Court was referring to, which must not be frustrated by decisions of a national authority, such acts would not include an exemption under art. 85 (3).

As against this, the view, and probably the majority view, is that an art. 85 (3) exemption, which is conditional upon the agreement being found to improve production, distribution, or technical or economic progress, involves a finding by the Commission that the agreement is positively beneficial. One author supporting this view has also commented that in practice art. 85 (3) is the tool of a real economic policy by which the Community seeks to improve the competitive structure of European industry.[2]

It is to be noted that the Court did not in the *Walt Wilhelm* Case follow the Advocate General in his reasoning that the application of national competition law stricter than Community competition law would not prejudice the latter since both Community and national systems were concerned to prevent restrictions of competition.[3]

For our part we consider that signature of the Treaty by the member states implies their acceptance of competition policy (as formulated and implemented by the Community authorities) as one of the means

---

1 [1974] CMLRev. 92, at p. 95.
2 See Mégret, *op. cit.*, p. 184, para. 113.
3 [1969] CMLR 100, at p. 109.

of achieving the aims set out in art. 2 of the Treaty and that accordingly the positive aspects of the policy must be given the same weight as its negative aspects. A balance must be struck between too little competition at the expense of the consumer and too much competition leading in certain circumstances to inefficiency. If it is right that the Commission's actions should not be frustrated by the application of incompatible national legislation in relation to the former it must also be right that the Commission should have an equally free hand in relation to the latter. The driver must have the use of the accelerator as well as the brake. Moreover, it would go against the principle of the full and uniform application of Community law required by the *Walt Wilhelm* Case if an agreement approved by the Commission under art. 85 (3) were to be permitted to operate in some member states but not in others. It is not thought that a contrary opinion should be based on too literal an analysis of the Treaty or of the Judgment in question (which in any event (as stated above) was not dealing with the exact point here under discussion) as such an interpretation would ignore the broad teleological approach to be adopted in relation to the interpretation of Community law.[1] However, complete certainty must await further clarification by the Court of Justice.

It seems therefore that when an agreement subject to the RTPA has been notified with the Commission (i.e. exemption under art. 85 (3) is requested) the Restrictive Practices Court should not prohibit it for so long as the Commission has not made a decision refusing the exemption – since, until an unfavourable decision is made, the possibility exists that the exemption will be granted. It is only possible to wait and see what the Director General of Fair Trading and the Restrictive Practices Court will do when faced with such a situation, since the consequence of inaction under the RTPA is that an agreement which is presumed to be contrary to United Kingdom policy as infringing the RTPA can continue in force for so long as the Commission has not reached a decision, which may take some considerable time.[2] The position is all the more unsatisfactory in that notification of an agreement to the Commission with a claim for exemption will not always be soundly based. In this connection it is to be noted that fines cannot be imposed by the Commission in respect of a notified agreement, subject to certain conditions,[3] so that notification could be used as a means of enabling the parties to prolong their operation of an agreement which would otherwise be condemned under the

1 See p. 7, para. 10, above.
2 See pp. 267, 270, below.
3 Reg. 17, art. 15 (5) (a); see p. 265, below.

RTPA. However, in practice it is to be expected that there will be co-operation between the Director General of Fair Trading and the Commission, possibly within the framework of the consultations provided for in Regulation 17,[1] and where in the opinion of the Commission, after a preliminary investigation, the notification has little or no chance of resulting in an exemption, this information would no doubt be communicated to the Director General, leaving him free to proceed against the agreement under the RTPA. Furthermore in such a case the Commission may communicate its opinion to the parties that exemption will not be justified, thus rendering them liable to fines as from that date should they not abandon the agreement.[2]

In so far as a national authority considers that the procedures discussed above will not avoid intolerable delays during which an agreement infringing national anti-trust law can continue to operate, it may, of course, proceed against the agreement under the national law, bearing in mind that if the agreement is eventually exempted by the Commission, the national authority will have to reverse its decision. In any event the national authority would clearly be unwise to take such action after the Commission had issued a communication under Regulation 17, art. 19 (3), indicating its intention to grant exemption under art. 85 (3).[3] This, of course, will only be so if the correct interpretation of the *Walt Wilhelm* Case is that given above, namely that an exemption under art. 85 (3) is a positive act of the Community, not to be frustrated at the national level.

From what has been said above based on our interpretation of the *Walt Wilhelm* Case, it follows that when an agreement benefits from exemption by category the national authority should take no action in respect of the agreement under national law, unless and until the Commission withdraws the benefit of group exemption from the agreement by individual decision.[4] No doubt, however, a national authority will wish to undertake a preliminary investigation of the agreement in order to satisfy itself of the validity of a submission by the parties that their agreement qualifies for the exemption.

It is interesting to note in this connection a certain lack of parallelism between the case now under discussion where the Restrictive Practices Court is asked to reach a decision on a matter which is also under examination by the Commission, and the case discussed in Chapter 4 above where an English court of ordinary jurisdiction (that is a court

---

1 Reg. 17, art. 10; see pp. 274, 275, below.
2 Reg. 17, art. 15 (6); see p. 265, below.
3 As to which, see p. 285, below.
4 Reg. 67/67, art. 6; Reg. 2799/72, art. 5; and see pp. 107 and 114, above.

other than the Restrictive Practices Court) has to decide upon the effect of art. 85 (1) as between the parties in relation to an agreement under consideration before it, when that agreement is also under examination by the Commission. In the former situation, if the above interpretation of the *Walt Wilhelm* Case is correct, it would seem to be necessary for the Restrictive Practices Court to hold its hand, while in the latter situation the *SABAM* Case[1] encourages such court of ordinary jurisdiction to reach a decision, without regard to the possible consequences of any subsequent Commission decision.

Article 85 (3) confers exemption in relation to an agreement which is within art. 85 (1); but if an agreement is not in any event within art. 85 (1), in the present context Community law has no application to it. A negative clearance issued in respect of an agreement is a declaration by the Commission that it does not consider the agreement to be within art. 85 (1).[2] A negative clearance does not then, in principle, inhibit the national authority from applying its domestic legislation with regard to the same agreement.[3]

The question of the overlap between Community competition law and national competition law has been discussed above in the particular context of a possibility of conflict in effect between the application of the RTPA by the Restrictive Practices Court and the application of art. 85 by the Commission to the same set of facts. There is a similar possibility of conflict when a national court of ordinary jurisdiction is asked to apply the consequences of an agreement infringing the provisions of its domestic competition law and that agreement is under consideration by the Commission. It is submitted that such a potential conflict could only arise in the United Kingdom where a court of ordinary jurisdiction is asked to apply RTPA 1968, s. 7. For example where A and B have accepted restrictions such that their agreement is registrable under the RTPA, but the agreement is not registered, does s. 7 (1) apply to the effect that the agreement is void *ab initio*, and its enforcement illegal, even where the agreement has been duly notified to the Commission, and is liable to be, or has actually been, exempted? Further, by s. 7 (2) third parties may have claims for breach of statutory duty against the parties for any damage caused them by the past performance of the agreement. Does an exemption, or the possibility of one, under art. 85 (3) prevent these consequences being applied by the United Kingdom court? These questions are also pertinent to

---

1 *Belgische Radio en Televisie* v. *SV SABAM and NV Fonior*, 30 January 1974, [1974] ECR 51; [1974] 2 CMLR 238, para. 22; see p. 129, above.
2 See p. 252, below.
3 See Mégret, *op. cit.*, p. 185 and the Report there cited.

the case where an agreement benefits from exemption, not by an individual decision of the Commission, but by virtue of exemption by category. The answer to all these questions, however, will depend on the approach developed by the United Kingdom courts with regard to the inter-action of Community law generally and national law.

Chapter 5

Article 86—The Abuse of a Dominant Position

SECTION 1 INTRODUCTION

The authentic English text of art. 86 of the Treaty states:

"Any abuse by one or more undertakings of a dominant position within the Common Market or in a substantial part of it shall be prohibited as incompatible with the Common Market in so far as it may affect trade between Member States. Such abuse may, in particular, consist in:

(a) directly or indirectly imposing unfair purchase or selling prices or other unfair trading conditions;
(b) limiting production, markets or technical development to the prejudice of consumers;
(c) applying dissimilar conditions to equivalent transactions with other trading parties, thereby placing them at a competitive disadvantage;
(d) making the conclusion of contracts subject to acceptance by the other parties of supplementary obligations which, by their nature or according to commercial usage, have no connection with the subject of such contracts."

While art. 85 prohibits the restriction of competition by agreement between undertakings, art. 86 prohibits the abuse (whether or not by agreement with any other undertaking) of market power by one or more dominant undertakings. In short, art. 86 is to art. 85 what in the United Kingdom the provisions in the Fair Trading Act 1973, relating to monopoly control, are to the Restrictive Trade Practices Acts.

In contrast to art. 85 there is no provision for exemption under art. 86 corresponding to art. 85 (3). It would indeed be surprising if it were possible to obtain relief in respect of an abuse of economic power. In so far as an undertaking may be in doubt as to whether a particular

147

practice is prohibited by the article, it has the possibility of seeking "negative clearance" under art. 2 of Regulation 17.[1]

Infringement of art. 86 is visited with fines.[2] Article 86 (in contrast to art. 85) does not declare the nullity of an act prohibited by it. It has been stated[3] that the absence of this provision is to be explained by the fact that the abuse of a dominant position is not a juridical act and that therefore the question of its nullity does not arise.[4]

However, the implementation of an abuse of a dominant position may well be by means of a juridical act, that is an act recognised by a national court as having certain legal consequences, e.g. a contract or an assignment, as in the *SABAM* Case,[5] where composers forfeited their rights to their works by agreement with SABAM, an authors' rights society, for five years after leaving the society. Where there are juridical acts the question can arise as to how such acts are affected by a finding that they were the means of implementing an abuse of a dominant position. It is thought that in such a situation either a party or a third party could invoke the abuse before a national court as a ground for claiming the nullity of the act in question and ensuing consequences. Whether such a claim is sustainable and what would be the consequences are questions for the national courts.

Further, whether or not the infringement of art. 86 involves a juridical act, an action for breach of statutory duty may lie by a third party, or indeed by a party to a juridical act if there was such an act (considerations thought to bar the claim of one party to an agreement prohibited by art. 85 against another party to the agreement[6] not being applicable where the plaintiff is *ex hypothesi* the victim of an abuse constituting an infringement of art. 86).

In order that art. 86 should be applicable it is necessary that:

(1) one or more undertakings should hold a dominant position in the Common Market or in a substantial part of it;

(2) there should have been an abuse by one or more undertakings of such a dominant position which may affect trade between member states.

---

1 See pp. 251ff. and in particular p. 254, below.
2 See pp. 293ff., below.
3 See, e.g., Goldman, *op. cit.*, para. 422.
4 A similar argument is put forward for the absence of a declaration of nullity of a concerted practice infringing art. 85; see p. 116, above.
5 *Belgische Radio en Televisie* v. *SV SABAM and NV Fonior,* 30 January 1974, [1974] ECR 51; [1974] 2 CMLR 238,
6 See p. 126, above,

SECTION 2 MARKET DOMINANCE

"a dominant position within the Common Market or in a substantial part of it"

The dominant position

The Commission in its *Continental Can* Decision[1] defines a dominant position in the following terms:

> "3. Undertakings are in a dominant position when they have the power to behave independently, which puts them in a position to act without taking into account their competitors, purchasers or suppliers. That is the position when, because of their share of the market, or of their share of the market combined with the availability of technical knowledge, raw materials or capital, they have the power to determine prices or to control production or distribution for a significant part of the products in question. This power does not necessarily have to derive from an absolute domination permitting the undertakings which hold it to eliminate all will on the part of their economic partners, but it is enough that they be strong enough as a whole to ensure to those undertakings an overall independence of behaviour, even if there are differences in intensity in their influence on the different partial markets."

While the Decision was overruled on other grounds on appeal to the Court of Justice[2] this definition was not questioned and may therefore be accepted as the most authoritative and valuable definition available to date of the concept of market domination. The definition may be considered in the context of a more general statement of the Commission's standpoint in relation to dominant positions set out in its "Memorandum on the Concentration of Enterprises in the Common Market",[3] which includes the following paragraph:

> "[63] **Market Domination**
>
> Although Article 86 does not speak of a market-dominating, but only of a dominant, position, it is generally assumed that an enterprise occupies a dominant position within the meaning of Article 86 if it is market-dominating. Market domination cannot be defined solely in terms of the market share of an enterprise or of other quantitative elements of a particular market structure. It is primarily a matter of economic potency, or the ability to exert on the operation of the market an influence that is

1 *Re Continental Can Company Incorporated*, 9 December 1971, JO 1972 L7/25; [1972] CMLR D11, at p. D27.
2 *Europemballage Corporation and Continental Can Company Incorporated* v. *EC Commission*, 21 February 1973, [1973] ECR 215; [1973] CMLR 199.
3 Translation taken from CCH Common Market Reports, No. 26, 17 March 1966, at p. 28.

substantial and also in principle foreseeable for the dominant enterprise. This economic ability of a dominant enterprise influences the market behaviour and the economic decisions of other enterprises, irrespective of whether it is used in a specific sense. If an enterprise is able, at its pleasure, to oust a competing enterprise from the market, it might already occupy a dominant position and exert a controlling influence upon the practices of other enterprises even if its own share of the market is still relatively small."

It is seen that the definition of "dominant position" in the *Continental Can* Decision reflects the statement in the Memorandum that market domination cannot be defined solely in terms of market shares: an undertaking is not dominant merely because of the market share it holds – but it will be dominant if the market share by itself or coupled with other factors confers market power such as to enable the undertaking to determine its pricing, production or distribution policies without due regard to competitors.

Thus in the *Continental Can* Case[1] market shares[2] of between 70% and 80% were the sole reasons given by the Commission for holding that Schmalbach-Lubecca-Werke AG (SLW)[3] had a dominant position on the German market for metal containers for meat and fish products.[4] But substantially lower percentages may suffice depending on the structure of the market (on a market comprising, say, 99 firms supplying 80% of the market and one firm supplying 20% of the market, the latter will usually be dominant).

As regards other factors which may be coupled with the market share to produce market power, the Commission, referring to the position of Continental Can itself (the parent company of SLW) states:[5]

> "14. Continental Can's important shares in the market, its production programme covering all the part markets and some substitution products, its supply of machines for manufacturing and using its products, its technical lead and its economic and financial power based on a very large size, ensure for that undertaking possibilities of independent action which give it a very strong position on the German market in light containers for meat and fish preserves as well as in metal covers."

Other factors would be: the number of undertakings competing

---

1 See pp. 161ff., below, for the facts of the case.
2 As to method of calculation of market share, see below.
3 In which Continental Can Co. had acquired an 85.8% holding.
4 See also *Re European Sugar Cartel*, 2 January 1973, OJ 1973 L140/17, at p. 39; [1973] CMLR D65; where market shareholdings of 90–95% were conclusive of market power without additional factors.
5 [1972] CMLR D11, at p. D30.

on the market; the price-cost relationship; the profitability of the undertaking; the elasticity of demand; the power to determine prices freely; the power to determine the terms of entry into the industry; the size of the undertaking.[1]

In the *Continental Can* Decision the undertaking's market power was considered solely "statically" in terms of market shares, technical efficiency and economic power – which were considerable enough to permit by themselves the inference of market power. There will be cases, however, where the market shares are substantially smaller and where the other factors taken together with the market shares are less telling. The question of whether or not an undertaking is dominant would then need to be tested also dynamically in terms of the market history of the undertaking and/or its behaviour on the market. As Deringer writes: ". . . domination of the market is nothing static; it is not a status of permanent duration, but a potential which manifests itself in a certain development and in the conduct of the enterprise."[2] Further, the Commission in its above mentioned Memorandum also stated:[3]

> "The causes of a dominant position may lie in the sphere of production, of distribution, or of financial power. That is why developments on the market must always be taken into account and why the enterprise must be viewed within the context of its economic relations. Thus, it would appear that as a rule an enterprise that acts as the 'price leader' in an oligopolistic situation occupies a market-dominating position."

According to Deringer the history of the growth of the undertaking and the development in time of the structure of the market in which the undertaking operates is relevant to the dynamic analysis of the undertaking's market power, for "a rise in the market share, in the prices and in the profits throughout [a period of observation leading up to the time of the action in which the question is relevant] would, as a rule, seem to be a clear indication that an enterprise occupies a market-dominating position"[4] although for ourselves we would prefer to say an "indication" rather than "a clear indication".

On the other hand, militating against market dominance is the danger of competition from potential competitors. Thus in the *Continental Can* Case[5] the Court of Justice held that the market

---

1 Taken from a list given by Jean-Pierre Dubois, "La position dominante et son abus dans l'article 86 du Traité de la CEE", Librairie Technique, Paris 1968.
2 Deringer, *op. cit.*, para. 527.
3 "Memorandum on the Concentration of Enterprises in the Common Market", CCH Common Market Reports, No. 26, 17 March 1966, para. 63.
4 Deringer, *op. cit.*, para. 527.
5 *Europemballage Corporation and Continental Can Company Incorporated v. EC Commission,* 21 February 1973, [1973] ECR 215; [1973] CMLR 199, at p. 227, para. 33.

dominance of SLW as regards light metal containers for meat and fish products was not decisive for so long as it had not been proved that competitors in other parts of the market for light metal containers could not by simply adapting their production enter the market in sufficient strength to constitute a serious counterweight to SLW's market power. It would have to be shown, however, it is submitted, that not only should the competitors be able to adapt technically but further that they would have some advantage from doing so and themselves be sufficiently strong, once having entered the market, to maintain their position in it in the face of the undertaking or undertakings already dominant on that market. Unless some such test is applied so as to exclude potential competition which is merely theoretical, it will only rarely be possible for the Commission to prove that an undertaking is dominant.[1]

While most cases of market dominance will concern the supply side of the market, buyers may also have such a strong market position as to be able to dictate the terms of supply. A buyer in a monopoly position must therefore have regard to art. 86. For an example of an abuse of dominant position by a buyer see *Re Eurofima*.[2]

The relevant market

It has been seen that there is no easy, ready-made formula which if satisfied will determine whether or not a dominant position exists when the market share of the undertaking or undertakings concerned is not so high as by itself to be conclusive of market dominance. Each case will depend on its own special circumstances and require exhaustive economic analysis. In any event it is clear from the *Continental Can* definition[3] that to determine whether or not there is a dominant position susceptible of abuse by one or more undertakings it is first necessary to determine the market share of the undertaking or undertakings alleged to be dominant; such a market share can only be determined in terms of a particular market – the relevant market, a concept which, being equally applicable to art. 85, is discussed below.[4]

Within the Common Market or in a substantial part of it

In order that art. 86 should apply, it is necessary that the dominant position which is being abused should exist in the Common Market or in a substantial part of it.

---

1 As to the reality of potential competition, see p. 38, above.
2 16 April 1973, [1973] CMLR D217; 1 P (73) 67; and see p. 164, below.
3 Given at p. 149, above.
4 See Ch. 6, below.

We have seen that the ascertainment of a dominant position depends on determining a relevant market and establishing that in relation to such market the undertaking concerned is dominant by reason of its market share or such share coupled with other factors.

It follows that for art. 86 to apply the relevant market must comprise a substantial part of the Common Market.

As to the relationship between a particular market and the Common Market as a whole, various territories or whole countries comprising the relevant market have been held to constitute substantial parts of the Common Market in the Commission's decisions to date on art. 86; such territories are the Federal Republic of Germany,[1] the southern part of Germany (Bavaria, Baden-Württemburg and parts of Hessen),[2] Belgium and Luxembourg taken together,[2] Belgium[3] and Holland.[2]

It is not entirely clear whether, in finding that such territories or countries constituted substantial parts of the Common Market, the Commission was comparing their respective territorial areas or whether it was making some form of economic comparison.

If the former is what the Commission intended no doubt in practical terms in the particular cases a correct result was reached. However, the logic of a purely geographic comparison may be doubted, for an economically significant market on which an undertaking is dominant may have an insignificant geographic dimension. It may be, therefore, that in finding that the areas in question constituted substantial parts of the Common Market, the Commission had in mind, apart from the geographic element, some other basis of comparison; but, if this is so, the decisions give no indication of what the basis could be. It is to be hoped, therefore, that further guidance as to how the notion of a "substantial part of the Common Market" is to be interpreted will be given by the Commission or by the Court of Justice when a suitable case presents itself, i.e. when a purely geographic comparison would produce a manifestly unsatisfactory result.

---

1 *Re GEMA (No. 1)*, 2 June 1971, JO 1971 L134/15; [1971] CMLR D35; and *Re Continental Can Co. Inc.*, 9 December, 1971 JO 1972 L7/25; [1972] CMLR D11.
2 *Re European Sugar Cartel* 2 January 1973, OJ 1973 L140/17; [1973] CMLR D65.
3 *Belgische Radio en Televisie* v. *SV SABAM and NV Fonior*, 30 January 1974, [1974] ECR 51; [1974] 2 CMLR 238; and *Re General Motors Continental*, 19 December 1974, OJ 1975 L29/14; [1975] 1 CMLR D20.

SECTION 3   ABUSE OF MARKET DOMINANCE

"Any abuse by one or more undertakings . . . in so far as it may affect trade between Member States"

One or more undertakings

An undertaking which by itself would not be dominant may nevertheless enjoy market power by reason of belonging to a grouping of undertakings – whether this be a group of undertakings under common control or two or more independent undertakings which together hold a sufficient share of a market to constitute an oligopoly. If such one or more undertakings within the grouping abuse the market power derived from it, art. 86 will be infringed.

The question has been discussed whether, if there is competition among the oligopolists, the oligopoly can be said to have a dominant position. Thus according to Deringer:[1] "to the extent that several enterprises belonging to a combine nevertheless compete with one another . . . there is no need to treat them together as occupying a dominant position in the market within the meaning of Article 86 . . ." As against this, it has been pointed out that even though there is competition between the members of an oligopolistic group such competition may be lacking in relation to their dealings with others, e.g. customers and suppliers, and art. 86 will be infringed if undue advantage is taken of this.

Absence of competition between the oligopolists implies agreement or concerted practice between them, which will be subject to art. 85. In so far as the evidence of agreement or concerted practice may not be sufficient, e.g. in the face of an argument by the parties that their prices result not from agreement or concertation but from the operation of market forces[2] the Commission has in art. 86 an alternative basis on which to proceed.

Which may affect trade between member states

As in the case of art. 85, the application of art. 86 depends on the possibility that trade between member states may be affected. As regards the use of the word "may" and the meanings of the expressions "trade" and "member states" the remarks made in relation to art. 85[3]

---

1 *Op. cit.*, para. 547.
2 See pp. 20, 21, above.
3 See pp. 26–34, above.

apply equally here, though the existing cases under art. 86 provide no authority as to whether the likely effect on trade between member states must be perceptible for the article to apply.

An important interpretation of the criterion of effect on intra-Community trade was given by the Court of Justice in the *Zoja* Case[1] on appeal from the Commission's Decision.

The Commission found that the abuse by a dominant undertaking (CSC-Istituto) consisting of the refusal to supply an essential product, aminobutanol, to the manufacturer, Zoja, of the drug ethambutol was such as to affect trade between member states because the manufacturer was an exporter or potential exporter of ethambutol from Italy to other member states. The Court found that the criterion of possible effect on intra-Community trade should not be judged merely by reference to the actual or even potential exports to other member states; the Court stated.[2]

> "By prohibiting the abuse of a dominant position within the market in so far as it may affect trade between Member States Article 86 therefore covers abuse which may directly prejudice consumers as well as abuse which indirectly prejudices them by impairing the effective competitive structure as envisaged by Article 3 (f) of the Treaty.
>
> "The Community authorities must therefore consider all the consequences of the conduct complained of for the competitive structure in the Common Market without distinguishing between production intended for sale within the market and that intended for export. When an undertaking in a dominant position within the Common Market abusively exploits its position in such a way that a competitor in the Common Market is likely to be eliminated, it does not matter whether the conduct relates to the latter's exports or to its trade within the Common Market, once it has been established that this elimination will have repercussions on the competitive structure within the Common Market."

But trade would also be affected by the abuse if the aminobutanol were supplied at a cost such as to render the ethambutol produced by Zoja unmarketable.

Examples of abuse

Article 86 sets out a non-exhaustive list of examples of what constitutes an abuse of a dominant position. These examples reflect in the context of art. 86 those set out in art. 85.

---

1 *Istituto Chemioterapico Italiano Spa and Commercial Solvents Corp.* v. *EC Commission*, 6 March 1974, [1974] ECR 223; [1974] 1 CMLR 309; the facts are given at p. 158, below, where the Decision of the Commission is discussed.
2 *Ibid.*, at paras. 32 and 33.

Thus no alteration was necessary to examples (d) (discrimination) and (e) (tying) of art. 85 which are reproduced verbatim in art. 86 as examples (c) and (d). It is relevant to remark in this connection that while under art. 85 some argument may be possible as to whether or not tying by a non-dominant undertaking is prohibited even in the absence of agreement,[1] art. 86 categorically forbids tying (except to the limited extent stated in the example) by a dominant undertaking and while there may be doubt as to whether discrimination is forbidden under art. 85 in the absence of agreement[2] there is no doubt that discrimination by a dominant undertaking is in all circumstances forbidden under art. 86.

Examples (a) (price fixing, etc.) and (b) (limiting production, etc.) of art. 85, however, were modified by the addition of a qualitative factor, to take account of the purpose of art. 86, which is to prohibit only the improper use of market power, not merely its possession, nor even its use. Hence the conditions or prices imposed must be "unfair" and the limitation of production, etc. must be "to the prejudice of consumers".

Article 86 has no example corresponding to (c) of art. 85, relating to the sharing of markets and sources of supply, presumably because the notion of sharing is incompatible with the unilateral exercise of market power envisaged by art. 86.

Although the cases decided under art. 86 contain clear instances of certain of the circumstances contemplated by the examples, they are so few in number that it has been thought appropriate to deal with them individually, rather than in relation to each of the examples, as was more feasible under art. 85; accordingly summaries of the existing cases are given below, illustrating generally the notion of abuse as interpreted by the Commission and, in the two cases, by the Court of Justice.

RE GEMA[3]

This Decision concerned the Gesellschaft für musikalische Aufführungs- und mechanische Vervielfältingungsrechte (GEMA) – the German music performing rights society for the protection of authors and the safeguard of their rights in German territory. The Commission held that GEMA, being the only such society in Germany, had a

---

1 See p. 66, above.
2 See p. 64, above.
3 2 June 1971, JO 1971 L134/15; [1971] CMLR D35.

dominant position within the terms of art. 86 and that it had abused that position in the following respects:

(A) By discriminating against authors from other member states, who in practice could not become members of GEMA and thereby suffer financial and other prejudices.

(B) By binding its members to unjustified obligations, in particular by hindering the transfer of members to another society by the require- ment, amongst others, that the author assigns all his rights to GEMA. The Commission stated:[1]

> "the present decision does not question GEMA's dominant position as such but only its improper exploitation of it, for even after amendment of the assignment contracts in the terms of this decision GEMA will continue to occupy a dominant position in Germany. The complaint against GEMA is precisely that it wants to turn its dominant position into an absolute monopoly through certain provisions in the assignment contracts."

Other unjustified obligations imposed were the exclusion of the right of a member to have recourse to the courts and a provision made for the payment of loyalty bonuses out of contributions of members not themselves eligible for the bonus. The Commission also objected to the refusal of ordinary membership for composers and publishers who are economically dependent on a user of musical works; for while this prohibition was intended to avoid the exercise of undue influence by such user it was found excessive. A precaution of this kind in the Commission's view should be reasonable such as would be the refusal of voting rights to the members in question in cases of voting on the conclusion of contracts with such users.

(C) By preventing the creation of a single market for the services of music publishers, in that foreign publishers could not become ordinary members of GEMA and thereby enjoy the rights attaching to such membership as regards a say in the management of GEMA, with the consequence that their services were less valuable to authors.

(D) By extending copyright contractually to non-copyright works, by requiring record manufacturers to pay royalty on the part of a record reproducing a work which was free of copyright.

(E) By applying dissimilar conditions to equivalent transactions with other trading parties, viz:

(i) by requiring payment of licence fees by German importers of

---

records even though such fees had already been paid once, either to GEMA or to another authors' rights society abroad, whereas the records distributed directly in Germany by foreign manufacturers were subjected to such fees only once, in the country of manufacture;

(ii) by requiring payment of a higher fee under s. 53 (5) of the German Copyright Act from importers of recording equipment than that required from the German manufacturers of such equipment.[1]

The Commission pointed out that transactions do not have to be in all respects identical in order to be equivalent – and equivalence must be tested by reference to the objectives of the Treaty, so that "with regard to Article 86, which aims at preventing undertakings in a dominant position from making more difficult the establishment of a system ensuring that competition is not distorted, the services of the manufacturers are thus equivalent to those of the importers."[2]

The condition that the abuse should be capable of affecting trade between member states was found to be satisfied in the following respects:

The inhibition on GEMA members becoming members of other authors' rights societies in other member states was an obstacle to the establishment of a single market in the supply of the services of publisher of musical works in the Community.

The practice referred to in paragraph (D) above also applied to records exported from Germany to other member states, and in that it caused such records to be unjustifiably more expensive was likely to have repercussions on intra-Community trade.

Trade between other member states and Germany was restricted by the double payment of licence fees referred to in paragraph (E) (i) above; likewise the discrimination referred to in paragraph (E) (ii) above restricted the import of recording equipment from other member states to Germany.

THE ZOJA CASE[3]

Commercial Solvents Corporation (CSC) held a world monopoly in the production and sale of nitropropane and aminobutanol, essential

---

1 German Copyright Act, s. 53 (5), provides that authors, via an authors' rights society, may claim an indemnity from manufacturers and importers of recording equipment for all reproductions which may be made by purchasers of such equipment.

2 [1971] CMLR D35, at p. D55.

3 *Zoja* v. *Commercial Solvents Corporation*, 14 December 1972, JO 1972 L299/51; [1973] CMLR D50; on appeal *sub nom. Istituto Chemioterapico Italiano Spa and Commercial Solvents Corp.* v. *EC Commission*, 6 March 1974, [1974] ECR 223; [1974] 1 CMLR 309.

products for the manufacture of ethambutol, a drug used in the treatment of tuberculosis. Laboratorio Chimico Farmaceutico Giorgio Zoja (Zoja) was a manufacturer of ethambutanol within and outside the Common Market. Zoja obtained its supplies of nitropropane and aminobutanol from Istituto Chemioterapico Italiano (Istituto), a 51% subsidiary of CSC, Istituto being also a manufacturer of ethambutanol and competing with Zoja in Italy.

In 1969 Istituto made an abortive attempt to merge with Zoja, who soon after the breakdown of negotiations found its supplies of aminobutanol cut off by the CSC-Istituto group and in the absence of alternative sources of supply its business would have been seriously prejudiced on the exhaustion of existing stocks.

The Commission found that CSC and Istituto, by virtue of the control exercised by the former over the latter, constituted a single group[1] and that as a consequence of CSC's world monopoly, the group *ipso facto* had a dominant position in the Common Market with respect to the supply of the raw materials for the production of ethambutol.

On appeal from the Commission's Decision, CSC argued that it did not have a dominant position in the supply of the raw materials for the production of ethambutol on the basis that ethambutol could be manufactured otherwise than from nitropropane and aminobutanol. However such other methods of production were not established commercially and in any event would require adaptations in the installations and processes used by Zoja. The Court held:[2] "It is only the presence on the market of a raw material which could be substituted without difficulty for nitropropane and aminobutanol for the manufacture of ethambutol which could invalidate the argument that CSC has a dominant position within the meaning of Article 86".

The Commission proceeded to find that the CSC-Istituto group had abused its dominant position in the following respects:

(A) The group's behaviour was such as to bring about the elimination of one of its principal competitors, thus seriously prejudicing effective competition within the Common Market. On appeal from the Decision the Court of Justice confirmed that such was the effect of the group's behaviour, and stated:[3]

". . . an undertaking which has a dominant position in the market in raw materials and which, with the object of reserving such raw material for

---

1 See Ch. 2, Section 6, "Agreements between groups of companies", p. 67, above.
2 [1974] ECR 223; [1974] 1 CMLR 309, at para. 15.
3 *Ibid.*, at para. 25.

the manufacturing of its own derivatives, refuses to supply a customer, which is itself a manufacturer of these derivatives, and therefore risks eliminating all competition on the part of this customer, is abusing its dominant position . . ."

(B) The group's conduct limited the outlets for nitropropane and aminobutanol and the production of ethambutol. The Court of Justice held on appeal that the abuse of a dominant position on the market in the raw materials can have effects restricting competition on the market for the end-product and that such effects must be taken into account.

As to the condition that the abuse should be capable of affecting trade between member states, Zoja was an exporter of ethambutol to France and Germany and a potential exporter to other EEC countries. In so far as the withholding of raw materials by CSC-Istituto prevented this trade the condition was satisfied.[1]

The effect on trade resulting from abuse must be considered in the light of actual market conditions. Thus another manufacturer of ethambutol held patents in certain of Zoja's potential export markets. The validity of such patents was, however, in dispute and therefore in the Commission's view, not such as to preclude Zoja from exporting.

It would seem possible to infer that if Italy was surrounded by a ring of valid patents[2] in all other EEC countries and Zoja was not licensed thereunder, the abuse by CSC-Istituto would not have been within the scope of art. 86, since there would be no actual or potential trade between member states capable of being affected.

While the abuse in (B) above is an instance of example (b) of art. 86, as regards the abuse in (A) it is interesting to note that the *Zoja* Decision, endorsed by the Court of Justice on appeal, follows the Commission's *Continental Can* Decision in which the Commission first maintained that the complete elimination of competition resulting from the takeover of a competitor was an abuse of a dominant position. The *Zoja* Decision is analogous in that CSC, having failed to eliminate Zoja by merger, attempted to eliminate it as a competitor by the withholding of essential supplies.

The *Zoja* Case also raises other questions which show the width of application of art. 86; thus while CSC was condemned for refusing to sell to Zoja in the particular circumstances of the case it may be asked whether any refusal to sell involves an infringement of the article. Can, for example, a dominant undertaking refuse to enter into a distribution agreement whether exclusive or non-exclusive?

---

1 But see also p. 155, above.
2 I.e. patents other than patents held by CSC-Istituto or their licensees.

And if a distribution agreement subsists, can it be terminated at the will of the licensor subject only to proper notice? Does this case more generally involve the inclusion into EEC law of an existing principle under French law, namely the prohibition of what is termed "*refus de vente*"?

For the present authors, it would be consistent with the general philosophy of the Commission to extend the *CSC-Zoja* principle to every case where it could reasonably be shown that the refusal to sell was contrary to the general aims of the Treaty as set out in its preamble and in art. 2. These aims, as will be seen below from the Court of Justice's Judgment in the *Continental Can* Case, govern the interpretation to be given to art. 86, the article being one of the instruments referred to in art. 3 for bringing about the broad economic objectives as specified in art. 2 of the Treaty. Such a wide interpretation of the scope of the *Zoja* Case would moreover be consistent with the principle by which under certain national laws, in particular English law, a monopolist under an industrial property right, e.g. a patentee, can be required in certain circumstances, in the public interest, to grant a compulsory licence.[1]

Extreme instances of the extension of art. 86 beyond the scope of the examples given in the article arise out of the *Continental Can* Case by which the merger of a dominant undertaking with a competitor was held to constitute the abuse of a dominant position and likewise the mere strengthening of the position of a dominant undertaking (regardless of the means employed) where prejudicial consequences to competition ensued. This extension obviously raises many important questions which are best considered after an account of the facts of the case and the legal background to it.

THE CONTINENTAL CAN CASE[2]

Continental Can Company Inc. (Continental), one of the world's leading undertakings in the packaging industry, acquired control over substantially the whole of the share capital of Thomassen & Drijver-Verblifa NV (TDV), a Dutch company engaged in the same industry. The Commission decided that, together with Schmalbach-Lubeca-Werke AG (SLW), Continental held dominant positions on various product markets within the EEC and that the acquisition infringed art. 86 as an abuse of these dominant positions. In so far as

---

1 Patent Act 1949, s. 49.
2 *Re Continental Can Company Incorporated*, 9 December 1971, JO 1972 L7/25; [1972] CMLR D11; and *Europemballage Corporation and Continental Can Company Incorporated* v. *EC Commission*, 21 February 1973, [1973] ECR 215; [1973] CMLR 199.

TDV and SLW were in a position to supply in each other's respective territories, their merger, by eliminating this competition, affected this actual and potential trade between member states.

The undertakings appealed to the Court of Justice on the grounds that:

(a) the Decision constituted an attempt by the Commission to control mergers by an unwarranted extension of the provisions of art. 86; and

(b) the Commission had in any event failed to prove market dominance by the undertaking concerned.

As regards (a) the undertakings argued that such an extension of the provisions of art. 86 was not justified either by the wording of art. 86 or by comparable provisions in the ECSC Treaty and national legislations; that specific examples of abuse given in art. 86 confirmed this in that they all related to market practices affecting trading partners and consumers but made no reference to competitors; that art. 86 required a direct causal link between a dominant position and its abusive exploitation, which was not the case where a dominant undertaking merely strengthened its market position. The undertakings succeeded in their appeal under (b)[1] but failed under (a), with the important consequence that the principle is established that art. 86 can be invoked by the Commission against certain mergers (using the term to include all manner of concentrations) involving a dominant undertaking, namely mergers which substantially eliminate competition or potential competition.

Considering that the literal wording of art. 86 hardly supports such an interpretation, it is interesting to see the Court of Justice's reasoning which may be briefly summarised as follows:

It is necessary to consider the issue having regard to the spirit, structure and wording of art. 86 taking account of the system set up by the Treaty and its objectives.

The promotion of the harmonious development of economic activities within the whole of the Common Market required by art. 2 of the Treaty is to be achieved (*inter alia*) by the institution, under art. 3 (f), of a system ensuring that competition in the Common Market is not distorted. This implies that it must not be eliminated altogether. While art. 85 is concerned with agreements between undertakings and art. 86 with unilateral action, they are both concerned with the maintenance of effective

---

1 See p. 168, below.

competition in the Common Market, so that prejudice to competition resulting from practices forbidden under art. 85 cannot be lawful when it is the consequence of concentration brought about by a dominant undertaking; and in the absence of specific provision it cannot be that while art. 85 forbids decisions of associations which do not go so far as to eliminate competition, art. 86 should permit the realisation by concentration of a degree of market power such as to eliminate any serious possibility of competition.

The Court concluded, in the light of the preceding considerations, that there may be abuse of a dominant position when a dominant undertaking increases its dominance to the extent that its market power is such as substantially to prevent competition, i.e. by eliminating all but those undertakings whose economic behaviour is dependent on that of the dominant undertaking: and it is immaterial how this is brought about, so that Continental Can's arguments based on the need of a direct causal link between a dominant position and its abusive exploitation are not valid. Article 86, therefore, covers not only practices resulting in immediate prejudice to consumers, but also those which prejudice them by impairing a market structure ensuring effective competition.

In the case before the Court an alleged dominant undertaking had increased its market power, and assuming that the Commission had satisfied the Court as to the facts on which the dominance was claimed to exist, the acquisition of control over TDV would have been held to infringe art. 86.

On the basis of the Court's Judgment, art. 86 is therefore only applicable where an already dominant undertaking strengthens that dominant position to the extent that competition is substantially obstructed. When a non-dominant undertaking does so, art. 86 on the basis of the *Continental Can* Case has no application. The scope of the decision is therefore extremely narrow and it is not surprising to find that the Commission should have wished to institute a full control of mergers, and a proposal for a Regulation[1] is at present before the Council for consideration, the object of which is the control of mergers which may impede competition in the Common Market or in a substantial part of it. It may be asked, however, whether in the event of delay in the adoption of the Regulation and in any event in the case of concentrations which will be outside the scope of the Regulation[2] the *Continental Can* interpretation of art. 86 could not be

---

1 See pp. 199ff., below.
2 I.e. by reason of the quantitative criteria, see p. 201, below.

extended by the Court of Justice in an appropriate case, to include cases where market dominance is the consequence of a merger between two or more non-dominant undertakings. Could it for example be argued that art. 86 applies to mergers not only when one of the merging undertakings is dominant during the period leading up to the merger but also when the dominant position is created by the merger, and the elimination of competition is concomitant with the merger. Such an interpretation, in our opinion, is sustainable, since a dominant position will be created by the act of the merging undertakings, the immediate and abusive effect of such dominant position being the elimination of competition.

Pending the adoption of such a Regulation, art. 86 as interpreted by the *Continental Can* Case is a factor to be taken into account by dominant undertakings planning mergers where it is not evident that substantial competition will subsist after the merger; and it is to be borne in mind in this connection that it is not necessary for the merger to result in the complete elimination of competition for the article to apply, the Court of Justice having further stated in its Judgment that since the Commission had based its case on the complete elimination of competition it had to establish this, "although such a restrictive condition as the elimination of *all* competition need not be fulfilled in all cases".[1]

RE EUROFIMA[2]

As mentioned above, a dominant position may be abused by a buyer. Thus a dominant buyer of railway rolling stock in the Common Market imposed on the contractors entrusted with a development contract a condition that the buyer should have unlimited rights to all patents resulting from the contracts, including the right to sub-license to third parties, without additional payment. The Commission warned that this would infringe art. 86 and the provision was modified to enable the buyer (i) to claim only the patent rights that were justified by its own requirements, (ii) to grant sub-licences to third parties, in order to promote standardisation, only by agreement with the contractor and against payment of compensation to him.

RE SUGAR CARTEL[3]

The *Sugar Cartel* Decision provides further examples of the abuse of a dominant position. The Raffinerie Tirlemontoise (RT) was held by the Commission to have a dominant position on the Belgian and

---

1 [1973] ECR 215; [1973] CMLR 199, at para. 29.
2 16 April 1973, [1973] CMLR D217; IP (73) 67; Bulletin 1973, No. 4, point 2105.
3 *Re European Sugar Cartel*, 2 January 1973, OJ 1973 L140/17; [1973] CMLR D65. For other aspects and a summary of the facts, see pp. 58–60, above.

Luxembourg sugar markets and to have abused this position by threatening to withhold supplies from the undertakings Export and Hottlet, two firms of Belgian sugar dealers, so as to oblige them only to re-sell the sugar which RT supplied to certain clients and for certain uses, and to impose these limitations on their customers.

Similarly the dominant Dutch producers, SU and CSM, were held to have abused their positions by threatening Dutch dealers' sources of supply if they sold certain stocks of sugar at prices substantially lower than those of SU and CSM and did not observe certain other restrictions on their commercial freedom.

GENERAL MOTORS CONTINENTAL[1]

In this case General Motors Continental NV, which was entrusted by Adam Opel AG with the issue of certificates required under Belgian law as to compliance of vehicles made by companies in the General Motors group with special technical standards, was held to have abused its dominant position[2] by charging more for certificates in respect of vehicles manufactured by General Motors imported into Belgium than for locally manufactured General Motors vehicles, thus prejudicing parallel imports of General Motors vehicles into Belgium.

Finally in relation to art. 86 the question has been raised as to the extent to which, if at all, a dominant position may be constituted by the ownership of industrial property rights and also as to the extent to which there may be an abuse of a dominant position by means of the exercise of such rights; this is discussed in Chapter 8, below, relating to Industrial Property Rights.[3]

---

1 19 December 1974, OJ 1975 L29/14; [1975] 1 CMLR D20.
2 See further p. 173, text and n. 4, below.
3 See pp. 225ff., below.

Chapter 6

The Relevant Market

SECTION 1 INTRODUCTION

This chapter is concerned with the notion of relevant market. The point has already been made in relation to art. 85 that competition cannot be restricted in the abstract, but only on a particular market. Similarly for the purposes of art. 86 it is necessary to determine the relevant market in order to evaluate whether an undertaking's share of such market is, coupled with other factors, such that it is dominant.

A market is said to exist when buyers wishing to exchange money for a product or service are in contact with sellers wishing to exchange goods or services. A market has also been referred to as a network of dealings in any factor or product, and in the Report of the [US] Attorney General's National Committee to Study Anti-trust Laws[1] "market" is defined in these terms:

> "For purposes of economic analysis, the 'market' is the sphere of competitive rivalry within which the crucial transfer of buyers' patronage from one supplier of goods or services to another can take place freely. The boundaries of an 'industry' or 'market' will often be uncertain and controversial, and a definition appropriate in one case may be inappropriate in another. For our purposes, a market is an economic relationship among sellers and buyers, whose boundaries are not necessarily defined by geographical area alone, nor by conventional product classifications. To ascertain whether a firm or group of firms acting in concert has monopoly power, the 'market' should include all firms whose production has so immediate and substantial an effect on the prices and production of the firms in question that the actions of the one group cannot be explained without direct and constant reference to the other. One should include in a market all firms whose products are in fact good and directly available substitutes for one another in sales to some significant group of buyers, and exclude all others. Where the products of different industries compete directly as alternatives for the same use, the market for that class of products should include the rival goods supplied by different industries.

1 Washington DC, US Government Printing Office 1955, ch. 7.

166

One should combine into one market two or more products (or two or more areas) if an appreciable fall in the price of one product (or in one area) will promptly lead to a relatively large diversion of purchasers from the other product (or area). The appropriate market area may be international, national, regional or local."

To define a market it is necessary, therefore, to establish both the goods or services which are the subject of offer and demand (the product market); and since the goods sought to be purchased are required to satisfy the needs of one or more buyers at a particular place or more generally within a particular area, it is also necessary to define a market by reference to such place or area (the geographic market).

SECTION 2   THE PRODUCT MARKET

In the US Department of Justice "Guidelines for the Control of Mergers", issued in 1968,[1] a product market is said to be constituted by the sale of any product or service which is distinguishable as a matter of commercial practice from other products or services; and further that the sales of two distinct products to a particular group of purchasers can be grouped into a single market where two products are reasonably interchangeable for that group in terms of price, quality and use. Such definition of a product market is, it is submitted, equally apt to describe the product market for the purposes of arts. 85 and 86, and it follows that any enquiry as to what constitutes a product market involves ascertaining the product in function of the consumer and the consumer in function of the product. Thus by way of a hypothetical example S may be the manufacturer of a product, say steel wool suitable for scouring; the determination of the relevant product market involves determining:

(1) who are the consumers; and

(2) what are the products which, from the point of view of such consumers, compete with S's product, viz. similar products made by other manufacturers and products which are interchangeable.

It may be found that steel wool has both domestic and industrial uses. For the domestic consumer a plastic product may be an adequate substitute, while for industrial uses scouring steel wool may be essential.

---

1 Reprinted in CCH 1973, Trade Regulations Reports, para. 4510.

Thus S's product caters for two distinct product markets according to the category of consumer. In one, the domestic market, S's metal product competes with a competitor's plastic product so that the product market comprises both types of scouring materials; in the other, the industrial market, S's product is not subject to competition from substitute plastic products and the relevant product market will be limited to steel wool, unless a substitute product other than plastic is available, when steel wool and such substitute product would comprise the relevant product market.

A particular product market may, however, require further definition by reference to certain other factors mentioned below,[1] and the delimitation of the product market by reference to the interchangeability of products may therefore represent only a first approximation or the outer boundary of the product market which will need to be analysed further into sub-markets, any one of which may, according to the circumstances, be the only or one of several relevant product markets in relation to which a restriction of competition or an abuse has to be considered.

It hardly needs saying that an undertaking's market share may be very different according to whether one or another product market is taken into consideration, to the extent that in relation to one product market the undertaking may be dominant but not in relation to the other. Thus in the *Continental Can* Case[2] the Commission had imputed dominant positions to SLW[3] by reason of its share of the markets for light containers for canned meat products, for light containers for canned fish products and (subject to an exception) for metal caps for use in the canned food industry – but the Court of Justice was not satisfied that such allocation to separate product markets had been justified by the Commission and suggested that only one product market for light metal containers could be involved, not to speak of an even wider product market comprising substitute products such as glass and plastic containers. It was necessary, the Court said, for the possibilities of competition to be assessed having regard to the characteristics of the relevant products by virtue of which they were particularly fit for certain specified purposes and not easily interchangeable with other products.

The Court has thus laid down a test by reference to the characteristics

---

1 See discussion of *Brown Shoe Co.* v. *US*, 370 US 294 (1962), US Supreme Court, at pp. 169, 170, below.
2 *Re Continental Can Company Incorporated*, 9 December 1971, JO 1972 L7/25; [1972] CMLR D11; and see p. 161, above.
3 Schmalbach-Lubeca-Werke AG, the 85·8% controlled subsidiary of Continental Can Company.

and uses of a product for determining the scope of a product market – but are there others? The Commission in Regulation 2779/72[1] gives as one of the criteria for exempting specialisation agreements from notification that the market shares of the parties do not exceed a percentage of the product market defined in terms of the agreement products and products considered similar by the consumer by reason of their characteristics, price and use. By this test a luxurious family type motor car and a low or medium priced car are not in the same relevant product market, for while in each case products having essentially the same properties and use are involved (motor vehicles for the ordinary carriage of passengers), the price differential is such that one of the conditions in the test is not satisfied.

It does not follow, however, that because their price is the same that two motor-car models are in the same product market. A family saloon and a sports car may carry the same price tag but each caters for a specific sub-market.[2]

Conversely it is not in all cases that a substantial price difference will prevent products being in the same product market. The income group to which a person belongs will be less decisive in relation to the purchase of a product representing a small proportion of his income. A person of average income would presumably not mind paying three times as much for a diamond gramophone stylus as for a sapphire one on the basis that it will last three times as long. He might not, however, pay three times as much for a car lasting three times longer.

Further, different product markets may subsist in relation to the same product according to the trading level. Thus in the *Consten-Grundig* Case,[3] where Grundig, in answer to the charge of infringement of art. 85 (1) by reason of steps taken to prevent parallel imports of Grundig recording equipment into the territory of its exclusive French distributor, pleaded *inter alia* the existence of competition between Grundig products and the products of other manufacturers, the argument was rejected.

The US Supreme Court judgment in the *Brown Shoe* Case[4] under the Clayton Act (where the definition of the relevant market is necessary to determine whether competition is reduced by a merger or other concentration of undertakings) gave the following tests as relevant for defining the product market: industry recognition of a

---

1 See the text of the Regulation, discussed at p. 112, above.
2 For application by the Commission of these principles of market delimitation in the motor industry, see *Re Bayerische Motoren Werke AG*, 13 December 1974, OJ 1975 L29/1, at para. 31.
3 *Etablissements Consten SA and Grundig Verkaufs-GmbH* v. *EEC Commission*, 13 July 1966, XII Rec. 429; [1966] CMLR 418.
4 *Brown Shoe Co.* v. *US*, 370 US 294 (1962). For facts of the case, see p. 170, below.

sub-market as a separate economic entity; public recognition of a sub-market as such; peculiar characteristics of the product; peculiar uses of the product; unique production facilities; distinct customers; distinct prices; sensitivity to price changes; and specialised vendors. The reader will recognise certain of the above tests which have already been discussed above.

It is only possible to wait and see to what extent the Court of Justice and the Commission will consider tests other than the substitutability of products considered similar by the consumer by reason of their characteristics, price and use, as relevant bearing in mind that they were evolved in relation to a foreign body of law with a purpose not identical to that of arts. 85 and 86, and generally having regard to the more flexible attitude adopted by the Commission in relation to restriction of competition. However, whether the product market is defined for the purposes of the Clayton Act or of arts. 85 and 86, in each case the delimitation of the product market is relevant for assessing the competitive position of an undertaking on a market. There appears therefore to be no reason of principle why tests evolved in relation to the Clayton Act should not be equally relevant to the ascertainment of the relevant market for the purposes of arts. 85 and 86. If this is correct the study of American case law under the Clayton Act may be found to be a rewarding exercise in seeking the solution to particular problems arising under arts. 85 and 86 – particularly until a substantial body of European case law is built up. In this context the following few examples of American decisions are given to show in particular both how narrowly and in certain cases how widely, certain product markets have been defined.

THE BROWN SHOE CASE[1]

Men's, women's and children's shoes were held to be three distinct product markets. Each of these product markets or lines of commerce (in American terminology) "was recognised as distinct by the public, was manufactured in separate factories, had characteristics rendering it generally non-competitive with the others, and was directed towards a distinct class of customer. Brown argued that the relevant markets should be broken down still further into high, medium and low-price varieties of each of the three classes of shoe, and that the category of children's shoes should be spread into three further sub-markets (namely infants' shoes, misses' and children's shoes, and youths' and boys' shoes). These refinements were, however, dismissed by the Court as 'unrealistic' and 'impractical' ".[2] No wonder! But the quota-

---

1 370 US 294 (1962), US Supreme Court.
2 A. D. Neale, *The Antitrust Laws of the USA*, Cambridge University Press, 1970, p. 195.

tion is given as the kind of argument which may be put up in support of a particular delimitation of a product market.

THE CONTINENTAL CAN CASE[1]

The District Court found that the metal-container and glass-container industries were each a relevant line of commerce and that beer containers (both glass bottles and cans) also constituted a distinct sub-market. The Supreme Court did not agree, Justice White finding "a rather general confrontation between metal and glass containers and competition between them for the same end-uses which is insistent, continuous, effective and quantity-wise very substantial".[2] He conceded that glass and metal containers have different characteristics which might disqualify one or the other from particular uses, and that for various reasons many users of glass or cans could not switch at will from one kind of container to another. But, nevertheless, he reiterated that there was sufficient inter-industry competition to justify treating "glass and metal containers" as a sub-market within the larger packaging-industry classification. Justices Harlan and Stewart, however, agreed with the District Court in their minority dissenting opinion and said that the majority view read the " 'line of commerce' element out of section 7,[3] destroying its usefulness as an aid to analysis"; the present authors would support with the minority view.

E.I. DU PONT DE NEMOURS – CELLOPHANE CASE[4]

The relevant market was held to be the flexible package industry as a whole and not merely the cellophane industry.

The Court stated:[5]

> "But where there are market alternatives that buyers may readily use for their purposes, illegal monopoly does not exist merely because the product said to be monopolized differs from others. If it were not so, only physically identical products would be a part of the market. To accept the Government's argument, we would have to conclude that the manufacturers of plain as well as moistureproof cellophane were monopolists ... for each of these wrapping materials is distinguishable ... What is called for is an appraisal of the 'cross-elasticity' of demand in the trade ... In considering what is the relevant market for determining the control of price and competition, no more definite rule can be declared than that

1 378 US 441 (1964).
2 A. D. Neale, *op. cit.*, p. 196.
3 Clayton Act, s. 7, prohibits mergers and acquisitions which may substantially lessen competition ". . . in any line of commerce, in any section of the country . . ."
4 351 US 377 (1956).
5 *Ibid.*, at p. 394, [15–17].

commodities reasonably interchangeable by consumers for the same purposes make up that 'part of the trade or commerce' monopolization of which may be illegal."

US V. CROWELL COLLIER AND MACMILLAN INC.[1]

Band uniforms generally and not all made-to-measure uniforms were held to constitute the relevant market. The District Court rejected the contention of the Government that blazers (as opposed to military type uniforms) sold and used for band uniforms should be excluded from the relevant market, thereby narrowing it. On the other hand, the court also rejected the defendants' attempt to enlarge the product market to include the entire made-to-measure uniform industry.

The relevant passages in the District Court's reasoning are as follows:[2]

"The essence of S7 is competition, and only those products that actually compete for sales should be grouped and analyzed within the same commercial or product line. Defendant's argument for defining the product market as made-to-measure uniforms ignores this point. As discussed heretofore, there is a good deal of similarity in appearance and manufacture between various types of uniforms, and, as defendant asserts, it would be relatively easy for a maker of one variety to expand his line to others. But, to put the matter somewhat simplistically, there is no competition between usher and firefighter uniforms; policemen do not consider band garb an alternative to their traditional blues . . .

"This principle works in the converse as well. The government here would eliminate from consideration blazers sold and used for band uniforms. It argues that in both appearance and price, band blazers differ extensively from traditional military type band garb. This, however, does not negate the fact that blazers are a viable alternative to the more common uniform replete with shako and overlay, and are preferred by a good number of bands in the north-east."

The reader will recognize in the finding that blazers are a viable alternative to the more common uniform the Commission's criterion[3] of defining for certain purposes the product market by reference to the products which are the subject of the relevant agreement and products which the consumer considers to be similar. Admittedly, however, the question remains as to who is the consumer. Bands in

---

1 361 F. Supp. 983 (SDNY 1973).
2 361 F. Supp. 983, at pp. 990, 991, [1, 2].
3 See p. 168, above.

the north-east are happy with a blazer uniform. By inference it may not be possible to say the same of a bandsman in the south-west.

Very narrow definition of the relevant product market in assessing the impact of anti-competitive practices as exemplified by the preceding American examples has at least been matched by the Commission in *Re Filipacchi*,[1] where classical music, light music and pop were treated as separate markets; and moreover within the pop music market the records of star performers were held to constitute a separate market from pop records by other performers. In defining the relevant product market the Commission has also distinguished between standard-type ball bearings and bearings of other types[2] and between Dutch preserved mushrooms and French and Taiwanese preserved mushrooms[3]. Further, the service provided by a company in the General Motors group in issuing conformity certificates for the group's vehicles was held to be a product market distinct from the market for the group's vehicles.[4]

In the *Zoja* Case,[5] the Court of Justice distinguished the market in the raw materials (aminobutanol and nitropropane) necessary for the manufacture of a product (ethambutol) from the market on which the product is sold, i.e. the market for anti-tuberculosis drugs generally.

It will be clear that very different results may ensue according to whether a product market is defined narrowly or broadly. A broad definition in relation to art. 86 means that an undertaking has a smaller market share, so that the chances of it being held to be dominant are reduced. On the other hand the broader the definition the more are the competing goods on the market, so that if in spite of the smaller market share the undertaking is nevertheless held to be dominant, the greater the possibility of abuse being committed by any particular action of the undertaking since the action can have repercussions in relation to goods which on the basis of a narrower definition of the relevant market would not be subject to the undertaking's dominance. Therefore an undertaking defending proceedings for breach of art. 86 may wish to maintain a broad definition of the product market with a view to establishing a smaller market share

---

1 *Re WEA-Filipacchi Music SA*, 22 December 1972, JO 1972 L303/52; [1973] CMLR D43.
2 *Re Franco-Japanese Ballbearings Agreement*, 29 November 1974, OJ 1974 L343/19; [1975] 1 CMLR D8.
3 *Re Preserved Mushrooms*, 8 January 1975, OJ 1975 L29/26.
4 *Re General Motors Continental*, 19 December 1974, OJ 1975 L29/14; [1975] 1 CMLR D20.
5 *ICI-CSC* v. *EC Commission*, 6 March 1974, [1974] ECR 223; [1974] 1 CMLR 309. The facts of the case are discussed at p. 158, above.

and thereby to be in a position to deny dominance of the market in question; or on the other hand it may wish to maintain a narrow definition of the product market enabling it to deny dominance not on the basis of its small market share, but on the basis that it is not even present on the market wherein a dominant position is alleged to have been abused.

The above considerations would seem to be equally applicable in relation to art. 85, e.g. where it is necessary to establish the market shares of undertakings which have entered into restrictive agreements with a view to seeing whether the agreement can be said to be of minor importance, and to be within the provisions of the Commission's Communication of 27 May 1970.[1] The Communication established criteria for treating certain agreements as not normally within art 85 (1) when certain market shares are not exceeded which necessarily involves the consideration of the way in which the relevant market is to be defined. What is involved, for the purpose of both articles is the definition of the field within which the existence or otherwise of an anti-competitive situation is to be assessed.

The way the relevant market is defined can also be important in relation to the question whether an agreement within art. 85 (1) satisfies the condition for exemption under art. 85 (3) that the agreement does not eliminate competition "in respect of a substantial part of the products in question". Thus in Re Kali und Salz-Kali Chemie[2] the Commission distinguished "straight" potash fertiliser from compound fertiliser on the grounds that the consumer did not consider them substitutes because of the higher price of the latter, and since the effect of the agreement was to eliminate Kali Chemie as a competitor with respect to straight fertiliser, it was not necessary to argue (as the undertakings did in support of their claim for exemption) that Kali Chemie continued to compete as producer of compound fertiliser.

It is to be noted in relation to what has been said above that parties under investigation under arts. 85 and 86 are not in any way precluded from advancing arguments relating to the extent of the product market, and an appeal is available to the Court of Justice if the parties are dissatisfied with the Commission's decision in this regard. The position contrasts with that under the Fair Trading Act 1973, where in relation to monopoly references, the extent of the relevant market to be taken into account is determined by the enforcement authorities.[3]

---

1 JO 1970 C64; [1970] CMLR D15; discussed at p. 75, above.
2 Re Agreement of Kali und Salz AG and Kali Chemie AG, 21 December 1973, OJ 1974 L19/22; [1974] 1 CMLR D1.
3 S. 10 (7).

SECTION 3   THE GEOGRAPHIC MARKET

When undertakings engaged in selling goods or services (products) make significant sales of a product to purchasers in a geographic area, such an area will constitute a geographic market to the extent that trade takes place under the same conditions throughout the area. If the conditions are not the same, different geographic markets may be involved, which need to be treated separately in computing market shares and drawing the necessary consequences as regards art. 85 (perceptible restriction of competition on such market) or art. 86 (market dominance on such market and its abuse).

There are various reasons why trading conditions may differ within a global area in which sales are made, requiring the area to be broken down into sub-areas or sub-markets, e.g. different market structures, different price levels, consumer preferences, etc. The exact limitation of each sub-market would be a matter of economic analysis. In most cases the relevant geographic market, within the Common Market as it is today, will not extend beyond the frontiers of a particular state, for in spite of the elimination of customs duties there subsist a great number of differing technical, fiscal and economic requirements and situations to be met in the member states, tending to compartmentalise the states concerned. In due course, if and when Europe becomes fully integrated economically, national boundaries will have no significance from the point of view of market delineation. In the meantime, it is by reference to national markets or parts of national markets, that, in all cases dealt with to date by the Commission under art. 86, the relevant geographic markets have been defined, as a first step in establishing market dominance within a substantial part of the Common Market.[1] Correspondingly, in relation to art. 85 it will in most cases be within the state boundaries that the relevant geographic market will be situated.

The "measure" of a market is the monetary value of the transactions in the product effected in the geographic market, though in particular instances other yard-sticks may be more appropriate, e.g. total deposits in the case of banks.

It follows that when a geographic area overspills into one or more other member states, the value of the total transactions in the enlarged geographic market and the value of a particular undertaking's share in it can differ materially from those values computed by reference to the seller's national market.

---

1 See p. 153, above.

In the same way that in relation to the product market an undertaking may have advantage in establishing a wider or narrower market,[1] so it may be advantageous for an undertaking to establish a wider or narrower geographic market in defending charges of infringement of art. 85 or art. 86.

Apart from cases when the geographic market is limited by the frontiers of member states by reasons outside the control of the undertakings, undertakings may themselves limit a market to an area within the said boundaries artificially by agreement or concerted practice as when undertakings agree to refrain from competing in each other's countries. In such case, the national undertakings concerned may each become dominant in their respective countries and each by its action will have brought itself within the scope of art. 86 should its subsequent market behaviour be held to be abusive in the light of the undertaking's self-imposed market dominance.

---

1 See pp. 173, 174, above.

Chapter 7

Co-operation and Concentration between Undertakings

SECTION 1 INTRODUCTION

The economic aim of the EEC is the creation of an integrated market of the member states. This necessarily involves the adaptation of industrial structures to meet both the opportunities and risks implicit in such integration.

The opportunities for undertakings to strengthen their position in the EEC should increase as further progress is made, beyond the existing elimination of customs duties, in removing all artificial barriers to trade; but, correspondingly, the risk of an undertaking ceasing to be able to hold its own in the integrated market will be greater as more intense competition is met not only from other EEC undertakings but also increasingly from non-EEC undertakings seeking to take advantage of the integrated European market.

EEC undertakings must, therefore, if they wish to remain competitive, enhance their ability both to penetrate the enlarged EEC market and to meet competition on their home ground. They may seek to achieve this by co-operating with other undertakings in such matters as research and development; by limiting their activities, in the interests of efficiency, through specialisation arrangements entered into with other undertakings; or by increasing their production and/or marketing potential through mergers or other forms of concentration; or by a combination of some of the above methods.[1]

It is the object of this chapter to study the extent to which such measures are compatible with the EEC competition rules. Consideration is therefore given, in section 2, to the application of art. 85 to co-operation agreements – discussed under the headings of research and development agreements and specialisation agreements.[2] Concentration between undertakings may be total, i.e. a merger of two or more undertakings, or partial, e.g. where two or more undertakings

---

1 See *Re Rank/Sopelem*, 20 December 1974, OJ 1975 L29/20, which concerned research, development, manufacture, exclusion dealing and specialisation.

2 Though these headings do not cover all co-operation agreements, which, as is indicated by the Commission's Communication on Co-operation Agreements (see Appendix IV, p. 408, below), is an all-embracing term. For a case falling squarely under neither heading, see *Re Agreement of SARL Wild Paris and SA E. Leitz France*, 23 February 1972, JO 1972 L61/27; [1972] CMLR D36, combining in one agreement co-operation and joint sales promotion.

agree to set up a joint venture; the application of arts. 85 and 86 to both forms of concentration is considered in section 3, which ends with an outline of the Commission's proposal for a Regulation on the control of concentrations between undertakings.

SECTION 2 CO-OPERATION BETWEEN UNDERTAKINGS

With regard to co-operation agreements generally, the Commission has in the past refuted criticism levelled against it that the EEC anti-trust rules create difficulties in connection with them, pointing to the liberal attitude reflected in its Communication on Co-operation Agreements,[1] and to the fact that even where competition is appreciably affected by a particular agreement or practice, it remains open to the parties to seek individual exemption under art. 85 (3). Nor does the Commission accept that its application of the Treaty rules discriminates against co-operation by agreement in favour of concentration, which implies the partial or total passing of control of an undertaking.

> "Generally speaking, firms in the Community have overestimated the administrative or legal difficulties [of the notification procedure of Regulation 17] or have read into it prejudice on the part of the Community against such agreements ... The various interpretations of Articles 85 and 86 may have led to the belief that the EEC Treaty [has] forced the Commission to adopt a sterner attitude towards co-operation than concentration. This is not the Commission's own interpretation, which is conscious of the fact that co-operation agreements are often the prelude to closer forms of integration and that it is not always possible for undertakings to change over to concentration without going through a transition stage. Even where there is no ultimate prospect of concentration, Article 85 (3) allows co-operation if it produces the desired economic effects."[2]

Research and Development

The Commission has made it clear that co-operation agreements between undertakings relating to the joint execution of research or the joint development of the results of research up to the stage of industrial development do not affect the competitive position of the parties and are unobjectionable under art. 85 (1); the provisions of the article are applicable, however, to agreements governing the use to which the results of such research and development are put.[3] Regula-

---

1 JO 1968 C75/3, mentioned on p. 79, above, and set out in Appendix IV, p. 407, below.
2 Industrial Policy in the Community, Memorandum from the Commission to the Council, Brussels 1970, pp. 144, 145.
3 Commission, 1st Report on Competition Policy, April 1972, sec. 31.

tion 17 contains provisions by which certain agreements in this field are exempt from notification[1]. But whilst such automatic exemption from notification is an indication of the Commission's positive approach to research and development and confirms that the prohibition is not likely to apply so long as the terms of the Regulation are met, the consequence of the provision, both in its original and revised form, has been that many such agreements have never been brought to the Commission's attention, with the result that the sources which normally indicate the Commission's application of the anti-trust rules to agreements (i.e. the Commission's decisions) are in this field limited. For this reason the Communication on Co-operation Agreements which the Commission issued in 1968 is of considerable importance;[2] further clarification of the basis on which the Commission applies the rules is found in the individual exemptions it has granted under art. 85 (3), and in the comments it has made from time to time in official statements and publications.

The Commission's Communication is stated to apply to all undertakings, irrespective of their size (though with reservations as indicated by the Commission in its First Report on Competition Policy[3]) and is expressed to be without prejudice to any interpretation by the Court of Justice; as has been pointed out in connection with communications of the Commission,[4] they should only be relied upon with caution.

However, the decisions of the Commission which have been taken to date support the views expressed in the Communication; so long as there is equal access to the results of a research and development programme which does not have the object of restricting, and has not restricted, the parties to it from undertaking their own research and development, it is not, in principle, restrictive of competition.[5] In this connection reference should be made to the comments of the Commission which accompany the Communication in which it outlines what is, and what is not, permitted in such a programme of research.

RE HENKEL–COLGATE[6]

This Decision is an interesting example of the approach the Commission adopts in justifying a co-operation agreement in the field of research and development under art. 85 (3) even where the agree-

---

1 Art. 4 (2) (3) (b) as amended, as to which see p. 262, below.
2 JO 1968 C75/3, set out in Appendix IV, p. 407, below, and see p. 79, above.
3 April 1972, sec. 32, 3rd para., though the grounds for the reservations are not specified; and see *Re Henkel-Colgate,* below.
4 See p. 5, para. 5, above.
5 *Re Eurogypsum,* 26 February 1968, JO 1968 L57/9; [1968] CMLR D1.
6 23 December 1971, JO 1972 L14/14.

ment relates both to joint research undertaken by the parties and the exploitation and utilisation of the results emanating from such joint effort, and notwithstanding the size and importance of the undertakings concerned. What mattered were the effects of the agreement on the distribution and marketing of the products, and whether or not the agreement might contribute to the division of the market by preventing or impeding parallel imports of the products between member states through the use of patent or knowhow rights. Since the parties had equal access to the results of the research, and there was no restriction either on production or distribution of products which result from the research, i.e. the parties were free to compete at the distribution level, the Commission was prepared to accept that the restrictions inherent in the joint venture operation were acceptable in the circumstances.[1]

The agreement related to a joint research programme by Colgate and Henkel operated through the medium of a jointly owned company, set up to achieve technical advances in order to increase the competitiveness of each partner as against the two other major producers of detergents, Unilever and Proctor and Gamble, on the world market.

The Commission considered that the intended form of co-operation between the partners through the joint company involved restrictions on competition within the Common Market and affected trade between member states. Indeed, while each partner reserved the right to undertake research on its own, this was unlikely to take place in view of the high cost involved, and, as there was an obligation to license the joint company to exploit the results of individual research, neither party could achieve a technical advance over the other, so that in practice the partners had contracted out of individual research in the field covered by the agreement. Moreover, whilst hoped-for improvements in quality and method of use of products would enhance the competitive position of the partners as against third parties, it eliminated competition between the partners themselves.

Henkel and Colgate both being major international companies (Colgate holding some 10% of the detergent market in the EEC, and Henkel holding 27%, although in three individual member states the percentage of the market held by one or other was in excess of 50%), the restrictions on competition between them necessarily affected trade between member states.

However, applying the four tests under art. 85 (3) the Commission found:

---

1 See pp. 196–198, below, for further comments on joint ventures.

(1) that the agreement was such as to lead to technical and economic improvements;
(2) that in the competitive situation existing as between four major detergent manufacturers consumers would benefit from the marketing of the technically improved products expected to result from the Colgate-Henkel co-operation;
(3) the agreement did not impose any unnecessary restrictions since:

    (a) the parties remained free to undertake their own research, and

    (b) the parties were entitled to obtain in each country, on the same terms, licences to exploit the results of the joint research, the royalty payable to the joint company being limited to the period of patent protection in the country concerned, even in the case of licences for unpatented knowhow, and

    (c) the agreement imposed no limitation on production and sale of products resulting from the joint research;

(4) the agreement did not eliminate competition in respect of a substantial part of the products in question: while each of the parties had strong market positions in all countries of the Common Market, jointly they did not have a dominant position on any market within the Community. Nevertheless the danger of concerted market behaviour as a consequence of cross-holdings or personal relationships existed and the Commission therefore imposed an obligation on the parties to keep it informed of all developments in these respects.[1]

RE RESEARCH AND DEVELOPMENT[2]

In another case the Commission commented on a similar type of agreement between two undertakings, but which it refused to approve since the parties were not equally entitled to the benefits of the research and development programme: more particularly, the agreement provided that either party could only obtain a licence to exploit in the other's territory the processes and knowhow derived from the arrangement on payment of a royalty not exceeding 2%. The effect of this financial provision, together with the possible use to which the patents and knowhow might be put, was that each party was, as a result, effectively precluded from exploiting the rights in the territory of the other, to the detriment of the integration of the market.

---

1 As to conditions attaching to the grant of exemption generally, see p. 289, below.
2 EC Bulletin 1971 No. 5, p. 39; [1971] CMLR D31.

RE ACEC-BERLIET[1]

This Decision concerns an agreement relating both to joint research and development and specialisation between the parties (for comments on specialisation generally see pp. 184ff., below).

ACEC of Belgium, who had invented a particular type of electric transmission system for commercial vehicles, particularly for use in buses, entered into a 10 year agreement with Berliet of France whereby each would co-operate in perfecting and marketing buses equipped with the system. Berliet agreed to study ACEC's transmission system with a view to making a prototype vehicle which used the system for later production, and for its part ACEC undertook to study and adapt its system for Berliet's vehicles and to produce them for buses bearing Berliet's trade mark. It was agreed that the field of collaboration could be widened to other forms of road transportation or types of electric transmission, with priority sharing between the parties of any new solutions under consideration and with complete exchange of technical information, (with the proviso that Berliet's information could not be used in studies which ACEC might undertake with other makers of buses).

In the event of manufacture on a production line basis, ACEC was to supply electric transmissions, (at a mutually agreed price) and Berliet would be responsible for mechanical parts of vehicles, more particularly internal combustion engines, chassis, coach-work and various accessories. Berliet would be entitled to enjoy most favoured client treatment.

Apart from a limited number of Belgian users, ACEC undertook to restrict its deliveries of transmissions in France to Berliet alone and to one manufacturer in each other member state (the original agreement, whereby ACEC was restricted to supplying one undertaking only in Germany and Italy, to a limited number of customers in Belgium and to Berliet in France, had been amended at the request of the Commission); elsewhere in the world ACEC's customers were limited in number. ACEC was obliged to keep Berliet informed of any contract relating to such matter.

Berliet was bound to purchase electric transmissions from ACEC alone but was to be subject to no territorial or other restrictions with regard to their resale. Each was to be the sole holder of the industrial property rights resulting from the inventions and developments which it had conceived or studied.

---

1 Re Agreement of Ateliers de Constructions Electriques de Charleroi and Berliet, 17 July 1968, JO 1968 L201/7; [1968] CMLR D35.

The Commission considered that the freedom of action of the parties was restricted by the provisions in the agreement for collaboration and division of labour. Third parties were also affected by the agreement in that (1) manufacturers of other electric transmission systems and their distributors would be prevented from selling their products to Berliet, and (2) other manufacturers of commercial vehicles would be restricted in their freedom to purchase electric transmission systems, since the agreement limited ACEC in the sale of its systems to such manufacturers in member states other than Belgium; this restriction would in turn restrict the choice for consumers.

Further, the agreement was capable of affecting trade between member states, since (1) Berliet alone in France would be able to purchase the transmission systems from ACEC, and (2) the possibility of exporting the system to member states other than France would be restricted by the very limited number of purchasers elsewhere in the Common Market.

However, the Commission specifically stated that the provision restricting the use of Berliet information and the obligation regarding most favoured client treatment would not restrict or distort competition within the meaning of art. 85 (1) both because of the necessity for confidence between the parties, and because of the risk inherent in mounting a programme involving substantial development effort and investment. Berliet could not reasonably be expected to contribute its services and knowhow under the agreement if, when the development came to a successful conclusion, Berliet's competitors could not only make use of the results of the research but could also obtain the electric transmissions from ACEC at a lower price than Berliet paid.

The Commission proceeded to find that the four tests of art. 85 (3) were satisfied:

(1) *Improvement in production and promotion of technical progress* – Specialisation and division of labour for research and manufacture would enable each party to adapt itself to the tasks to which it is best fitted, the intention being to perfect a product superior to those hitherto in existence.

(2) *Benefit to consumers* – Since all technical research carried the risk that a successful conclusion would not result, an appreciation of the result could only be based on probabilities; but it was reasonable to anticipate that the hoped-for results would be obtained more rapidly as a result of joint research. In the present case consumers would benefit because of availability of a product with new characteristics, and competition met from products incorporating more traditional features should ensure that terms of sale remained reasonable.

(3) *No unnecessary restrictions accepted* – The reciprocal restrictions by which on the one hand ACEC agreed to deliver its transmission system in France to Berliet only and Berliet on the other hand was prohibited from purchasing electric transmissions from suppliers other than ACEC gave a reasonable opportunity to both parties to recoup their investments in a new development – investments which, failing such security, they would be inhibited from making.

The obligation of ACEC to deliver its transmission system within the Common Market to one single manufacturer in each member state (other than France and Belgium) enabled such manufacturers to achieve the necessary production runs for profitable exploitation. If production were dispersed among a large number of manufacturers none of them would have been able to produce sufficient vehicles to make the new project a success.

(4) *No substantial elimination of competition* – Competition would exist from buses equipped with other systems of mechanical transmissions, and there would be no restriction, either territorial or otherwise, imposed on manufacturers using the ACEC system in the EEC and preventing them from distributing such buses where they wish.

In the circumstances, therefore, the Commission agreed to grant an exemption under art. 85 (3), requiring ACEC and Berliet to report to it on the application of the agreement, and limiting the duration of the Decision to 5 years[1].

Although the Commission has been authorised by the Council of Ministers[2] to adopt a Regulation granting exemption by category in the research and development field, to date it has taken no action in this respect.

Specialisation

Specialisation agreements are agreements whereby undertakings, in the interests of greater efficiency, mutually give up the manufacture of certain ranges of goods to be manufactured only by the other party to the agreement usually giving the other exclusive rights to distribute such goods in return for the right to distribute the latter's goods in the home territory. Such agreements are prima facie prohibited by art. 85 (1) (b)[3]. The Commission takes the view, however, that such agreements can improve production by enabling undertakings to

---

1 This period has now expired and no renewal of the Decision would appear to have been sought.
2 Under Reg. 2821/71, as to which see pp. 96, 97, above.
3 See p. 54, above.

specialise in those fields for which they are best equipped, with consequent increase in output and reduction in unit costs from which consumers, in competitive conditions, should benefit.

Specialisation agreements may come within the provisions of the group exemption[1] in which case they are exempt from the prohibition contained in art. 85 (1) without the need for any action by the parties. If a specialisation agreement does not qualify for exemption by category, it may nevertheless fall within Regulation 17, art. 4 (2) (3) (c),[2] in which case it need not be notified to the Commission.

However, if the agreement falls within neither of these special provisions the parties must – and in any event, if in doubt as to the status of the agreement, the parties may – formally notify the agreement to the Commission, in order to obtain the benefit of exemption from the prohibition of art. 85 (1) pursuant to art. 85 (3).[3] Such exemption will only be forthcoming if the specialisation results in benefits which are available not only to the undertakings but to consumers as well, or there must at least be a sufficient probability that such benefits will be available in the future.[4] The Commission has to date taken a number of decisions relating to specialisation agreements, and it is proposed to set out at some length three of these decisions in order to demonstrate the Commission's approach in considering specialisation agreements for exemption. Though some factors emerge as being of particular importance, in the final analysis each case turns a great deal on its facts. Little purpose is therefore served by setting out at length further decisions of the Commission, though short particulars of some are given, either as particularly clear examples of beneficial co-operation, or because of the particular point of interest they raise.

RE FN–CF[5]

The parties, Fabrique Nationale d'armes de guerre (FN) and Cartoucherie française (CF), were respectively Belgian and French manufacturers of ammunition.

Before the relevant agreement, entered into in 1968, each company manufactured a full range of ammunition for sporting, personal defence and industrial purposes. While FN was concerned primarily with complete cartridges (the FN range) CF's production was related more specifically to certain components for cartridges and to rifle

---

1 Reg. 2779/72, as to which see p. 108, above.
2 See p. 263, below.
3 See pp. 255, 256, below.
4 Commission's 1st Report on Competition Policy, April 1972, sec. 28.
5 *Re Agreement of Fabrique Nationale d'armes de guerre and Cartoucherie française*, 28 May 1971, JO 1971, L134/6.

ammunition (the CF range). These being complementary, the parties agreed to specialise in the production of their respective ranges and to rationalise distribution, on the basis that CF operated a developed sales network in France and its overseas territories while the emphasis of FN's distribution system was in Benelux and certain other countries (outside of France and its former territories); to this end FN was appointed CF's exclusive distributor for Benelux, and CF was appointed FN's exclusive distributor for France and its overseas territories. As regards other countries the distribution was entrusted to the company with the strongest local representation. Further, each party agreed to purchase exclusively from the other all products of the kind covered by the agreement.

The companies agreed to exchange technical information and to work together to develop new products and to grant each other royalty-free, non-exclusive licences in respect of products developed together and to keep the exchanged knowhow secret for the duration of the agreement and five years thereafter. As a result of their co-operation various measures of standardisation were effected and the manufacture of new products resulting from their joint research had been allotted to one or other of the partners.

As a result of the mutual designation of each party as the other's distributor, FN's sales network in France was wound up, sales being effected through CF's network and conversely CF's network in the Benelux countries no longer existed since FN's network in that area became available to CF as well as the former's network in Germany, Italy and in non-EEC countries where CF was not previously represented.

The agreement provided for publicity in common to advertise the full range of products available as a result of the co-operation, each party being free to advertise separately.

Market information was to be exchanged to enable sales promotion to be intensified. The agreement contained no restrictions against parallel imports. But each party was to fix its own selling price for its own products and those which it resold as distributor.

The agreement was clearly within art. 85 (1) involving as it did limitations of production inherent in the specialisation and limitation of sales outlets inherent in the exclusive mutual distribution of each party's specialised production: and the exclusive distribution could not but affect the flow of trade between member states.

However the Commission found that the four tests of art. 85 (3) were satisfied:

(1) *The specialisation resulted in improved production and distribution and technical progress*

Improvement in production – As a result of the agreement each party concentrated on the product ranges it was best equipped to produce; this enhanced output and production capacity and saved labour. These factors in turn resulted in lower unit costs, the accelerated writing down of investments and more efficient quality control; all of which resulted in a more intensive, rational and economic use of resources.

Improvement in distribution – Reciprocal distribution ensured that each party could offer a complete range of products – its own and that of the other party.

Distribution by each party in areas in which it was best represented ensured greater market penetration.

Further, joint advertising reduced advertising costs, enabling the parties to intensify their sales effort in other directions.

Technical progress – This resulted from the technical co-operation between the parties: each party benefited from information received from the other. Better results in the development of new products ensued from the single research team with avoidance of unnecessary dispersal of effort – and the resulting economies permitted new investments which made possible, since the agreement took effect in 1968, the standardisation in sizes and ballistic characteristics of the relevant products, improved products, greater automation and the formation of a more specialised labour force.

(2) *Benefit to consumers*

Consumers benefited:

(a) by lower prices made possible by greater efficiency resulting from the specialisation,

(b) by reason of the improved quality of the products.

(3) *No unnecessary restrictions accepted*

(a) The various restrictions (other than those related to exclusive dealing) were inherent in the specialisation and technical co-operation between the parties.

(b) As regards exclusive dealing, but for each party's obligation to purchase exclusively from the other, there would not be an assured market for the increased production resulting from specialisation; and but for each party's obligation to sell exclusively to the other, the profit from sales in a party's territory of products which it had ceased to produce by reason of the specialisation and of new products developed in common, would accrue to third parties.

(4) *No substantial elimination of competition*

Neither FN nor CF as producers dominated the market in any country: there was ample competition both from other national producers and foreign producers. At distribution level competition was safeguarded by the possibility of parallel imports and as retailers were not tied, competition subsisted at all levels of trading.

RE MAN-SAVIEM[1]

This concerned an agreement between a German and a French manufacturer for co-operation in research and development, design, manufacture, assembly, sale and after-sales services all in relation to a common range of industrial vehicles of over 7·5 tons of which the following were the main provisions:

(a) Each party was to manufacture and sell all vehicles within the range developed in common but Saviem was to be design leader for vehicles between 7·5 tons and 12 tons ("the middle range") and Man for vehicles over 12 tons ("the upper range").

(b) The manufacture of engine and other units for all vehicles was allocated to each party broadly according to the range for which he was design leader: thus engines for the medium range were made by Saviem under licence from Man and engines for the upper range were made by Man.

(c) Each party would be supplied by the other with his requirements of all units for use in his vehicles but not for resale.

(d) A party was not to sell engines or other units made by him to third parties except with the consent of the other party, the consent always to be given unless a refusal could be justified for important reasons.

(e) The whole range of vehicles for the French market was to be assembled and distributed by Saviem and correspondingly by Man as regards the German market, and the assembly for export of vehicles within the upper and middle ranges would be by Man and Saviem respectively.

(f) In the assembly only units developed in common or by each of them within his allocated range would be used.

(g) Each party was precluded from technical co-operation with others.

(h) While the parties were to be able to undertake research in common to be agreed as need arose they were each restricted from designing vehicles within the other's range.

---

1 *Re MAN-SAVIEM*, 17 January 1972, JO 1972 L31/29; [1974] 2 CMLR D123.

(i) Sub-contract work was to be offered first to the other party.

(j) The parties were to treat as secret information resulting from the co-operation.

The Commission found that restriction of competition was involved as follows:

The parties were not free to design or develop or manufacture vehicles except within their allotted ranges or to use engines or other units except those developed in common or by each party in his specified field ((a), (b) and (f) above). The vehicles made by each party would therefore differ less and less to the detriment of available choices open to users. The allocation of sales territories ((e) above) deprived users of the benefit of competition between the manufacturers. Third party enterprises were restricted in their ability to tender for sub-contract work as a result of the preference which the parties had to give to each other as regards sub-contracts ((i) above).

The reason for a party's refusal to consent to a sale by the other party of engines or other units made by him ((d) above) could be the desire to restrict competition from the third parties.

Restriction of competition was involved in the resale prohibition as regards units supplied by one party to the other ((c) above). The benefits in the fields of research and development, manufacture and distribution which could have ensued from co-operation with third parties were precluded by the veto on such co-operation ((g) above).

The Commission also found trade between member states to be affected through the alteration in the currents of trade resulting from the provisions of the agreement.

No restrictions on competition were found with respect to:

Research in common ((h) above) in the absence of demarcation of the areas of research and of any prohibition on individual research; and it was relevant that the parties were entitled to the free use of resulting patents and knowhow.

Obligations as to secrecy ((j) above).

The following reasons were given for exempting the agreement under art. 85 (3):

(1) *The agreement was found to result in improved production and distribution*

Improvement in production – The co-operation in design whether effected in common or separately promoted technical progress and improved products.

Co-operation in development would lead to common conception for the vehicles designed in common and would form a basis for co-operation in the subsequent stages of production, assembly and sales.

The co-operation would lead to standardisation which would enhance production of a wider range of vehicles and stock management would be simplified.

Since the parties would continue to manufacture vehicles within their existing production possibilities the co-operation would not involve substantial investments such as to detract from the advantages of the scheme.

The specialisation in manufacture would increase productivity and reduce costs.

The specialisation would better allow the parties to produce a large number of different models as dictated by market requirements.

The advantages to be derived from the specialisation in production would outweigh the additional costs involved in the transport of parts between the two manufacturing and assembly centres.

Improvements in distribution – Each party would have an outlet for its products in the other's country, as a consequence of its products being incorporated in vehicles assembled by the latter and sold through its already established distribution channels with the benefit of the after-sales services essential for successful marketing of vehicles.

(2) *Benefit to consumers*

Competition from other manufacturers would ensure that saving in costs would be passed on to users.

Users would also benefit from the agreement in that they would find throughout the Common Market an after-sales organisation qualified to service the vehicles developed in common.

(3) *No unnecessary restrictions accepted*

The terms of the agreement were all necessary to strengthen and to achieve the results expected from the co-operation, and in particular:

The provisions conferring exclusive selling rights were necessary in so far as each party would benefit from sales of vehicles in both ranges, which would compensate it if the range in which it specialised was less successful.

Co-operation with other parties (prohibited by the agreement) would prejudice the co-operation and thereby reduce the parties' competitiveness as against other manufacturers.

(4) *No substantial elimination of competition*

At least ten other important undertakings were potential competitors as suppliers of industrial vehicles of over 7·5 tons. While hitherto in certain EEC countries competition had been potential rather than actual owing to technical barriers and lack of after-sales and repairs service available to importers, the Commission anticipated an evolution towards more competitive conditions through increase in trade between member states.

RE PAPETERIES BOLLORE[1]

In this case five French companies participated in an agreement whereby in its final version they co-operated in specialising in the production and marketing of fine papers, carbon paper and cigarette paper. The agreement contained terms relating to technical and commercial assistance and co-operation for obtaining orders in non-EEC markets. Each party limited its production to certain sorts and quantities of thin paper. Production of the participants represented over 50% of Community production of cigarette paper of which 80% was exported, 10% to the EEC and 70% to non-member states; the participants produced about 15% of Community production of carbon paper, exporting about 15% from France, nearly half of which went to other EEC countries.

The Commission considered that art. 85 (1) applied by reason of the restriction of competition between the participants resulting from specialisation – with repercussions on the position of consumers owing to the reduction in the number of suppliers of each kind of paper – trade between member states being also affected by the resultant changes in the pattern of exports within the EEC.

On the other hand, the Commission did not consider trade between member states to be affected by co-operation between the participants as regards export to non-EEC countries, having regard to the abolition of previously existing arrangements for sharing export markets through quotas coupled with a system for the equalisation of profits.

The Commission, however, granted exemption under art. 85 (3) on the ground of improvement in production achieved by economies of scale resulting from the specialisation; the resulting reduced costs led to reduced prices, thus benefiting consumers. Technical progress might also result from improvement in production.

The restrictions imposed in the agreement were inherent in the specialisation; the agreement therefore did not contain any unnecessary restrictions.

As regards the requirement for exemption under art. 85 (3) that competition should not be eliminated in respect of a substantial part of the products in question, the Commission considered that, for

---

1 26 July 1972, JO 1972 L182/24; [1972] CMLR D94.

thin paper other than cigarette paper, no problem arose in view of the weak market strength of the participants; but that, for cigarette paper, it was necessary to analyse the market both in the light of its history and recent developments. The Commission found:

(1) The French cigarette paper industry which previously commanded the market lost that position after 1945 and this led it to develop other papers.

(2) The participants faced strong competition from other manufacturers of cigarette paper both in the EEC and elsewhere – in particular from German and Italian manufacturers, in addition to competition in the Common Market to be expected from Austrian and American concerns. It was essential therefore for the participants to be competitive.

(3) On the demand side the market comprised on the one hand a few very substantial cigarette manufacturers (e.g. state monopolies in France and Italy and other manufacturers linked to multi-national companies) and on the other smaller manufacturers for whom it was essential to buy supplies of paper from the most competitive source.

(4) In the circumstances a balance existed between the forces of supply and demand on the market for cigarette paper, which is world-wide.

The Commission concluded:

"[24] In sum, in spite of the strong position of the participants in certain territories of the Common Market, the analysis of the market in question and of its special peculiarities does not give ground to fear that competition will be eliminated in a substantial part of the products in question on the Common Market by reason of the position of the purchasers, of the potential competition which exists between the parties to the agreement and the pressures exerted by the producers of other countries of the Common Market where no undertaking participates in the agreement, as well as by producers of non-member countries, none of them ignoring any market because, for the products in question, it is at the world level that competition plays."[1]

On the basis that full competition between the participants could be restored if the specialisation agreement was terminated by the parties at any time, the Commission granted exemption subject to certain obligations.[2] These were that the parties had to notify the Commission of:

(1) arbitral awards made with regard to interpretation or application of the provisions in the agreement regarding specialisation;

---

1 [1972] CMLR D94, at p. D101.
2 As to the power to impose obligations, see p. 289, below.

(2) the way in which the arrangements concerning specialisation worked after two years;

(3) the taking up of shares or any personal links between management organs of the participants, and any proposal for merger or takeover liable to occur between them or one of them and a third party in the thin paper sector.

Another Decision relating to an arrangement which contains an element of specialisation and which was approved by the Commission is *ACEC – Berliet*.[1] This has already been referred to in the section "Research and Devlopment".[2]

The following are short particulars of further Decisions relating to specialisation and other co-operation agreements where art. 85 (3) exemption has been given:

Re Jaz-Peter[3] – This was a specialisation agreement between French and German manufacturers of time pieces of all kinds allocating the manufacture of large mechanical clocks and electric clocks to Peter and Jaz respectively. Provision was made for the exchange of know-how and information and for exclusive dealing, each party distributing the other's products in the distributor's country under the latter's name. Exemption was granted on the ground of resulting improvement of distribution, production and technical progress, the other conditions for exemption also being found to be satisfied.

Re Clima-Buderus[4] – This was an agreement between French and German manufacturers of different types of temperature control, ventilation and heating apparatus by which each party was precluded from manufacturing specified apparatus within the other's range of products. Provision was made for exclusive dealing between the parties, each party also having preference for the supply to the other of products not covered by the agreement. Specialisation in research and development was implicit in the agreement. Exemption was granted in view of:

elimination of duplication in research and development expenditure and in investments;

increased sales resulting in greater productivity through economies of scale and better use of existing facilities;

consequent reduction of unit costs resulting in lower selling prices rendering the products more competitive;

---

1 *Re ACEC-Berliet*, 17 July 1968, JO 1968 L201/7; [1968] CMLR D35.
2 See p. 182, above.
3 *Re Agreement of Jaz SA*, 22 July 1969, JO 1969 L195/5; [1970] CMLR 129.
4 *Re Agreement of Clima Chappée SA*, 22 July 1969, JO 1969 L195/1; [1970] CMLR D7.

better production planning through assurance of orders consequent
on exclusive dealing;

greater client satisfaction by reason of offer of full range of products
by each party;

all of which *taken together* contributed to improvement of production
and distribution. The other conditions for exemption being satisfied,
the agreement was exempted under art. 85 (3).

Re Prym-Beka[1] – The benefit of specialisation was claimed in respect
of an agreement where one of the parties (Prym – a German manufacturer of needles for domestic sewing machines) ceased to manufacture altogether and transferred its manufacturing plant to its
competitor (Beka) (a Belgian undertaking) from which thereafter
Prym agreed to purchase all its supplies. The Commission exempted
the relevant agreement under arts. 85 (3) stating:

" . . the concentration of manufacturing agreed on by Prym and Beka
has, from the point of view of the improvement of production, favourable
effects analogous to those of specialization; it causes an increase of at
least 50 per cent in the quantity of needles to be manufactured in the Eupen
factory, which makes it possible to make more intensive use of the
existing plant and to introduce production-line manufacture.

This rationalization of production has in particular made it possible to
reduce the very large proportion of labour costs in the producer's cost
price."[2]

Re S.P.C.A. – Kali und Salz[3] – This is a case where exemption
sought under art. 85 (3) on the grounds of specialisation was not granted.

The agreement was between French (S.P.C.A.) and German (Kali
und Salz) trade associations of producers of potassium salts and provided for the control of production and of access to each other's national
markets. The parties pleaded that a consequence of the agreement
was that it allowed them to concentrate production (by not manufacturing a full range of products) and consequently to sell their own
products at lower prices. The Commission held that "in view of the
favourable supply situation . . . , there is no reason to suppose that,
were each undertaking acting on its own, it would be obliged, under
pressure of its customers' requirements, to manufacture products
whose cost of production would either in itself be excessive or would
have an unfavourable effect on the undertaking's prices".[4]

---

1 *Re Agreement of Prym-Werke KG, and SA Manufacture Belge d'Aiguilles Beka,* 8 October
1973, OJ 1973 L296/24; [1973] CMLR D250.
2 *Ibid.*, at p. 26.
3 11 May 1973, OJ 1973 L217/3; [1793] CMLR D219.
4 *Ibid.*, at p. 5.

Thus the participants' claim that the agreement led to improvement of production with ensuing benefit to consumers was not substantiated on the facts and exemption was accordingly refused.

SECTION 3 CONCENTRATION OF UNDERTAKINGS

Agreements relating to research and development and specialisation are forms of co-operation which do not usually imply any loss of ownership or control of the undertakings concerned, but merely constitute a means of regulating the competitive relationship between them. The present section is concerned with the application of arts. 85 and 86 to actual concentration of undertakings, that is, the act of bringing two or more undertakings under common control; the application of art. 85 to agreements between two or more undertakings already under common control has already been discussed.[1]

Under article 85

The EEC Commission issued in 1965 to the governments of member states a "Memorandum on the Concentration of Enterprises in the Common Market",[2] setting out the Commission's views regarding concentrations and the incidence thereon of arts. 85 and 86. The principal points made by the Memorandum were that:

(1) Concentrations, particularly across the internal EEC boundaries, are in principle desirable to enable undertakings to attain the necessary size to take advantage of the Common Market and to meet the competition of large undertakings from "third" countries.

(2) A concentration involves a permanent change in the internal structure of the undertakings concerned brought about by the transfer of property (shares or assets) or of management powers. While restriction of competition may result from concentrations, the restriction is the consequence of this structural change and not of an agreement between independent undertakings. Concentration and a restrictive agreement are therefore two essentially different things, although capable of having the same effect.

(3) While there are bound to be border-line cases where it will not be clear whether a particular grouping of businesses or undertakings or management powers involves concentration or a disguised form of restrictive agreement, if it is a concentration art. 85 will not apply even though brought about by agreement.

---

1 See Ch. 2, Section 6, p. 67, above.
2 A translation will be found in CCH Common Market Reports, No. 26, 17 March 1966, at p. 28.

The Commission's view that art. 85 does not apply to concentrations was contrary to the majority view of a working party of legal experts appointed by the Commission to study the question. While on a literal reading art. 85 could be said to apply to a concentration brought about by agreement, the true construction of the Treaty involves more than a literal interpretation and the Commission set out in the Memorandum various reasons why in its opinion a literal reading of the article would not be correct: the fact that mergers and restrictive agreements are usually treated under separate heads of legislation under national laws (e.g. in the United Kingdom, where the RTPA constitutes a distinct body of law from the monopolies and mergers legislation); and that states which have enacted legislation against restrictive practices have not always attempted to control concentrations, which the Memorandum attributes to the fact that while restrictive agreements are generally considered harmful until proved otherwise, concentrations are generally only considered harmful where they result in permissible limits of market power being exceeded. In the absence therefore of specific reference to concentrations in art. 85, its application to them cannot be implied; particularly as in the forerunner of the EEC Treaty, the ECSC Treaty, concentrations are specifically subject to the control of the Commission (art. 66). The Commission adduced certain other reasons of a technical nature tending to show that art. 85 cannot be made to apply to a merger.

All commentators do not agree with the Commission in its interpretation, but in practice the question must be treated as settled by the view which the Commission itself takes of the matter, as the enforcement authority.[1]

JOINT VENTURES

There is concentration where the undertakings concerned or all but one of them come under common control and cease to be independent. A joint venture, for example through a jointly owned company, is a special case of concentration in that there is only partial abandonment of independence by the founders who continue in business as independent undertakings. In such cases the Commission warns that it will be necessary to examine carefully whether in addition

---

1 See *Re SHV-Chevron*, 20 December 1974, OJ 1975 L38/14. Two suppliers of petroleum products, Chevron and SHV, vested their respective distribution systems in jointly owned subsidiaries (with SHV ceasing to be an independent wholesaler of such products), and the Commission treated this as a concentration between Chevron, SHV and the subsidiaries. While the Commission considered certain restrictions on competition with the subsidiaries accepted by Chevron and SHV (see p. 197, n. 3, below) under art. 85, the concentration itself was not questioned under art. 85.

to the structural changes brought about by the transfer of property to the joint company, there subsist agreements or concerted practices between the undertakings within the meaning of art. 85.[1]

Re Henkel-Colgate[2] involved exemption under art. 85 of a joint venture agreement relating to joint research. This case, however, gives no guidance in relation to the more usual types of joint ventures, e.g. those concerned with trading activities – so that the extent of the incidence of art. 85 to such ventures is still very much a matter of conjecture. It is on this conjectural basis that the following points are discussed in relation to art. 85.

(1) In so far as a joint venture can properly be classified as a concentration art. 85 does not apply to the mere setting up of the joint venture.

(2) Nevertheless it must be rare that a joint venture does not imply the acceptance of some restriction on competition by one or more of the undertakings concerned, i.e. the founders and the joint company itself, viz. restrictions on competition:

(a) by the founders against the jointly owned company;
(b) by the jointly owned company against the joint founders;
(c) between the founders.

(a) *Restrictions on competition by the joint founders against the jointly owned company*

The creation of a joint venture company involves the investment by each founder of money and other resources which are pooled within the joint company, the joint venturers reciprocally standing to profit from each other's contribution. But for the expectation of mutual benefit, the investments would never have been made so that restriction on competition by the founders against the jointly owned company should logically be permitted to ensure the success of the venture undertaken in common.[3]

As against this, it is said that a restriction on the joint venturers from competing against the joint venture company is only warranted

---

1 Memorandum on Concentration, p. 58; see p. 195, n. 2, above.
2 23 December 1971, JO 1972 L14/14; see p. 179, above.
3 For support of the view that the founders can properly be restrained from competing against the joint company, see P. van Ommeslaghe, "L'application des articles 85 et 86 du Traité de Rome aux fusions, pour groupes de societes et aux entreprises communes", 1967 Revue Trimestrielle de Droit Européen, 458. In Re *SHV-Chevron*, 20 December 1974, OJ 1975 L34/14, such restrictions by founders were given negative clearance, but only on the basis that they were not perceptible. The Decision does not, therefore, support the above submission; it does, however, include the statement that such restrictions ensure that the assets transferred to the joint company maintain their value.

if the joint venture is "deserving", in the sense that it enables an activity to be undertaken which would not otherwise be possible. A joint venture company could on the other hand be no more than a means employed by the founders for exploiting a market in co-operation rather than in competition.[1]

An example of the "deserving" joint venture would be the case of a United Kingdom company setting up a manufacturing plant in another EEC country by joining forces with a local company in the framework of a joint company, to which the United Kingdom company subscribes patent licences, knowhow, etc., and the local company land, buildings and essential local knowledge and connections. In such a case the agreement not to compete with the joint venture company should qualify for art. 85 (3) exemption.

(b) *Restrictions on competition by the jointly owned company against the joint founders*

If the founders wish to eliminate the risk of competition by their jointly owned company, they can achieve this by various devices written into its memorandum and articles of association – a limited objects clause, unanimous voting, etc. If this is permissible, no objection can logically be raised to an agreement by the founders that they will procure that the joint company will not compete against them. However, the joint venture may not be deserving and if it is correct that deserving joint ventures must be distinguished from those that are not the admissibility or otherwise of the restrictions accepted by the jointly owned company must be assessed in the context of all the circumstances.

(c) *Restrictions on competition between the joint founders*

It must be clear that any agreement between the joint founders restricting competition between them beyond the strict limits essential for the achievement of the objectives of the joint venture company will be within art. 85.[2]

Under article 86

If art. 85 is not considered by the Commission to be applicable to concentrations, contrary to the view of the group of experts mentioned above, the Commission has adopted their view that concentrations in which undertakings occupying a dominant position take part can in

---

1 For this view, see J. Mégret, *op. cit*, p. 261, where it is suggested that a restriction on competition by joint venturers against the joint company may be justifiable in certain cases but not in others.
2 *Re SHV-Chevron*, 20 December 1974, OJ 1975 L38/14.

certain circumstances be prohibited under art. 86 – a view endorsed by the Court of Justice, as we have seen in the *Continental Can* Case.[1] As already mentioned, the possible application of art. 86 to concentrations is extremely restricted since it is necessary that an already dominant undertaking should be involved in the concentration. The article has no application to a merger between two non-dominant undertakings notwithstanding that competition in the relevant market might as a result be completely eliminated – unless the interpretation of the article is further extended by the Court of Justice possibly along the lines already discussed.[2] Article 86 will, however, no longer need to be relied on to the same extent in relation to concentrations if the Regulation on the control of concentrations referred to below, is adopted.

The Regulation will confer on the Commission power, in effect, to prohibit concentrations where certain minima are exceeded in terms of the turnover and market shares of the undertakings concerned. Article 86 will however continue to be applicable in relation to concentrations which are outside the scope of the Regulation because such minima are not exceeded – the fact that they are not exceeded does not mean necessarily that one or more of the undertakings involved in the merger is not dominant – domination not being, as we have seen, necessarily dependent on a minimum market share or size of the undertaking.

PROPOSAL FOR A REGULATION ON THE CONTROL OF CONCENTRATIONS BETWEEN UNDERTAKINGS

The spread of concentrations in the EEC in recent years, many of them involving major undertakings, and the continuing trend towards concentration, with its concomitant threat to competitive conditions, has led the EEC to decide to institute a system of merger control; this decision was taken at the Paris Summit Conference of October 1972, in terms of the communique,[3] which states:

"The Heads of State or of Government consider it necessary to seek to establish a single industrial base for the Community as a whole. This involves the formulation of measures to ensure that mergers affecting firms

---

1 *Re Continental Can Co. Inc.*, 9 December 1971, JO 1972 L7/25; [1972] CMLR D11; on appeal *sub nom. Europemballage Corp. and Continental Can Co. Inc.* v. *EC Commission*, 21 February 1973, [1973] ECR 215; [1973] CMLR 199.
2 See pp. 163, 164, above.
3 Final Communiqué issued by the Heads of State or Government of the countries of the enlarged Community at their meeting in Paris on 19 and 20 October 1972, point 7.

established in the Community are in harmony with the economic and social aims of the Community, and the maintenance of fair competition as much within the Common Market as in external markets in conformity with the rules laid down by the treaties."

The communique further stated:

"it was desirable to make the widest possible use of all the provisions of the Treaties, including Article 235 of the EEC Treaty".

Article 235 to which reference is made above provides:

"If action by the Community should prove necessary to attain, in the course of the operation of the common market, one of the objectives of the Community and this Treaty has not provided the necessary powers, the Council shall, acting unanimously on a proposal from the Commission and after consulting the Assembly, take the appropriate measures."

The article is invoked in the present context having regard to the inadequacies of arts. 85 and 86 for the purpose of merger control. Article 85, as we have seen, is held by the Commission to be inapplicable to concentrations and, as we have also seen, the scope of art. 86, requiring as it does that an already dominant undertaking should be involved, is extremely restricted, not to speak of the general feeling that the extension of art. 86 to cover the *Continental Can* situation was at the limit of generally understood principles of legal construction.

In these circumstances, the Commission has now proposed for consideration by the Council of Ministers a draft Regulation on the Control of Concentrations between undertakings.[1] In view of the current climate favouring competition policy as a means of fighting inflation and the level at which the decision was taken, it may be anticipated that the Regulation will be adopted in the reasonably near future, albeit with some modifications, and the proposed Regulation is, therefore, set out in full in Appendix III, p. 393, below.

Essentially, the EEC scheme provides for a system of notification of mergers which, like the British, but unlike the US system, allows each merger to be considered on its merits.

The main provisions of the proposed Regulation are as follows:

(1) Under art. 1, the general principle is laid down that concentrations (defined in art. 2) involving at least one undertaking or group of undertakings established in the Common Market which give the power or enhance the power to hinder effective competition in the Common Market, or a substantial part thereof, are in effect prohibited –

---

1 OJ 1973 C92/1; see also the official explanatory memorandum to the Regulation in European Parliament Working Documents, 1 October 1973, doc. 170/73.

in so far as trade between member states may be affected. The article sets out considerations by reference to which the existence or otherwise of such power is to be assessed.

A concentration which does hinder effective competition will nevertheless not be caught:

(a) When the aggregate turnover of the undertakings participating in the concentration is less than 200 million units of account[1] *and* the goods or services concerned by the concentration do not account in any member state for more than 25% of the turnover in identical goods or services or, in short, goods which the consumer considers as substitutes.

It follows that the exception does not apply where an undertaking having a 25% market share of the relevant goods in, for example, France, but no market share in the United Kingdom, proposes to acquire an undertaking with a very small market share in the United Kingdom – such concentration would be within the Regulation but outside the Fair Trading Act (the 25% test under s. 64 (1) (a) not being satisfied), if it is assumed that the assets taken over do not exceed £5 million.[2]

The turnover, it will be noted, is to be general and not restricted to the goods or services concerned by the concentration.

(b) When the concentration is indispensable for attaining a priority Community objective. For the exception to apply a specific Decision of the Commission granting an individual authorisation will be required under art. 3 (4).

(2) Article 2 defines the concentrations which are to be within the Regulation as those whereby a person or an undertaking or group of persons or undertakings acquires control of one or several undertakings.

The article proceeds to define what constitutes (A) control, (B) acquisition of control.

(A) *Control*

Control is constituted by all such rights and contracts which, either separately or jointly, legally or in practice make it possible to determine how an undertaking shall operate. Article 2 (2) sets out a non-exhaustive list of rights and contracts constituting control which the report accompanying the draft Regulation explains to be largely inspired

---

1 The value of the unit of account is explained at p. 294, below.
2 Fair Trading Act 1973, s. 64 (1) (b).

by the notion of control developed in applying art. 66 (1) of the ECSC Treaty,[1] viz.:

  (i) ownership or the right to use all or part of the assets of an undertaking;
 (ii) rights or contracts which confer power to influence the composition, voting or decisions of the organs of an undertaking;
(iii) rights or contracts which make it possible to manage the business of an undertaking;
 (iv) contracts made with an undertaking concerning the computation or appropriation of its profits;
  (v) contracts made with an undertaking concerning the whole or an important part of supplies or outlets, where the duration of these contracts or the quantities to which they relate exceed what is usual in commercial contracts dealing with those matters.

The list extends, of course, the notion of control well beyond its meaning in the United Kingdom, particularly item (v).

(B) *Acquisition of control*

There may be acquisition of control not only by virtue of direct proprietary or contractual rights but also when the rights are capable of indirect exercise by virtue of powers or fiduciary relationships.

(3) Article 3 specifies that a decision "condemning" a concentration does not automatically render void the legal transactions relating to the concentration but when a concentration has already occurred the Commission may make such orders as may be necessary to restore conditions of competition, including orders for "unscrambling".[2]

(4) Under art. 4 concentrations involving undertakings whose aggregate turnover is not less than 1,000 million units of account[3] *must* be notified to the Commission.[4] Further concentrations need not, however, be notified when the turnover of undertakings to be acquired does not exceed 30 million units of account. Failure to notify a concentration intentionally or negligently is visited by fines.[5]

---

1 See, in particular, Decision No. 24/54 of 6 May 1954, JO ECSC, 11 May 1954, 345, laying down a regulation on what constitutes control of an undertaking.
2 The European Parliament has proposed that the text submitted by the Commission to the Council of Ministers should be amended to the effect that the Regulation applies even in the case of concentrations put into effect before the Regulation comes into force (OJ 1974 C23/19).
3 See p. 201, n. 1, above.
4 The European Parliament proposes that this sum should be the aggregate *annual* turnover.
5 Art. 13 of the proposed Regulation; cf. position under Reg. 17, p. 256, below.

Concentrations other than the above *may* be notified to the Commission.

The effect of the notification provisions has to be assessed in the light of arts. 6 and 17. Article 6 imposes on the Commission the obligation to commence proceedings within three months of notification or, if later, the date when full information required by the Commission is supplied or at any later date in a case where false or misleading information has been supplied. Without prejudice to the latter provision, a concentration will be automatically allowed if the Commission has not instituted proceedings within the three months or extended period above referred to.

Under art. 17 the Commission must publish its decision within 9 months after commencement of proceedings, subject to extension when the Commission has been forced to require formally the production of information by a decision or when it has found it necessary to order an investigation (under art. 12).

Thus even without any default on the part of the undertakings, an investigation of the proposed merger may take up to 12 months (3 months within which the Commission can decide to take proceedings plus the 9 months referred to above). This delay corresponds with a maximum period of 12 months in the United Kingdom under the Fair Trading Act (6 months within which a merger reference must be made[1] and 6 months within which the Monopolies Commission has to adjudicate on the reference[2]).

In summary, therefore, there are three degrees of concentration to be taken into account:

(a) concentrations which are outside the Regulation by reason of the limits stated in Article 1 not being attained;

(b) concentrations which by reason of the size of the undertakings have to be notified under art. 4;

(c) concentrations intermediate between (a) and (b): the concentration need not be notified but it may be subject to subsequent challenge by the Commission with possible disastrous results for the undertakings concerned. In such cases, therefore, undertakings would be advised to take advantage of the optional notification provision referred to because if this is done the Commission is required to start proceedings (as we have seen)

---

1 Fair Trading Act 1973, s. 64 (4) (a) and (b).
2 *Ibid.,* s. 70, but see subs. (2) which allows an extension of up to 3 months.

within three months of notification or "forever after hold its peace".

The remaining articles of the Regulation are concerned with procedural questions (which essentially follow the corresponding provisions of Regulation 17), and are set out in Appendix III, p. 339, below.

Chapter 8

Industrial Property Rights

SECTION 1 INDUSTRIAL PROPERTY RIGHTS AND THE RESTRICTION OF TRADE BETWEEN MEMBER STATES

In general

Industrial property rights in the terminology of the Rome Treaty are rights such as patents, trade marks and copyright[1] for which the more usual expression in the United Kingdom is "intellectual property rights". The expression industrial property right is used in the authentic English version of the Treaty and it is therefore used here.

The essential feature of an industrial property right is that it is a monopoly or exclusivity granted by the state or recognised by law, conferring on the owner special rights or protection within the boundary of the state. Only the patentee or his assignee or licensee can make articles or carry out processes in accordance with the patented invention in the United Kingdom or import such articles into the United Kingdom for the duration of the patent. Only the registered owner of the trade mark or his assignee or licensee can mark products with the trade mark in the United Kingdom. No person other than the author or his licensee can reproduce his work in the United Kingdom. The words "in the United Kingdom" are common to each industrial property right described and reflect the territorial principle of industrial property rights.

Industrial property rights have also this in common: that while only the owner of the right or his licensee is entitled to sell in the first instance the product protected by the relevant industrial property right in the United Kingdom, the product can be resold thereafter by any person who has acquired the product legitimately, at any rate in the absence of some agreement or other legal provision to the contrary binding on the reseller. If, however, the resale were to

---

1 But see p. 261, below, for other rights which may also be considered to be industrial property rights.

involve the delivery of the goods abroad (eg. to another EEC country) where they might be protected by a corresponding patent or registered trade mark, their importation into that country could, subject to the provisions of the relevant national law, be prohibited as infringing the corresponding foreign patent or trade mark or other industrial property right.

It is seen therefore that industrial property rights on the one hand constitute legal means of preventing the movement of goods across international borders and on the other that, in so far as the ideal of the Common Market is to establish one undivided market, national industrial property legislation can be inconsistent with this ideal – an ideal which requires that circulation of goods protected by industrial property rights should be at least as free within the boundaries of the EEC as within the boundaries of the individual state which has granted the rights.

The Treaty specifically recognises national industrial property rights under art. 222 of the Treaty[1] and a reconciliation has to be attempted between, on the one hand, the exercise of such rights and, on the other hand, a basic principle of the Common Market, namely the free movement of goods within its borders. This was not a simple task having regard to art. 36 of the Treaty,[1] which, after providing that the prohibitions to the free movement of goods within the Common Market can, in spite of the specific provisions of arts. 30 to 34, in fact be derogated from "for the protection of industrial property rights", adds that the derogation shall "not constitute a means of arbitrary discrimination or a disguised restriction on trade between Member States". Where is the line to be drawn? This question has been the subject of several judgments of the Court of Justice, the effect of which may be summarised as follows: the existence of industrial property rights is recognised by EEC law; but their exercise may be prevented or restricted when (1) it is abusive, that is the exercise is made otherwise than for the *bona fide* protection of the particular right which it is the *essential purpose* of the relevant industrial property right to protect; and (2) its effect is to frustrate the objectives of the EEC's competition policy – as when the exercise of the right prevents the free movement of goods. Metaphorically, the conception is that while the ownership of a motor car is allowed, its use may in certain circumstances be prevented, e.g. when the alcohol content of the driver's blood exceeds a certain level.

The distinction between the existence of an industrial property right on the one hand and its exercise on the other as a means of bringing about the reconciliation referred to in the preceding para-

---

1 Set out in Appendix I, below.

graph was first drawn by the Court of Justice in the *Grundig* Case[1] in relation to trade marks; the *Parke Davis* Case[2] in relation to patents; and the *Deutsche Grammophon* Case[3] as regards copyright (at any rate as regards a special kind of copyright known to German law, which, it is submitted, for present purposes is essentially indistinguishable from ordinary copyright). But whatever the industrial property right, the underlying principle is the same, namely that the exercise of the right is not *per se* prohibited. It can be exercised when, but for the exercise, the owner of the right would be deprived of the essential protection or benefit which it is the purpose of the relevant industrial property right to confer – i.e., in the case of a patent and copyright, proper financial reward to be expected from the monopoly position of the patent or copyright owner; in the case of a trade mark protection against deception.

The use of an industrial property right to obtain something more or collateral out of the exercise of the right is however forbidden. For example, in relation to patents it is forbidden for a patentee who has received (or, perhaps, who has been in a position to claim) the reward of his patent monopoly to use the patent or a corresponding patent to isolate a particular national market within the EEC; and similarly, in relation to trade marks, it is forbidden for the owner of a trade mark to use it in order to isolate a national market by preventing the importation of goods bearing the mark where the mark is used under authority from the trade mark owner or his predecessor in title.

Since the subject of this book is essentially the EEC's competition policy under arts. 85 and 86, the reader naturally will expect to find an agreement or concerted practice or the abuse of a dominant position at the root of an improper use of an industrial property right in the way described above. As regards art. 86, the reader is referred to p. 225, below, but as regards the incidence of art. 85, it is important to point out that while the improper use in the way described above of an industrial property right will more often than not result from an agreement, the existence of an agreement is not essential. In the absence of an agreement, the prohibition of such improper use results from art. 36 which, as we have seen, provides that the exercise of an industrial property right "must not constitute a means of arbitrary discrimination or a disguised restriction on trade between Member States".

---

1 *Etablissements Consten SA and Grundig Verkaufs-GmbH* v. *EEC Commission,* 13 July 1966, XII Rec. 429; [1966] CMLR 418; see p. 14, above.
2 *Parke, Davis & Co.* v. *Probel,* 29 February 1968, XIV Rec. 81; [1968] CMLR 47.
3 *Deutsche Grammophon GmbH* v. *Metro-SB-Grossmärkte GmbH,* 8 June 1971, XVII Rec. 487; [1971] CMLR 631.

These general remarks will, it is hoped, become clear in the context of the actual decided cases which are summarised below.

Trade marks

THE CONSTEN-GRUNDIG CASE[1]

The reader will have seen from the facts more fully set out at p. 14, above, that Grundig's trade mark "GINT" was registered in France by agreement with Grundig in the name of Consten (Grundig's French distributor) so that the latter could use it to prevent the parallel import into France of Grundig products bearing the same mark. Such use (by agreement between Grundig and Consten) of the trade mark not for the purpose of preventing the public being misled or confused as to the origin of the goods, but to isolate the French market, was held to infringe art. 85 (1).

RE TRANSOCEAN MARINE PAINT[2]

The fact that the mark "Transocean", which was registered in the names of the members of the Transocean Marine Paint Association in their respective countries, could have been used to prevent imports into one member state of the EEC from another member state, was nevertheless held not to prevent the exemption of the association agreement under art. 85 (3)[3] – since to have used the mark in this way would have constituted an abuse prohibited as a result of the *Consten-Grundig* Case.

RE REMINGTON RAND[4]

The Italian subsidiary of the Sperry Rand Corporation and licensed user of the trade mark "Remington" in Italy brought infringement proceedings against another Italian company which had imported Remington razors from another EEC country. The proceedings were abandoned on the Commission taking the view that the licensing agreement, as interpreted and applied by the parties, infringed art. 85 (1) in that the use made of the agreement against the importer

---

1 *Re Grundig*, 23 September 1964, JO 1964 161,2545; [1964] CMLR 489; on appeal *sub. nom. Etablissements Consten SA and Grundig Verkaufs-GmbH* v. *EC Commission*, 13 July 1966, XII Rec. 429; [1966] CMLR 418.
2 *Re Transocean Marine Paint Association*, 27 June 1967, JO 1967 163/10; [1967] CMLR D9; the facts of the Decision are fully explained at p. 87, above.
3 See p. 90, above.
4 Bulletin 1969 No. 8, p. 40.

"was not concerned with action against imitations, since the electric razors imported into Italy legitimately bore an authentic Remington trade mark, but the intention was to prevent him from importing razors into Italy from other Common Market countries. The agreement thus applied, ensuring absolute territorial protection to Remington Rand Italia, affected trade between Member States and restricted competition in the products in question, by pursuing objectives unconnected with the proper function of the trade mark."[1]

THE SIRENA CASE[2]

This case is illuminating not only in relation to what is an improper use of a trade mark but also as to what constitutes an "agreement" for the purposes of art. 85.[3] The case came before the Court of Justice on reference from an Italian Court under art. 177.

The Italian Court wished to know whether arts. 85 and 86 prevented the Italian undertaking Sirena from asserting its registered trade mark "Prep" to prevent the sale in Italy under the same trade mark of similar products made in Germany by another manufacturer – the German manufacturer being entitled to the use of the same trade mark in Germany under rights derived from an American firm, being the same firm which had previously, indeed as far back as 1937, also conferred the right on Sirena to use the trade mark in Italy.

The problem arose when the German "Prep" product began to be imported into Italy at prices considerably lower than Sirena's "Prep" product and Sirena wished to prevent these imports by an infringement action. The importer set up the defence that Sirena's action was in breach of art. 85. The question asked of the Court of Justice under art. 177 was in particular whether arts. 85 and 86 must be interpreted to the effect that they prevent the owner of a trade mark validly registered in one member state from exercising the corresponding absolute right to prohibit third parties from importing from other member states of the Community products bearing the same trade mark *originally lawfully affixed*.

To this question the Court of Justice answered that art. 85 "applies where, by virtue of trade mark rights, imports of products originating in other member-States bearing the same trade mark because their owners have acquired the trade mark itself or the right to use it through agreements with one another or with third parties, are prevented".[4]

---

1 Bulletin 1969 No. 8, p. 40.
2 *Sirena SRL* v. *Eda SRL,* 18 February 1971, XVII Rec. 69; [1971] CMLR 260.
3 Discussed in this connection at p. 17, above.
4 [1971] CMLR 260, at p. 275.

This answer, to be fully understood, must be read in conjunction with the reasoning of the Court expressed in the Judgment. It may be analysed as follows:

(a) a trade mark right is a right granted by the state and is not as such any kind of agreement which could bring art. 85 into play;

(b) agreements however can come into being in connection with licences or assignments of the trade mark;

(c) if by reason of licences or assignments, i.e. by agreement, trade mark rights become exercisable by different persons, the intent of the agreement constituted by the licence or assignment could be that the trade mark rights should be used to prevent imports; that is to say, the agreement would have as its *object* the prevention of competition within the Common Market;

(d) that in any event such might be the *effect* of licences or assignments, i.e. agreements;

(e) accordingly when, as a result of a licence or assignment, a trade mark comes to be owned or exercisable by different persons, the licence or assignment may constitute an agreement caught by art. 85 (1) – unless it escapes because some other criterion of applicability is not satisfied, such as that it does not in fact restrict competition (which could be the case where the parties have agreed that the trade mark rights should not be asserted within the EEC against parallel imports) or there is in fact no appreciable effect on trade between member states by reason of any exercise of the trade mark rights.[1]

It must be emphasised that in the *Sirena* Case as in the cases mentioned above the imported German "Prep" product bore the relevant trade mark legitimately. Here again, however, we have no doubt that Sirena would not have been impeded by art. 85 from pursuing its infringement action against a mere infringer, that is to say someone having no right or title whatsoever to the use of the trade mark "Prep". In such case Sirena would have been protecting the very right which is the essence of a trade mark.

THE HAG CASE[2]

While in the preceding cases the use of trade marks to prevent imports involved infringement of art. 85 on the basis that the use for that purpose was the consequence or effect of an agreement, in the

---

1 *Re Advocaat Zwarte Kip*, 24 July 1974, OJ 1974 L237/12; [1974] 2 CMLR D79, shows that an appreciable effect on trade always results from the exercise of trade mark rights.
2 *Van Zuylen Frères* v. *Hag AG*, 3 July 1974, [1974] ECR 731; [1974] 2 CMLR 127.

present case such use of a trade mark, even in the absence of agreement, was held by the Court of Justice to be prohibited on the basis of art. 36 of the Treaty.

HAG AG, a German company, was the original patentee of a process for the manufacture of decaffeinated coffee; HAG AG marketed the coffee under the name HAG, which was registered as a trade mark in Germany, Belgium and Luxembourg. In 1927 the Belgian and Luxembourg marks were transferred by HAG AG to its Belgian subsidiary HAG SA. As a consequence of the second world war the shares of HAG SA vested in the Belgian Custodian of Enemy Property who sold them to a Belgian family. In 1971 HAG SA sold the Belgian and Luxembourg trade marks (but not its business) to a private company, Van Zuylen Frères (VZF), under which VZF would market decaffeinated coffee purchased from HAG SA.

In 1972 HAG AG began to export to Luxembourg decaffeinated coffee under its original German HAG trade mark. VZF instituted infringement proceedings before the Luxembourg courts and the question arose whether VZF's infringement action could be maintained in view of the provisions of art. 85 and/or arts. 5, 30 and, particularly, 36 of the Treaty. The question was referred to the Court of Justice for a ruling under art. 177.

The Court considered that HAG SA, though originally a subsidiary of HAG AG, had become independent by operation of law and found, considering the absence of any legal, financial, technical or economic link between the German and Belgian trade mark owners, that art. 85 did not apply. Thus the question fell to be answered only in the context of the rules relating to the free circulation of goods. The Court held that it was incompatible with the provisions of the Treaty relating to the free circulation of goods to prevent the sale in a member state of a product originating from another member state under a trade mark which is lawful in the exporting country on the grounds only of the existence in the importing country of an identical mark having the same origin; and the situation is the same whether the goods bearing the foreign trade mark are sold by the owner of the trade mark or by his successors in title.

Thus in relation to trade marks, in so far as any doubts subsisted prior to the *HAG* Case as to the significance to be attached to the proviso concerning industrial property rights in art. 36 of the Treaty, these have been conclusively resolved by the *HAG* Case, which confirms that trade mark rights can only be invoked against purely spurious products. The Court was not concerned that imports into one EEC country of other goods of different origin bearing the same trade mark might cause confusion, stating "if the indication of the origin of a product is useful, the information can be ensured by means which do not hinder the free movement of goods." This aspect of the Court's Judgment is further referred to below in relation to *Re Advocaat*.

RE ADVOCAAT[1]

In this Decision the Commission applied the principle, confirmed by the Court of Justice in the *Sirena* Case, that there is no objection to the assignment or sub-licensing of a trade mark as such, provided the protection afforded by trade mark registration in different member states is not used in a manner which derogates from the principle of the primacy of the free movement of goods within the Community. The Decision also illustrates the *HAG* Case, in so far as it held that consumer protection through trade marks must be subordinated to the principle of the free movement of goods within the Community.

In 1938 VB Van Olffen of Hattem (Van Olffen), a Dutch company manufacturing the liqueur advocaat and owner of the registered trade mark "Advocaat Zwarte Kip" in various countries, entered into an agreement with Thissen transferring to the latter the right to manufacture and sell advocaat in Belgium and Luxembourg under such trade mark provided nothing was done to damage the reputation of the mark. Various assignments of the Belgian and Benelux trade marks took place and in 1955 Cinoco SA of Brussels (Cinoco) became the registered owner of the trade marks. In 1971 a quantity of Advocaat Zwarte Kip manufactured by Van Olffen under its Dutch trade mark was imported by a dealer into Belgium and Cinoco sued for infringement of the Belgian mark. The Commission was apprised and found, on the basis of the wording of the 1938 agreement, subsequent events and correspondence between Van Olffen and Cinoco, that the agreement was intended to partition the Common Market and caused a substantial restriction of potential competition and affected trade between member states and therefore infringed art. 85. The Commission also refused exemption under art. 85 (3) for the technical reason that the agreement had not been notified and for the further reason that the agreement did not contribute to any improvement in the production or distribution of goods, or promote either technical or economic progress, but that, on the contrary, the effect of the agreement was to hinder the distribution of advocaat.

In the proceedings before the Commission Cinoco argued that in this case the partitioning of the markets was justified by the quality

---

1 *Re Advocaat Zwarte Kip*, 24 July 1974, OJ 1974 L237/12; [1974] 2 CMLR D79.

difference between the Dutch and the Belgian products, in particular that the Dutch product contained about 14° of alcohol whilst the Belgian product contained 18°. The Commission stated in its Decision that a difference of quality could not justify a partitioning of markets explaining that:

> "A supplier is entitled to indicate on the packaging of his product its composition, origin, and alcoholic content. Van Olffen in fact states the alcoholic content on the bottle, whilst Cinoco indicates the origin of the products sold by it. The consumer is in danger of being misled only if the supplier omits to state either the composition or the origin of a product. The importation by Soenen of advocaat manufactured and put into circulation by Van Olffen has not harmed the interest of the consumer, but has, if anything, benefited it, by allowing the consumer the opportunity of purchasing advocaat manufactured by Van Olffen's new processes – and moreover at a lower price. It is ultimately for the consumer to decide the effect he will allow a difference in quality to have on the choice he alone must make."[1]

The *HAG* Judgment and the *Advocaat* Decision have caused some consternation. Any lingering hopes that traders may have had that *Sirena* was but an aberration have been dashed – and within the EEC we may well see products with identical names, with identiacl get-up, posing "traps" for the unwary buyer. The circumspect buyer will, of course, read carefully the information which manufacturers cannot hereafter but display prominently on their goods as to their quality and origin in order to prevent foreign competitors from benefiting gratuitously from the goodwill of a national producer acquired laboriously and/or at great expense over the years. But the process is reciprocal, and if the United Kingdom market can be invaded by, say, Dutch products of the same name and presentation as the corresponding United Kingdom product, to the confusion of the English housewife, her counterpart in Holland will have to face the same hazards. There is, of course, a difference between cases where a product which is put on the market under the same name is essentially the same product as where companies in the same group manufacture to the same general specification, subject only to very minor variations to take account of local conditions at the point of sale, and cases where, as in *Sirena*, the German and Italian "Prep" products developed quite separately so that between the German and Italian products there was perhaps nothing in common but the name "Prep", and that both products were in fact after-shave preparations.

---

1 *Ibid.*, at p. 14.

It is difficult to see a solution to this particular problem and it would seem that the possibilities of confusion described above have to be accepted, at any rate if the view is taken that they appear to be relatively insignificant when measured against the advantages of a common market in Europe.

THE CENTRAFARM/WINTHROP CASE[1]

This case is one of two cases decided by the Court of Justice as this book was going through the press. Both cases enshrine the principle of the primacy of the free movement of goods over industrial property rights – the *Centrafarm/Winthrop* Case in relation to trade marks, and the *Centrafarm/Sterling* Case[2] in relation to patents.

The *Centrafarm/Winthrop* Case concerned a drug marketed in Holland by Winthrop BV under the trade name Negram, of which it is the registered owner in that country – Winthrop BV being the wholly-owned subsidiary of Sterling Winthrop Group Limited (an English Company) which markets the drug in the United Kingdom under the same trade mark. Centrafarm BV (a Dutch company) purchased the product in the United Kingdom for resale in Holland where it fetched higher prices than in the United Kingdom, the price in the United Kingdom being lower as a result of the government's price control policies. Winthrop BV, on the importation of the goods into Holland, brought infringement proceedings in respect of its Dutch trade mark, and on reference by the Dutch Court under art. 177 of the Treaty the Court of Justice held:

(A) The exercise of trade mark rights by their owner in a member state to prevent the sale of a product first sold in another member state by such owner or with his consent, is incompatible with the rules relating to the free circulation of goods.

(B) It is immaterial that a lower price ruling in the exporting country is due to price controls operated by the authorities of that country.

While distortion of competition through subsidies and price controls is very much the concern of the EEC the solution lies in measures to bring about harmonisation in economic policy and in the granting of state aids. In the meantime distortion in one member state should not allow another member state to maintain or introduce measures contrary to the rules relating to the free movement of goods, in particular

---

1 *Centrafarm BV and Adriaan de Peijper* v. *Winthrop BV,* 31 October 1974, [1974] 2 CMLR 480.
2 *Centrafarm BV and Adriaan de Peijper* v. *Sterling Drug Inc.,* 31 October 1974, [1974] 2 CMLR 480; this Case is discussed at p. 220, below.

in the area of industrial and commercial property rights (paragraphs 16 and 17 of the Judgment).

> (C) The owner of a trade mark relating to a pharmaceutical product cannot be exempted from the rules relating to the free circulation of goods on the ground of the need to protect the public against defective products.

While it is correct that art. 36 permits derogation from the rules relating to the free movement of goods in the interests of the protection of public health, this is to be achieved through the enforcement by national health authorities of appropriate regulations and not by misapplication of the rules governing the scope of industrial property rights (paragraphs 20 and 21 of the Judgment).

> (D) Article 42 of the Accession Treaty of the three new member states does not apply to prevent imports into the Netherlands prior to 1 January 1975 of goods put on the market in the United Kingdom by the owner of a trade mark or with his consent.

> (E) Article 85 of the Treaty is not directed at agreements or concerted practices between undertakings in the relationship of parent and subsidiary, if the undertakings together form an economic unit within which the subsidiary does not enjoy real autonomy in determining its conduct on the market.

Whilst it is possible for a group of companies without infringing art. 85 to regulate internally their marketing arrangements, e.g., to the effect that Company A will only supply Country A, the group must not attempt to prevent imports in derogation of the rules relating to the free movement of goods as interpreted by the Court and not least in the Judgment now discussed. This ruling is in line with previous decisions of the Commission and judgments of the Court of Justice in relation to the application of art. 85 where groups of companies are concerned.[1]

Finally it will be remembered that a derogation from the principle of free movement of goods within the Community is permitted under art. 36 of the Treaty where this is justified on the ground of the "protection of industrial and commercial property" – but that such protection can only be invoked in relation to what is inherent in or specific to the relevant property. The Court of Justice in paragraph 8 of the *Centrafarm/Winthrop* Judgment defined the specific object of a trade mark as the exclusive right to use the trade mark for the purpose of effecting the first sale of a product, thus protecting the owner of the

---

1 See p. 67, above.

trade mark against competitors who would abuse the status and reputation of the trade mark by the sale of products improperly bearing such trade mark.

Copyright

THE DEUTSCHE GRAMMOPHON CASE[1]

Briefly the facts of the case are that Deutsche Grammophon (DG), a manufacturer of records, itself effected t!.e distribution of its records in Germany by selling to retail and wholesale trade outlets on terms involving the imposition of a fixed selling price to the ultimate consumer of the records – a retail price maintenance system then permitted, under certain conditions, in Germany. As regards other countries, including EEC countries, the distribution was through licensees of DG (both DG's own subsidiaries and also other companies) under which the licensees were given the exclusive right in their respective territories to exploit DG's recordings. These recordings were protected in Germany by an industrial property right akin to copyright conferred by art. 85 of the German Copyright Law by virtue of which the manufacturer of a recording has the exclusive right of reproduction and distribution.

Metro, another German company, obtained DG recordings from Polydor, DG's French subsidiary and licensee, being records which DG had delivered to Polydor. Metro was not bound by any agreement with DG regarding resale price maintenance and proceeded to resell the records in Germany at considerably less than the maintained price.

DG brought proceedings before the German court alleging infringements of its rights under the German Copyright Law. Metro contended that such rights had been "exhausted" by the marketing of the recordings by Polydor. DG contested this on the ground that a German industrial property right could not be affected, in view of the territorial basis of the application of such rights, by anything done outside Germany – in this case by the first marketing of the records outside Germany.

On reference from the German court under art. 177 the Court of Justice held:

> "1. It conflicts with the provisions regarding the free movement of goods in the Common Market if a manufacturer of recordings so *exercises*[2]

---

1 *Deutsche Grammophon GmbH* v. *Metro-SB-Grossmärkte GmbH*, 8 June 1971, XVII Rec. 487; [1971] CMLR 631.
2 Authors' emphasis.

the exclusive right granted to him by the legislation of a member-State to market the protected articles as to prohibit the marketing in that member-State of products that have been sold by him himself [*sic*] or with his consent in another member-State solely because this marketing has not occurred in the territory of the first member-State."[1]

In other and plainer words, in relation to the special German copyright in question, it is not permissible for the owner of such right to exercise it in relation to products first sold outside Germany *when the seller is the owner of the right or when the products were sold under licence from the owner.*

The Judgment is not explicit as to the reason for this qualification but from the general discussion below of the *Parke Davis* Case, decided before the present Case, it may be assumed that the underlying thinking was that DG had the possibility of benefiting from its copyright in Germany and that if it voluntarily denied itself this possibility by first distributing the products in France, through its French subsidiary, there was no longer any good reason for derogating from the principle of the free movement of goods within the Community.

The question which immediately arose after the *Deutsche Grammophon* Case was whether it was relevant not only to the special case of German copyright attaching to records but also to copyright in general and to patents and trade marks. Spokesmen of the Commission,[2] as the enforcing authority of the competition policy of the EEC, were not prepared to find any essential difference between the German copyright in question and general copyright, patent and trade mark protection, such that the *Deutsche Grammophon* Case would not be applicable to the latter, but certain other opinion has contested this. However, this question must now be regarded as settled by the recent *Centrafarm/Sterling*[3] and *Centrafarm/Winthrop*[4] Cases, which apply the *Deutsche Grammophon* principle to patents and trade marks respectively.

Patents

THE PARKE DAVIS CASE[5]

Parke Davis owned Dutch patents in relation to an antibiotic. Probel and others imported into Holland antibiotics covered by the

1 [1971] CMLR 631, at p. 659.
2 See the 5th Annual General Report, p. 452/3, and the Commission's 1st Report on Competition Policy, April 1972, sec. 67.
3 *Centrafarm BV and Adriaan de Peijper* v. *Sterling Drug Inc.*, 31 October 1974, [1974] 2 CMLR 480; see p. 220, below.
4 *Centrafarm BV and Adriaan de Peijper* v. *Winthrop BV*, 31 October 1974, [1974] 2 CMLR 480; see p. 214, above.
5 *Parke, Davis & Co.* v. *Probel*, 29 February 1968, XIV Rec. 81, [1968] CMLR 47.

patent which had been made in Italy, where no patent protection for drugs is available. Parke Davis brought proceedings against the importers in Holland in respect of the infringement of its Dutch patents. The Dutch court requested a ruling from the Court of Justice under art. 177, as to whether the infringement action brought to prevent imports of a product from an EEC country where it is not patentable was contrary to the Treaty, having regard to the provisions of arts. 85 and 86, considered, if necessary, in conjunction with arts. 36 and 222 of the Treaty.

The Court of Justice held (1) that the rights granted by member states to the holder of a patent are not affected as regards their *existence* by the prohibitions of art. 85 or 86 of the Treaty, and (2) the *exercise* of those rights would not in itself fall under art. 85 (1) in the absence of any agreement, decision or concerted practice referred to in that provision, or under art. 86 in the absence of any improper exploitation of a dominant position.

The Court of Justice's answer opened the way for the Dutch court to find in favour of Parke Davis provided it was satisfied, on the one hand, that apart from the exercise of the patent right there was no infringement of art. 85, and, on the other, that the circumstances of the exercise of the patent right were not such as to constitute improper exploitation of a dominant position – as to which see p. 225 below.

However, it is essential to note that one of the premises of the *Parke Davis* Judgment was that the goods in question were manufactured in a member state of the EEC in which the relevant product was not patentable and that another premise was that there was no connection between Parke Davis and the manufacturer of the goods. If the Court had dealt with the question raised by the assertion of Parke Davis of its patent rights on the assumption that patent protection was available in the country where the product was first marketed and/or that this marketing had been effected by a firm connected with Parke Davis – it is difficult to say what conclusion the Court would have reached at the time (1968) having regard to the difficulties of the questions raised by these assumptions and the opposing opinions held at the time in relation to the relative importance to be attached to the maintenance of industrial property rights on the one hand and the free movement of goods within the EEC on the other.

The questions in issue here originate in the very nature of patent rights. A patent right may be regarded as a monopoly granted by the state for a limited period to encourage invention (by the enhanced pecuniary reward to be expected by the patentee as a result of the monopoly which his patent confers) and to encourage public disclosure of inventions. In the framework of a national system, the patentee can claim this reward at various stages of the production and marketing arrangements applicable to the patented product (e.g. as part of the purchase price on the sale of the product or as royalty for a licence to manufacture or use) but once a patented product has come into the hands of a purchaser, it ceases, subject to any limitations on the rights of a purchaser imposed under a national law, to be subject to the patentee's rights either by reason of an implied licence granted by the seller, as under the British system, or by virtue of the principle of exhaustion of the patent right as under German and other continental systems. In so far as the patentee has on or before the sale to a first purchaser failed to reap the benefit of his patent monopoly, he cannot do so thereafter from any subsequent purchaser and the product must then be able to circulate freely within the boundaries of the state which has granted the patent.

It follows that if the EEC is to constitute a single market, the free circulation of a patented product once it has been marketed should extend to the whole of the EEC. This concept will pose no problem when the whole of the territory of the Common Market is the subject of a unitary patent system.

As we shall see, such a patent system will in all probability be adopted, though the expected date of coming into force (1976) seems, at present, optimistic. In the meantime, the position is that in different EEC states not only does the extent of patent protection vary enormously (in some states such as Germany a patent is practically a guarantee of its validity while in others it is little more than evidence of registration) but, further, in certain states a particular type of product or process may not be patentable at all (as in the case of pharmaceutical products in Italy) while it is in others, and it follows that in a country where patent protection is weak, or not available, the patentee may not be able to command the same reward for his invention as in a country where the patent is strong.

The fact that the *Parke Davis* Case was concerned with pharmaceutical products originating in a country where they were not patentable made it relatively easy for the Court of Justice to reach the conclusion which it did, particularly on the basis that the marketing in Italy was not done by, or under licence from, Parke Davis. The Court argued that since Parke Davis had not received the reward attributable to its patented process when the product in question was put on the market in Italy, it was entitled to claim it on the entry of the product into Holland where Parke Davis did enjoy patent protection.

But what would be the case if a product is patentable in another EEC state but protection under such patent is either not applied for, or if applied for is refused? Could Parke Davis in such a case assert its

Dutch patent on the entry of the infringing products into Holland?
Or would this be an unwarranted interference with inter-state trade?
And does the answer depend on who has marketed the product in the
other EEC state, i.e. an independent third party or a licensee of Parke
Davis or a company associated with Parke Davis? A first indication
of how these questions should be answered was given by the Court of
Justice in the *Deutsche Grammophon* Case, discussed above, and many,
though not all, of these questions have been resolved by the recent
Centrafarm/Sterling Case, decided by the Court of Justice as this book
was going through the press, which is discussed immediately below.

THE CENTRAFARM/STERLING CASE[1]

Sterling Drug Inc. was, in relation to the process of manufacturing
a certain drug (the subject of the *Centrafarm/Winthrop* Case already
discussed[2]), the registered owner of patents in various countries
including the United Kingdom and the Netherlands. Centrafarm BV
(a Dutch company) purchased the patented product in the United
Kingdom for resale in Holland where it fetched higher prices than in
the United Kingdom, the price in the United Kingdom being lower
as a result of the government's price control policies. Sterling Drug
Inc. sued for infringement of its Dutch patent and on reference by the
Dutch court under art. 177 of the Treaty the Court of Justice held:

(A) The exercise of patent rights by a patentee in a member state
to prevent the sale of a product which has first been sold in
another member state by the patentee or with his consent, is
incompatible with the rules relating to the free circulation of
goods.

The following points may be noted in connection with this ruling:

(a) It is immaterial whether a patentee (or licensee) using the patent
to prevent imports of a product is a manufacturer of the same product
or not. The Danish government submitted to the Court that to prevent
the use by a manufacturer of his patent to stop the importation of goods
manufactured in another EEC country in the circumstances stated in
the Court's ruling would undermine "the legal basis and the economic
conditions of the exploitation of patents by industry" – and pointed
to the Protocol of the Community Patent Convention which contemplated a transitional period before such a fundamental change in

---

1 *Centrafarm BV and Adriaan de Peijper* v. *Sterling Drug Inc.*, 31 October 1974, [1974]
2 CMLR 480.
2 See p. 214, above.

the law is made.[1] The Court did not accept the Danish government's submission, drawing in its ruling no distinction between patentees who were manufacturers and those who were not.

(b) Patent rights may, however, be exercised so as to prevent the free movement of goods within the Community against a product emanating from a member state where it is not patentable and which has been manufactured without the consent of the patentee. This is stated in paragraph 11 of the Judgment and is a reference back to and confirmation of the Court's Judgment in the *Parke Davis* Case[2].

It seems, then, that if a patentee in country A wishes to prevent imports from country B where the relevant goods are patentable he must actually take out a parallel patent in country B as a pre-condition of exercising his patent rights in country A. Could the Court be said to be treating the failure of a patentee in one member state to take out a parallel patent in another member state as an implicit licence to persons in that other member state to make and sell the goods protected by the patent?

(c) In the same paragraph 11 the Court, assuming that it was possible for separate patents to exist in different countries but which covered the same invention and which had originally been taken out by legally and economically independent persons, considered that in such a case the exercise of patent rights against imports could also be justified.

(d) Sterling Drug Inc. submitted to the Court that insofar as a patentee may be permitted (as in the *Parke Davis* Case) to exercise his patent to prevent imports from a country where he does not enjoy parallel protection, the divergencies in the various member states as to the conditions of the grant of a patent and the extent of the protection conferred by the patent raised difficult questions for a national court called upon to determine the scope of any patent protection conferred in the exporting country. The Court of Justice in paragraph 14 of the Judgment held, with regard to this submission (amounting in the Court's view to the proposition that truly parallel patents did not exist), that what matters is the equivalence of the invention covered under each patent and that this was a matter for the appreciation of the national court.

(e) It is to be noted that what is prohibited under the Court's ruling is the use of patent rights to prevent imports where the relevant goods have first been sold in another member state by the patentee or with his consent. This seems to allow the use of patent rights to prevent

---

1 The Convention and Protocol are discussed at pp. 223–225, below.
2 See pp. 217ff, above.

direct exports by the patentee or his licensees to a member state from another member state.

In this connection it will be remembered that an exclusive distribution agreement does not forfeit the exemption by category under Regulation 67/67 by reason of the prohibition on the exclusive distributor against "invading" the territory of another distributor.[1] Correspondingly there would seem to be no reason why, in the case where a patentee has granted licences under parallel patents for different member states, it should not be legitimate for the licensees to be required to respect each other's territories and likewise for the patentee to respect the territories of his licensees.[2] It is logical, it is submitted, that the prohibition under the Court's ruling should apply (as it does according to its terms) only after the goods have been the subject of a sale in another country – which must, of course, imply a *bona fide* sale. It is understood, however, that views have been expressed to the effect that the Court's ruling prevents even such direct exports, e.g., by a licensee into the territory of another licensee.

(B) It is immaterial in relation to the Court's ruling at (A) that the patentee and his licensees belong to the same group.

It would seem indeed to be anomalous if a subsidiary in an international group of companies could use a parallel patent to partition the market while such use of the patent would be prohibited in the case of a licensee which is not in the same group.

In the remainder of the Judgment the Court of Justice dealt in essentially identical terms to those used in its *Centrafarm/Winthrop* Judgment[3] with the questions raised concerning the effect of state price-control policies, the need to protect the public against defective pharmaceutical products, the effect of art. 42 of the Accession Treaty and the incidence of art. 85 to groups of undertakings.

Finally, it will be remembered that in the *Centrafarm/Winthrop* Case the Court of Justice defined the specific object of trade mark protection. Similarly, in paragraph 9 of the *Centrafarm/Sterling* Judgment the Court defined the specific object of a patent as being to ensure that the creative effort of the inventor is rewarded by the grant of the exclusive right to use an invention for the purpose of making and effecting a first sale of industrial products either directly or by the grant of licences to third parties and by conferring the right on the patentee to prevent imitations.

---

1 See p. 103, above.
2 See also p. 237, text and n. 1, below.
3 As to which see pp. 214, 215, above.

THE FUTURE APPLICATION BY CONVENTION OF THE
EXHAUSTION OF RIGHTS PRINCIPLE TO PATENTS

Convention for a European System for the Grant of Patents – It is necessary
for the purposes of the present discussion to explain that at the Munich
Diplomatic Conference on 5 October 1973, a Convention establishing
a European System for the Grant of Patents ("the Patents Grant Convention") was agreed between nineteen European states and was open
for signature.[1]

The aim of the Convention is to provide for a uniform filing,
examination and grant procedure, all to be carried out by the international patent office to be established in Munich on the basis of
uniform and common requirements for patentability. The patent
granted will be a "European patent", which in the individual country
or countries designated in the application will have the effect of a
national patent.

Convention for the European Patent for the Common Market – In
addition, and more directly relevant to the subject of this chapter,
the text of the Convention for the European Patent for the Common
Market ("the Community Patent Convention") has been agreed.[2]
The effect of the Convention is to create a unitary patent covering
the combined territories of the nine member states, in the same way
that a United Kingdom patent covers each of its constituent parts.

The provisions which are relevant for present purposes are arts. 32
and 78 of the Community Patent Convention:

> "32 (1) The rights attached to a Community Patent shall not extend to
> acts concerning a product covered by that patent which are done in the
> territory of the contracting States after the proprietor of the patent has
> put that product on the market in one of these States.
>
> (2) The provisions of paragraph (1) also apply with regard to a product
> put on the market without infringement of the Community Patent by a
> contractual licensee or by a licensee under Article 44.[3]"

> "78. (1) The rights attached to a national patent in a contracting State
> shall not extend to acts concerning a product covered by that patent

---

1 In 1972 the Government of the Federal Republic of Germany arranged for the publication of the drafts of the Convention in English, French and German, bearing the title:
  "Preparatory Documents M/1 to M/8 for the Munich Diplomatic Conference for the
  setting up on a European System for the Grant of Patents (1973);" published by
  Wila Verlag für Wirtschaftswerburg, Wilhelm Lampl, Munich 21.
2 Published by the Official Publications Office of the European Communities, Luxembourg, 1973.
3 Provision for compulsory licensing.

which are done in the territory of such contracting State after the proprietor of the patent has put that product on the market in a contracting State.

(2) The provision of paragraph (1) shall also apply with regard to a product put on the market by the proprietor of a national patent granted for the same invention in another contracting State who has economic connections with the proprietor of the patent referred to in paragraph (1). For the purpose of this paragraph (2) persons shall be deemed to have economic connections where one of them is in a position to exert a decisive influence on the other directly or indirectly with regard to the exploitation of a patent, or when a third party is in a position to exert such influence on both parties.

(3) The provisions of paragraphs (1) and (2) shall also apply with regard to a product put on the market without infringement of the relevant patent by a contractual licensee or by a licensee of right."

The message of these two articles is clear. When these articles come into force it will not be possible to assert either a national patent or the Community patent to prevent the importation into one EEC state of a product marketed in another EEC state by either a patentee or a licensee or, in the case of a national patent, also by a person with whom the patentee has economic connections.

The two Conventions were to come into force in 1976, the adoption of the Community Patent Convention being conditional on the Patents Grant Convention coming into force,[1] but, as mentioned above, these dates seem optimistic.

Protocol to the Convention: Suspension of the exhaustion of rights principle as regards patents – However by a Protocol to the Community Patent Convention the provisions of arts. 32 and 78 are to be postponed for a transitional period of five years (subject to possible reduction or extension). During this period the provisions of national law will apply to the Community Patent which during such period will be treated as a national patent in each contracting state; and likewise national law, and not art. 78, will apply in relation to national patents. Now, national law, at any rate national domestic law, will in many cases permit the assertion of national patent rights against the importation from abroad of a product protected by the national patent, whether it was marketed abroad by the patentee or his licensee, or not.

However, as national law incorporates EEC law[2] the question arises whether during the transitional period such marketing in another EEC state does or does not result in the "exhaustion" of the relevant national patent right, on the basis of the *Centrafarm/Sterling* Case.

1 Article 89 and Annex I of the Convention.
2 See Ch. 1, pp. 5, 6, above.

Since the effect of this Judgment is to establish the applicability of the exhaustion of rights principle to patents, the reference to national law under the Protocol strictly speaking has (by reason of the incorporation of EEC law into national law) the effect of circumventing the apparent intention of the Protocol to delay for five years the application of the relevant rule. To reconcile the provisions of the Protocol with good sense, it seems necessary to interpret the Protocol, if eventually adopted in its present form, as a "statutory" postponement of any such effect of the Judgment as far as patents are concerned.

However, the Commission has delivered a formal opinion[1] to the effect that the Protocol in attempting to postpone the exhaustion of rights principle in relation to patents is contrary to Community law as authoritatively interpreted by the Court of Justice.[2] Therefore, the Commission argues, for a member state to adopt the Protocol would be a breach of its obligation not to jeopardise the attainment of the objectives of the Treaty under art. 5. Nor in the Commission's opinion could the Protocol be justified as an amendment to the Treaty, which it considers can only take place in accordance with certain procedures set out in art. 236. In the last resort the question of the legality of the Protocol must be one for the determination of the Court of Justice.

Industrial property rights in relation to article 86

In the *Parke Davis* Case[3] the Court of Justice established that although a patent confers on its holder a special protection within the framework of the state, it does not follow that the exercise of the right conferred by the patent implies the presence of the three elements for bringing art. 86 into play: the existence of a dominant position; abuse of that position; and the possibility that trade between member states may be affected. It could only do so if the exercise of the patent degenerated into an improper exploitation of the protection.

With regard to the existence of a dominant position the Court of Justice repeated, in almost identical terms, in the *Sirena*[4] and *Deutsche Grammophon*[5] Cases that the mere ownership of an industrial property right does not constitute a dominant position. Thus the owner of a trade mark does not enjoy a dominant position merely because he can prohibit third parties from marketing products bearing the same trade

---

1 OJ 1974 L109/34, issued before judgment was delivered in the *Centrafarm/Sterling* Case.
2 This being a reference at the time to the *Deutsche Grammophon* Case.
3 *Parke, Davis & Co.* v. *Probel*, 29 February 1968, XIV Rec. 81; [1968] CMLR 47.
4 *Sirena SRL* v. *Eda SRL*, 18 February 1971, XVII Rec. 69; [1971] CMLR 260.
5 *Deutsche Grammophon GmbH* v. *Metro-SB-Grossmärkte GmbH*, 8 June 1971, XVII Rec. 487; [1971] CMLR 631.

mark in the territory of a member state.[1] Nor does a manufacturer of
recordings who has a protection right analogous to copyright have a
dominant position merely because he exercises his exclusive right to
market the protected articles.[2]

The owner of an industrial property right will, however, have a
dominant position if in addition to the power conferred by the industrial property right, or exceptionally, it is submitted, by means of that
power alone, he is able to prevent the maintenance of effective competition in a considerable part of the relevant market, e.g. if he is able
to exclude competition in such market from the products of other
manufacturers.

Where it is established that the owner of an industrial property right
has a dominant position then according to the *Sirena*[3] and *Deutsche
Grammophon*[4] Cases, such a position is not abused merely because a
higher price is charged for the protected product, although this may
be the case if the price differential is excessive, or in the words of the
Judgment in *Deutsche Grammophon* "cannot be explained on any
objective grounds".[5]

SECTION 2   PATENT AND KNOWHOW LICENSING
AGREEMENTS

We have been discussing in the previous section the way in which
Community law has developed to forbid the use of industrial property
rights to restrict trade between member states where such use goes
beyond the interest intended to be protected by the grant of the
industrial property right concerned – and it has been seen that the
prohibition of what may be termed the abuse of the industrial property
right for such a purpose is not dependent on the existence of an
agreement and is therefore possible irrespective of the application of
art. 85.

Alongside the development of Community law in such cases as
Consten-Grundig,[6] *Parke Davis*,[7] *Sirena*,[3] *Deutsche Grammophon*,[4]

---

1 [1971] CMLR 260, at p. 275.
2 [1971] CMLR 631, at p. 658.
3 *Sirena SRL* v. *Eda SRL*, 18 February 1971, XVII Rec. 69; [1971] CMLR 260.
4 *Deutsche Grammophon GmbH* v. *Metro-SB-Grossmärkte GmbH*, 8 June 1971, XVII Rec.
487; [1971] CMLR 631.
5 [1971] CMLR 631, at p. 659.
6 *Etablissements Consten SA and Grundig Verkaufs – GmbH* v. *EEC Commission*, 13 July
1966, XII Rec. 429; [1966] CMLR 418.
7 *Parke, Davis & Co.* v. *Probel*, 29 February 1968, XIV Rec. 81; [1968] CMLR 47.

Centrafarm/Winthrop,[1] and *Centrafarm/Sterling*,[2] which are concerned with impediments to intra-Community trade by the use of industrial property rights as against third parties to the contract, if any, between undertakings, Community law has also developed the principle that the owner of an industrial property right cannot grant a licence under it containing restrictions on the licensee which infringe art. 85, bearing in mind that a licence under an industrial property right constitutes an agreement between undertakings.

Just as in the circumstances contemplated in the preceding section it was necessary for Community law to reconcile the industrial property right monopoly on the one hand with the principle of free movement of goods on the other, so in the case of the licensing of industrial property rights a reconciliation was necessary under Community law between the right to exploit such rights and the need for the licence not to infringe art. 85.

In the former case the reconciliation was effected by distinguishing between the existence of the industrial property right and its use; and in the latter by developing the principle that all those restrictions on a licensee which are co-extensive with the grantor's monopoly are permissible, but that anything beyond would infringe art. 85. For example in the case of a patent licence, provision for royalty payments thereunder after the expiry of the patent will infringe art. 85. Conversely, while a patent confers privileges on a patentee, it does not subject him to restrictions, with the consequence that restrictions accepted by the patentee under a licence may infringe art. 85, these being unrelated to the patent grant.

Patent licensing agreements

The principle that only those restrictions in a licence which are co-extensive with the rights of the grantor under an industrial property right are permitted is not, however, easy to apply in practice, particularly in relation to patents. In view of their great industrial importance the Commission issued on 24 December 1962[3] a Communication, specifying certain provisions in a patent licence which in its opinion were permissible and the reasons for this. The Commission

---

1 *Centrafarm BV and Adriaan de Peijper* v. *Winthrop BV,* 31 October 1974, [1974] 2 CMLR 480.
2 *Centrafarm BV and Adriaan de Peijper* v. *Sterling Drug Inc.,* 31 October 1974, [1974] 2 CMLR 480.
3 JO 1962 139/2922. This Communication supersedes two earlier pronouncements of the Commission concerning patent licensing agreements not discussed here, but which can be found in Campbell, *op. cit.*, Vol. I, paras. 4.3, 4.4.

is further planning the adoption of a Regulation to provide for group exemption for certain patent licensing agreements.[1]

The Communication is now set out in full. Since section I merely lists the various permitted clauses, it is helpful to read the relevant paragraph of explanation contained in Section IV, p. 232, below, immediately after each of the paragraphs I, A to E.

NOTICE ON PATENT LICENSING AGREEMENTS[2]

I. On the basis of the facts known at present, the Commission considers that the following clauses in patent licensing agreements are not caught by the prohibition laid down in Article 85 (1) of the Treaty:

A. Obligations imposed on the licensee which have as their object:

1. Limitation of the exploitation of the invention to certain of the forms which are provided for by patent law (manufacture, use, sale).

2. Limitation:
   (a) of the manufacture of the patented product,
   (b) of the use of the patented process, to certain technical applications.

3. Limitation of the quantity of products to be manufactured or of the number of acts constituting exploitation.

Although patent licensing agreements often contain provision for a minimum quantity to be produced in order to secure for the patentee adequate reward through royalties, etc., the wording of paragraph 3 would appear wide enough also to permit the patentee to impose a ceiling on the licensee's production. However, it is understood that such an upper limit would only in exceptional circumstances be viewed with favour.

4. Limitation of exploitation:
   (a) in time
       (a licence of shorter duration than the patent);
   (b) in space
       (a regional licence for part of the territory for which the patent is granted, or a licence limited to one place of exploitation or to a specific factory);

---

1 See pp. 96, 97, above.
2 Translation taken from "Competition Law in the EEC and the ECSC", published by the Office for Official Publications of the European Communities, available from HMSO.

(c) with regard to the person
(limitation of the licensee's power of disposal, e.g., prohibiting him from assigning the licence or from granting sub-licences).

B. Obligations whereby the licensee has to mark the product with an indication of the patent.

It appears from *Re Burroughs-Delplanque*[1] and *Re Burroughs-Geha*[2] that additional identification marks may be marked on the licensed product to facilitate quality and quantity control by the licensor.

C. Quality standards or obligations to procure supplies of certain products imposed on the licensee – in so far as they are indispensable for the technically perfect exploitation of the patent.

D. Undertakings concerning the disclosure of experience gained in exploiting the invention or the grant of licences for inventions in the field of improvements or applications; this, however, applies to undertakings entered into by the licensee only if such undertakings are not exclusive and if the licensor has entered into similar undertakings.

E. Undertakings on the part of the licensor:

1. Not to authorize anyone else to exploit the invention,

2. Not to exploit the invention himself.

It is now the Commission's view that an exclusive licence may be restrictive of competition as the licensor is disabled from granting licences to others with the consequent elimination of other potential suppliers of the patented products. This emerges from *Re Davidson*,[3] *Re Raymond-Nagoya*[4] and *Re Burroughs-Delplanque*.[5]

In *Re Davidson*[6] the Commission stated:

"[36] A patent confers on its holder the exclusive right to exploit the invention covered by it. The holder may cede, by licences, for a given territory, the use of the rights derived from its patent. However, if it undertakes to limit the exploitation of its exclusive right to a single undertaking in a territory and thus confers on that single undertaking the right

1 *Re Agreement of Burroughs AG and Ets. L. Delplanque*, 22 December 1971, JO 1972 L13/50; [1972] CMLR D67.
2 *Re Agreement of Burroughs AG and Geha GmbH*, 22 December 1971, JO 1972 L13/53; [1972] CMLR D72.
3 *Re Agreement of the Davidson Rubber Co.*, 9 June 1972, JO 1972 L143/31; [1972] CMLR D52.
4 *Re Agreement of A. Raymond and Co.*, 9 June 1972, JO 1972 L143/39; [1972] CMLR D45.
5 *Re Agreement of Burroughs AG and Ets. L. Delplanque*, 22 December 1971, JO 1972 L13/50; [1972] CMLR D67.
6 [1972] CMLR D52, at p. D59.

to exploit the invention and to prevent other undertakings from using it, it thus loses the power to contract with other applicants for a licence. In certain cases such exclusive character of a licence relating to industrial property rights may restrict competition and be covered by the prohibition set out in Article 85 (1)."

The principle was also applied to knowhow licences in *Re Raymond-Nagoya* in almost identical terms.

The exclusive licence will nevertheless not be within art. 85 unless the other conditions of its application are met; thus in *Raymond-Nagoya* an exclusive licence to a Japanese manufacturer to make plastic attachment components used in the construction of cars granted by the French licensor was held not to be within art. 85 since the restrictions on competition in Japan resulting from the exclusivity had no repercussions in the Common Market. The licence in this case was a knowhow licence but the principle will be the same in the case of a patent licence. In *Burroughs-Delplanque* the exclusive licence granted by Burroughs for the manufacture of certain specialised carbon papers to licensees in Common Market countries was held not to be within art. 85 on the ground that the resulting restrictions on competition were not perceptible.

Where the exclusive licence is within art. 85 (1) it may nevertheless be exempted under art. 85 (3). Thus in *Davidson*, having established that the exclusive licence granted by Davidson to Happich in Germany and Maglem in Belgium to manufacture under Davidson's patents and knowhow padded, seamless objects (especially elbow rests and cushions for motor cars) did perceptibly restrict competition in the Common Market and affect trade between member states, the Commission proceeded to grant exemption under art. 85 (3). The Commission found that the licensed process brought about technological improvements from which consumers benefited, thus satisfying the two positive conditions for the application of art. 85 (3).[1]

In examining whether the two negative conditions for the application of art. 85 (3)[1] were also satisfied, the Commission found first that no unnecessary restrictions were imposed in the licence. In particular, the Commission held that the restriction on Davidson from granting other licences was indispensable, stating that:[2]

"given the situation of the market in those products in 1959, the Davidson Rubber Company would not have succeeded in having its new process used in Europe by third parties if it had not agreed to limit its licensees

---

1 See pp. 81, 82, above.
2 [1972] CMLR D52, at p. D62, para. 47.

in that part of the world to a small number of undertakings by giving them an assurance that in the territories assigned to them it would not cause them to have competition from new licensees. Indeed, in the present case, without exclusivity the licensees would not have agreed to make the investments necessary to develop the process and adapt it to the requirements of the European market".

It may be asked whether almost every exclusive licence cannot be justified on such grounds. There must indeed be very few licensees prepared to invest in the development of a market for a licensed product without the safeguard of exclusivity. But to qualify for exemption under art. 85 (3) the agreement must also satisfy the second negative condition that it does not eliminate competition in a substantial part of the products in question.

In *Davidson* the Commission found this condition satisfied since there were other competing processes operated by a dozen other undertakings with a substantial share in the Common Market. Further, the products manufactured by the exclusive licensees in different EEC countries competed amongst themselves by export into each other's territories. It is interesting, however, to speculate how it could be possible to satisfy the condition of art. 85 (3) that the agreement does not afford to the undertakings concerned the possibility of eliminating competition in respect of a substantial part of the products in question in the case of a completely novel product, such, for example, as the wireless was when first invented. Maybe the solution is that if the product is so completely novel, there is no competition, actual or potential, which can be restricted as a consequence of the exclusive licence, so that art. 85 (1) does not apply in any event.

> II. This Notice is without prejudice to the legal appraisal of clauses other than those referred to at I (A) to (E). Moreover, a general appraisal does not appear possible for agreements relating to
>
> 1. Joint ownership of patents,
> 2. Reciprocal licensing,
> 3. Multiple parallel licensing. The appraisal of the clauses referred to at I (A) to (E) is confined to obligations of a duration not exceeding the period of validity of the patent.

It is seen that the Commission intended that the criteria in section I, A to E should apply to individual licences only, and not to licences forming part of schemes such as those described above, which may be, though not necessarily so, the means of vertical or horizontal market sharing, excluding competitors from a market, etc. As will be seen from the Commission's comment in the penultimate paragraph of section III, the Commission in 1962 hoped to revert to the questions raised by such schemes, but to date no general guidelines have been formulated.

III. The object of this Notice is to give enterprises some indication of the considerations by which the Commission will be guided when interpreting Article 85 (1) of the Treaty and applying it to a number of clauses often found in certain patent licensing agreements. So long as and in so far as such agreements do not contain restrictions other than those resulting from one or more of the clauses mentioned above, the Commission considers that they are not affected by the prohibition of Article 85 (1). The situation having thus been clarified, it will as a general rule no longer be useful for enterprises to obtain negative clearance for the agreements mentioned, nor will it be necessary to have the legal position established through a Commission decision on an individual case; this also means that notification will no longer be necessary for agreements of this type. This Notice is without prejudice to any interpretation that may be made by other competent authorities, and in particular by the courts.

A decision is to be made later on the question of the application of Article 85 (1) of the Treaty to clauses of the types mentioned above which are contained in agreements relating to joint ownership of patents, to the grant of reciprocal licences or multiple parallel licences, to agreements relating to the exploitation or other industrial property rights or of attainments not protected by law and constituting technical improvements, and to any clauses other than those mentioned above. This Notice is without prejudice to the interpretation of Article 4 (2) (2) (b), of Regulation No. 17.

IV. The obligations listed at I (A) do not fall under the prohibition of Article 85 (1) because they are covered by the patent. They entail only the partial maintenance of the right of prohibition contained in the patentee's exclusive right in relation to the licensee, who in other respects is authorised to exploit the invention. The list at I (A) is not an exhaustive definition of the rights conferred by the patent.

The obligations imposed on the licensee to mark the product with an indication of the patent (point I (B)) is in accordance with the patentee's legitimate interest in ensuring that the protected articles are clearly shown to owe their origin to the patented invention. As long as the licensee is also free to make distinguishing marks of his own choice on the protected article, this provision has neither the object nor the effect of restricting competition.

The licensee's undertakings, mentioned at I (C), concerning compliance with certain quality standards for the protected products or for semi-products, raw materials or auxiliary materials, cannot restrict competition worthy of protection, where they are intended to prevent technically incorrect application of the invention. The undertaking to procure supplies of certain products is relevant only where quality cannot be established by objective standards, in which case such an undertaking has the same scope as the prescription of quality standards.

The undertakings given by the licensee and mentioned at I (D) have in any case no restrictive effect on competition when the licensee retains the possibility of disclosing experience gained or of granting licences to third parties and is entitled to participate in the licensor's future stock of experience and inventions. With regard to undertakings given by the licensor concerning the disclosure of experience or the grant of a licence, as mentioned at I (D), these seem to be unexceptionable from the angle of the rules of competition, even without that limitation. In this connection point I (D) only relates to the obligation to disclose experience or to grant licences; this is without prejudice to the legal appraisal of any restrictions imposed on the parties involved concerning the utilization of such experience or inventions.

By the undertaking mentioned at I (E) – not to authorise anyone else to exploit the invention – the licensor forfeits the right to make agreements with other applicants for a licence. Leaving out of account the controversial question whether such exclusive undertakings have the object or affect of restricting competition, they are not likely to affect trade between Member States as things stand in the Community at present.[1] The undertaking not to exploit the patented invention oneself is closely akin to an assignment of the right and accordingly does not seem to be open to objection.

There are also certain other clauses (apart from those contained in the Communication) imposing obligations or prohibitions on the licensee, which are normally acceptable:

(1) An obligation on the licensee to manufacture only in accordance with the licensor's technical instructions; the purpose of such obligation being to ensure that the products made under the licence are technically satisfactory.[2]

(2) An obligation to refer disputes to arbitration.[2]

It is not clear why a straightforward arbitration clause should in itself have any repercussions on competition. Presumably, however, an award by the arbitrator inconsistent with the provisions of the Treaty would be unenforceable, e.g. an award of damages for a breach of a clause prohibited under art. 85.

On the other hand, a prohibition on the licensee against challenging

---

1 But see p. 229, above, and cases cited there decided since the Communication was issued.
2 *Re Agreement of Burroughs and Delplanque,* 22 December 1971, JO 1972 L13/50; [1972] CMLR D67; *Re Agreement of Burroughs and Geha,* 22 December 1971, JO 1972 L13/53; [1972] CMLR D72.

the validity of a patent is not permitted.[1] This type of clause is restrictive of competition in that –

(i) if the challenge is successful the licensee may be relieved from obligations under the licence thereby enhancing his competitiveness, and

(ii) the invention is no longer protected by the patent and third parties become free to market the relevant invention to the benefit of consumers.

An important question in relation to patent licensing is the extent, if any, to which an exclusive licensee may be contractually protected from direct exports into his territory by the licensor and other licensees, as to which see pp. 221, 222, above.

Knowhow licensing agreements

While the Commission's Communication of 24 December 1962 gives guidance as to the provisions which may be included in a patent licence (and the position will be clarified further when a Regulation granting exemption by category for certain licences is issued)[2] no overall guide lines as yet exist as to what is and what is not permissible in a *knowhow* licence by way of restrictions imposed on the licensee or licensor, although certain specific provisions have been the subject of decisions by the Commission as will be seen below.

That the Commission should have difficulty in formulating a policy in relation to knowhow licensing is not entirely surprising as difficult issues are involved. Public policy requires the widest possible dissemination of technical information so that it is available to any person in a position to exploit it. On the other hand, unpatented knowhow is a valuable asset, its owner enjoying a *de facto* monopoly in respect of it so long as it remains secret – a position of strength he will often be loath to prejudice by communicating the knowhow to a licensee, with the attendant danger of the knowhow becoming public knowledge, even though he himself is not in a position for financial or other reasons to exploit it fully. The encouragement in the interests of technical progress of the dissemination of knowhow through licensing thus requires that the legitimate interests of the owner of the knowhow are protected. Accordingly under many national laws provisions in knowhow licensing agreements designed to ensure such protection are

---

1 *Re Agreement of A. Raymond and Co.*, 9 June 1972, JO 1972 L143/39; [1972] CMLR D45; though in this case the clause was permitted as the avoidance of this patent would not have affected competition within the EEC. See also *Re Agreement of Davidson Rubber Co.*, 9 June 1972, JO 1972 L143/13; [1972] CMLR D52, para. 50.
2 This is discussed at pp. 96, 97, below.

generally enforceable, with the result that knowhow, while secret, enjoys a special status as, so to speak, a quasi industrial property right.[1] The EC Commission is equally concerned that knowhow should be disseminated and exploited in the interests of technical progress within the Common Market and accordingly accepts that certain provisions can be included in knowhow licensing agreements for the protection of the legitimate interests of the owner of the knowhow. But the delimitation between acceptable restrictions and those which are not, by reference as in the case of patents to what is inherent in the patent right, is difficult in the absence of consensus as to what are the rights attaching to undisclosed knowhow and consequently as to what the rights of its owner should be. That he is entitled to have the secrecy of the knowhow maintained appears to be generally accepted, but it is not clear what other restrictions he should be entitled to impose on the licensee or to accept himself.

The more general opinion among commentators is that, with some caution, restrictions which can be included in a patent licence should *mutatis mutandis* be capable of inclusion in a knowhow licence – this being the position under German law from which much of the EEC's competition law is inspired. In contrast, both the United States and United Kingdom anti-trust laws are very much stricter.

US anti-trust law and doctrine in this area are unsettled veering from an extreme position (now apparently abandoned) condemning all licensing of unpatented knowhow to a more cautious view that limitations as to territory, field of use and quantity can be defended in licences if the knowhow is (1) essential to the licensee's ability to manufacture the product, (2) truly unavailable to other producers, and (3) related to only one or very few products representing either a new enterprise for the licensee or a significant improvement over anything he has produced before. The limitations should not extend in time beyond the period when the knowhow has satisfied all the above criteria. These provisions fall far short of what would be permitted in a patent licence. Moreover certain commentators in the United States deny that the owners of secret knowhow need any particular encouragement for its dissemination. For example, R. H. Stern writes,[2]

---

1 It has been argued (for example in the United States, see further below) that the only proper means of protecting knowhow is through the patent system, all other methods being restrictive of competition. But many types of knowhow are not suitable for patent protection. Perhaps the law will eventually distinguish between knowhow which "ought" to be patented (where no other protection will be available) and types of knowhow entitled to protection as knowhow.

2 R. H. Stern, Chief of the Patent Unit, Antitrust Division, US Department of Justice, in Les Nouvelles, Vol. 5, No. 5, at p. 223.

"Nor is any broader or longer territorial restriction to be justified by reference to public policies favouring the dissemination of technology. In fact, there are strong incentives for the sale or licensing of technology, which assure that it will normally take place to a substantial extent without the inducement of allowing continuing anti-competitive arrangements. These incentives include the advantage to the licensor of royalty payments, the demand by customers for alternative sources of supply, the licensor's unwillingness to invest in additional production facilities, and the licensor's concern about competitors' inventing around the technology. Moreover, the licensor will seek to recoup, by means of the royalty charge, any economic loss anticipated by reason of the licensee's competition. The existence of substantial domestic patent and know-how licensing programmes of American corporations would seem to indicate that the prospect of licensing competition, in general, does not unduly hinder the transfer of technology in return for the payment of reasonable royalties."

In the United Kingdom the position is governed by RTPA 1956, s. 8 (5), to the effect that in an agreement for the exchange of knowhow a restriction can be imposed as to the kind of goods which can be produced with the knowhow; the imposition of any other restriction renders the licence registrable.

There is therefore respectable precedent for far greater stringency in relation to permissible restrictions in knowhow licensing than under German law, and the view that clauses which are permissible in a patent licence should also be allowed in a knowhow licence must therefore be treated with caution pending guidance from the Commission – which, let it be hoped, will not be delayed much longer so that undertakings should at least know what is the law which they are required to observe. Nothing is worse than uncertainty. While this prevails it would be advisable for the parties to knowhow agreements to agree the consequences which are to ensue in the event that it is found that the knowhow licence infringes art. 85. It is arguable that any such agreement should be included in a collateral agreement to avoid the nullity of the licence agreement (in so far as the offending provisions are not severable)[1] affecting also a clause in the agreements setting out the consequences of such nullity.

In the meantime the Commission has in *Re Burroughs-Delplanque*[2] allowed clauses to ensure the secrecy of the knowhow on the ground that "the essence of the technical know-how, which is an ensemble of industrial processes unprotected by legal provisions on industrial

1 Severance depends on the domestic law concerned, see pp. 136, 137, above.
2 *Re Agreement of Burroughs AG and Ets. L. Delplanque*, 22 December 1971, JO 1972 L13/50; [1972] CMLR D67, at p. D70.

property, is secrecy. The secrecy is a necessary condition for the owner of technical know-how to grant it to other undertakings for its full exploitation and it is therefore a precondition for any marketing of technical know-how, so long as the latter has not fallen into the public domain."

The permitted clauses were:

(1) The licensee of knowhow may during the currency of the agreement and for a period thereafter be prevented from disclosing the knowhow communicated during the currency of the agreement and from using the knowhow after the end of the agreement. In the Burroughs-Delplanque licence the period of continuing secrecy at the end of the agreement was ten years, and this was approved by the Commission, but it is understood that the ten year period is not a maximum. What is a reasonable period depends on the circumstances of each particular case. The prohibitions on the use or disclosure of the knowhow cannot however be indefinite.

(2) The licensee may be prevented from granting sub-licences as the secrecy cannot be guaranteed unless the licensor knows to whom the secret will be communicated.

Finally, the remarks made at pp. 221, 222, above, relating to the protection of an exclusive patent licensee from direct exports into his territory by the licensor and other licensees should, it is submitted, apply equally to exclusive knowhow licensees. It is interesting to note that in 1968 the Commission indicated its intention to give a favourable decision where the licensor imposed on his licensees a prohibition against direct exports into each other's territories, but the decision was never made, and no explanation for not proceeding has been given by the Commission.[1]

---

1 *Re Scott Paper*, 24 October 1968, JO 1968 C110/2.

Chapter 9

Transport, Agriculture and Public Undertakings

SECTION 1 TRANSPORT

Article 3, paragraph (e), of the Treaty has laid down a common policy in the sphere of transport as one of the areas of Community action essential for achieving the broad objectives of the Treaty set out in art. 2 – on a par with the other "foundations of the Community" in Part II of the Treaty: the free movement of goods (Title I), agriculture (Title II) and the free movement of persons, services and capital (Title III), transport being the subject of Title IV.

Under art. 84 (1), in Title IV, the scope of the common transport policy was limited to transport by rail, road and inland waterway. Sea and air transport (owing to their extension beyond the EEC) are excluded under art. 84 (2), until the Council of Ministers should determine to what extent and by what procedure appropriate provisions (within the framework of a common transport policy – art. 74) should be laid down.

Competition is an aspect of a common transport policy, but in view of the distinctive features of transport it was considered necessary to draw up special competition rules derogating to a certain extent from the general rules of competition as constituted by arts. 85 and 86 in conjunction with Regulation 17. Thus, by Regulation 141 of 1962,[1] the Council exempted transport from the provisions of Regulation 17 as regards agreements the effect of which was to fix transport rates and conditions, to limit and control the supply of transport or to share transport markets and as regards the abuse of dominant positions in the transport market. By this means more time was available within which the ground rules of a common transport policy could develop and with them a clearer idea of the modifications required to be made to the general rules of competition. Subsequently by Regulation 1002

---

1 Art. 1, OJ 1962 124/2751, set out in Appendix II, p. 343, below.

of 1967[1] the Council determined that as regards transport by rail, road and inland waterway the exemption under Regulation 141 was not to extend beyond 30 June 1968 and in that year the Council, under arts. 75 and 87 adopted Regulation 1017[2] constituting a self-contained "code" of the competition rules to be applied in the field of transport by rail, road and inland waterway in so far as the general competition rules were excluded by Regulation 141. Thus, at any rate in theory the general rules are not totally excluded with respect to transport undertakings. It is difficult, however, to give realistic examples of agreements and practices relating to transport undertakings which could be subject to the general rules in view of the comprehensive scope of the agreements and practices within Regulation 1017; and for all intents and purposes the latter Regulation incorporates the competition rules as regards transport by rail, road and inland waterway (to which modes of transport the term "transport" is exclusively applied below).

The present position with regard to sea and air transport is more complex. In *Commission* v. *French Republic*[3] the question before the Court of Justice was whether arts. 48 to 51 of the Treaty apply to sea transport. The Court ruled that sea transport,[4] in so far as it is excluded from the common transport policy, remains "subject to the general rules of the Treaty".[5] It is submitted that, within the meaning of the Judgment, the general rules of the Treaty include the competition rules, and if this is so it follows that the competition rules apply to sea and air[4] transport, although, since the Judgment leaves unaffected art. 1 of Regulation 141,[6] the rules cannot at present, it seems, be implemented with regard to these forms of transport.

Similarities and differences between Regulations 1017 and 17

Regulation 1017, art. 1 – the basic provision – delimits the scope of the Regulation as described above, but so as to include in addition "the operations of providers of services ancillary to transport". The article also refers to certain forms of co-operation and financial agreements, as to which see below, to be considered in applying the Regulation.

Article 2 prohibits as incompatible with the Common Market (in the same way as art. 85) agreements which may affect trade between

---

1 JO 1967 306/1.
2 JO 1968 175/1, set out in Appendix II, p. 360, below.
3 4 April 1974, [1974] ECR 359.
4 It is submitted that the same considerations apply to air transport: see *ibid.,* para. 32.
5 *Ibid.,* para. 32.
6 See p. 238, n. 1, above.

member states and whose object or effect is the restriction of competition within the Common Market; and, still following the pattern of art. 85, art. 2 sets out a non-exhaustive enumeration of practices (corresponding to those in art. 85 but adapted to the particular circumstances of the transport industry) which are prohibited.

By art. 7 all such agreements are, as under art. 85 (2), declared to be automatically void.

Regulation 1017, art. 5, incorporates a provision (corresponding to art. 85 (3)) exempting from art. 2 agreements from which specified beneficial effects can be shown to result (improvement in the quality of transport services, continuity and stability of the market in certain circumstances, increased productivity, furtherance of technical and economic progress) which at the same time take account of the interests of transport users and do not involve the acceptance of any unnecessary restrictions nor the elimination of competition in a substantial part of the transport market concerned. Exemption on these grounds can be granted only by the Commission.[1]

There are, however, important differences between the provisions of art. 85 (supplemented by Regulation 17) and the corresponding provisions of Regulation 1017:

(a) Notification of an agreement is not a prerequisite to obtaining exemption under art. 5, and accordingly undertakings can practise agreements which are within Regulation 1017 until "challenged" by the Commission, when the exemption can be claimed. Undertakings may however in the interests of legal security, initiate a procedure under art. 12 requiring the Commission to determine whether or not the agreement is within art. 2 and, if so, whether it qualifies for exemption under art. 5.

As under art. 85 (3) the exemption may be retroactive – not to the date of notification since there is no requirement as to notification – but to a prior date determined by the Commission in its decision and the position in this respect is the same when the exemption is granted by the Commission otherwise than on application by the undertakings.[2]

(b) Regulation 1017 includes detailed exceptions for technical and co-operation agreements and exemption for specified groups of small and medium-sized undertakings, which exceptions and exemptions reduce considerably the areas of application of art. 2. Thus art. 3 provides that art. 2 does not apply to agreements, etc., the object or

---

1 Reg. 1017, art. 15, corresponding to Reg. 17 art. 9.
2 Reg. 1017, art. 11.

effect of which is to apply technical improvements or to achieve technical co-operation by means of:

(i) the standardisation of equipment, transport supplies, vehicles or fixed installations;

(ii) the exchange or pooling, for the purpose of operating transport services, of staff, equipment, vehicles or fixed installations;

(iii) the organisation and execution of successive, complementary, substitute or combined transport operations, and the fixing and application of inclusive rates and conditions for such operations, including special competitive rates;

(iv) the use, for journeys by a single mode of transport, of the routes which are most rational from the operational point of view;

(v) the coordination of transport timetables for connecting routes;

(vi) the grouping of single consignments;

(vii) the establishment of uniform rules as to the structure of tariffs and their conditions of application, provided such rules do not lay down transport rates and conditions.

Further, art. 4 provides that art. 2 does not apply to agreements whose purpose is:

—the constitution and operation of groupings of road or inland waterway transport undertakings with a view to carrying on transport activities;

—the joint financing or acquisition of transport equipment or supplies, where these operations are directly related to the provision of transport services and are necessary for the joint operations of the aforesaid groups;

subject however to the limitations that the total carrying capacity of groupings does not exceed:

—10,000 metric tons in the case of road transport;

—500,000 metric tons in the case of transport by inland waterway;

and the individual capacity of each undertaking belonging to a grouping does not exceed 1,000 metric tons in the case of road transport or 50,000 metric tons in the case of transport by inland waterway.

(c) Article 6 and art. 14 introduce yet another and more fundamental exception. As mentioned, the competition rules in relation to transport are intended to take effect in the framework of a common transport policy, including the establishment of a stable transport market. Until the Community has introduced measures to ensure such a market, art. 2 may be declared to be inapplicable to any agreement which tends to reduce disturbances on the market in question. However, art. 6 will only apply if the Council has found, on the basis of a report by the Commission, that a state of crisis exists in all or part of a transport market. Exemption under art. 6 takes effect only from the date of the Commission's decision and, subject to renewal, may not exceed three years.[1]

Article 8 corresponds verbatim to art. 86 save that the non-exhaustive list of examples of abuse are adapted to the special circumstances of the transport industry. It is not possible, however, to obtain under Regulation 1017 negative clearance in respect of a particular practice in the absence of provisions in Regulation 1017 corresponding to art. 2 of Regulation 17 – the above mentioned procedure under art. 12 being applicable only to agreements within art. 2 of Regulation 1017.

Article 9 (corresponding to art. 90 of the Treaty) prohibits States from granting or maintaining in respect of public undertakings in the field of transport measures contrary to the provisions of Regulation 1017, but this provision is subject to certain exceptions in the case of undertakings entrusted with the operation of services of general economic interest.[2]

The remaining provisions of Regulation 1017 are procedural and are in line with corresponding provisions of Regulation 17 (including provisions as to fines and penalty payments)[3] up to the same maximum amounts as under Regulation 17.

In the absence, however, from Regulation 1017 of provisions for notification of agreements, there is no provision in Regulation 1017 corresponding to art. 15 (5) of Regulation 17 (exempting notified agreements from fines with respect to acts done after notification but before the Commission's decision).[4]

SECTION 2   AGRICULTURE

The importance of agriculture to the economies of the original member states and to the well-being of their citizens is reflected in the Treaty, where the authors of the Treaty placed the title relating to agriculture second only to the free movement of goods in order of priority as constituting one of the foundations of the Community.

Agricultural products of the soil, of stock farming and of fisheries and products of first stage processing directly related to these products[5]

---

1 Reg. 1017, art. 14.
2 See Section 3, p. 245, below.
3 Arts. 22 and 23, corresponding to Reg. 17, arts 15 and 16.
4 See p. 265, below.
5 Art. 38 (1) of the Treaty.

(consisting of the products listed in Annex II of the Treaty) are subject to common rules. These are designed on the one hand to ensure that farmers and consumers benefit from the advantages to be achieved by increased productivity[1] and the stability of the markets in the Community[2] (so ensuring a fair standard of living for the agricultural Community,[3] availability of supplies,[4] and availability of products to consumers at reasonable prices[5]), whilst at the same time regulating imports and exports both between member states and between the Community and countries elsewhere in the world.

It is beyond the scope of this book to detail the arrangements that have been developed in order to achieve the common agricultural policy in the various sectors of agricultural products covered by the Treaty; suffice it to say that it was envisaged that the competition rules contained in the Treaty should apply in part, at least in so far as the Council of Ministers determined,[6] to the production of, and trade in, agricultural products.

In defining a common competition policy to be applied in the agricultural sector the Council of Ministers had to balance the desire to achieve competition in agricultural products against the overriding necessity to buttress the national organisations (which are responsible for implementing Community policy) from the effects of excessive competition, which could undermine the stability of the market. In the event the measure which was adopted in April 1962 (Regulation 26[7]) applies arts. 85 to 90 of the Treaty to all agreements (i.e. agreements, decisions and concerted practices) and practices referred to in arts. 85 (1) and 86 which relate to the production of, or trade in, the products listed in Annex II, subject to the exception provided for.[8]

The exception is that art. 85 (1) does not apply to such agreements as form an integral part of a national market organisation *or* which are necessary to attain the objectives set out in art. 39 (see above).[9] In determining whether or not an agreement is necessary for the attainment of the objectives set out in art. 39, the Commission will be guided by such directions as the Council may have given for the agricultural product in question; if there are alternative or better means

---

1 Art. 39 (1) (a) of the Treaty.
2 *Ibid.*, art. 39 (1) (c).
3 *Ibid.*, art. 39 (1) (b).
4 *Ibid.*, art. 39 (1) (d).
5 *Ibid.*, art. 39 (1) (c).
6 *Ibid.*, arts. 42 and 43.
7 OJ 30/993; set out in Appendix II, p. 332, below.
8 Reg. 26, art. 1.
9 Reg. 26, art. 2 (1).

of attaining these objectives, the agreement cannot be regarded as necessary for their attainment. Further, the Commission examines an agreement for which the benefit of the exception is claimed in the light of *each* objective and it is only if the agreement is shown to be necessary for the attainment of *all* the objectives that the benefit of the exception is available.[1]

If the objectives of art. 39 are to be met to the satisfaction of the Commission, it appears that it is of paramount importance whether or not the products subject to the agreement are those produced within the Community. In *Re FRUBO*[1] the Commission held that produce imported from elsewhere in the world neither increased Community agricultural production nor contributed to ensuring a fair standard of living for the Community's agricultural work force and thus the agreement could not be considered necessary for the attainment of two of the objectives of art. 39. Further, the reference to market stabilisation, when considered in the context of the provisions relating to agriculture as a whole (as set out in arts. 38 to 47 of the Treaty), is directed at the marketing of Community – as opposed to world – production at remunerative prices which are not subject to excessive fluctuation. With regard to assuring the availability of supplies, this objective is mainly directed at ensuring that the supply to the Community market does not depend on the importation of agricultural products from third countries. Article 39 must be read as a whole, and the objectives there expressed construed in that context; so that the intention of the Community in ensuring the availability of supplies to consumers at reasonable prices is that the interests of the consumer should not be overlooked in the course of developing the common agricultural policy; for this objective to be met it must be shown that consumers enjoy reasonable prices only as a result of the agreement.

It is provided in art. 2 (1) that the exception applies in particular to agreements between farmers, farmers' associations or associations of such associations belonging to a single member state which are concerned in the production or sale of agricultural products or the use of joint facilities for the storage, treatment or processing of agricultural products where no obligation to charge identical prices is imposed. Producers, therefore, or those engaged in trade in agricultural products, are unaffected by the provisions of art. 85 (1) so long as they belong to one member state, and their agreements form an integral part of a national market organisation and do not relate to price fixing. However, the Commission is exclusively authorised to apply the competition rules in the agricultural sector and remains at liberty to hold by

---

1 *Re FRUBO*, 25 July 1974, OJ 1974 L237/16; [1974] 2 CMLR D89; and see *Re Preserved Mushrooms*, 8 January 1975, OJ 1975 L29/26.

decision that such agreements exclude (as opposed to restrict) competition or that the objectives of art. 39 are jeopardised.[1]

With regard to such decision the Commission may act on its own initiative, at the request of a competent authority of a member state, or of an interested undertaking or association of undertakings,[2] and must publish its decision[3] after consulting member states and hearing the parties concerned and any other natural or legal person that it considers appropriate.[4] Its decision is subject to review by the Court of Justice.

If an agreement cannot be shown to be necessary for the attainment of the objectives set out in art. 39 (1), the Commission will not apply the exception contained in Regulation 26, art. 2 (1), and will apply art. 85 (1) in the normal way. The consequences which result from the implementation of an agreement which is brought within the prohibition of art. 85 (1) of Regulation 26, art. 1, are the same as those discussed elsewhere.[5] Regulation 26 also contains rules relating to dumping and to state aids[6] which are, however, outside the scope of this book.

SECTION 3   PUBLIC UNDERTAKINGS

The authentic English text of art. 90 of the Treaty states:

"1. In the case of public undertakings and undertakings to which Member States grant special or exclusive rights, Member States shall neither enact nor maintain in force any measure contrary to the rules contained in this Treaty, in particular to those rules provided for in Article 7 and Articles 85 to 94.

2. Undertakings entrusted with the operation of services of general economic interest or having the character of a revenue-producing monopoly shall be subject to the rules contained in this Treaty, in particular to the rules on competition, in so far as the application of such rules does not obstruct the performance, in law or in fact, of the particular tasks assigned to them. The development of trade must not be affected to such an extent as would be contrary to the interests of the Community.

---

1 Reg. 26, art. 2 (1).
2 Reg. 26, art. 2 (3).
3 Reg. 26, art. 2 (2).
4 *Ibid.*, this would appear to be wider than the corresponding provision under Reg. 17; see pp. 284, 285, below.
5 As regards nullity see Ch. 4, above, and as regards liability to fines see Ch. 11, Section 6, p. 293, below.
6 Reg. 26, arts. 3 and 4.

3. The Commission shall ensure the application of the provisions of this Article and shall, where necessary, address appropriate directives or decisions to Member States."

The object of the competition rules of the Treaty is to bring about at the level of intra-community trade a free market economy, but the Treaty does not purport to regulate the economic system within any particular state: each state is free to determine the respective spheres of public and private enterprise in its economy. In particular, art. 222 provides that the Treaty "shall in no way prejudice the rules in Member States governing the system of property ownership".

But if the public and private sectors are to compete on fair terms they must, in principle, be subject to the same competition rules, particularly where a public undertaking in one state is competing with a private undertaking in another. Thus the general rule is that arts. 85 and 86 apply without distinction to public and private undertakings.

In order to give effect to the general rule art. 90 (1) prohibits states from protecting from the effects of the Treaty public undertakings (an expression which is not defined but which would appear to mean no more than that the state or a subdivision of the state has an interest in the undertaking by reason of ownership, control or the function performed by the undertaking) and the other undertakings specifically referred to in the article[1] (in so far as they are not in any event public undertakings). The distortion of competition which would otherwise result is obvious. Indeed art. 90 (1) was incorporated in the Treaty at the instigation of Belgium which feared the effects of unequal competition between its largely privately owned industry and French and Italian industry in which the state plays a more important role.

Article 90 (1) would seem to supplement art. 37 which provides for the progressive adjustment of state monopolies; under art. 37, for example, the French match and tobacco monopoly (SEITA) was adjusted to ensure that foreign suppliers have access to the French market in reasonably competitive conditions. In the absence of art. 37 it is thought that the same adjustment could have been brought about under art. 90 (1).

However, trading activities by undertakings may include the rendering of some service of general economic benefit to the community – as in the case of a public utility. In such a case the authors of the Treaty considered that the strict application of the competition rules could be inconsistent with the performance of the services in question. Article 90 (2) therefore provides that where "undertakings entrusted with the

---

1 I.e. undertakings to which states grant special or exclusive rights, e.g. see the *Port de Mertert* Case, p. 248, below.

operation of services of a general economic interest or having the character of a revenue producing monopoly" are concerned, the competition rules apply only so far as performance of "the particular task assigned to them" is not prejudiced, subject always to the overall proviso that the non-observance of the competition rules does not affect the development of trade to an extent contrary to the interests of the Community.

An example of a revenue producing monopoly would be the French match and tobacco monopoly (SEITA) mentioned above; there are no such monopolies in the United Kingdom, however, and they can accordingly be ignored for the present purposes.

The expression "undertakings entrusted with the operation of services of general economic interest" has been especially coined for the purposes of the article, having no counterpart in any of the legal systems of the original six signatory states. It is to be noted in the first instance that the undertakings concerned need not be public undertakings in the sense that they are publicly owned or controlled. Whether the undertakings are public or private, they must have been entrusted by some competent public authority with the operation of the relevant services – so that it was not possible for SABAM, a Belgian performing rights society, to claim the benefit of the exemption, the Court of Justice holding[1] that the society had not been *entrusted* with rendering the services: its task was self-imposed.

It is to be noted that it is only where the services rendered by the undertaking are of a general *economic* nature that the derogations in art. 90 (2) can apply. Thus in *Re GEMA*[2] the Commission rejected the claim of the German music performing rights society of that name to be within art. 90 (2) on the ground (*inter alia*) that its activities were of general cultural and social interest only. The same point was taken by the Court of Justice in *SABAM*.[1]

On the other hand, the Court of Justice held art. 90 (2) to apply to an undertaking which enjoyed certain exclusive rights for operating port facilities on the Moselle[3] and to a commercial television undertaking in so far as the provision of facilities for publicity was a service of general economic interest with which the undertaking was entrusted by the Italian State.[4]

---

1 *Belgische Radio en Televisie* v. *SV SABAM and NV Fonior,* 27 March 1974, [1974] ECR 313; [1974] 2 CMLR 238.
2 2 June 1971, JO 1971 L134/15; [1971] CMLR D35; and see pp. 156 ff., above, for the facts and other aspects of this case.
3 *Ministère public Luxembourgeois* v. *M. Muller, veuve Hein,* 14 July 1971, XVII Rec. 723.
4 *Giuseppe Sacchi,* 30 April 1974, [1974] ECR 409; [1974] 2 CMLR 177.

Apart from what appears from the preceding cases, there is only speculation amongst legal writers as to the scope of the meaning to be given to the expression "services of general economic interest" in the absence of available guidance in other legal systems. Authoritative definition of the expression therefore must be developed case by case by the Court of Justice and by the Commission under the control of the Court.

Article 90 (1) is directed at the state itself, prohibiting it from enacting, or enjoining it to repeal, measures restricting competition in relation to public undertakings, while art. 90 (2) is aimed at regulating derogation from the rules of competition by the undertakings referred to in that article. But the reference in art. 90 (1) to the rules contained in the Treaty includes art. 90 (2) so that a state could defend measures restrictive of competition taken by it or which it refrains from abolishing on the ground that the relevant undertaking is within art. 90 (2). Thus in the *Port de Mertert* Case[1] the Court of Justice, on reference under art. 177 in a case where the question was whether certain legislation of the Luxembourg State conferring exclusive rights on an undertaking to operate port facilities on the Moselle infringed the competition rules under art. 90 (1) and whether art. 90 was directly applicable, gave its ruling on the basis that art. 90 (2) was available to the state as a defence in so far as the services to be rendered pursuant to the grant of the exclusive rights were of general economic interest.

Compliance with the provisions of arts. 90 (1) and 90 (2) is ensured by the powers of the Commission under art. 90 (3), i.e. by appropriate directives or decisions addressed to member states, as specifically provided in art. 90 (3) or, which is implied, by the Commission instituting proceedings pursuant to its powers under Regulation 17 against any undertaking infringing the competition rules applicable to them by virtue of art. 90 (2).

The question arises, however, as to whether arts. 90 (1) and 90 (2) are directly enforceable by competitors, suppliers or consumers claiming to be prejudiced by breaches of the article.

In the *Television* Case,[2] on reference under art. 177, the question arose as to whether the enforcement by the Italian State Television Authority (Radio Audizione Italiana) of its monopoly was contrary to art. 86 so that a person operating a tele-distribution organisation illegally, in so far as doing so contravened the state monopoly, could plead infringement of art. 86 by the state as a ground for escaping from the consequences of his otherwise illegal act. The Court, having first

---

1 *Ministère public Luxembourgeois* v. *M. Muller, veuve Hein*, 14 July 1971, XVII Rec. 723.
2 *Giuseppi Sacchi*, 30 April 1974, [1974] ECR 409; [1974] 2 CMLR 177.

found that the grant or extension of exclusive rights by a state does not by reason of art. 90 *per se* infringe the competition rules, held that, in so far as the grantee subsequently abused a resulting dominant position, a breach of art. 86 was involved conferring directly enforceable rights on persons affected to which national courts must give effect.

It would be open, however, to an undertaking against which breaches of art. 85 or 86 are alleged to plead in justification that observance of the articles in the particular case would be inconsistent with the task of general economic interest with which the undertaking had been entrusted.

The question then arises as to whether it would be within the competence of a national court before which this inconsistency is pleaded to determine the issue. In the *Television* Case[1] it was held that, where the television undertaking is entrusted by the state with the operation of its services as services of general economic interest, then, even as regards such of the services as are commercial, and in particular those which relate to publicity, the competition rules apply to the undertaking by virtue of art. 90 (2), for so long as it has not been shown that the application of the rules would be incompatible with the task with which the undertaking has been entrusted. There is nothing in the judgment to suggest that the national court should not be competent to determine the issue, but in the *Port de Mertert* Case where the question of direct applicability of art. 90 (2) also arose, the Court of Justice held that a justification of breaches of the competition rules on the ground of inconsistency with the task entrusted to the relevant undertaking, involved an appreciation of the general economic policy followed by member states under the supervision of the Commission and was not therefore of a nature such as to confer directly applicable rights on persons affected.

It remains to be seen whether this is still good EEC law or whether, in the *Television* Case, the Court intended to say that notwithstanding the *Port de Mertert* Case the national court should decide the issue when it was raised. It may be that while the national court could properly be considered competent to decide the question of any possible prejudice to the task of general economic interest with which the undertaking is entrusted resulting from the observance of the competition rules, consideration of the overall proviso should be left to the Commission.

---

1 *Giuseppe Sacchi,* 30 April 1974, [1974] ECR 409; [1974] 2 CMLR 177, para. 15.

Chapter 10

Negative Clearance, Notification and Form A/B

SECTION 1 INTRODUCTION TO REGULATION 17

The basic rules governing competition in the Common Market are contained in arts. 85 and 86; but the authors of the Treaty were under no illusion that these articles provided anything more than a framework of principles, and that the means of applying these principles would have to be worked out subsequently in much greater detail. Accordingly, the Treaty provided, by art. 87,[1] that within three years of its entry into force the Council should adopt provisions to give effect to the principles contained in arts. 85 and 86; it is to the provisions which have been adopted under art. 87 that detailed consideration is now given.

In 1962 the Council of Ministers adopted Regulation 17 which, despite subsequent amendments, remains the single most important legislative act adopted by the Communities to give effect to the competition rules.

The Regulation is of interest in that not only does it vest in the Commission the necessary means by which to administer the competition rules, but it also grants to it powers[2] not referred to in the Treaty so as to enable it to regulate competition affairs with as much flexibility as possible. In addition to, or as a consequence of, these provisions the Commission attempts to delineate the areas of application of national competition law and the Community rules and to provide for co-operation with those responsible for administering national law in member states.

More specifically, Regulation 17 empowers the Commission –

(1) to issue decisions stating that the prohibitions contained in arts. 85 (1) and 86 do not apply;

(2) to rule whether or not the prohibitions contained in arts. 85 (1)

---

1 Set out in Appendix I, p. 314, below.
2 For example to issue a "negative clearance", as to which see Section 2, p. 251, below.

250

and 86 do apply and, in the case of an agreement[1] subject to art. 85 (1), whether that prohibition should be declared inapplicable pursuant to art. 85 (3), thereby rendering the agreement in question valid;

(3) to carry out investigations into the activities of undertakings, with powers of search in member states;

(4) to administer the competition rules in accordance with an established procedure;

(5) to enforce compliance with arts. 85 (1) and 86 by means of fines or periodic penalty payments;

(6) to adopt implementing provisions with regard to procedural aspects.

It is proposed to consider first in Section 2 of this chapter the purpose and effect of a negative clearance (that is, the declaration by the Commission as to the non-applicability of art. 85 (1) or art. 86) and then to consider in Section 3 what agreements must be notified to the Commission in order for exemption from the prohibition in art. 85 (1) to be granted pursuant to art. 85 (3). The procedural steps to be taken by undertakings in order to obtain a negative clearance or the grant of an exemption are virtually the same, and these are described and commented on in Section 4. The reader is referred to Chapter 11 for a survey of the procedures which must be followed by the Commission in its administration and enforcement of the competition rules.

SECTION 2   NEGATIVE CLEARANCE

As will be apparent from the introductory comments, a distinction must be drawn between an exemption from the prohibition contained in art. 85 (1) granted by the Commission pursuant to art. 85 (3), and a negative clearance relating to both arts. 85 (1) and 86. The authority of the Commission to issue a negative clearance derives from Regulation 17 itself,[2] and not from the Treaty in implementation of which Regulation 17 was adopted. The intention of the Commission in including this power in the Regulation is clearly stated in the preamble to the Regulation: it is in the interests of undertakings to know whether any agreements to which they are party, or propose to become party, may lead to action on the part of the Commission under arts. 85 and 86.[3]

---

1 The reader is reminded that the term "agreement" is used as including an agreement, decision or concerted practice.
2 Art. 2.
3 The Preamble is set out in Appendix II, p. 318, below.

Whereas in the case of an exemption the Commission confirms that the prohibition contained in art. 85 (1) applies, but is prepared to permit the agreement in question to continue because of the positive benefits deriving from it, a negative clearance is a statement from the Commission that on the basis of the facts in its possession there are no grounds for action on its part in respect of an agreement or practice, i.e., it is a statement that the prohibitions of arts. 85 (1) and 86 do not apply.

The Commission alone has competence to issue a negative clearance and can only do so if specifically requested;[1] application for exemption under art. 85 (3) does not constitute a request for a negative clearance.[2] The Commission need only rely on the information made available to it when considering whether or not to issue the clearance.

The effect of a negative clearance is that undertakings which are parties to an agreement or are responsible for a practice liable to be within art. 86, and which notify the agreement or practice,[3] where no change in circumstances takes place, may rely on the terms of the Commission's decision by which the clearance is granted, as constituting confirmation from the Commission that it will not take action pursuant to arts. 85 (1) and 86 with regard to the agreement or practice.

The issue of a negative clearance by the Commission does not, however, prevent it from taking action pursuant to arts. 85 and 86 where there is a factual change in circumstances or incorrect information has been supplied to the Commission; in such circumstances it may take a decision[4] finding that the prohibition contained in art. 85 (1) or art. 86 applies. It is submitted, however, that in the absence of such circumstances the Commission cannot revoke its decision, although the Commission has stated that a change in case law may lead it to re-examine the merits of its decision.[5]

It may be noted that application for negative clearance which is subsequently refused does not in theory prevent the Commission from imposing fines for the period between the date of application and its decision, whereas there is a restriction on imposing fines for the same period in respect of a notification for exemption under art. 85 (3).[6]

---

1 Reg. 17, art. 2.
2 But see further, p. 267, below.
3 As to the procedure for negative clearance, see Section 4, p. 267, below.
4 Under Reg. 17, art. 3.
5 Commission's Practical Guide to Articles 85 and 86 of the Treaty of Rome (1962) Part III, VII, 4, unofficially translated in the Board of Trade Journal, 9 October 1962 and reprinted in Campbell, *op. cit.,* Vol. II, para. 2605, at para. 2654. Commercial undertakings are entitled to rely on statements in the Guide: *per* the Advocate General in *Parfums Marcel Rochas Vertriebs – GmbH* v. *Bitsch,* 30 June 1970, XVI Rec. 515; [1971] CMLR 104, at p. 111.
6 Reg. 17, art. 15 (5); though in practice both applications will now normally be made at the same time—see p. 267, below.

Additionally, fines may be imposed on undertakings which supply incorrect or misleading information.[1] In practice, however, it is most unlikely that the Commission would seek to impose fines in the case of an agreement or practice which has been formally submitted to it in accordance with the provisions of Regulation 17.

Whilst Regulation 17, art. 2, refers to applications by the undertakings or associations of undertakings concerned, in fact *any* undertaking which is party to the agreement or responsible for the practice may seek a negative clearance,[2] subject to notice being given to any other undertakings concerned in the agreement or practice that such application has been made.[3]

Whereas, in the case of exemption under art. 85 (3), the national courts or authorities must exercise their competence under domestic competition legislation subject to the exemption granted by the Commission[4] the issue of a negative clearance does not preclude them from taking action in accordance with such legislation. The national authorities (as to which see p. 292, below, but used here to include the Restrictive Practices Court) in the United Kingdom, in applying the provisions of the RTPA and monopolies and mergers legislation are in no way concerned with the prohibitions of arts. 85 (1) and 86,[5] which in any event the negative clearance has confirmed as not applying. Likewise the national courts in civil proceedings remain free to consider and to apply the provisions of the RTPA and the consequences which flow therefrom, notwithstanding the issue of a negative clearance. It is submitted, however, that in proceedings before a national court where a party disputing the validity of an agreement or practice invokes the provisions of arts. 85 and 86, the court is properly entitled to reject the point if a negative clearance has been issued in respect of that agreement or practice; but in any event the court should not, in the interests of consistent application of the articles, hold that the prohibitions contained in the articles apply with regard to the same facts as those for which the Commission has already issued a negative clearance.

The question may be asked whether, as between the parties themselves, the issue of a negative clearance inhibits either, both or all from seeking to invoke the prohibitions contained in arts. 85 and 86 at

---

1 Reg. 17, art. 15 (1) (a), and see p. 294, below.
2 Reg. 27, art. 1 (1).
3 *Ibid.*; see p. 268, below.
4 See Ch. 4, Section 3, particularly pp. 141 ff., above.
5 See discussion at p. 293, below.

some future date; but even if the national authorities and courts do permit such plea to be raised it is submitted that they should consider it on the basis stated in the preceding paragraph.

As regards art. 85, the Commission assesses the implication of the agreement on the basis of information supplied to it or in its possession; apart from factual data on the particular circumstances, of importance may be the degree of competition encountered from similar products,[1] the duration of an agreement[2] and the importance of the parties in the market in question.[3]

The Commission has only to determine that one of the two conditions necessary for applying art. 85 (1) is not met in order to be able to issue a negative clearance. After reviewing the factual situation, the first question the Commission examines is whether or not the agreement has the object or effect of appreciably restricting competition in the Common Market;[4] if not, clearance will be issued.[5]

If it takes the view that the agreement does have such an object or effect, the Commission then examines whether or not it is such that it may have an appreciable effect on trade between member states; if not, a clearance will again be forthcoming since the two conditions necessary for art. 85 (1) to apply are not met[6].

With regard to art. 86, the Commission will not be prepared to certify that there are no grounds for action on its part unless full disclosure of the facts is made, which must include details of the practices in question and the position of the undertakings within the Common Market or a substantial part thereof in regard to products or services

---

1 *Re Grosfillex,* 11 March 1964, JO 1964 58/915; [1964] CMLR 237; *Re Agreement of Rieckermann KG and AEG-Elotherm GmbH,* 6 November 1968, JO 1968 L276/25; [1968] CMLR D78.

2 *Re Agreement of Nicholas Frères,* 30 July 1964, JO 1964 136/2287; [1964] CMLR 505.

3 *Re SOCEMAS,* 17 July 1968, JO 1968 L201/7; [1968] CMLR D28; *Re Alliance de constructeurs français de machines-outils,* 17 July 1968, JO 1968 L201/1; [1968] CMLR D23.

4 See p. 27, above.

5 *Re Grosfillex* (above); *Re Agreement of Mertens and Straet,* 1 June 1964, JO 1964 92/1426; [1964] CMLR 416; *Re DECA,* 22 October 1964, JO 1964 173/2761; [1965] CMLR D50; *Re Eurogypsum,* 26 February 1968, JO 1968 L57/9; [1968] CMLR D1; *Re SOCEMAS* (above); *Re Alliance de constructeurs français de machines-outils* (above); *Re Rieckermann* (above); *Re Christiani and Nielsen,* 18 June 1969, JO 1969 L165/2; [1969] CMLR D36; *Re Pirelli-Dunlop,* 5 December 1969, JO 1969 L323/21; *Re Vereniging van Vernis- en Verffabrikanten,* 25 June 1969, JO 1969 L168/22; [1970] CMLR D1; *Re Supexie's Agreement,* 23 December 1970, JO 1971 L10/12; [1971] CMLR D1; *Re Dupont de Nemours (Deutschland) GmbH,* 14 June 1973, OJ 1973 L194/27; [1973] CMLR D226.

6 *Re Comptoir Français de l'Azote,* 6 November 1968, JO 1968 L276/29; [1968] CMLR D57; *Re Chaufourniers' (Limeburners') Agreement,* 5 May 1969, JO 1969 L122/8; [1969] CMLR D15; *Re Kodak,* 30 June 1970, JO 1970 L147/24; [1970] CMLR D19; *Re SEIFA,* 30 June 1969, JO 1969 L173/8; *Re ASPA,* 30 June 1970, JO 1970 L148/9; [1970] CMLR D25.

to which the practice relates.[1] There have been no such decisions to date.

SECTION 3 NOTIFICATION FOR EXEMPTION UNDER ARTICLE 85 (3)

The conditions laid down in art. 85 (3) which an agreement must satisfy before it can be exempted from the prohibition of art. 85 (1), together with the generally retroactive effect of such an exemption on the validity of the exempted agreement, have already been discussed.[2] It has been stated that if an agreement is notifiable, its notification to the Commission is a pre-condition to the grant of an individual exemption; and further, if the agreement is notifiable (and is not an old or accession agreement) and it is notified only on a date after its inception, then, in the event of subsequent exemption, the agreement cannot be validated retroactively to a date earlier than the date of notification.

It is the purpose of this section to examine the provisions contained in Regulation 17 which establish whether an agreement is notifiable or not. Further consideration will then be given to the effect of this distinction and the advantages to be derived from notifying an agreement.

Agreements requiring notification

REGULATION 17, ARTICLE 4 (1)

This article provides:

> "Agreements, decisions and concerted practices of the kind described in Article 85 (1) of the Treaty which come into existence after [13 March, 1962][3] and in respect of which the parties seek application of Article 85 (3) must be notified to the Commission. Until they have been notified, no decision in application of Article 85 (3) may be taken."

Formal notification of a new agreement[4] must be made if exemption is to be sought from the prohibition contained in art. 85 (1), and art. 4 (1) specifically states that the Commission cannot take a decision under art. 85 (3) with regard to an agreement in the absence of such notification. However, the apparently absolute requirement that

---

1 Reg. 27, art. 4 (4).
2 See Ch. 3, above.
3 The date of entry into force of Reg. 17, see p. 105, n. 2, above.
4 I.e. an agreement entered into on or after 13 March 1962 but which is not an accession agreement; see p. 272, n. 2, below.

notification must be made if art. 85 (3) is to be applied by individual decision of the Commission is qualified by the provisions of Regulation 17, art. 4 (2) (discussed immediately below) and by specific provisions in the Regulations conferring exemption by category on certain types of agreement (which provisions allow the Commission to withdraw the exemption by category in a particular case and to consider whether the agreement qualifies for exemption under art. 85 (3) on an individual basis, the requirements as to notification being dispensed with).[1]

Whilst the onus is on the participants to an agreement to notify if they wish to obtain the benefit of individual exemption under art. 85 (3) there is no *obligation* to notify an agreement; nowhere in the Treaty or the secondary legislation under it is such an obligation imposed. Regulation 17 does not give the Commission power to impose fines for non-notification but only in respect of a breach of the prohibition contained in art. 85 (1).[2]

Notification is merely the procedural means by which exemption under art. 85 (3) may be sought. It follows that in the absence of notification, a notifiable agreement which is subject to the prohibition contained in art. 85 (1) will remain prohibited, since art. 85 provides for the automatic prohibition of the relevant agreement and Regulation 17, art. 1, confirms that no prior decision with regard to the prohibition is required.

REGULATION 17, ARTICLE 5 (1)

This Article provides:

> "1. Agreements, decisions and concerted practices of the kind described in Article 85 (1) of the Treaty which are in existence at the date of entry into force of this Regulation and in respect of which the parties seek application of Article 85 (3) shall be notified to the Commission before [1 November 1962][3]. [However, notwithstanding the foregoing provisions, any agreements, decisions and concerted practices to which not more than two undertakings are party shall be notified before 1 February 1963.]"[4]

The requirement that an agreement must be formally notified to the Commission if it is to benefit from individual exemption under art. 85 (3) is accordingly applied to old agreements[5] with the exception

---

1 Reg. 67/67, art. 6, and Reg. 2779/72, art. 5, discussed respectively at pp. 107 and 114, above.
2 Subject always to the imposition of fines for failure to comply with procedural requirements—see p. 294, below, on fines; contrast position under the Commission's proposal for a regulation on the control of concentrations between undertakings, discussed at p. 202, above.
3 As amended by Reg. 59, art. 1 (1), OJ 1962 58/1655.
4 As added by *ibid.*, art. 1 (2).
5 That is agreements entered into before 13 March 1962.

of those agreements falling within art. 5 (2) (discussed below); the latest date for notification of these agreements was as specified in the amended article above. Article 25 (2)[1] extended this requirement for notification to accession agreements[2] which had to be notified by 30 June 1973.

In the absence of notification old and accession agreements remain prohibited in the same way as new agreements, although the notification of old and accession agreements, unlike that of new agreements, has substantive as well as procedural advantages.[3]

Agreements not requiring notification

REGULATION 17, ARTICLE 4 (2)

This article provides:

> "Paragraph 1 shall not apply to agreements, decisions or concerted practices where . . ."

These words introduce three short sub-paragraphs which indicate certain types of new agreements which are exempted from the requirement of notification of art. 4 (1); art. 5 (2) extends this exemption from notification to old and accession agreements falling within the sub-paragraphs of art. 4 (2). Agreements falling within art. 4 (2) *may* nevertheless be notified to the Commission, so that in a case of doubt the parties can notify the agreement, thereby ensuring that exemption under art. 85 (3) is not forfeited as a result of a mistaken interpretation of art. 4 (2) of Regulation 17.

The Court of Justice originally held that an agreement falling within the terms of art. 4 (2) and not notified to the Commission requesting exemption under art. 85 (3) remained fully effective until such time as the agreement was held to be void; no distinction was made between an old agreement and a new agreement;[4] subsequently, however, the Court held in the *de Haecht* (No. 2) Case[5] that distinction must be made, in considering the effect of art. 85 (2), between such agreements. Though the Court did not specifically indicate, with regard to old agreements, that in the absence of notification in reliance on art. 4 (2)

---

1 Added to Reg. 17 by Annex I to the Act of Accession.
2 That is agreements entered into before 1 January 1973 which were not then within art. 85 (1) and which were brought within the scope of the article by virtue of the accession of the new member states.
3 See discussion in Ch. 4, above as to the validity of notified old and accession agreements; and, see below under "Effect of Notification", p. 264.
4 *Brauerei A. Bilger Söhne GmbH* v. *Jehle,* 18 March 1970, XVI Rec. 127; [1974] 1 CMLR 382; *Béguelin Import Co.* v. *GL Import-Export SA,* 25 November 1971, XVII Rec. 949; [1972] CMLR 81.
5 *Brasserie de Haecht* v. *Wilkin-Janssen (No. 2),* 6 February 1973, [1973] ECR 77; [1973] CMLR 287.

they retained validity until such time as the Commission takes a decision declaring them void, it is submitted that this must follow from what the Court said with reference to old agreements generally.[1]

On the other hand, in the case of new agreements (and, it is submitted, agreements coming into existence after 1 January, 1973 and which are subject to the rules of competition as a result of accession of the new member states) the Court made it absolutely clear that such agreements are void *ab initio* under art. 85 (2) since exemption from notification under art. 4 (2) "merely constitutes an inconclusive indication that the agreements referred to are generally less harmful to the smooth functioning of the Common Market".[2]

Where an agreement comes within the terms of art. 4 (2), there is no necessity for the parties to notify it for the purposes of obtaining individual exemption under art. 85 (3), but this in no way restricts the Commission's freedom of action with regard to the agreement. Where the facts in the possession of the Commission lead it to undertake a full investigation of an agreement and it concludes that the prohibition of art. 85 (1) applies, it is not precluded from declaring that the agreement satisfies the conditions of art. 85 (3) and therefore granting it exemption from the prohibition.[3]

Whilst it is unlikely, in the case of an agreement which might reasonably be thought to be within the provisions of art. 4 (2), that the Commission will impose fines where no notification has been made, there is no express limitation on the Commission's power to do so and the implication is that in such a case the Commission retains its general discretion to fine, subject always to the right of appeal to the Court of Justice.

Agreements falling within art. 4 (2) are dealt with in three sub-paragraphs which are disjunctive, no notification being necessary for any agreement meeting the specific requirements of any one of the sub-paragraphs:

"(1) the only[4] parties thereto are undertakings from one Member State and the agreements, decisions or practices do not relate either to imports or to exports between Member States."

The purpose of this provision is to exempt from notification agreements which by their nature are unlikely to have any appreciable

---

1 *De Haecht* (*No. 2*), above, para. 9.
2 *Ibid.*, para. 13; see pp. 121, 122, above; and see, generally, Ch. 4, above, on the nature of the invalidity of the agreements, notifiable and non-notifiable, found to infringe art. 85 (1).
3 See Reg. 17, art. 6 (2).
4 Thus the sub-paragraph cannot apply where a non-EEC undertaking participates in the agreement: *Bégudin Import Co.* v. *GL Import-Export SA,* 25 November 1971, XVII Rec. 949; [1972] CMLR 81.

effect on intra-Community trade. The rather cryptic expression "from one Member State" renders the French "ressortissant à un seul Etat membre" which the Practical Guide explains as referring to undertakings within the jurisdiction of a single member state.[1]

A more difficult problem arises in determining to what extent an agreement does or does not "relate to imports or exports between Member States". In its Practical Guide[2] the Commission has stated that ". . . purely regional arrangements for specialisation or exclusive rights within one country, which only indirectly affect imports and exports, are not subject to notification: nor are price arrangements or arrangements limiting production between undertakings in a single Member State, provided that these arrangements do not concern either imports or exports". Further the Commission stated that an agreement permitting exports but prohibiting re-imports requires notification as it affects imports and exports more than merely indirectly.

The Court of Justice has distinguished between the factor of "affecting trade between Member States" which is relevant in deciding the applicability of art. 85 (1) of the Treaty,[3] on the one hand, and that of "relating to imports and exports" which is relevant in deciding the applicability of art. 4 (2) (1), on the other. Thus in the *Bilger* Case[4] it held that an exclusive supply agreement, between a brewery and an innkeeper in the same member state as the brewery, by which the innkeeper agreed to purchase all his beer from the brewery, could affect trade between member states. In the case in question since the parties were in the same member state and the beer did not have to be imported from elsewhere in the EEC, the Court indicated that the agreement fell within the provisions of art. 4 (2) (1), and was thus exempt from notification.

"(2) not more than two undertakings are party thereto, and the agreements only:

(a) restrict the freedom of one party to the contract in determining the prices or conditions of business upon which the goods which he has obtained from the other party to the contract may be resold; or

(b) impose restrictions on the exercise of the rights of the assignee or user of industrial property rights – in particular patents, utility models, designs or trademarks – or of the person entitled under a

---

1 Commission's Practical Guide (1962), Part II, III, 3; Campbell, *op cit.*, para. 2620.
2 *Ibid.*
3 See pp. 30ff., above.
4 *Brauerei A. Bilger Söhne GmbH* v. *Jehle,* 18 March 1970, XVI Rec. 127; [1974] 1 CMLR 382.

contract to the assignment, or grant, of the right to use a method of manufacture or knowledge relating to the use and to the application of industrial processes."

Under art. 4 (2) (2) the jurisdiction to which the parties to the agreement are subject is immaterial so long as there are only two parties thereto; one or both parties may be within the Common Market, or both may be outside the territory of the Community.[1]

The agreements must contain no restriction other than that stipulated in either sub-paragraph (a) or (b), that is the sole effect of the agreements must be limited to the provisions of one or other of the sub-paragraphs.

Sub-paragraph (a) exempts from notification agreements which might nevertheless be within art. 85 (1) (a), which prohibits, inter alia, agreements directly or indirectly fixing selling prices; accordingly, no notification of the agreement is required where the party who is purchasing the goods for resale is obliged to observe the requirements of the other party to the agreement as to the resale price of the goods or as to the conditions on which they may be resold. It is to be noted that the wording is wide enough to include a prohibition imposed by the seller on the buyer against exporting the purchased goods to another member state. It is only in a most exceptional case that such an agreement would qualify for exemption under art. 85 (3), but the exemption, if claimed, could not be refused on the technical ground that the agreement had not been notified.

The sub-paragraph should not, of course, be taken to represent tacit Commission approval or otherwise of resale price maintenance.[2]

Sub-paragraph (b) concerns agreements relating to the use of industrial property rights, and the conditions and restrictions that may be imposed on the user of such rights by the owner in an agreement, without the agreement being notifiable; the question as a matter of substance of whether art. 85 (1) applies to such agreements has been discussed in Chapter 8, above.

An agreement, which on its face might appear to be exempt from notification under art. 4 (2), may be held to be outside the scope of the article by reason of the *effect* (as opposed to the expressed object) of the agreement. Thus in *Re Advocaat*[3] a licence to use a trade mark was held not to be exempt from notification when its *effect*[4] was to

---

1 For territory, see pp. 28–30, above. For extra-territorial application of the competition rules see pp. 23ff., above; *ICI Ltd* v. *EC Commission,* 14 July 1972, XVIII Rec. 619; [1972] CMLR 557.
2 See p. 50, above.
3 24 July 1974; OJ 1974 L237,12; [1974] 2 CMLR D79; see pp. 212ff., above.
4 See pp. 41–42, above.

impose restrictions on imports within the EEC of goods bearing the same trade mark by the assignor and/or third parties, the exemption of art. 4 (2) (2) (b) being applicable to an assignment or licence imposing restrictions only on the person exploiting the industrial property right, and not on the grantor or assignor of the right.

The sub-paragraph defines industrial property rights as including patents, utility models, designs or trade marks or the right to use a manufacturing method or knowledge relating to the use and application of industrial processes. The last phrase would seem to refer to what is generally known as knowhow. The list given of particular types of industrial property rights is stated to be non-exhaustive. There is no reason to distinguish between the interpretation of this term in the present context and for the purpose of the competition rules generally. Thus, though not specifically mentioned, an agreement limiting the exercise of copyright would be covered by the sub-paragraph. However, no comprehensive definition of industrial property rights has been issued by the Commission.

When an agreement contains restrictions additional to those referred to in the sub-paragraph notification is necessary under art. 4 (1); the need for such notification depends on whether or not two tests have been satisfactorily met. These are:

(i) does the agreement in question contain any restriction other than a restriction on the exercise of the industrial property right; and
(ii) are the restrictions relating to the exercise of the industrial property right contained in the agreement limited to those which are inherent in the right itself?

In so far as the second test is concerned, it is generally satisfied if the restriction is prescribed or authorised by national legislation and the owner of the right is permitted by such legislation to impose certain restrictions or obligations on the user. But the restrictions imposed on the user must have a direct bearing on the exercise of the right, and those which go beyond this requirement are not covered by the sub-paragraphs with the result that they must then be considered in the light of art. 4 (1).[1]

What, then, is inherent in an industrial property right, and what goes beyond it? The Court of Justice has stated that different forms of industrial property rights merit different degrees of protection,[2] and reference should be made to Chapter 8 above for a discussion of what

1 Commissions Practical Guide (1962), Part II, III 3; Campbell, *op. cit.*, para. 2620.
2 *Sirena SRL* v. *Eda SRL*, 18 February 1971, XVII Rec. 69; [1971] CMLR 260.

is inherent in the grant of rights relating to patents,[1] trademarks[2] and knowhow rights.[3]

> "(3) they have as their sole object:
> (a) the development or uniform application of standards or types; or"

Although the three paragraphs contained in art. 4 (2) may be applied disjunctively, since agreements falling within art. 4 (2) (3) must have as their sole object provisions specified in each of the sub-paragraphs thereto, it is submitted that if the agreement contains any restriction other than those specified in one or other of sub-paragraphs (a), (b) or (c) of art. 4 (2) (3) then the benefit of art. 4 (2) cannot be safely claimed. In such case it would be prudent to notify the agreement with a request for individual exemption under art. 85 (3).

Thus there is no necessity to notify to the Commission agreements whose sole purpose is to limit the parties to producing goods which meet an agreed standard or design (for example, of size, type or kind); sub-paragraph (a) presupposes that the parties must adhere to the agreed criteria, and are not permitted to produce the goods otherwise than in accordance with them.[4]

> "(b) joint research and development;"

Article 4 (2) (3) (b) as originally adopted stipulated that the only research agreements which could be exempted from notification were those concerned with joint research for improvements to techniques. This provision was subsequently amended[5] since it was considered that agreements relating to all aspects of joint research and development do not, as a rule, restrict competition, thereby necessitating notification.[6]

---

1 *Centrafarm BV and Adriaan de Peijper* v. *Sterling Drug Inc.,* 31 October 1974, [1974] 2 CMLR 480, para. 9; see p. 222, above
2 *Centrafarm BV and Adriaan de Peijper* v. *Winthrop BV,* 31 October 1974, [1974] 2 CMLR 480, para. 8; see pp. 215–216, above.
3 *Re Agreement of Burroughs AG and Delplanque,* 22 December 1971, JO 1972 L13/50; [1972] CMLR D67; and see pp. 234ff., above.
4 It may be noted that by Reg. 2821/71 (set out in Appendix II, p. 380, below) the Commission is authorised to adopt a regulation granting exemption by category to agreements which have as their object the application of standards or types; no such regulation has as yet been adopted, see pp. 96–97, above.
5 By Reg. 2822/71 OJ 1971 L285/49.
6 There is provision under Council Reg. 2821/71 (set out in Appendix II, p. 380, below) for the Commission to adopt a Regulation granting exemption by category to agreements which have as their object the research and development of products or processes up to the state of industrial application, and exploitation of the results, including provisions regarding industrial property rights and confidential technical knowledge; no such Regulation has as yet been adopted, see pp. 96–97, above.
    See further Ch. 7, Section 2, p. 178, above, on research and development generally.

The original text also contained the proviso that the results of the research should be accessible to all parties and usable by them; the omission of this proviso in the amended text is not thought to be of any substantive significance, since if the agreement regulates not only the implementation of research and development but also the exploitation of the results achieved then it falls outside art. 4 (2) (3) (b) by virtue of the opening words to sub-paragraph 3; such an agreement is therefore notifiable.

> "(c) specialisation in the manufacture of products including agreements
>   necessary for achieving this,
>   – where the products which are the subject of specialisation do
>   not, in a substantial part of the Common Market, represent
>   more than 15% of the volume of business done in identical
>   products or considered by consumers to be similar by reason
>   of their characteristics, price and use, and
>   – where the total annual turnover of the participating under-
>   takings does not exceed 200 million units of account."[1]

This sub-paragraph, not originally contained in Regulation 17, was added by Council Regulation 2822/71[2] and the format is similar to that adopted in the Regulation granting exemption by category to certain specialisation agreements;[3] both the market share and the assets figure are higher but so long as the sole object of the agreement is specialisation in the manufacture of products, and both the defined limits are not exceeded, there is no necessity to notify such agreements to the Commission. It may be noted that, in contrast to the Regulation granting exemption by category,[4] there is no extended definition of undertaking to include other undertakings in the same group.[5]

See Chapter 7, Section 2[6] for comments on specialisation agreements generally.

---

1 The value of the unit of account is explained at p. 294, below.
2 OJ 1971 L285/49.
3 Commission Reg. 2779/72; see art. 3 (1) (a) and (b), OJ 1972 L292/23; commented on at pp. 112 and 113, above; compare also the similar format of the Commission's Communication on Agreements of Minor Importance, p. 77, above.
4 Reg. 2779/72, art. 4, pp. 113, 114, above.
5 See also an identical extended definition in the Communication on Agreements of Minor Importance, at p. 78, above.
6 At p. 184, above.

Effect of notification

General consideration of the effect of art. 85 (2) on a prohibited agreement and the effect achieved by notifying it is the subject of an earlier chapter;[1] it may be useful, however, to refer briefly to the matter again in order to outline the provisions of Regulation 17 which deal with the procedural effect of notification, where the agreements are notifiable under art. 4 (1) or 5 (1) and have been notified.

Distinction must be made between old, new and accession agreements.[2] As is explained in Chapter 4, above, the technical amendment to art. 5 of Regulation 17, by the new art. 25, has the effect of putting the parties to an accession agreement in the same position as the parties to an old agreement enjoyed when Regulation 17 was first adopted.[3] So long as notification was made by 1 November 1962[4] in the case of old agreements, and by 1 July 1973 in the case of accession agreements,[5] the Commission may specify that any decision it takes granting exemption under art. 85 (3) may take effect from a date earlier than the date of notification,[6] i.e. the prohibition contained in art. 85 (1) may be declared inapplicable from 13 March 1962 in the case of old agreements and 1 January 1973 in the case of accession agreements.[7]

In the case of old and accession agreements not notified within the time limits specified above, and in the case of new agreements the Commission may date its decision, and thus the exemption, back to the date of notification and no earlier.[8]

Where agreements are covered by art. 4 (2) (being either new agreements, or old or accession agreements brought within art. 4 (2) by virtue of art. 5 (2)) they are exempt from notification but if the Commission subsequently grants exemption under art. 85 (3) it may be back-dated to the date on which the agreements were entered into, or, if later, 13 March 1962 or 1 January 1973 depending on which is the relevant date.[9]

The date of submission of an application or notification is taken as being the date on which it is received by the Commission unless trans-

---

1 Ch. 4; see particularly the summary at pp. 123–124, above.
2 These terms are explained on p. 117, above.
3 See p. 119, above.
4 Reg. 17, art. 5 (1), as amended by Reg. 59, art. 1 (1); though in the case of two-party agreements the date 1 February 1963 was substituted by *ibid.*, art. 1 (2).
5 Reg. 17, art. 25 (2).
6 Reg. 17, art. 6 (2).
7 Art. 85 not being applicable to such agreements prior to those dates for reasons previously explained at p. 106, above.
8 Reg. 17, art. 6 (1). For an example, see *Re Sopelem-Langen*, 20 December 1971, JO 1972 L13/47; [1972] CMLR D77; where two agreements were entered into on 3 and 9 February 1965, and notified to the Commission on 8 February 1967; the Decision of the Commission took effect from the date of notification.
9 Reg. 17, art. 6 (2), and see n. 7, above.

mission is by registered post, in which case the date of submission is taken as being the date shown on the postmark of the place of posting.[1]

In the case of duly notified agreements, whether old, new or accession agreements, until such time as the Commission determines that exemption cannot be granted under art. 85 (3), the parties to the agreement may continue their activities in so far as such activities are covered by the scope of the notification, and no fines will be imposed on the parties by the Commission;[2] it may be noted, however, that whilst the Commission has no power to impose fines after the date of notification and before it takes its decision, if, after preliminary examination of the notified agreement, it informs the parties that application of art. 85 (3) is not justified, the parties run a substantial risk of the imposition of fines if they disregard the warning expressed by the Commission and continue to adhere to the terms of the agreement.[3]

In an effort to encourage compliance with art. 85, Regulation 17 provided that where notification of an old agreement[4] or accession agreement[5] was made within the stipulated time limit, the prohibition contained in art. 85 (1) can be retrospectively annulled to a date prior to the date of the notification if *either* the parties no longer give effect to provisions in the agreement which are prohibited by art. 85 (1) *or* they modify the agreement so as to bring it into line with what is permitted by art. 85 (1) or so that it meets the conditions contained in art. 85 (3). Likewise agreements in existence on 13 March 1962 which fall within art. 4 (2) may benefit from this provision,[6] if notified to the Commission by 1 January 1967.[7] Accession agreements are brought within this provision if notified by 1 July 1973.[8] A further inducement to notify by the specified dates is that no fine can be imposed in respect of any act taking place prior to the notification.[9]

---

1 Reg. 27, art. 3.
2 Reg. 17, art. 15 (5) (a), as extended to accession agreements by art. 25; where nullity of such agreements is retroactive (see pp. 123–124, above) and exemption is not granted, the parties may be faced with civil claims (see pp. 131ff., above); for a case where the Commission held that the activities of the undertakings exceeded those described in the notification and imposed fines, see *Re Belgian Wallpaper Manufacturers' Agreement* (*Papiers peints de Belgique*), 23 July 1974, OJ 1974 L237/3; [1974] 2 CMLR D102.
3 Reg. 17, art. 15 (6); the warning must be given in a formal decision, which must be adequately reasoned; *Cement Manufacturers* v. *EC Commission,* 15 March 1967, XIII Rec. 93; [1967] CMLR 77.
4 Art. 7 (1), as amended by Reg. 59, art. 1 (3).
5 Art. 7 (1), as extended by Reg. 17, art. 25 (2).
6 Reg. 17, art. 7 (2).
7 Reg. 118, art. 1, OJ 1963 162/2696.
8 Reg. 17, art. 25 (2).
9 Reg. 17, arts. 15 (5) (b) and 25 (3).

The effect of the procedure contained in art. 7 (1) is that where the agreement does not meet the requirements of art. 85 (3) (i.e. no exemption may be granted without modification) so long as the parties modify the agreement the Commission will annul the prohibition for the period following notification to the time the Commission demands amendment, even though during that period the parties have given full effect to the terms of the agreement.[1] The Commission has even invoked the principle of art. 7 (1) in cases where agreements have been submitted to it within the time limits, but only with a request for negative clearance. On the terms of the original agreements being modified to take them outside the scope of art. 85 (1) altogether, the Commission issued negative clearances which were retrospective back to 13 March 1962.[2]

Article 7 (1) specifically provides that such retrospective annulment of the prohibition applies only to the undertakings and associations of undertakings which are party to the notification: undertakings which have not expressly consented to the notification are not able to seek the benefit of the retrospective authorisation in respect of the agreement. The effect of this provision is to ensure that where there is an agreement which cannot as it stands be exempted under art. 85 (3), and the parties thereto refuse to comply with its terms in the belief that continued observance of them may render them liable to fines imposed by the Commission, refusal to consent to notifying the agreement under art. 7 will protect such parties from consequences in civil law, e.g., damages in respect of breach of contract in the event that the Commission grants retrospective authorisation of the agreement. By consenting to notify the Commission of the agreement the parties implicitly accept the terms and conditions of the agreement and continue to be subject to its provisions for the period up to the date on which a decision is taken.

Advantages of notification

Receipt by the Commission of a notification for exemption under art. 85 (3) confers limited rights on the parties so notifying the agreement. Unless the notification was made prior to 1 November 1962 in the case of an old agreement or, in the case of an accession agreement, prior to 1 July 1973, such notification does not confer provisional validity on the agreements;[3] further, the special provisions contained

---

1 For a case where Reg. 17, art. 7 (1), was not applied, though the parties had notified within the time limits see *Re Belgian Central Heating Agreement,* 20 October 1972, JO 1972 L264/22; [1972] CMLR D130.
2 *Re Pirelli-Dunlop,* 5 December 1969, JO 1969 L323/21; *Re ASPA,* 30 June 1970, JO 1970 L148/9; [1970] CMLR D25; *Re Supexie's Agreement,* 23 December 1970, JO 1971 L10/12; [1971] CMLR D1.
3 *Brasserie de Haecht* v. *Wilkin-Janssen (No. 2),* 6 February 1973, [1973] ECR 77; [1973] CMLR 287; and see p. 121, above.

in Regulation 17 regarding amendment of old and accession agreements found to be incompatible with the requirements of art. 85 (3) or for the issue of a negative clearance (see art. 7) do not apply.

Even where an agreement cannot benefit from provisional validity and the consequences of the application of art. 7 (1), there is still advantage to be derived from notification, since no exemption can be obtained under art. 85 (3), nor will a negative clearance under Regulation 17, art. 2, be given, in the absence of formal application, and the Commission will not impose fines for infringement of art. 85 (1) or art. 86 after the date of notification and before its decision under art. 85 (3).[1]

SECTION 4 METHOD OF NOTIFYING FOR EXEMPTION AND APPLYING FOR NEGATIVE CLEARANCE: FORM A/B

A request for exemption and/or for negative clearance must be made on the prescribed form. It will be noticed that the text of Regulation 17 distinguishes between "applying" for a negative clearance and "notifying" for exemption under art. 85 (3). This distinction was reflected in the existence of two separate forms, Form A and Form B, for negative clearance and exemption respectively. This led to a certain amount of confusion, and a single form, Form A/B, suitable for either or both procedures, was adopted in 1968.[2]

It may be noted that in a number of instances where undertakings did not originally apply for negative clearance, the Commission has in fact issued a negative clearance where the information submitted to it clearly showed that the intention was to request a negative clearance, or where discussions with the Commission have indicated that such a request was in fact being made.[3] However in general the Commission will not treat an application for negative clearance as a notification,[4] leaving it open to the undertakings concerned to apply for either or both. In practice the safest course to adopt is to request both, at least where the facts lend some justification.

Notification made for the purposes of obtaining exemption under art. 85 (3) is not treated as an admission on the part of the undertakings concerned that the provisions of art. 85 (1) are fulfilled, i.e., that the

---

1 Reg. 17, art. 15 (2).
2 Reg. 1133/68: OJ 1968 L189/1.
3 *Re Agreement of Nicholas Frères,* 30 July 1964, JO 1964 136/2287; [1964] CMLR 505; *Re Cement Makers' Agreement,* 5 May 1969, JO 1969 L122/8; [1969] CMLR D15; *Re Cobelaz (No. 2),* 6 November 1968, JO 1968 L276/19; [1968] CMLR D68; *Re Pirelli-Dunlop,* 5 December 1969, JO 1969 L323/21.
4 Commission's Explanatory Memorandum to Form A/B.

parties are carrying on prohibited practices, accordingly the Commission sees no conflict in applying for a negative clearance on the one hand and at the same time making a notification for exemption on the other hand.[1]

It is not necessary that every undertaking which is party to an agreement must be party to an application or notification made on Form A/B.[2] In such event an indication must be given of the manner in which the application or notification has been made known to the other undertakings. Where Form A/B is submitted on behalf of an undertaking, it must be accompanied by written proof that such person is authorised to represent the undertaking.[3] Seven copies of the Form must be submitted to the Commission and must be supported by a similar number of supporting documents which, if copies, must be certified as true copies.[4] Applications and notifications must be in one of the official working languages of the Community (i.e., English, French, German, Italian, Dutch, Danish)[5] and translations of documents not in these languages must be submitted.[6] Where the agreements in question have not been reduced to writing, in whole or in part, the Commission requires an outline of the agreements in respect of which notification is made.[7] Submission to the Commission of a standard contract in a form frequently entered into by the notifying party covers all such copy contracts as from the date of notification.[8]

With regard to the requirement to supply information as to whether or how far the agreements in question relate to restrictive practices, the limitation on the power of the Commission to impose fines will only apply to practices which fall within activities described in the notification.[9] It is of considerable importance, therefore, to ensure that Form A/B is completed as accurately as possible. Further the supply of incorrect or misleading information may result in the imposition of fines.[10] Information may be supplied by third parties or other information may already be in possession of the Commission or come to its

---

1 Commission's Explanatory Memorandum to Form A/B.
2 Reg. 27, art. 1 (1).
3 Reg. 27, art. 1 (2).
4 Reg. 27, art. 2 (2).
5 Council Reg. 1, art. 1, of 15 April 1958, OJ 1958 17/385, as amended by the Accession Treaty.
6 Reg. 27, art. 2 (3).
7 Form A/B, section II, question 2.
8 *Brasserie de Haecht* v. *Wilkin-Janssen (No. 2)*, 6 February 1973, [1973] ECR 77; [1973] CMLR 287, at p. 303, para. 21; cf. Form A/B, Part II (1) (b).
9 Reg. 17, art. 15 (2) (a); and see p. 265, n. 2 and text, above.
10 Reg. 17, art. 15 (1) (a); and see pp. 294, 295, below.

attention, particularly following publication of a summary of the facts in the Official Journal.[1]

In the case of a request for exemption under art. 85 (3), this will not be granted unless the positive and negative criteria are met;[2] accordingly the Commission requires an explanation as to the extent to which the agreement in question meets such requirements. The positive requirements may be satisfactorily met, for example, by improvement in quality of products, the introduction of new technical processes or reduction in costs, and of particular significance may be cost reductions which are passed on to the consumer; also material is the extent to which competition is faced from other manufacturers who supply competing products. Application of art. 85 (3) is based largely on economic considerations, and the following matters are those to which the Commission is likely to give particular consideration in determining whether or not exemption can be granted in any particular case:[3]

(a) The size of the participating undertakings, their turnover for the product or service in question, and what share it represents of the total production or supply of the product or service in question;

(b) the economic situation on the relevant market;[4]

(c) the structure of the relevant market (degree of concentration, problems of adapting to conditions in the Common Market);

(d) the volume of trade between member states on the relevant market and the influence of the agreement on such trade;

(e) effects of the agreement on the market (for example, on prices, quality, quantities, distribution methods, consumer choice);

(f) the degree of competition subsisting between the parties under the agreement;

(g) the degree of competition subsisting between persons who are not parties to the agreement.

There appears to be no hard and fast rule determining the length of time which the Commission takes in considering agreements or practices submitted to it under arts. 85 and 86; it may be safely assumed, however, in the absence of exceptional circumstances, and certainly if no direct approach is made to the Commission requesting expedited

---

1 Pursuant to Reg. 17, art. 19 (3), as to which see p. 285, below.
2 See comments on art. 85 (3) generally, pp. 81ff., above.
3 Commission's Explanatory Memorandum to Form A/B.
4 For the meaning of relevant market, see Ch. 6, above.

attention,[1] that the delay can be measured in terms of years (as likely as not many)[2] rather than in months. In any event a minimum delay of at least six months between the submission of Form A/B and the Commission decision should be anticipated even if the formal decision-taking procedures[3] are observed without undue interruptions.

---

1 As, for example, was made in *Re Henkel-Colgate*, 23 December 1971, JO 1972 L14/14.
2 E.g., *Re Supexie*, 23 December 1970, JO 1971 L10/12; [1971] CMLR D1: negative clearance requested 30 October 1962, Commission Decision dated 23 December 1970; *Re ASPA*, 30 June 1970, JO 1970 L148/9; [1970] CMLR D25; negative clearance requested 31 October 1962, Commission Decision dated 30 June 1970; *Re Duro-Dyne/Europair*, 19 December 1974, OJ 1975 L29/11; exemption requested 31 October 1962; Commission's Decision dated 19 December 1974.
3 As to which see Ch. 11, below.

Chapter 11

Commission Procedure

It is the purpose of this chapter to consider the way in which the Commission determines whether or not the prohibitions contained in arts. 85 and 86 are applicable to agreements or practices which come to its attention.

SECTION 1   INTRODUCTION

Organisation of Commission

The Commission maintains a permanent department (at present, and referred to herein, as Directorate-General IV – DG IV) which supervises the administration of the competition rules contained in the Treaties establishing the European Communities; the department is under the overall supervision of one of the members of the Commission.

The department is responsible for the day-to-day supervision of problems relating to competition rules, maintaining such contact as is necessary with other departments in the Commission which may have an interest in any matter under scrutiny by DG IV As has been stated earlier, the competition policy of the Community cannot be considered in isolation from the other areas of activity of the Community; for example, when the Commission published an announcement recommending that self-restraint marketing agreements[1] should be notified to the Commission under Regulation 17, DG IV conferred with other Commission departments, particularly those dealing with external relations and external trade, before the announcement was made.

At all times, and particularly during the formal Commission procedure which results in the taking of a formal decision,[2] DG IV maintains close contact with the Commission's Legal Service, in which

---

1 OJ 1972 C111; and see now *Re Franco-Japanese Ballbearings Agreement*, 29 November 1974, OJ 1974 L343/19; [1975] 1 CMLR D8.
2 Described at p. 280, below; for a detailed analysis of the decision-making procedure, see Frances Graupour, "Commission Decision-making on Competition Questions" (1973), 10 CML Rev. 291.

a specialist team of lawyers is responsible for working with, and approving the activities of, DG IV. The Legal Service plays a significant role in the Commission infra-structure, since it is always consulted by the Commission acting as a collegiate body before it takes a decision as proposed by DG IV.

Commission's general approach in administering the Competition Rules

Whilst the Commission is armed with the power to investigate alleged infringements of the competition rules, to ban certain practices and to approve others, and to impose fines,[1] its primary function is not that of processing and approving every aspect of commercial activity, but rather that of ensuring that agreements or practices which have or are likely to have a significant effect on the unity of the Common Market comply with the competition rules.

That the Commission is prepared to adopt a pragmatic approach in its task of applying the rules contained in arts. 85 and 86 is apparent from the manner in which it has set about implementing the tasks assigned to it. In applying its powers it exercises considerable procedural flexibility in defining the scope of arts. 85 (1) and 86 when issuing, or refusing to issue, a negative clearance.[2] Further, it has accepted substantial limitation on the scope of the prohibition contained in art. 85 (1), as is indicated by the provisions of the Communications on co-operation agreements between undertakings,[3] and on agreements of minor importance.[4] The Court of Justice likewise accepts the need for a flexible approach to determining and assessing the appreciable effect of an agreement in any particular set of circumstances.[5]

Additionally, the power to determine whether or not exemption should be granted under art. 85 (3) has enabled the Commission to define the limits of what will be permitted under art. 85 (1), and to indicate what may be permitted even though technically within the prohibition. Thus group exemptions enable automatic approval to be given to whole categories of similar agreements (such as exclusive distribution agreements[6] and specialisation agreements[7]).

---

1 As to all of which see below.
2 See p. 251, above.
3 JO 1968 C75/3; [1968] CMLR D5; and see p. 79, above.
4 JO 1970 C/64; [1970] CMLR D15; and see p. 74, above.
5 *Franz Völk* v. *Etablissements Vervaecke*, 9 July 1969, XV Rec. 295; [1969] CMLR 273; *Béguelin Import Co.* v. *GL Import-Export SA*, 25 November 1971, XVII Rec. 949; [1972] CMLR 81.
6 See p. 97, above.
7 See p. 108, above.

Perhaps one of the most important aspects of the Commission's approach to its task is its recognition that informal discussion can be every bit as effective as reliance on formal procedures. It has on numerous occasions agreed that certain aspects of an agreement or practice can be altered to make it acceptable without even resorting to the formal procedure laid down in Regulation 17 and elsewhere. Indeed, the value of an approach to the Commission to discuss informally problems which may arise through the subsequent application of the competition rules cannot be overstressed, especially in view of the considerable amount of time that is likely to elapse if a formal decision is to be sought. Whilst such an approach may not always produce a definite answer, particularly in the case of contacts made on a "no-names" basis, early consultation with DG IV will enable the undertakings to enter into agreements at a later date in the knowledge that no objection is likely to be forthcoming from the Commission. Whilst the advantages of obtaining confirmation in this way from the Commission that it will not invoke the prohibitions contained in arts. 85 (1) and 86 are that the procedure is informal, speedier and usually avoids detailed publicity, the disadvantage is that the parties will not obtain the security of a formal decision granting exemption under art. 85 (3) which will also regulate the position of the parties in the event of subsequent civil proceedings in relation to the same agreement.

In a number of instances the Commission has published brief details of agreements and practices, which have either been notified to it or which have come to its attention and which, following informal bilateral contacts between the Commission and the parties, have been modified or terminated so as to comply with art. 85 (1) or art. 86; in some cases it has been possible to determine the attitude of the Commission with regard to a particular type of agreement or practice even though no formal decision has hitherto been adopted. Reference to the Bulletin which the Commission publishes each month can be an invaluable source of information on current Community development in the competition sector.

SECTION 2   THE COLLATION OF THE INFORMATION NECESSARY TO TAKE A DECISION

Initial sources of Commission's information

In considering the possible application of the competition rules, the Commission is most likely to derive information leading it to suspect an infringement of art. 85 or art. 86 from one or more of the following sources:

(a) Full disclosure of agreements and practices is required where the Commission is requested to give an exemption under art. 85 (3), or a negative clearance. In either case the information may be made available to the Commission by one or more of the parties to such agreements or practices.[1]

(b) Member states or natural or legal persons who claim a legitimate interest may apply to the Commission to find that there is infringement of arts. 85 and 86; whereas a member state may make such application even if its legitimate interests are not prejudiced by the agreement or practice in question, an undertaking or individual must show that he is able to claim such an interest.[2] Although the complainant must be able to show that he has a justified interest in termination of the alleged infringement (e.g., on the grounds that he is suffering damage by its continuance),[3] in practice any legitimate grievance is of interest to the Commission even if it does not enable it to issue an immediate decision holding that the prohibitions contained in art. 85 (1) and art. 86 have been breached. Such information may constitute sufficient grounds for the Commission to open its own investigation.[4] The Commission advises that such complaints be made on Form C, in seven copies, and the same procedure as regards completion and submission of this form applies as in the case of Form A/B.[5] It will be noted that it is not necessary for such a person to *prove* the validity of an interest in applying to the Commission to find such infringement in contrast to the position with regard to entitlement to be heard at a Commission hearing,[6] where sufficient interest must be *shown*. The Commission has absolute discretion, subject only to appeal to the Court of Justice, to determine what evidence is sufficient for its deliberations before taking a decision based on that evidence.

(c) The Commission maintains both formal and informal contact with the authorities responsible for administering the national antitrust legislation in each member state.[7]

---

1 Reg. 27, art. 1 (1); and see p. 268, above.
2 Reg. 17, art. 3 (2).
3 Commission's Practical Guide (1962), Part II, I, Campbell, *op. cit.*, Vol. II, para. 2615; see, e.g., *Re Preserved Mushrooms,* 8 January 1975, OJ 1975 L29/26.
4 Reg. 17, arts. 11, 12 and 14, see pp. 276ff., below.
5 See Ch. 10, Section 2, p. 267, above.
6 See p. 284, below, on Reg. 17, art. 19 (2).
7 Reg. 17, art. 10.

This close and constant liaison is maintained by means of:

(i) the existence of the Advisory Committee on Restrictive Practices and Monopolies to which each member state appoints a representative who is competent in restrictive practices and monopolies legislation.[1] The Committee must be consulted by the Commission before it takes any decision[2] and, although the opinion of the Committee is not binding on the Commission, its views carry considerable weight.

(ii) the transmission by the Commission to national authorities of documentation it receives in connection with an application for exemption under art. 85 (3), a request for a negative clearance or where such documents are lodged in connection with a possible infringement of arts. 85 or 86.[3]

Such liaison ensures that information is channelled back to the Commission from the national authorities, and vice versa; this information is subject to rules relating to improper disclosure, whether by the Commission, national authorities or the servants of either.[4]

Additionally, governments of member states and national authorities responsible for administering restrictive trade practices and monopolies legislation are required to give all necessary information in assisting the Commission to carry out its duties in applying the competition rules.[5] The Commission is fully entitled to rely on the results of investigations carried out by the national authorities in implementing the Community rules of competition.[6]

(d) Objections and queries raised by individuals, whether customers or competitors, who consider that they have been prejudiced by behaviour form a valuable source of information which may enable the Commission to take action. Questions to the Commission from members of the European Parliament also may lead to Commission inquiry.

(e) The Commission, where it suspects that competition is being restricted or distorted within the Common Market because of circumstances prevailing in any sector of the economy, may inquire generally

---

1 Reg. 17, art. 10 (3) and (4).
2 Reg. 17, art. 10 (3) and see p. 285, below.
3 Reg. 17, art. 10 (1).
4 Reg. 17, art. 20.
5 Reg. 17, art. 11 (1).
6 *Francolor* v. *EC Commission*, 14 July 1972, XVIII Rec. 851; [1972] CMLR 557; *Hoechst* v. *EC Commission*, 14 July 1972, XVIII Rec. 927; [1972] CMLR 557.

into the sector in question.[1] Among inquiries undertaken so far by the Commission are those relating to the margarine sector (as a result of which an undertaking in a dominant position terminated a practice of paying bonuses for exclusive purchase) and to the brewery sector.[2]

Commission's powers to require supply of information

In carrying out its duties in implementation of the competition rules, the Commission may obtain all necessary information from the governments and competent authorities of the member states, and from undertakings and associations of undertakings.[3]

In requesting information from an undertaking or association of undertakings, a copy of which request must be sent by the Commission to the competent national authority,[4] the Commission must state why the request is being made and the authority for such request, and must also point out that fines may be imposed for the supply of incorrect information.[5] If the undertaking or association of undertakings fails to reply within the time stipulated by the Commission, it may take a decision requiring the disclosure of the requested information. The decision must specify what information is required, indicate the time in which it is to be supplied and state that penalties may be imposed.[6] The procedure is not frequently used, since in practice the Commission has found that in the majority of cases undertakings supply the requested information within the stipulated time limit.[7]

Information may be required to be supplied not only by the undertakings to which the request is addressed, but by their representatives as well, and in the case of legal persons, companies or firms or associations without legal personality, by the persons authorised to represent them by law or by their constitution.[8]

Information received in the course of an investigation may be used

---

1 Reg. 17, art. 12; and see p. 277, below.
2 Commission's 1st Report on Competition Policy (April 1972), sec. 124.
3 Reg. 17, art. 11 (1).
4 Reg. 17, art. 11 (2).
5 Reg. 17, art. 11 (3).
6 Reg. 17, art. 11 (5).
7 Though the Commission has found it necessary to threaten the imposition of fines or periodic penalty payments, e.g., in the course of carrying out a general enquiry into the beer industry (Decisions of 18 June 1971, JO 1971 L161/2, 6 and 10). See also Decisions of 1 February 1971, JO 1971 L34/13 and of 2 July 1971, JO 1971 L161/32.
8 Reg. 17, art. 11; Reg. 17, art. 20 (1).

for no purpose other than the investigation in question,[1] although this does not preclude the transmission of that information to national authorities. Disclosure of any information obtained by officials of the Commission and competent authorities in the course of such investigation is forbidden.[2]

It is submitted that art. 11 cannot be used by the Commission as a means of obtaining information on the offchance that it might reveal the existence of an infringement of art. 85 or art. 86. On the other hand where the Commission suspects that competition is being restricted or distorted within the Common Market because of circumstances prevailing in any sector of the economy, it may, under art. 12 (1), inquire generally into the sector in question. In so doing, the Commission may require undertakings to supply information to enable it to determine whether or not there is an infringement of the articles for the purposes of taking a decision pursuant to art. 3. It may call on undertakings to communicate agreements which do not require notification under arts. 4 (2) and 5 (2) of Regulation 17.[3]

The procedure adopted is that the Commission requests the information from the undertakings in the sector concerned, sends a copy of such request to the national authorities, and in the event of the undertakings failing to supply the information within the required time limit, takes a decision requiring supply of the requested information. Failure to supply it renders the undertakings concerned liable to fines and periodic penalty payments; the decision may be reviewed, on appeal, by the Court of Justice. The Commission must consult the Advisory Committee on Restrictive Practices and Monopolies before taking its decision.[4]

The meaning of "sector of the economy" is not specified in Regulation 17 or elsewhere, but is broad enough to cover any market situation which suggests to the Commission, whether on the grounds of the actual trend of trade between member states, price movements, inflexibility of prices or any other reason, that competition in the Common Market is being restricted.[5] Whilst the provisions of the article are so wide that the Commission is at liberty to demand information in almost any circumstances, it is our view that such an inquiry cannot be instigated by the Commission as a means of enabling it to extract information from undertakings or groups of undertakings

---

1 Reg. 17, art. 20 (1).
2 Reg. 17, art. 20 (2).
3 Reg. 17, art. 12 (2).
4 Reg. 17, art. 12 (4).
5 Reg. 17, art. 12 (1).

where their size suggests that they hold a dominant position in the
sector in question – the inquiry must cover the whole of the sector,
and not be directed at the main undertakings who operate in that
sector. This does not mean to say that the Commission will not
uncover practices which are prohibited by art. 86, and, indeed, is
entitled to demand details of the structure of undertakings in a dominant
position and particulars of their behaviour,[1] but such requests can
only be made in the context of the inquiry into the economic sector
concerned. The Commission is not entitled to cast around for information from the largest undertakings under the guise of carrying out a
sectorial market investigation in the hope that it will uncover matters
subject to the prohibitions; any such attempt could be the subject of
appeal to the Court of Justice under art. 173 of the Treaty, as being a
misuse by the Commission of its powers.[2]

Commission's powers of investigation

In ensuring that the provisions of arts. 85 and 86 are observed,
the Commission may undertake all necessary investigations into
undertakings and associations of undertakings;[3] national authorities must undertake such investigation if so requested by the
Commission.[4]

Before carrying out any investigation the Commission must take a
formal decision, specifying the subject matter and purpose of the
investigation and the date on which it is to begin.[5] The decision, a copy
of which is sent to the undertakings concerned, must also state that the
undertakings to which the decision is addressed may appeal to the
Court, and that fines and periodic penalty payments[6] may be imposed
for intentionally or negligently refusing to submit to such an investigation.

Prior to taking a decision to carry out such an investigation,
the Commission must consult with the competent authorities
of the member state in which the investigation is to be carried out.[7]

Accordingly, the Commission is precluded from mounting an
investigation without notice either to national authorities or the

---

1 Reg. 17, art. 12 (3).
2 See Ch. 12, Section 1, p. 302, below.
3 Reg. 17, art. 14 (1).
4 Reg. 17, art. 13 (1).
5 Reg. 17, art. 14 (3).
6 As to which, see pp. 294, 295 and 298, 299, below.
7 Reg. 17, art. 14 (4).

undertaking or undertakings concerned; no undertaking will ever find itself subject to a formal investigation without receiving intimation of the fact.

Officials of the national authorities are required to carry out the investigation at the request of the Commission, subject to producing to the undertaking concerned written authorisation from the relevant national authority of the member state in whose territory the investigation is to be made;[1] Commission officials may assist national officials in carrying out an investigation, subject to giving due notice to the national authorities of their proposed action.[2]

Receipt of notice by an undertaking that an investigation is to be made should not be used by the undertaking as a reason for destroying incriminating evidence; not only may the Commission already be in possession of evidence against the undertaking concerned, but, further, the intentional or negligent production of incomplete business records may lead to the imposition of fines.[3]

Officials authorised by the Commission to conduct an investigation have power to:

(i) examine books and other business records;
(ii) take copies of or extracts from books and business records;[4]
(iii) ask for oral explanations on the spot;[5]
(iv) enter any premises, land and means of transport of undertakings.

Where the Commission takes a decision under art. 14 (3) undertakings and associations of undertakings have no option but to submit to an investigation; such decision is subject at all times to appeal to the Court of Justice, but an undertaking has no formal right to be heard by the Commission before it takes a decision requiring an investigation to be held. Refusal to submit to an investigation thereafter may result in the imposition of fines.[6]

---

1 Reg. 17, art. 13 (1).
2 Reg. 17, art. 14 (5).
3 Reg. 17, art. 15 (1) (c), ranging from 100 to 5,000 units of account, and see pp. 294, 295, below.
4 In practice the Commission has found this power to be too limited; it may be noted that, in its proposal for a regulation on the control of concentrations between undertakings, it is seeking the power to request that undertakings should prepare copies of or extracts from books, etc., art. 12 (1) (b), in Appendix III, p. 400, below. As regards professional privilege, see p. 297, below.
5 For an example where the Commission used this power, see Re Preserved Mushrooms, 8 January 1975, OJ 1975 L29/26.
6 Reg. 17, art. 15 (1) (c), ranging from 100 to 5,000 units of account.

SECTION 3 THE DECISION-TAKING PROCESS

The formal stages of Commission procedure by which it may implement the competition rules are mainly determined by the provisions of Regulations 17 and 99/63 (set out at pp. 318 and 345, below), and by the Commission's internal procedural rules.

The Commission may commence its formal procedure with regard to the activities of an undertaking or undertakings with a view to achieving one of the following ends:

(a) to issue a negative clearance under Regulation 17, art. 2;[1] or
(b) to declare under Regulation 17, art. 6, that the prohibition of art. 85 (1) is inapplicable pursuant to art. 85 (3); [2] or
(c) to require termination under Regulation 17, art. 3, of an infringement of arts. 85 or 86.

The purpose of a decision taken by the Commission under Regulation 17, art. 3, is to enforce the application of the prohibitions contained in arts. 85 and 86; the decision itself does not constitute the prohibition, but is merely a declaratory statement to the undertaking or undertakings concerned, and to the world in general, that the parties to whom the decision is addressed are in breach of the prohibitions. Fines[3] or periodic penalty payments[4] may be imposed by the Commission to enforce compliance with the competition rules.

Whilst the Commission may intervene under art. 3 when it believes that there is a breach of either art. 85 or art. 86, it is under no obligation to take simultaneous action with regard to identical or similar breaches committed by other undertakings, though this does not relieve those undertakings from observing rules to which they are bound to conform.[5]

It may be noted that the Commission may take a decision under art. 3 and may impose fines under art. 15, even if undertakings have put an end to the prohibited practices prior to the date of adoption of a formal decision.[6]

During the course of taking a formal decision with regard to the

---

1 As to which, see Ch. 10, Section 2, p. 251, above.
2 As to which, see Ch. 3, Section 1, p. 81, above.
3 Reg. 17, art. 15 (2) (a); p. 296, below.
4 Reg. 17, art. 16 (1) (c); p. 298, below.
5 *Federal Republic of Germany* v. *EC Commission,* 16 June 1966, XII Rec. 228; [1967] CMLR 22.
6 *Chemiefarma, Buchler and Boehringer* v. *EC Commission,* 15 July 1970, XVI Rec. 661, 733 and 769, at pp. 703, 764 and 811; Cf. RTPA 1956; *Re Newspaper Proprietors' Agreement,* [1964] 1 All ER 55; [1964] 1 WLR 31, HL.

implementation of arts. 85 and 86 the following formal steps must be taken:

Formal opening of proceedings and transmission by Commission of its statement of objections to undertakings concerned

Formal proceedings are commenced either by the Commissioner responsible for DG IV signing a form to that effect upon receipt of a complaint, or by a formal decision being taken by the Commission to institute proceedings on its own initiative. In either case, the Commission is required to inform the competition authorities of member states of the opening of proceedings,[1] and the undertakings concerned are likewise informed.

Prior to reaching the stage of formal proceedings, the Commission will usually have already been in contact with the undertakings concerned either by way of correspondence, or informal meetings between them and representatives of the Commission, or formal contact may have been made during the course of an investigation instigated by the Commission in accordance with art. 14 (1). Such contact between the undertakings and the Commission will normally have enabled both sides to establish the areas of dispute in question.

The Commission must then inform the undertakings in writing of the practices to which objection is made; this is done by a statement of objections.[2] It is irrelevant that the Commission notifies the undertakings of the opening of proceedings at the same time as it forwards its statement of objections.[3] As an alternative, in appropriate circumstances (particularly where notice has to be given to a number of undertakings for which no joint agent has been appointed) the undertakings may be informed by means of a notice published in the Official Journal.[4] Not only is the Commission required to pay due regard to the legitimate business secrets of the undertakings if notice is given in this manner, but, further, no fine or periodic penalty payment may be imposed.[5]

Service of the Commission's statement of objections is properly made on an undertaking in a territory outside the EEC even where the national law of that third country does not recognise the form in which such service is made. It is the aim of the Community's

---

1 Reg. 17, art. 10.
2 Reg. 99/63, art. 2 (1); the statement must indicate the matters to which the Commission objects sufficiently clearly to enable the undertakings concerned to determine the extent to which they wish to make representations to the Commission.
3 *Azienda Colori Nazionali Affini SpA (ANCA)* v. *EC Commission,* 14 July 1972, XVIII Rec. 933; [1972] CMLR 557.
4 Reg. 99/63, art. 2 (2).
5 Reg. 99/63, art. 2 (3).

competition rules to prevent distortions to competition within the
Common Market, and since proceedings relating to these rules are
regulated by procedural steps which give the undertakings concerned
the opportunity to explain their position[1], service in a non-EEC
country in accordance with Community law and not in accordance
with the national law of that country has been held not to invalidate
subsequent administrative proceedings.[2]

The statement of objections may be signed by an authorised official
of the Commission.[3] It is this statement which determines the position
of the Commission vis-à-vis the undertakings in relation to
which proceedings for infringement have been initiated; the
Commission decision initiating a procedure is not determinative in
this respect.[4]

Proceedings before the Commission with regard to arts. 85 and
86 are administrative and not judicial proceedings; the Commission
is obliged to inform the undertakings of the essential factual elements
on which it bases its complaint, but it is not necessary that the whole
Commission file should be communicated to the undertakings.[5]
The statement of objections should detail all the facts on which the
Commission relies in making its case and fix a time limit within which
the undertakings concerned must notify the Commission of their
views on that statement.[6] Where the Commission is obliged to initiate
new investigations in the course of proceedings already commenced,
the statement of objections need not be amended unless the Commission considers that the undertaking concerned must be charged
with infringement based on new facts or it bases its proof of infringement on substantially different grounds.[7]

The time limit for preparation of the undertaking's comments may
not be less than two weeks,[8] time running from the day following
receipt of a communication.[9] In practice, the Commission usually
allows a delay of three weeks for such observations.

---

1 At a formal hearing under Reg. 17, art. 19; see below.
2 *J. R. Geigy AG* v. *EC Commission*, 14 July 1972, XVIII Rec. 787; [1972] CMLR
  557.
3 *ICI Ltd* v. *EC Commission*, 14 July 1972, XVIII Rec. 619; [1972] CMLR 557.
4 *Ibid.*
5 *Etablissements Consten SA and Grundig Verkaufs-GmbH* v. *EEC Commission,* 13 July
  1966, XII Rec. 429; [1966] CMLR 418, at p. 469; *ICI Ltd.* v. *EC Commission* (above).
6 Reg. 99/63, art. 3 (1).
7 *Farbenfabriken Bayer AG* v. *EC Commission*, 14 July 1972, XVIII Rec. 745; [1972]
  CMLR 557.
8 Reg. 99/63, art. 11 (1).
9 Reg. 99/63, art. 11 (2).

At the same time as commenting on the Commission's statement of objections the undertakings may forward to the Commission documentary evidence on which they might wish to rely[1] and may ask that they, or other persons, be heard in corroboration of these facts[2] (see below). In practice the fact that objection is not taken to the Commission's statement of objections in the reply of the undertakings will not bar subsequent objection being raised at the oral hearing.

Commission hearing of the parties and third parties

HEARING OF THE PARTIES

The Commission is bound to hear the parties on its objections, if so requested, before it takes a decision with regard to an exemption under art. 85 (3), the grant of a negative clearance or the taking of a decision requiring the termination of an infringement.[3] An opportunity to be heard must also be afforded to undertakings where the Commission proposes to take a decision renewing, revoking or amending a decision, or by which it proposes to impose fines or periodic penalty payments.[4] The opportunity for such a hearing must be given irrespective of whether or not the Commission ultimately takes a favourable decision; the meeting is held on a date determined by the Commission.[5]

Persons appearing before the hearing (which is usually chaired by a representative of DG IV) may be represented by legal representatives.[6] In the case of undertakings they may only be represented by a "duly authorised agent in their regular employment and by a statutorily or otherwise properly admitted representative ..."[7] The Court of Justice proceeded to justify this provision by pointing out that such persons are usually the best instructed as regards the facts and technical or economic aspects of the activities of their undertakings.

Persons appearing at the hearing, whether in a representative capacity or not, may be assisted by lawyers or university teachers entitled to plead before the Court of Justice.[8] The Commission is not entitled to dictate to an undertaking how it should be represented in proceedings.[9]

---

1 Reg. 99/63, art. 3 (3).
2 *Ibid.*
3 Reg. 17, art. 19 (1); and Reg. 99/63, art. 7 (1). Undertakings, individuals and interested third parties appearing at a Commission hearing do so at their own expense.
4 *Ibid.*; the Commission must give any person whose interests are perceptibly affected by its decision the opportunity to make his point of view known: *Transocean Marine Paint Association* v. *EC Commission*, 23 October 1974, [1974] 2 CMLR 459, para. 15.
5 Reg. 99/63, art. 8 (1).
6 Reg. 99/63, art. 9 (2).
7 *Ibid.*, *BASF AG* v. *EC Commission*, 14 July 1972, XVIII Rec. 713; [1972] CMLR 557, at p. 631, para. 11.
8 Reg. 99/63, art. 9 (2); and see p. 306, text and n. 9, below.
9 *BASF AG* v. *EC Commission* (above).

The hearing is in private;[1] a note is kept of the proceedings and copies of the record are circulated to the parties for approval.[2] The purpose of this provision is to indicate to the person heard that the minutes are in accordance with his essential statements.[3] Delay in circulation of the minutes until shortly before the Commission takes its decision will not constitute grounds for invalidating the decision unless there is doubt as to the accuracy of the reproduction of the statement.[4]

It appears that an undertaking may refute statements made at the oral hearing by writing to the Commission at a later stage[5] or may present its case at a subsequent date to the hearing if unable to arrange for due representation in time.[6]

Representatives of the member states may attend the hearing, and make their point of view known.[7]

Information derived from the meeting is subject to rules of professional and business secrecy which bind officials of the Commission with regard to information acquired in implementing and administering the competition rules.[8]

If an undertaking is given at the oral hearing that the parties will correct the matters complained of, it is not likely that the Commission will proceed to take a formal decision under Regulation 17, arts. 2, 3 or 6.

HEARING OF THIRD PARTIES

If either the Commission (or the competent authorities of the member states)[9] considers it necessary, third persons may be given the opportunity to be heard subject to their being able to show "a sufficient interest".[10] "Sufficient interest" is not defined but it is submitted that the interest must be such that the person concerned is directly affected by the agreement or practice which is the subject of the hearing.[11] Whilst it is desirable that the Commission should make the fullest possible enquiries with regard to the implications

---

1 Reg. 99/63, art. 9 (3).
2 Reg. 99/63, art. 9 (4).
3 *ICI Ltd.* v. *EC Commission*, 14 July 1972, XVIII Rec. 619; [1972] CMLR 557.
4 Ibid.
5 *Farbenfabriken Bayer AG* v. *EC Commission*, 14 July 1972, XVIII Rec. 745; [1972] CMLR 557.
6 *Hoechst v. EC Commission*, 14 July 1972, XVIII Rec. 933; [1972] CMLR 557.
7 Reg. 99/63, art. 8 (2).
8 Reg. 17, art. 20; Reg. 99/63, art. 9 (3).
9 Reg. 17, art. 19 (2); and see *Deutscher Komponistenverband eV* v. *EC Commission*, 13 July 1971, XVII Rec. 705; [1973] CMLR 902.
10 Reg. 99/63, art. 7(2).
11 For support of this view, see *Transocean Marine Paint Association* v. *EC Commission*, 23 October 1974, [1974] 2 CMLR 459, para. 15.

of practices complained of, a third party will not have sufficient interest merely because he will derive advantages if the agreement or practice is declared illegal.[1]

Third parties showing a sufficient interest are entitled to make their views known in writing within a time limit fixed by the Commission.[2]

Request by Commission for comments from interested third parties on proposed application of article 85 (3) or issue of a negative clearance

In cases where the Commission proposes to grant an exemption under art. 85 (3) or a negative clearance, it must publish a summary of the application or notification inviting observations on its proposed decision within a period of time of not less than one month.[3] The summary which is published in the Official Journal of the European Communities[4] contains a statement to the effect that the Commission proposes to make a favourable decision with regard to the agreement or practice of which it publishes brief details in the notice. Comments are invited from interested third parties[5] to the statements made in the notice, with the request that they be sent, under the quoted reference, to DG IV.

The Commission is obliged to ensure that it does not publish details which may harm the legitimate interest of undertakings in protecting their business secrets.[6]

Opinion of Advisory Committee on Restrictive Practices and Monopolies

The Commission is obliged to consult this Committee before it takes any decision by which exemption is granted or a negative clearance given, or requiring termination of a prohibited practice, or relating to the renewal or revocation of, or amendment to, a decision taken pursuant to art. 85 (3),[7] or relating to the imposition of fines and periodic penalty payments;[8] and the Committee must also be consulted before the Commission decides to institute a sectorial inquiry.[9]

---

1 *Etablissements Consten SA and Grundig Verkaufs-GmbH* v. *EEC Commission,* 13 July 1966, XII Rec. 429; [1966] CMLR 418.
2 Reg. 99/63, art. 5.
3 Reg. 17, art. 19 (3).
4 Referred to as a communication, published in the "C" series.
5 It will be noted that there is no necessity to show "sufficient" interest as a prerequisite to commenting on the Commission's proposal; nor is the Commission bound to act upon such comments.
6 Reg. 17, art. 20.
7 Reg. 17, art. 10 (3); and see p. 275, above.
8 Reg. 17, arts. 15 (7) and 16 (3).
9 Reg. 17, art. 12 (4), and see p. 277, above.

The consultation takes place after the Commission has gathered all the material it requires and after it has decided in principle what action it proposes to take. The Commission is not entitled to publish details of the opinion,[1] and since the Committee is an institution formed for the purpose of safeguarding the interests of member states rather than of undertakings, the undertakings subject to the proposed decision have no right to consult the opinion.

The advice received from the Advisory Committee is of a consultative nature only; it does not bind the Commission.[2]

SECTION 4   RESULT OF THE PROCEDURE

Commission decisions: their content and effect

The Commission may require that an infringement of art. 85 or art. 86 shall be brought to an end by adopting a decision to that effect.[3]

A decision is binding in its entirety on the party to whom it is addressed[4] and in practice in the case of a trade association the Commission will address the decision not only to the association but also to each of the participating members.[5] Although the Treaty does not require a decision to be published in the Official Journal,[6] such an obligation is imposed by Regulation 17,[7] which requires that the Commission must publish decisions relating to the grant of a negative clearance, an exemption under art. 85 (3) or requiring termination of an infringement. The published decision must state the names of the parties and the main contents of the decision, but must pay proper regard to business secrets of the undertakings concerned. The obligation to publish such decisions does not extend to those imposing fines or periodic penalty payments. Thus when a procedural fine of 4,000 units of account was imposed on an undertaking under investigation in the Sugar Cartel, the only announcement of this fine was contained in a

---

1 Reg. 17, art. 10 (6).
2 *Chemiefarma, Buchler and Boehringer* v. *EC Commission*, 15 July 1970, XVI Rec. 661, 773 and 769.
3 Reg. 17, art. 3 (1).
4 Art. 189 of the Treaty; set out in Appendix I, pp. 316, 317, below.
5 For example, *Re Cematex*, 24 September 1971, JO 1971 L227/26; [1973] CMLR D135;
   Re German Ceramic Tiles, 29 December 1970, JO 1971 L10/15; [1971] CMLR D6.
6 See art. 191.
7 Reg. 17, art. 21 (1).

press release (subsequently published in the Bulletin of the European Communities).[1]

The only authentic text of a decision is that which is notified to the addressee;[2] irregularities in the procedure of the notification of a decision do not affect the validity of such a decision.[3] The decision must clearly state the legal basis on which it is taken and the factual reasons which led the Commission to adopt such a decision.

When giving the reasons for its decision, the Commission is not obliged to enter into all the arguments which the undertakings concerned may have used in their defence; it is sufficient if it refers to those facts and deals with such legal issues which are of essential importance as regards the substance of the decision.[4]

Where the Commission requires that undertakings bring to an end an infringement of arts. 85 and 86 such termination can be enforced by the imposition of periodic penalty payments,[5] and in many instances the Commission will not impose fines for past infringement where an undertaking voluntarily undertakes to amend its agreements or practices.

It will be noted that the Commission does not expressly have the power either under the Treaty or under Regulation 17 to order divestiture,[6] but merely to demand termination of practices which are prohibited; however, in practice the dividing line between the two is narrow, and the Commission, in requiring termination of prohibited practices, has resorted to imposing an obligation on the undertakings concerned to make their own proposals to the Commission as to how the arrangements can be rendered compatible with the rules.

Thus, in *Re GEMA*[7] the Commission ordered that the rules of the Society should be amended to make them compatible with art. 86 and subsequently modified its original requirements after further discussion with the Society.[8] In *Continental Can*[9] it required termination of violation of art. 86, demanding that Continental Can present

---

1 Bulletin 1971 No. 11, p. 55; and see p. 295, below.
2 *Etablissements Consten SA and Grundig Verkaufs-GmbH* v. *EEC Commission*, 13 July 1966, XII Rec. 429; [1966] CMLR 418.
3 *ICI Ltd* v. *EC Commission*, 14 July 1972, XVIII Rec. 619; [1972] CMLR 557.
4 *Farbwerke Hoechst AG* v. *EC Commission*, 14 July 1972, XVII Rec. 927; [1972] CMLR 557.
5 As to which, see p. 298, below.
6 Contrast the position envisaged in the proposal for a Regulation on the control of concentrations between undertakings, art. 3 (3), p. 202, above, and Appendix III, p. 397, below.
7 *Re GEMA*, 2 June 1971, JO 1971 L134/15; [1971] CMLR D35; see p. 156, above.
8 *Re GEMA (No. 2)*, 6 July 1972, JO 1972 L166/22; [1972] CMLR D115.
9 *Re Continental Can Co Inc.*, 9 December 1971, JO 1972 L7/25, [1972] CMLR D11; see p. 161, above.

its proposals to the Commission within six months of the date of the decision.[1] In *Zoja*[2] where the Commission held that the refusal by an undertaking in a dominant position to supply a competitor with certain raw materials violated art. 86, the undertaking concerned, jointly and severally with its parent company, was required to make prompt supply of the raw material to the competitor at a price no higher than the maximum which it normally charged for the products. Further, the undertakings were required to submit proposals to the Commission within two months of the date of the decision relating to future supplies of the raw material.[3]

Commission recommendations

Prior to taking a decision under Regulation 17, art. 3 (1), the Commission may make a recommendation; this has no binding force on the undertakings to which it is addressed,[4] and is not published. However, details may be given in the Bulletin, as in the case of the *Stoneware Conventions*,[5] where the Commission considered that exclusive and collective purchase and sales arrangements had the effect of contributing to the division of the market. Despite changes made to the arrangements following receipt of a recommendation, the Commission was still not satisfied that the revised arrangements complied with art. 85 (1), but during the course of its further investigation the arrangements were terminated. There can be little doubt but that had the failure to observe the terms of the recommendation been continued, the addressees would have been exposed to particularly severe fines in any subsequent decision finding that there was intentional infringement of art. 85 (1)[6] (the same would also apply in the case of art. 86). In the majority of cases, however, the Commission will proceed by way of the informal procedure[7] rather than by recommendation.[8]

---

1 The decision was subsequently overruled by the Court of Justice on a question of fact and was never implemented: *Europemballage Corporation and Continental Can Co. Inc.* v. *EC Commission*, 21 February 1973, [1973] ECR 215; [1973] CMLR 199.
2 *Zoja* v. *Commercial Solvents Corporation*, 14 December 1972, JO 1972 L299/51, [1973] CMLR D50; see p. 158, above.
3 The decision was upheld on appeal to the Court of Justice: *ICI SpA and CSC* v. *EC Commission*, 6 March 1974, [1974] ECR 223; [1974] 1 CMLR 309; see p. 158, above.
4 Art. 189 of the Treaty; set out in Appendix I, pp. 316, 317, below.
5 Bulletin 1971, No. 12, p. 44.
6 Subject always to appeal to the Court of Justice.
7 See p. 273, above.
8 See for example Deutsche Philips.

Duration of decisions under article 85 (3)

When applying art. 85 (3) the Commission may attach such conditions and obligations as it thinks fit to the decision it takes.[1]

The exemption granted under art. 85 (3) may be made conditional upon certain features in the notified agreement being modified or terminated altogether; in such circumstances the Commission may decree that the exemption will not become effective until steps have been taken to comply with its requirements.

The decision may also impose a continuing obligation upon the parties which must be met if the exemption is to remain in force, i.e., the parties may be required to supply details of the manner in which the agreement is operating, or to inform the Commission of the results of joint research.[2] Heavy fines may be imposed on undertakings which fail to comply with an obligation imposed upon them.[3]

In any event, regardless of whether or not conditions and/or obligations are imposed on the undertakings, the decision is issued for a specified period, usually a number of years; if the requirements of art. 85 (3) continue to be met, the decision can be renewed but only if specific application is made for such renewal.[4]

The Commission, subject to appeal to the Court of Justice, is free at any time to revoke or amend its decision or to direct that certain acts of the parties are prohibited where:[5]

(a) there has been any change in the facts which are fundamental to the decision: *ex hypothesi* such a change can only take place after the decision has been taken, assuming that all the relevant facts were supplied to the Commission at the time the decision was taken (as to which see under (c) below). Distinction must be made between facts which relate to the original decision on the one hand and, on the other hand, facts which are so completely different from those relating to the original decision as themselves to constitute a practice which requires new notification to the Commission. The distinction is not easily made; in our view, even in the case where no obligation is imposed upon the parties under art. 8 (1) to inform the Commission of what is happening pursuant to the agreement which is subject to the decision,

---

1 Reg. 17, art. 8 (1); for an example, see *Re Papeteries Bollore,* 26 July 1972, JO 1972 L182/24; [1972] CMLR D94, at p. 192, above.
2 *Re Omega Watches,* 28 October 1970, JO 1970, L242/22; [1970] CMLR D49; *Re Henkel-Colgate,* 23 December 1971, JO 1972 L14/14; *Re ACEC-Berliet,* 17 July 1968, JO 1968 L201/7; [1968] CMLR D35.
3 Reg. 17, art. 15 (2) (b); see p. 296, below.
4 Reg. 17, art. 8 (2); see, e.g., p. 184, text and n. 1, above.
5 Reg. 17, art. 8 (3) (a)–(d).

the Commission should be informed if the facts materially change, so as to ensure that the parties continue to enjoy the benefit of the exemption. If the Commission does take action to revoke or amend its decision, or prohibit an act of the parties where the facts have changed, the original decision can be revoked only from the date of the new decision prohibiting the act, in contrast to the position under (b), (c) and (d) below.[1]

(b) the parties commit a breach of any obligation attached to the decision. When this occurs the Commission may revoke the decision retroactively to the date from which the exemption was granted, with the result that the parties may find that under the system of law governing the agreement there are consequences arising from performance of an illegal agreement. Further, the Commission may impose fines or periodic penalty payments.[2]

(c) the decision is based on incorrect information or was obtained by deceit: not only is the supply of incorrect or misleading information in making a notification subject to fines,[3] but also the decision may be revoked with retroactive effect.

(d) the parties abuse the exemption from the prohibition contained in art. 85 (1) and granted by the decision: again the decision may be revoked retroactively.

SECTION 5   CONCURRENT JURISDICTION OF NATIONAL AND COMMUNITY AUTHORITIES TO APPLY ARTICLES 85 AND 86

Initiation of a procedure

The prohibitions contained in arts. 85 (1) and 86 are directly applicable, no national legislation being required to give effect to them in the member states;[4] upon entry into force of the Treaty authorities[5] in the member states responsible for administering domestic legislation on competition were competent both to rule on the admissibility of agreements and practices under arts. 85 and 86 and to grant exemption under art. 85 (3),[6] but these powers have been substantially curtailed by Regulation 17, which provides that such authorities remain competent to determine whether or not the prohibitions of arts. 85 (1) and 86 apply, but only until such time as the Commission initiates a

---

1 Reg. 17, art. 8 (3), final sentence.
2 Reg. 17, art. 15 (2) (b).
3 Reg. 17, art. 15 (1) (a).
5 Which term is discussed at p. 292, below.
4 See p. 4, para. 1, above.
6 Art. 88 of the Treaty, set out in Appendix I, p. 315, below.

procedure with regard to a request for a negative clearance or exemption under art. 85 (3) or requiring termination of an infringement.[1] In exercising its competence the national authority now has no means of granting exemption under art. 85 (3) or of issuing a negative clearance, since the right to declare the prohibition inapplicable pursuant to art. 85 (3) is exclusively reserved to the Commission[2] and a negative clearance is simply a statement *by the Commission* that there are no grounds under arts. 85 (1) or 86 for action on its part.[3]

Since authorities in member states remain competent to rule on the admissibility of agreements and practices under arts. 85 (1) and 86 until such time as the Commission has initiated a procedure, it is of considerable importance to know at what moment such a procedure commences. On this vital point Regulation 17 is silent, and it has been left to the Court of Justice to indicate what is meant by the term. In the *de Haecht (No. 2)* Case[4] the Court of Justice confirmed that mere acknowledgement by the Commission of an application for negative clearance or a notification requesting exemption under art. 85 (3) does not constitute an official act indicative of the Commission's intention to proceed to take a decision under Regulation 17, arts. 2, 3 or 6. Thus, quite apart from the formalities of submission and acknowledgement of Form A/B, any correspondence relating to its contents and formal transmission of such Form to the competent authorities in member states,[5] since the Commission can only take a decision after hearing the parties[6] and receiving the opinion of the Advisory Committee on Restrictive Practices and Monopolies,[7] only action which will result in these steps, i.e. steps which must be taken if a formal decision is to be taken, will normally constitute the initiation of proceedings. There must be active interest on the part of the Commission in proceeding – "some unequivocal and externally recognisable act towards dealing with the case" in the view of the Advocate General[8] – such as might be manifested by the demand for information from an undertaking[9] or investigations carried out by the Commission with regard to a specific matter or set of circumstances.[10]

---

1 Reg. 17, art. 9 (3).
2 Reg. 17, art. 9 (1).
3 Reg. 17, art. 2.
4 *Brasserie de Haecht* v. *Wilkin-Janssen (No. 2)*, 6 February 1973; [1973] ECR 77; [1973] CMLR 287, paras. 17, 18.
5 Under Reg. 17, art. 10.
6 Reg. 17, art. 19 (1).
7 Reg. 17, art. 10.
8 [1973] CMLR 287, at p. 296.
9 Under Reg. 17, art. 11.
10 Under Reg. 17, arts. 12–14.

It seems that the transmission of a statement of objections from the Commission to an undertaking[1] must be regarded as sufficient for the purposes of determining the competence of national authorities to act under arts. 85 and 86.[2]

Meaning of national authorities

Whether the Commission has initiated a procedure may be relevant in determining the competence of a national authority to rule on the admissibility of agreements or practices under arts. 85 (1) and 86: by national authority is meant the authority, whether judicial or administrative, or both, responsible for administering domestic competition legislation. Thus a national court, applying the prohibitions contained in arts. 85 (1) and 86 to an agreement or practice in civil proceedings before it, is not an "authority" for the purposes of Regulation 17, art. 9 (3), and the construction placed on the pronouncement of the Court of Justice in the *Bilger* Case[3] to this effect is no longer valid. In the *SABAM* Case[4] the Court held, on a preliminary question arising on a referral from a Belgian court of first instance under art. 177, that where the Commission has commenced a procedure under Regulation 17, art. 3, proceedings before a national jurisdiction to assess the civil consequence of the prohibition contained in art. 86 are not superseded or stayed by the Commission action,[5] the prohibitions in arts. 85 (1) and 86 take direct effect and give rise to rights and obligations which individuals are bound to observe and which must be upheld by national jurisdictions. Thus clear distinction must be drawn between national administrative authorities permitted under art. 88 and in accordance with Regulation 17 to determine whether or not agreements and practices are admissable under arts. 85 and 86 on the one hand and those responsible for determining the legal consequences of such agreements and practices in civil proceedings in accordance with national law on the other. In cases where the Commission has been requested to grant an exemption under art. 85 (3) it remains the case that the national courts are free to apply the prohibition of arts. 85 (1) and 86 although

---

1 See p. 281, above.
2 *Belgische Radio en Televisie* v. *SV SABAM and NV Fonior,* 30 January 1974; [1974] ECR 51; [1970] 2 CMLR 238.
3 *Brauerei A. Bilger Söhne GmbH* v. *Jehle,* 18 March 1970, XVI Rec. 127; [1974] 1 CMLR 382.
4 *Belgische Radio en Televisie* v. *SV SABAM and NV Fonior* (above).
5 The Court of Justice in *SABAM* considered the point with particular reference to Commission action under Reg. 17, art. 3 (termination of an infringement); it is submitted however that there is no logical reason for distinguishing in this respect between a procedure under this article and one under art. 2 or 6 (negative clearance and exemption).

doubtless due weight will be given to the suggestion made by the Court of Justice in *de Haecht* (*No.* 2)[1] that in such a case it could defer judgment until the Commission has ruled on the matter.

Position in the United Kingdom

It would seem that Regulation 17 does not, by itself, vest powers in the national authorities to initiate proceedings under arts. 85 (1) and 86 with regard to agreements or practices which are subject to these articles. If a national authority wishes to exercise the power reserved to it by Regulation 17, art. 9 (3), to initiate such proceedings, it must seek the authority to do so in its domestic legislation. It is submitted that under present legislation in the United Kingdom the Restrictive Practices Court has no jurisdiction to exercise the powers reserved to it by Regulation 17, art. 9 (3), except during the course of proceedings relating to the acceptability or otherwise of an agreement or practice under the provisions of the RTPA, and any consideration of arts. 85 (1) and 86 would in any event be suspended if the Commission had initiated a procedure under Regulation 17 with regard to the same set of circumstances. Further, any decision of the Restrictive Practices Court relating to the application of the RTPA must be in accordance with the European Communities Act 1972, s. 10[2]. In practice if the authorities in the United Kingdom consider that an agreement or practice infringes the Treaty the proper course for them to adopt is to refer the matter to the Commission requesting it to consider the matter in accordance with the provisions of the Treaty.

The position with regard to the jurisdiction of the national courts (or tribunals) concerned with the civil consequences of the prohibitions has already been discussed in Chapter 4, above[3].

SECTION 6 PECUNIARY SANCTIONS

Fines, which may be imposed by the Commission, after consultation with the Advisory Committee on Restrictive Practices and Monopolies,[4] and which may be the subject of appeal to the Court of Justice (Regulation 17, art. 17), fall into two categories:

(a) those resulting from procedural misbehaviour;[5] and

---

1 *Brasserie de Haecht* v. *Wilkin-Janssen* (*No.* 2), 6 February 1973; [1973] ECR 77; [1973] CMLR 287.
2 See pp. 138ff., above.
3 See Section 2, p. 124, above.
4 Reg. 17, art. 15 (3).
5 Reg. 17, art. 15 (1) (a)–(c).

(b) those imposed for infringement of art. 85 (1) or art. 86 or for failing to observe obligations imposed by a decision taken in application of art. 85 (3).[1]

Fines, together with the consequences of civil proceedings flowing from art. 85 (2),[2] are the means by which compliance with the competition rules can be ensured; but the imposition of fines by the Commission carries with it no connotation of a criminal sanction[3] and their enforcement is a matter for civil law.[4]

Whilst there is no obligation on the Commission to publish decisions by which fines are imposed, the Court of Justice has held that there is no reason why it should not publish them so long as business secrets are not disclosed.[5]

It may be noted from Regulation 17 that the Commission has no power to impose fines on officers of undertakings, but only on undertakings or associations of undertakings.

Fines and periodic penalty payments are expressed in terms of units of account, the unit of account being that adopted in drawing up the budget of the Community in accordance with arts. 207 and 209 of the Treaty.[6] The unit of account now has a different value depending on the field of Community activity in question, but for present purposes is equivalent to 0·88867088 grams of pure gold[7] – this being the value of the United States dollar before it was devalued in 1971.

Procedural fines

Fines ranging from 100 to 5,000 units of account may be imposed on undertakings or associations of undertakings where intentionally or negligently:[8]

(i) incorrect or misleading information is supplied in connection with notification for exemption under art. 85 (3) or application for the issue of a negative clearance;

(ii) incorrect information is supplied to the Commission in response to an enquiry instigated under art. 11 or in connection with

---

1 Reg. 17, art. 15 (2) (a) and (b).
2 See Ch. 4, Section 2, p. 124, above.
3 Reg. 17, art. 15 (4).
4 Art. 192 of the Treaty; and see p. 300, below.
5 *Francolor* v. *EC Commission*, 14 July 1972, XVIII Rec. 851; [1972] CMLR 557.
6 Reg. 17, art. 18.
7 Art. 18 of the Budgetary Rules adopted by the Council of Ministers on 15 November 1960, JO 83/1939.
8 Reg. 17, art. 15 (1) (a)–(c).

    a sectorial enquiry it is carrying out, or information is not supplied within the time limit fixed by the Commission for the supply of such information;

(iii) books or other business records requested by the Commission are supplied in incomplete form, or undertakings refuse to submit to an investigation ordered by decision of the Commission.

Further, periodic penalty payments of from 50 to 1,000 units of account may be imposed for each day of delay in complying with a Commission requirement to supply complete and correct information or to submit to an investigation.[1]

It is submitted that the reference to intentional behaviour in art. 15 (1) is intended to cover deliberate action by an undertaking to avoid the obligations to which it is subject; failure to act as required on account of *unwitting* mistake on the other hand does not necessarily bring such behaviour within the subparagraph since to be negligent the behaviour must indicate a culpable degree of inadvertence. The Commission has regard to the good faith of the undertakings in notifying an agreement. Vague statements and failure to reveal the existence of agreements may, it seems, constitute procedural misbehaviour justifying the imposition of procedural fines.[2]

The only instance to date in which the Commission has imposed a procedural fine on an undertaking arose during the course of the Commission investigations into the Sugar Cartel. In carrying out an investigation under Regulation 17, art. 14, for a "presumed infringement"[3] of the rules, authorised officials of the Commission sought to examine the business records of Raffinerie Tirlemontoise; those submitted were not complete. Considering that failure to retain official documents constituted negligent behaviour on the part of the undertaking, the Commission imposed a fine of 4,000 units of account pursuant to Regulation 17, art. 15 (1) (c).[4] It may be noted that Raffinerie Tirlemontoise, whilst maintaining that its failure to preserve the required document did not constitute negligence on its part, nevertheless did not appeal to the Court of Justice against the imposition of the fine.

---

1 Reg. 17, art. 16 (1) (c)–(d); and see p. 298, below.
2 *Re Belgian Wallpaper Manufacturers' Cartel (Papiers peints de Belgique)*, 23 July 1974, OJ 1974 L237/3; [1974] 2 CMLR D102, section IV, para. 2.
3 To use the terminology contained in the statement of the Commission on the matter; Bulletin 1971 No. 11, p. 55.
4 Bulletin 1971 No. 11, p. 55.

Substantive fines

Fines ranging from 1,000 to 1 million units of account, or a sum in excess thereof, but not exceeding 10% of the turnover in the preceding business year of each of the undertakings participating in the infringement, may be imposed by the Commission on undertakings where, either intentionally or negligently, they:

(i) infringe art. 85 (1) or art. 86;
(ii) commit a breach of any obligation imposed by the Commission in a decision applying art. 85 (3).[1]

As in the case of procedural misbehaviour, periodic penalty payments may also be imposed.[2]

The scope of art. 15 is not limited to the imposition of fines for infringement repeated after the Commission has taken a decision prohibiting the act complained of, since the threat that fines may be imposed with regard to the period before it is declared prohibited is intended to act as a deterrent.[3]

Regulation 17 requires that in determining the amount of a fine regard must be had both to the gravity and duration of the infringement.[4] In accordance with this requirement the Commission has considered the following to be material:

(i) the nature and duration of the restriction on competition;[5]
(ii) the number and size of the undertakings concerned;
(iii) the share of the market controlled by each undertaking in the EEC;
(iv) the situation in the market at the time the infringements were committed;[6] and
(v) the number and importance of the interventions made by the undertaking with regard to the prohibited practice.[7]

---

1 Reg. 17, art. 15 (2) (a), (b).
2 Reg. 17, art. 16 (1) (a) and (b); and see p. 298, below.
3 *BASF AG* v. *EC Commission*, 14 July 1972, XVIII Rec. 713; [1972] CMLR 557. The fact that steps have been taken to remedy a breach by partially reimbursing excessive charges may be a factor taken into account in determining the amount of a fine, but it does not alter the nature of the act in respect of which complaint is made: *Re General Motors Continental*, 19 December 1974, OJ 1974 L29/14; [1975] 1 CMLR D20.
4 Reg. 17, art. 15 (2); *ICI SpA and CSC* v. *EC Commission*, 6 March 1974, [1974] ECR 223; [1974] 1 CMLR 309.
5 But failure of the Commission to react promptly to allegations of breach may diminish the importance of the duration of the infringement as a material consideration: *ICI SpA and CSC* v. *EC Commission* (above).
6 *Chemiefarma* v. *EC Commission*, 15 July 1970, XVI Rec. 661; *Re European Sugar Cartel*, 2 January 1973, OJ 1973 L140/17; [1973] CMLR D65.
7 *ICI Ltd* v. *EC Commission*, 14 July 1972, XVIII Rec. 619; [1972] CMLR 557.

Although the importance to consumers generally of the product concerned and steps taken to restrict intra-Community trade are material, the Commission has indicated that account will be taken of trading habits which existed prior to the establishment of the EEC and which are only slowly changed to take account of the new marketing opportunities offered by the common market.[1]

Fines may only be imposed where the infringement of art. 85 (1) or art. 86 is intentional or negligent;[2] a determining factor is whether the undertaking knew or could have known of the effect of the restrictive agreement in question.[3] Whilst error on the part of an undertaking in continuing to maintain arrangements which the Commission has already condemned under art. 85 (1) may indicate that such infringement is not deliberate, nevertheless, maintenance of such agreements and practices may constitute lack of the degree of care required in operating its trading system, thus indicating negligence on the part of the undertaking, with the result that fines can be imposed by the Commission under art. 15 (2) (a).[4]

It may be noted that the Commission has relied on the fact that legal advice has been sought and given to undertakings as proof that they must have been aware of the implications of art. 85 (1), with the result that fines could be imposed under art. 15 (2) of Regulation 17.[5] In the *Sugar Cartel* the Commission went so far as to seize correspondence containing the advice of lawyers acting on behalf of one of the undertakings eventually fined, on the basis that this constituted prima facie evidence of intentional infringement of arts. 85 (1) and 86.

Negligent failure to comply with the requirements of the Commission[6] and deliberately not notifying to the Commission agreements which might subsequently result in the discovery of other agreements which themselves had not been notified have also been held to be indicative of the serious nature of behaviour.[7]

---

1 *Re European Sugar Cartel*, 2 January 1973, OJ 1973 L140/17; [1973] CMLR D65.
2 As is the case with procedural fines, see p. 295, above.
3 *Re European Sugar Cartel* (above).
4 *Re Deutsche Philips GmbH*, 5 October 1973, OJ 1973 L293/40; [1973] CMLR D241.
5 *Re Cartel in Quinine*, 16 July 1969, JO 1969 L192/5; [1969] CMLR D41.
6 *Re Deutsche Philips GmbH* (above).
7 *Re Cartel in Quinine* (above); and see *Re Belgian Wallpaper Manufacturers' Cartel*, 23 July 1974, OJ 1974 L237/3; [1974] 2 CMLR D102.

The Commission imposed a fine on an undertaking for the first time in 1969 for breach of art. 85 (1); the fines so far imposed are as follows:

Market sharing	Amount of Fine
Quinine Cartel[1]	10,000 – 210,000 ua[2]
Dyestuffs[3]	40,000 – 50,000 ua[4]
Sugar Cartel[5]	100,000 – 1,500,000 ua
Belgian Wallpaper Manufacturers' Cartel[6]	36,000 – 135,000 ua
Preserved Mushrooms[7]	2,000 – 32,000 ua
Distribution	
Filipacchi[8]	60,000 ua
Pittsburgh Corning[9]	100,000 ua
Deutsche Philips[10]	60,000 ua
Article 86	
Zoja/Commercial Solvents[11]	200,000 ua[12]
Sugar Cartel[5]	1,500,000 ua
General Motors[13]	

Periodic penalty payments

Periodic penalty payments ranging from 50 to 1,000 units of account per day, calculated from a date specified in the decision, may be imposed by the Commission on undertakings in order to secure.[14]

  (i) termination of an infringement of art. 85 or art. 86;

  (ii) abstention from any act prohibited in a decision granting exemption under art. 85 (3);

  (iii) supply of complete and correct information requested by decision under art. 11 (5);

  (iv) submission to an investigation ordered by the Commission under art. 14 (3).

---

1 *Re Cartel in Quinine*, 16 July 1969, JO 1969 L192/5; [1969] CMLR D41.
2 The fines on Buchler, Boehringer and Chemiefarma were all reduced by 10,000 ua on appeal to the Court of Justice: 15 July 1970, XVI Rec. 661; [1972] CMLR 557.
3 *Re Cartel in Aniline Dyes*, 24 July 1969, JO 1969 L195/11; [1969] CMLR D23.
4 The fine of 40,000 ua imposed on ACNA was reduced to 30,000 ua on appeal to the Court of Justice: 14 July 1972, XVIII Rec. 933; [1972] CMLR 557.
5 *Re European Sugar Cartel*, 2 January 1973, OJ 1973 L140/17; [1973] CMLR D65 (subject to appeal).
6 23 July 1974, OJ 1974 L237/3; [1974] 2 CMLR D102 (subject to appeal).
7 8 January 1975, OJ 1975 L29/26.
8 *Re WEA-Filipacchi Music* 22 December 1972, JO 1972 L303/52; [1973] CMLR D43.
9 23 November 1972, JO 1972 L272/35; [1973] CMLR D2.
10 5 October 1973, OJ 1973 L293/40; [1973] CMLR D241.
11 14 December 1972, JO 1972 L299/51; [1973] CMLR D50.
12 *ICI SpA and CSC* v. *EC Commission*, 6 March 1974, [1974] ECR 223; [1974] 1 CMLR 309.
13 *Re General Motors Continental*, 19 December 1974, OJ 1975 L29/14; [1975] 1 CMLR D20.   14 Reg. 17, art. 16.

Prior to taking a decision imposing periodic penalty payments, the Commission must consult the Advisory Committee on Restrictive Practices and Monopolies.[1]

The Commission has the option of lowering the amount of the period penalty payments from the amount originally fixed where the undertaking subsequently complies with the requirements of the Commission.[2]

The Commission has imposed a periodic penalty payment in one case to date[3] in which it held that an undertaking had abused its dominant position by refusing to supply an essential raw material to a competitor. Accordingly, in addition to imposing a fine of 200,000 units of account for the infringement of art. 86,[4] a daily penalty was imposed on Istituto and its American parent company, CSC, in order to restore such supply and to ensure that the undertakings submitted proposals relating to the subsequent supply of material so that the Commission could approve these proposals. Subsequently, on appeal, the Court stayed execution of the fine until the date set for the Commission to inform the Court of its opinion of the proposed scheme.[5]

Double jeopardy to sanctions

One of the undertakings fined in the *Dyestuffs* Case was subsequently fined in the United States under US anti-trust law; the undertaking concerned then applied to the Commission requesting that the amount of the US fines be deducted from the fine imposed by the Commission.

The Commission confirmed that it was aware of the anti-trust proceedings in the United States when it took its decision, but maintained that the Treaty and the implementing secondary legislation do not require that other penalties should be taken into account.[6] Whilst the Court of Justice had stated in the *Walt Wilhelm* Case[7] that penalties might be imposed for the same set of circumstances under both domestic and EEC legislation, that case was solely concerned with the possibility of two sets of fines being imposed under Community law and under the domestic legislation of one of the member states. Such was not the case where fines were imposed under Community law and under the law of a non-member state. Further, since the decisions of the Commission and the American Court were based

---

1 Reg. 17, art. 16 (3); and see p. 205, above.   2 Reg. 17, art. 16 (2).
3 *Zoja* v. *Commercial Solvents Corporation*, 14 December 1972, JO 1972 L299/51; [1973] CMLR D50; for full facts, see pp. 158ff., above.
4 Reduced on appeal to the Court of Justice; see p. 298, above.
5 *ICI SpA and CSC* v. *EC Commission*, 14 March 1973; [1973] ECR 357; [1973] CMLR 361.
6 *Re Boehringer Mannheim*, 25 November 1971, JO 1971 L282/46; [1972] CMLR D121.
7 *Walt Wilhelm and others* v. *Bundeskartellamt*, 13 February 1969, XV Rec. 1; [1969] CMLR 100; and see pp. 140, 141, above.

on facts which had different effects in different jurisdictions, the Commission refused to permit the US fine to be deducted from the fine it itself had imposed on the undertaking. This decision was upheld by the Court of Justice on appeal.[1]

In the case where the Court of Justice considered the possible double imposition of sanctions on an undertaking under both Community and domestic legislation,[2] the Court accepted that both national and Community authorities could have competence to act against measures restricting competition, but stated that, so as to ensure the full and uniform application of Community law, the primacy of the Community system must be observed. Whilst it is possible for two sets of sanctions to be imposed, general principles of equity require that in imposing a subsequent sanction any sanction already imposed should be taken into account.

Under art. 87 (2) of the Treaty,[3] the Council, on a proposal of the Commission, may define the relationship between Community and national law, but to date no proposals have been made by the Commission in this respect.

Implementation of fines and periodic penalty payments

Decisions of the Commission imposing fines (which are not of a criminal law nature)[4] or periodic penalty payments are enforceable in accordance with art. 192[5] of the Treaty which provides that such enforcement is governed by the rules of civil procedure in force in the state in the territory of which enforcement is carried out. Thus, so far as the United Kingdom is concerned, in the event of failure by the undertaking to pay, the recovery procedure is in accordance with the provisions of the European Communities (Enforcement of Community Judgments) Order 1972,[6] which provides that once the decision is registered with the High Court or the Court of Session in Scotland, it is to have the same force and effect as if it were a judgment or order given or made by that Court on the date of registration. This order was made pursuant to s. 2 (2) of the European Communities Act 1972.

SECTION 7   TIME LIMITS ON ACTION BY THE COMMISSION

Originally the Commission was not bound by any rule limiting the time in which it was obliged to initiate proceedings with regard to

1 *Boehringer* v. *EC Commission*, 14 December 1972, XVIII Rec. 1281; [1973] CMLR 864.
2 *Walt Wilhelm and others* v. *Bundeskartellamt*, 13 February 1969 XV Rec. 1; [1969] CMLR 100; and see pp. 140, 141, above.
3 Set out in Appendix I, p. 314, below.   4 Reg. 17, art. 15 (4).
5 Set out in Appendix I, p. 317, below.   6 SI 1972, No. 1590.

arts. 85 and 86; whilst the Court of Justice indicated that delay by the Commission in exercising its authority to impose fines and periodic penalty payments was unsatisfactory in the interests of legal security[1], the Court also stated that it was for the Community institutions themselves to adopt the legislation necessary in this respect.

Accordingly, on the proposal of the Commission, the Council of Ministers in November 1974 adopted Regulation 2988/74[2] introducing rules of prescription; the Regulation came into force on 1st January 1975, but applies to infringements committed before that date. The Regulation provides that the Commission may not impose fines or periodic penalty payments for infringement of the EEC anti-trust rules[3] unless proceedings are initiated within five years of the infringement of art. 85 (1) or art. 86, except in the case of procedural infringements, where the limitation period is three years. In the case of continuing infringements, the period begins to run on the date on which such infringements cease. Where the undertaking or undertakings concerned have been informed by the Commission, or by a member state at the request of the Commission, that any action is being taken with regard to an infringement (such as where the undertaking receives a written request for information from the Commission or from a member state acting on its behalf, or where authorisation is made to carry out an investigation or formal proceedings are commenced), the period is interrupted. Time commences afresh from each interruption. Further, measures taken against one undertaking have the effect of interrupting the period not only for that undertaking but for all other undertakings participating in the infringement as well[4]. Where the Commission has imposed fines or periodic penalty payments, the decision imposing them must be enforced within five years of the effective date of such decision[5], subject to interruption on grounds of, for example, alteration of, or refusal to alter, the size of the fine or action regarding enforcement of the sanction. Further, where time is allowed for payment to be made, or the Court of Justice suspends enforcement of the payment, the limitation period is also suspended.

---

1 *Chemiefarma, Buchler and Boehringer* v. *EC Commission,* 15 July 1970, XVI Rec. 661, 773 and 769, at pp. 685, 752 and 798; *ICI Ltd* v. *EC Commission,* 14 July 1972, XVIII Rec. 619; [1972] CMLR 557, paras. 45–50.
2 OJ 1974 L319/1, set out in Appendix II, p. 389, below.
3 Including the rules relating to the transport sector.
4 Including associations of undertakings.
5 The reference in the text to the date on which the decision becomes final is presumably to the date on which it is adopted.

Chapter 12

Appeals to the European Court of Justice

The many references throughout this book to the judgments of the Court of Justice by which it has interpreted and applied the EEC anti-trust rules merely emphasise the point that the Court serves as an indispensable link between the rights of individuals and undertakings in the member states on the one hand and the aims and objectives of the Community on the other.

The Treaty itself vests in the Court wide ranging powers with regard to the implementation of its provisions, and the obligations of member states in connection with them, charging it to ensure that in the interpretation and application of the Treaty the law is observed.[1] For the purposes of this chapter we are primarily concerned with the functions of the Court in anti-trust matters, which it performs either on appeal by a party aggrieved at the action or inaction of the Commission in administering the rules, under art. 173 or 175, or, alternatively, following a referral from a national court or tribunal under art. 177.

It will be recalled[2] that while a judgment of the Court of Justice is binding on the courts of the member states, the Court of Justice has not considered itself similarly bound by its own judgments.[3]

SECTION 1   THE COURT'S JURISDICTION UNDER ARTICLES 173 AND 175

The Court has an overriding function under the Treaty to ensure that acts of the Commission (and of the Council of Ministers, which for present purposes need not concern us further) are not only permitted but also properly adopted[4]. The term "acts" is undefined in

---

1 Art. 164.
2 P. 5, para. 7, above.
3 As in the case of *Brasserie de Haecht* (No. 2), 6 February 1973, [1973] ECR 77; [1973] CMLR 287.
4 Art. 173, set out in Appendix I, p. 316, below.

art. 173, but should be interpreted by reference to art. 189 of the Treaty, namely as including regulations, directives and decisions, but excluding (in accordance with art. 173) an act which can properly be termed a recommendation or opinion. The grounds (set out in art. 173) on which the Court may review the legality of all such acts are the following:

  (i) lack of competence; i.e., that the Commission does not have jurisdiction to take the measures complained of;
 (ii) infringement of an essential procedural requirement, as provided for by the Treaty;[1]
(iii) infringement of the Treaty or of any rule of law relating to its application; or
 (iv) misuse of powers, i.e., that the Commission takes a measure within its competence but for a reason other than that for which such competence exists.

In the event that the Court finds that the action is well-founded, it must declare the measure to be void.[2] The jurisdiction of the Court is unlimited with regard to fines or periodic penalty payments, which it may cancel, decrease or increase as it thinks fit.[3]

Member states and any individual (i.e., any natural or legal person) to whom a decision is addressed may institute proceedings; further, any natural or legal person, where a decision (and the nature of the act rather than its appearance is the decisive test) is addressed to another person but is of direct and individual concern to the former, may also institute proceedings on the same grounds.[4]

Whilst there should be no difficulty in determining the person to whom a decision is addressed, those to whom such a decision is not addressed have to be able to show that, even though the decision is not addressed to them personally, it concerns them individually as well as directly. In order to meet the requirement that he is individually concerned a party must be able to satisfy the Court that the act complained of has features which affect him because of particular circumstances or on account of a special factual situation which singles him out to the exclusion of others, thereby putting him in the same position as the addressee. It then usually follows that the provision in question directly concerns the individual as well.

---

1 Particularly where the decision is insufficiently reasoned, as to which, see, e.g., *Hoechst v. EC Commission*, 14 July 1972, XVIII Rec. 927; [1972] CMLR 557, and p. 287, above.
2 Art. 174, para. 1. The Court has, however, amended a decision where the Commission erroneously held that the whole of an agreement infringed art. 85 (1); the Court ruled that the agreement infringed art. 85 only in part: *Consten and Grundig v. EEC Commission*, 13 July 1966, XII Rec. 429, [1966] CMLR 418.
3 Art. 172, Reg. 17, art. 17.
4 Art. 173, para. 2.

The Treaty lays down strict rules with regard to time limits; an appeal to the Court against a decision of the Commission must be commenced within two months of its being notified to the undertaking or from the date of its publication.[1]

Failure of the Commission to act may itself constitute grounds of appeal to the Court, where it has been requested to do so, but has failed to take action within two months.[2] The action must be commenced within two months of termination of such notice,[3] and any natural or legal person may bring such an action where the act should have been addressed to him. As in the case of an appeal under art. 173, however, the procedure does not apply in the case of a recommendation or an opinion. Since no time limit is imposed on the Commission in taking a decision granting exemption under art. 85 (3) or a negative clearance, it is submitted that this procedure (under art. 175) would be of no avail except where the Commission has been supplied with, or is in possession of, sufficient information to enable it to take a decision to the effect that an agreement or practice is subject to art. 85 (1) or art. 86, but it fails to act, despite a request so to do as, for example, after the supply of information on Form C.[4] Indeed, where a member state or a natural or legal person who claims a legitimate interest[5] has applied to the Commission to find that there is an infringement of art. 85 (1) or art. 86, if the Commission considers that there are insufficient grounds for granting such application, it is bound to inform the applicant of its reasons and fix a time limit for it to submit further comments in writing.[6] It is considered that only the failure of the Commission to act notwithstanding the supply of such information would constitute sufficient grounds to rely on art. 175.

It will be evident, therefore, that any action taken by the Commission under or in implementation of Regulation 17 is subject to review by the Court of Justice and nothing in the Regulation in any way detracts from the unlimited jurisdiction which the Court enjoys under the Treaty. The following decisions by the Commission are specifically provided in Regulation 17 as being subject to appeal to the Court: decisions (a) requiring information to be supplied either on an individual basis[7] or in connection with a sectorial inquiry instigated by the Commission;[8] (b) ordering an investigation to be carried out by

---

1 Art. 173, para. 3: subject to extension on account of distance – a further 10 days for the United Kingdom: Rules of Procedure, art. 81 (2) and Annex II, as amended by the Decision of the Court of Justice, 9 May 1974, OJ 1974 L132/27.
2 Art. 175.   3 Ibid., para. 2.
4 See p. 274, above.   5 See p. 274, above.
6 Reg. 99/63, art. 6.   7 Reg. 17, art. 11 (5).
8 Reg. 17, art. 12 (4).

its officials or those of member states on its behalf;[1] (c) imposing fines or periodical penalty payments, which the Court may cancel, reduce or increase.[2]

Application for annulment of a Commission decision does not of itself have the effect of suspending the decision, and, under the Rules of Procedure, it is necessary to make separate application for interim measures pending the outcome of the substantive appeal.[3]

Outline of Court's procedures and requirements[4]

An action before the Court of Justice in accordance with the provisions of the Treaty, and as provided by the Protocol on the Statute of the Court[5] and the Rules of Procedure,[6] is commenced by the presentation of two copies of an application from the applicant, signed by a lawyer on behalf of the party (as to which see below) and accompanied by relevant documentation.[7]

The application (in one of the official working languages of the Community,[8] the applicant deciding which, except in specified cases[9]) must indicate:[10]

(i) the name and permanent address of the applicant;
(ii) the name of the party against whom the application is made;
(iii) the subject matter of the dispute and a brief statement of the grounds on which the application is based;
(iv) the submission of the applicant;
(v) an indication of the nature of any evidence relied upon;
(vi) the address for service in the place where the Court has its seat (i.e., Luxembourg) with a statement of the name of the person who is authorised and has shown willingness to accept service.

and must be accompanied by:

(1) The decision in respect of which annulment is sought or, in the case of an application against an implied decision,[11] by documentary evidence of the date on which the Commission was requested to act.[12]

---

1 Reg. 17, art. 14 (3).   2 Reg. 17, art. 17.
3 Rules of Procedure, arts. 83–90; see, e.g., *ICI SpA and CSC* v. *EC Commission*, 14 March 1973, [1973] ECR 351; [1973] CMLR 361, and p. 299, above.
4 See, for greater detail on the Court's composition and procedure, *Jacobs and Durand, References to the European Court: Practice and Procedure* (Butterworths, London, 1975), also in *Atkin's Court Forms*, 2nd Edn., Vol. 17 (1975 Issue).
5 Protocol attached to the Treaty of Rome.
6 Adopted by the Court of Justice pursuant to art. 188 of the Treaty; published in OJ 1974 L350/1, and Jacobs and Durand, *op. cit.*, Appendix 2B.
7 Rules of Procedure, art. 37.
8 I.e. Danish, German, English, French, Italian and Dutch: Reg. 1, art. 1, OJ 1958 17/385, as amended by Treaty of Accession.
9 Rules of Procedure, art. 29.   10 Rules of Procedure, art. 38.
11 This is the term used in the Annual Report of the Court of Justice, 1974, p. 27 (Luxembourg 1975) to refer to a failure by the Commission to act which is made the subject of proceedings under art. 175.   12 Protocol on the Statute of the Court, art. 19.

The Registrar of the Court may ask for the production of the material within a reasonable period, and if it is not so produced within the prescribed time, after hearing the Advocate General, he may decide whether or not to reject the application.[1]

(2) A document certifying that the lawyer signing the application is entitled to practise before a court of a member state.[2]

(3) Where the applicant is a legal person, the instrument or instruments constituting and regulating it, and proof that the authority granted to the applicant's lawyer has been properly conferred on him by someone authorised for the purpose.[3]

The Registrar of the Court notifies the Commission of the application, which must be lodged by the applicant within two months of notification of the decision. The Commission must answer the case put forward by the applicant within one month;[4] such time limit may be extended by the President of the Court on application of the Commission.[5] Thereafter the application may be supplemented by a reply to which the Commission may submit a rejoinder;[6] the President is required to fix the time limit within which the pleadings must be lodged.[7]

After the Court has made arrangements for the collection of any evidence, including that from experts,[8] usually an oral hearing is heard before the Court at which the parties may be represented by their legal representatives,[9] and thereafter the Advocate General[10] presents his conclusions to the Court which do not, however, bind the Court. Subsequently, the judgment of the Court is given by one of the judges, no dissenting judgment being permitted in principle. The judgment is binding from the date on which it is delivered.

The Court makes no charge in respect of proceedings brought before it[11] unless expenses which have been incurred could have been avoided or there have been unusually large copying or translation expenses.[12]

---

1 Rules of Procedure, art. 38 (7).
2 Rules of Procedure, art. 38 (3); it is clear from the annual report published by the Court that both barristers and solicitors are entitled to sign the application if properly qualified according to their national laws.
3 Rules of Procedure, art. 38 (5).
4 Rules of Procedure, art. 40.
5 Rules of Procedure, art. 40 (2).
6 Rules of Procedure, art. 41 (1).
7 Rules of Procedure, art. 41 (2).
8 Rules of Procedure, art. 49.
9 By the Protocol of the Court of Justice, art. 17, such a legal representative must be a lawyer entitled to practice before a court of a member state.
10 There are four Advocates General, one of whom is attached to each case.
11 Rules of Procedure, art. 72.
12 Ibid., art. 72 (a) and (b).

Normally the losing party bears the other party's costs of proceedings before the Court[1] unless the Court orders each party to bear its own costs after each has failed on one or more heads, or there are exceptional reasons.[2] Costs that may be recovered include the expenses of witnesses and experts, and such sums as are necessarily incurred by the parties for the purposes of the action, including travel and subsistence expenses and payment of agents, advisers or lawyers.[3]

Legal aid is available if a party finds itself wholly or partially unable to meet the costs of proceedings before the Court;[4] the application for such aid must be accompanied by a certificate from the competent national authority supporting the alleged lack of means.[5]

It may be noted that third party proceedings may be commenced by any natural or legal person to contest a judgment which has been given without their being heard and where it is prejudicial to their rights;[6] inability to appear or failure to have, or to have been in a position to have had, notice of the proceedings is sufficient.[7]

SECTION 2   THE COURT'S INTERPRETATIVE JURISDICTION UNDER ARTICLE 177[8]

As will be evident from the comments made elsewhere in this book national courts and tribunals may be required to implement the prohibitions contained in arts. 85 (1) and 86 during the course of proceedings before them. Since it was realised that the Treaty provisions would have to be incorporated and applied in a consistent manner in all the member states to ensure the uniform application and development of Community law, provision was made whereby, in matters relating, *inter alia*, to the interpretation of the Treaty or the validity and interpretation of acts of the Commission or Council of Ministers, the Court of Justice should have jurisdiction to give preliminary rulings. Courts and tribunals are at liberty to refer questions

---

1 Rules of Procedure, art. 69 (2); which of course includes the Commission, see, e.g., *Europemballage Corp. and Continental Can Co. Inc.* v. *EC Commission*, 21 February 1973, [1973] ECR 215; [1973] CMLR 199.
2 Rules of Procedure, art. 69 (3).
3 *Ibid.*, art. 73.
4 *Ibid.*, art. 76 (1).
5 *Ibid.*
6 Protocol on the Statute of the Court, art. 39.
7 *Belgium* v. *Vloeberghs and High Authority*, 12 July 1962, VIII Rec. 331; [1963] CMLR 44.
8 See further Jacobs and Durand, *op. cit.*

where a decision on such questions is necessary to enable them to give a judgment, and in the case of a court or tribunal from whose decision there is no right of appeal ("no judicial remedy under national law")[1] a referral must be made with regard to such questions.[2]

Except in the case of the national court of last instance there is no obligation, however, to make a referral. The questions must be formulated in such a way as to enable the Court of Justice to decide the questions relating to Treaty or secondary legislation interpretation.[3] The fact that a national court does refer questions to the Court of Justice in no way precludes the possibility of the case in question being the subject of further appeal before a higher national court or of the national courts referring the same or other questions requesting clarification of Community law to Luxembourg. The Court does not apply the Treaty to the specific facts of the case, but gives its judgment in the abstract, indicating what Community law states or requires.[4]

In the case of proceedings under art. 177 the usual procedure is for the Court of Justice to order that costs incurred in referring the case to Luxembourg should be treated as costs in the cause, leaving the national court which referred the matter to rule on the question of costs at the conclusion of the case. Costs incurred by an intervening party, which includes governments of member states, the Commission, and, where appropriate, the Council,[5] in submitting observations to the Court, are not recoverable.[6]

In consequence of this procedure the Court of Justice on a number of occasions has been requested by national courts to answer questions as to the interpretation of arts. 85 to 90 and art. 36 which have arisen during the course of proceedings: among examples of more recent cases referred to the Court are those relating to distribution

---

1 Art. 177, para. 3, set out in Appendix I, p. 316, below.
2 The Court of Justice has given guidance on when a reference should be made; see, notably, *Firma Rheinmühlen-Düsseldorf* v. *Einfuhr- und Vorratsstelle für Getreide und Futtermittel*, 16 January 1974, [1974] ECR 33; [1974] 1 CMLR 523. For a recent decision of the English Court of Appeal as to when referral should be made, see *H. P. Bulmer* v. *J. Bolinger SA*, [1974] 2 All ER 1226; [1974] 3 WLR 202.
3 Though the Court will not be deterred by the lack of precision in the questions put to it where the object of the referral is clear from the information supplied to the Court; see *Ministère public luxembourgeois* v. *Muller, veuve Hein*, 14 July 1971, XVII Rec. 723.
4 See Lipstein, *op. cit.*, pp. 32, text and nn. 4, 5, and 33, text and nn. 1, 2.
5 Protocol of the Court, art. 20.
6 For a recent example, see *Guiseppe Sacchi*, 30 April 1974, [1974] ECR 409; [1974] 2 CMLR 177.

arrangements,[1] patents,[2] trademarks[3] and abuse of a dominant position.[4]

Ultimately, the effectiveness of the Court of Justice in developing Community law by means of this procedure depends on the goodwill of the national courts and tribunals and their willingness to seek the assistance of another court – albeit a Community institution – in interpreting matters of Community law.

---

1 *Béguelin Import Co* v. *GL Import-Export SA*, 25 November 1971, XVII Rec. 949; [1972] CMLR 81; *Brasserie de Haecht* v. *Wilkin-Janssen (No. 2)*, 6 February 1973, [1973] ECR 77; [1973] CMLR 287.
2 *Parke, Davis & Co v Probel*, 28 February 1968, XIV Rec. 81; [1968] CMLR 47; *Centrafarm BV and Adriaan de Peijper* v. *Sterling Drug Inc.,* 31 October 1974, [1974] 2 CMLR 480.
3 *Sirena SrL* v. *Eda SrL*, 18 February 1971, XVII Rec. 69; [1971] CMLR 260; *Van Zuylen Frères* v. *Hag AG,* 3 July 1974, [1974] ECR 731; [1974] 2 CMLR 127; *Centrafarm BV and Adriaan de Peijper* v. *Winthrop BV*, 31 October 1974, [1974] 2 CMLR 480.
4 *Belgische Radio en Televisie* v. *SV SABAM and NV Fonior*, 27 March 1974, [1974] ECR 313; [1974] CMLR 238; *Guiseppe Sacchi*, 30 April 1974, [1974] ECR 409; [1974] 2 CMLR 177.

Treaty of Rome

Article 1

By this Treaty, the High Contracting Parties establish among themselves a EUROPEAN ECONOMIC COMMUNITY.

Article 2

The Community shall have as its task, by establishing a common market and progressively approximating the economic policies of Member States, to promote throughout the Community a harmonious development of economic activities, a continuous and balanced expansion, an increase in stability, an accelerated raising of the standard of living and closer relations between the States belonging to it.

Article 3

For the purposes set out in Article 2, the activities of the Community shall include, as provided in this Treaty and in accordance with the timetable set out therein

- (a) the elimination, as between Member States, of customs duties and of quantitative restrictions on the import and export of goods, and of all other measures having equivalent effect;
- (b) the establishment of a common customs tariff and of a common commercial policy towards third countries;
- (c) the abolition, as between Member States, of obstacles to freedom of movement for persons, services and capital;
- (d) the adoption of a common policy in the sphere of agriculture;
- (e) the adoption of a common policy in the sphere of transport;
- (f) the institution of a system ensuring that competition in the common market is not distorted;
- (g) the application of procedures by which the economic policies of Member States can be coordinated and disequilibria in their balances of payments remedied;
- (h) the approximation of the laws of Member States to the extent required for the proper functioning of the common market;

311

(i) the creation of a European Social Fund in order to improve employment opportunities for workers and to contribute to the raising of their standard of living;

(j) the establishment of a European Investment Bank to facilitate the economic expansion of the Community by opening up fresh resources;

(k) the association of the overseas countries and territories in order to increase trade and to promote jointly economic and social development.

Article 5

Member States shall take all appropriate measures, whether general or particular, to ensure fulfilment of the obligations arising out of this Treaty or resulting from action taken by the institutions of the Community. They shall facilitate the achievement of the Community's tasks.

They shall abstain from any measure which could jeopardise the attainment of the objections of this Treaty.

Article 7

Within the scope of application of this Treaty, and without prejudice to any special provisions contained therein, any discrimination on grounds of nationality shall be prohibited.

The Council may, on a proposal from the Commission and after consulting the Assembly, adopt, by a qualified majority, rules designed to prohibit such discrimination.

Articles 30 to 34

[Articles 30 to 34 impose obligations on Member States both not to introduce any new quantitative restrictions or like measures on imports and exports between Member States, and also to eliminate over a period of time all such existing measures.]

Article 36

The provisions of Articles 30 to 34 shall not preclude prohibitions or restrictions on imports, exports or goods in transit justified on grounds of public morality, public policy or public security; the protection of health and life of humans, animals or plants; the protection of national treasures possessing artistic, historic or archaeological value; or the protection of industrial and commercial property. Such prohibitions or restrictions shall not, however, constitute a means of arbitrary discrimination or a disguised restriction on trade between Member States.

Article 85

1. The following shall be prohibited as incompatible with the common market: all agreements between undertakings, decision by associations of undertakings and concerted practices which may affect trade between Member States and which have as their object or effect the prevention, restriction or distortion of competition within the common market, and in particular those which:

(a) directly or indirectly fix purchase or selling prices or any other trading conditions;
(b) limit or control production, markets, technical development, or investment;
(c) share markets or sources of supply;
(d) apply dissimilar conditions to equivalent transactions with other trading parties, thereby placing them at a competitive disadvantage;
(e) make the conclusion of contracts subject to acceptance by the other parties of supplementary obligations which, by their nature or according to commercial usage, have no connection with the subject of such contracts.

2. Any agreements or decisions prohibited pursuant to this Article shall be automatically void.

3. The provisions of paragraph 1 may, however, be declared inapplicable in the case of:

– any agreement or category of agreements between undertakings;
– any decision or category of decisions by associations of undertakings;
– any concerted practice or category of concerted practices;

which contributes to improving the production or distribution of goods or to promoting technical or economic progress, while allowing consumers a fair share of the resulting benefit, and which does not:

(a) impose on the undertakings concerned restrictions which are not indispensable to the attainment of these objectives;
(b) afford such undertakings the possibility of eliminating competition in respect of a substantial part of the products in question.

Article 86

Any abuse by one or more undertakings of a dominant position within the common market or in a substantial part of it shall be prohibited as incompatible with the common market in so far as it may affect trade between Member States.

Such abuse may, in particular, consist in:

(a) directly or indirectly imposing unfair purchase or selling prices or other unfair trading conditions;

(b) limiting production, markets or technical development to the prejudice of consumers;

(c) applying dissimilar conditions to equivalent transactions with other trading parties, thereby placing them at a competitive disadvantage;

(d) making the conclusion of contracts subject to acceptance by the other parties of supplementary obligations which, by their nature or according to commercial usage, have no connection with the subject of such contracts.

Article 87

1. Within three years of the entry into force of this Treaty the Council shall, acting unanimously on a proposal from the Commission and after consulting the Assembly, adopt any appropriate regulations or directives to give effect to the principles set out in Articles 85 and 86.

If such provisions have not been adopted within the period mentioned, they shall be laid down by the Council, acting by a qualified majority on a proposal from the Commission and after consulting the Assembly.

2. The regulations or directives referred to in paragraph 1 shall be designed in particular:

(a) to ensure compliance with the prohibitions laid down in Article 85 (1) and in Article 86 by making provision for fines and periodic penalty payments;

(b) to lay down detailed rules for the application of Article 85 (3), taking into account the need to ensure effective supervision on the one hand, and to simplify administration to the greatest possible extent on the other;

(c) to define, if need be, in the various branches of the economy, the scope of the provisions of Articles 85 and 86;

(d) to define the respective functions of the Commission and of the Court of Justice in applying the provisions laid down in this paragraph;

(e) to determine the relationship between national laws and the provisions contained in this Section or adopted pursuant to this Article.

Article 88

Until the entry into force of the provisions adopted in pursuance of Article 87, the authorities in Member States shall rule on the admissibility of agreements, decisions and concerted practices and on abuse of a dominant position in the common market in accordance with the law of their country and with the provisions of Article 85, in particular paragraph 3, and of Article 86.

Article 89

1. Without prejudice to Article 88, the Commission shall, as soon as it takes up its duties, ensure the application of the principles laid down in Articles 85 and 86. On application by a Member State or on its own initiative, and in cooperation with the competent authorities in the Member States, who shall give it their assistance, the Commission shall investigate cases of suspected infringement of these principles. If it finds that there has been an infringement, it shall propose appropriate measures to bring it to an end.

2. If the infringement is not brought to an end, the Commission shall record such infringement of the principles in a reasoned decision. The Commission may publish its decision and authorise Member States to take the measures, the conditions and details of which it shall determine, needed to remedy the situation.

Article 90

1. In the case of public undertakings and undertakings to which Member States grant special or exclusive rights, Member States shall neither enact nor maintain in force any measure contrary to the rules contained in this Treaty, in particular to those rules provided for in Article 7 and Articles 85 to 94.

2. Undertakings entrusted with the operation of services of general economic interest or having the character of a revenue-producing monopoly shall be subject to the rules contained in this Treaty, in particular to the rules on competition, in so far as the application of such rules does not obstruct the performance, in law or in fact, of the particular tasks assigned to them. The development of trade must not be affected to such an extent as would be contrary to the interests of the Community.

3. The Commission shall ensure the application of the provisions of this Article and shall, where necessary, address appropriate directives or decisions to Member States.

Article 173

The Court of Justice shall review the legality of acts of the Council and the Commission other than recommendations or opinions. It shall for this purpose have jurisdiction in actions brought by a Member State, the Council or the Commission on grounds of lack of competence, infringement of an essential procedural requirement, infringement of this Treaty or of any rule of law relating to its application, or misuse of powers.

Any natural or legal person may, under the same conditions, institute proceedings against a decision addressed to that person or against a decision which, although in the form of a regulation or a decision addressed to another person, is of direct and individual concern to the former.

The proceedings provided for in this Article shall be instituted within two months of the publication of the measure, or of its notification to the plaintiff, or, in the absence thereof, of the day on which it came to the knowledge of the latter, as the case may be.

Article 177

The Court of Justice shall have jurisdiction to give preliminary rulings concerning:

(a) the interpretation of this Treaty;
(b) the validity and interpretation of acts of the institutions of the Community;
(c) the interpretation of the statutes of bodies established by an act of the Council, where those statutes so provide.

Where such a question is raised before any court or tribunal of a Member State, that court or tribunal may, if it considers that a decision on the question is necessary to enable it to give judgment, request the Court of Justice to give a ruling thereon.

Where any such question is raised in a case pending before a court or tribunal of a Member State, against whose decisions there is no judicial remedy under national law, that court or tribunal shall bring the matter before the Court of Justice.

Article 189

In order to carry out their task the Council and the Commission shall, in accordance with the provisions of this Treaty, make regulations, issue directives, take decisions, make recommendations or deliver opinions.

A regulation shall have general application. It shall be binding in its entirety and directly applicable in all Member States.

A directive shall be binding, as to the result to be achieved, upon each Member State to which it is addressed, but shall leave to the national authorities the choice of form and methods.

A decision shall be binding in its entirety upon those to whom it is addressed.

Recommendations and opinions shall have no binding force.

Article 192

Decisions of the Council or of the Commission which impose a pecuniary obligation on persons other than States shall be enforceable.

Enforcement shall be governed by the rules of civil procedure in force in the State in the territory of which it is carried out. The order for its enforcement shall be appended to the decision, without other formality than verification of the authenticity of the decision, by the national authority which the Government of each Member State shall designate for this purpose and shall make known to the Commission and to the Court of Justice.

When these formalities have been completed on application by the party concerned, the latter may proceed to enforcement in accordance with the national law, by bringing the matter directly before the competent authority.

Enforcement may be suspended only by a decision of the Court of Justice. However, the courts of the country concerned shall have jurisdiction over complaints that enforcement is being carried out in an irregular manner.

Article 222

This Treaty shall in no way prejudice the rules in Member States governing the system of property ownership.

Appendix II

Regulations of the Council and Commission

REGULATION No 17

First Regulation implementing Articles 85 and 86 of the Treaty

THE COUNCIL OF THE EUROPEAN ECONOMIC COMMUNITY,

Having regard to the Treaty establishing the European Economic Community, and in particular Article 87 thereof;

Having regard to the proposal from the Commission;

Having regard to the Opinion of the Economic and Social Committee;

Having regard to the Opinion of the European Parliament;

Whereas, in order to establish a system ensuring that competition shall not be distorted in the common market, it is necessary to provide for balanced application of Articles 85 and 86 in a uniform manner in the Member States;

Whereas in establishing the rules for applying Article 85 (3) account must be taken of the need to ensure effective supervision and to simplify administration to the greatest possible extent;

Whereas it is accordingly necessary to make it obligatory, as a general principle, for undertakings which seek application of Article 85 (3) to notify to the Commission their agreements, decisions and concerted practices;

Whereas, on the one hand, such agreements, decisions and concerted practices are probably very numerous and cannot therefore all be examined at the same time and, on the other hand, some of them have special features which may make them less prejudicial to the development of the common market;

Whereas there is consequently a need to make more flexible arrange-

318

ments for the time being in respect of certain categories of agreement, decision and concerted practice without prejudging their validity under Article 85;

Whereas it may be in the interest of undertakings to know whether any agreements, decisions or practices to which they are party, or propose to become party, may lead to action on the part of the Commission pursuant to Article 85 (1) or Article 86;

Whereas, in order to secure uniform application of Articles 85 and 86 in the common market, rules must be made under which the Commission, acting in close and constant liaison with the competent authorities of the Member States, may take the requisite measures for applying those Articles;

Whereas for this purpose the Commission must have the co-operation of the competent authorities of the Member States and be empowered, throughout the common market, to require such information to be supplied and to undertake such investigations as are necessary to bring to light any agreement, decision or concerted practice prohibited by Article 85 (1) or any abuse of a dominant position prohibited by Article 86;

Whereas, in order to carry out its duty of ensuring that the provisions of the Treaty are applied, the Commission must be empowered to address to undertakings or associations of undertakings recommendations and decisions for the purpose of bringing to an end infringements of Articles 85 and 86;

Whereas compliance with Articles 85 and 86 and the fulfilment of obligations imposed on undertakings and associations of undertakings under this Regulation must be enforceable by means of fines and periodic penalty payments;

Whereas undertakings concerned must be accorded the right to be heard by the Commission, third parties whose interests may be affected by a decision must be given the opportunity of submitting their comments beforehand, and it must be ensured that wide publicity is given to decisions taken;

Whereas all decisions taken by the Commission under this Regulation are subject to review by the Court of Justice under the conditions specified in the Treaty; whereas it is moreover desirable to confer upon the Court of Justice, pursuant to Article 172, unlimited jurisdiction in respect of decisions under which the Commission imposes fines or periodic penalty payments;

Whereas this Regulation may enter into force without prejudice to any other provisions that may hereafter be adopted pursuant to Article 87;

HAS ADOPTED THIS REGULATION:

Article 1 Basic provision

Without prejudice to Articles 6, 7 and 23 of this Regulation, agreements, decisions and concerted practices of the kind described in Article 85 (1) of the Treaty and the abuse of a dominant position in the market, within the meaning of Article 86 of the Treaty, shall be prohibited, no prior decision to that effect being required.

Article 2 Negative clearance

Upon application by the undertakings or associations of undertakings concerned, the Commission may certify that, on the basis of the facts in its possession, there are no grounds under Article 85 (1) or Article 86 of the Treaty for action on its part in respect of an agreement, decision or practice.

Article 3 Termination of infringements

1. Where the Commission, upon application or upon its own initiative, finds that there is infringement of Article 85 or Article 86 of the Treaty, it may by decision require the undertakings or associations of undertakings concerned to bring such infringement to an end.

2. Those entitled to make application are:

(a) Member States;
(b) natural or legal persons who claim a legitimate interest.

3. Without prejudice to the other provisions of this Regulation, the Commission may, before taking a decision under paragraph 1, address to the undertakings or associations of undertakings concerned recommendations for termination of the infringement.

Article 4 Notification of new agreements, decisions and practices

1. Agreements, decisions and concerted practices of the kind described in Article 85 (1) of the Treaty which come into existence after the entry into force of this Regulation and in respect of which the parties seek application of Article 85 (3) must be notified to the Commission. Until they have been notified, no decision in application of Article 85 (3) may be taken.

2. Paragraph 1 shall not apply to agreements, decisions [and]¹ concerted practices where:

(1) the only parties thereto are undertakings from one Member

---

1 As amended by Regulation 2822/71, OJ 1971 L285/49.

State and the agreements, decisions or practices do not relate either to imports or to exports between Member States;

(2) not more than two undertakings are party thereto, and the agreements only:

   (a) restrict the freedom of one party to the contract in determining the prices or conditions of business upon which the goods which he has obtained from the other party to the contract may be resold; or

   (b) impose restrictions on the exercise of the rights of the assignee or user of industrial property rights—in particular patents, utility models, designs or trade marks—or of the person entitled under a contract to the assignment, or grant, of the right to use a method of manufacture or knowledge relating to the use and to the application of industrial processes;

(3) they have as their sole object:

   (a) the development or uniform application of standards or types; or

   [(b) joint research and development;

   (c) specialisation in the manufacture of products, including agreements necessary for achieving this,

      – where the products which are the subject of specialisation do not, in a substantial part of the common market, represent more than 15% of the volume of business done in identical products or those considered by consumers to be similar by reason of their characteristics, price and use,
      and
      – where the total annual turnover of the participating undertakings does not exceed 200 million units of account.][1]

These agreements, decisions and practices may be notified to the Commission.

Article 5 Notification of existing agreements, decisions and practices

1. Agreements, decisions and concerted practices of the kind described in Article 85 (1) of the Treaty which are in existence at the date of entry into force of this Regulation and in respect of which the

1 As amended by Regulation 2822/71, OJ 1971 L285/49.

parties seek application of Article 85 (3) shall be notified to the Commission before 1 [November]¹ 1962.

[However, notwithstanding the foregoing provisions, any agreements, decisions and concerted practices to which not more than two undertakings are party shall be notified before 1 February 1963.]¹

2. Paragraph 1 shall not apply to agreements, decisions or concerted practices falling within Article 4 (2); these may be notified to the Commission.

Article 6   Decisions pursuant to Article 85 (3)

1. Whenever the Commission takes a decision pursuant to Article 85 (3) of the Treaty, it shall specify therein the date from which the decision shall take effect. Such date shall not be earlier than the date of notification.

2. The second sentence of paragraph 1 shall not apply to agreements, decisions or concerted practices falling within Article 4 (2) and Article 5 (2), nor to those falling within Article 5 (1) which have been notified within the time limit specified in Article 5 (1).

Article 7   Special provisions for existing agreements, decisions and practices

1. Where agreements, decisions and concerted practices in existence at the date of entry into force of this Regulation and notified [within the time limits specified in Article 5 (1)]² do not satisfy the requirements of Article 85 (3) of the Treaty and the undertakings or associations of undertakings concerned cease to give effect to them or modify them in such manner that they no longer fall within the prohibition contained in Article 85 (1) or that they satisfy the requirements of Article 85 (3), the prohibition contained in Article 85 (1) shall apply only for a period fixed by the Commission. A decision by the Commission pursuant to the foregoing sentence shall not apply as against undertakings and associations of undertakings which did not expressly consent to the notification.

2. Paragraph 1 shall apply to agreements, decisions and concerted practices falling within Article 4 (2) which are in existence at the date of entry into force of this Regulation if they are notified before 1 January [1967].²

---

1 As amended by Regulation 59, OJ 58/1665.
2 As amended by Regulation 118/63, OJ 162/2696.

Article 8 Duration and revocation of decisions under Article 85 (3)

1. A decision in application of Article 85 (3) of the Treaty shall be issued for a specified period and conditions and obligations may be attached thereto.

2. A decision may on application be renewed if the requirements of Article 85 (3) of the Treaty continue to be satisfied.

3. The Commission may revoke or amend its decision or prohibit specified acts by the parties:

(a) where there has been a change in any of the facts which were basic to the making of the decision;
(b) where the parties commit a breach of any obligation attached to the decision;
(c) where the decision is based on incorrect information or was induced by deceit;
(d) where the parties abuse the exemption from the provisions of Article 85 (1) of the Treaty granted to them by the decision.

In cases to which subparagraphs (b), (c) or (d) apply, the decision may be revoked with retroactive effect.

Article 9 Powers

1. Subject to review of its decision by the Court of Justice, the Commission shall have sole power to declare Article 85 (1) inapplicable pursuant to Article 85 (3) of the Treaty.

2. The Commission shall have power to apply Article 85 (1) and Article 86 of the Treaty; this power may be exercised notwithstanding that the time limits specified in Article 5 (1) and in Article 7 (2) relating to notification have not expired.

3. As long as the Commission has not initiated any procedure under Articles 2, 3 or 6, the authorities of the Member States shall remain competent to apply Article 85 (1) and Article 86 in accordance with Article 88 of the Treaty; they shall remain competent in this respect notwithstanding that the time limits specified in Article 5 (1) and in Article 7 (2) relating to notification have not expired.

Article 10 Liaison with the authorities of the Member States

1. The Commission shall forthwith transmit to the competent authorities of the Member States a copy of the applications and notifications together with copies of the most important documents lodged

with the Commission for the purpose of establishing the existence of infringements of Articles 85 or 86 of the Treaty or of obtaining negative clearance or a decision in application of Article 85 (3).

2. The Commission shall carry out the procedure set out in paragraph 1 in close and constant liaison with the competent authorities of the Member States; such authorities shall have the right to express their views upon that procedure.

3. An Advisory Committee on Restrictive Practices and Monopolies shall be consulted prior to the taking of any decision following upon a procedure under paragraph 1, and of any decision concerning the renewal, amendment or revocation of a decision pursuant to Article 85 (3) of the Treaty.

4. The Advisory Committee shall be composed of officials competent in the matter of restrictive practices and monopolies. Each Member State shall appoint an official to represent it who, if prevented from attending, may be replaced by another official.

5. The consultation shall take the place at a joint meeting convened by the Commission; such meeting shall be held not earlier than fourteen days after dispatch of the notice convening it. The notice shall, in respect of each case to be examined, be accompanied by a summary of the case together with an indication of the most important documents, and a preliminary draft decision.

6. The Advisory Committee may deliver an opinion notwithstanding that some of its members or their alternates are not present. A report of the outcome of the consultative proceedings shall be annexed to the draft decision. It shall not be made public.

Article 11   Requests for information

1. In carrying out the duties assigned to it by Article 89 and by provisions adopted under Article 87 of the Treaty, the Commission may obtain all necessary information from the Governments and competent authorities of the Member States and from undertakings and associations of undertakings.

2. When sending a request for information to an undertaking or association of undertakings, the Commission shall at the same time forward a copy of the request to the competent authority of the Member State in whose territory the seat of the undertaking or association of undertakings is situated.

3. In its request the Commission shall state the legal basis and the purpose of the request and also the penalties provided for in Article 15 (1) (b) for supplying incorrect information.

4. The owners of the undertakings or their representatives and, in the case of legal persons, companies or firms, or of associations having no legal personality, the persons authorised to represent them by law or by their constitution shall supply the information requested.

5. Where an undertaking or association of undertakings does not supply the information requested within the time limit fixed by the Commission, or supplies incomplete information, the Commission shall by decision require the information to be supplied. The decision shall specify what information is required, fix an appropriate time limit within which it is to be supplied and indicate the penalties provided for in Article 15 (1) (b) and Article 16 (1) (c) and the right to have the decision reviewed by the Court of Justice.

6. The Commission shall at the same time forward a copy of its decision to the competent authority of the Member State in whose territory the seat of the undertaking or association of undertakings is situated.

Article 12   Inquiry into sectors of the economy

1. If in any sector of the economy the trend of trade between Member States, price movements, inflexibility of prices or other circumstances suggest that in the economic sector concerned competition is being restricted or distorted within the common market, the Commission may decide to conduct a general inquiry into that economic sector and in the course thereof may request undertakings in the sector concerned to supply the information necessary for giving effect to the principles formulated in Articles 85 and 86 of the Treaty and for carrying out the duties entrusted to the Commission.

2. The Commission may in particular request every undertaking or association of undertakings in the economic sector concerned to communicate to it all agreements, decisions and concerted practices which are exempt from notification by virtue of Article 4 (2) and Article 5 (2).

3. When making inquiries pursuant to paragraph 2, the Commission shall also request undertakings or groups of undertakings whose size suggests that they occupy a dominant position within the common market or a substantial part thereof to supply to the Commission such particulars of the structure of the undertakings and of their behaviour as are requisite to an appraisal of their position in the light of Article 86 of the Treaty.

4. Article 10 (3) to (6) and Articles 11, 13 and 14 shall apply correspondingly.

Article 13 Investigations by the authorities of the Member States

1. At the request of the Commission, the competent authorities of the Member States shall undertake the investigations which the Commission considers to be necessary under Article 14 (1), or which it has ordered by decision pursuant to Article 14 (3). The officials of the competent authorities of the Member States responsible for conducting these investigations shall exercise their powers upon production of an authorisation in writing issued by the competent authority of the Member State in whose territory the investigation is to be made. Such authorisation shall specify the subject matter and purpose of the investigation.

2. If so requested by the Commission or by the competent authority of the Member State in whose territory the investigation is to be made, the officials of the Commission may assist the officials of such authorities in carrying out their duties.

Article 14   Investigating powers of the Commission

1. In carrying out the duties assigned to it by Article 89 and by provisions adopted under Article 87 of the Treaty, the Commission may undertake all necessary investigations into undertakings and associations of undertakings. To this end the officials authorised by the Commission are empowered:

   (a) to examine the books and other business records;
   (b) to take copies of or extracts from the books and business records;
   (c) to ask for oral explanations on the spot;
   (d) to enter any premises; land and means of transport of undertakings.

2. The officials of the Commission authorised for the purpose of these investigations shall exercise their powers upon production of an authorisation in writing specifying the subject matter and purpose of the investigation and the penalties provided for in Article 5 (1) (c) in cases where production of the required books or other business records is incomplete. In good time before the investigation, the Commission shall inform the competent authority of the Member State in whose territory the same is to be made of the investigation and of the identity of the authorised officials.

3. Undertakings and associations of undertakings shall submit to investigations ordered by decision of the Commission. The decision shall specify the subject matter and purpose of the investigation, appoint the date on which it is to begin and indicate the penalties

provided for in Article 15 (1) (c) and Article 16 (1) (d) and the right to
have the decision reviewed by the Court of Justice.

4. The Commission shall take decisions referred to in paragraph 3
after consultation with the competent authority of the Member State
in whose territory the investigation is to be made.

5. Officials of the competent authority of the Member State in whose
territory the investigation is to be made may, at the request of such
authority or of the Commission, assist the officials of the Commission
in carrying out their duties.

6. Where an undertaking opposes an investigation ordered pursuant
to this Article, the Member State concerned shall afford the necessary
assistance to the officials authorised by the Commission to enable them
to make their investigation. Member States shall, after consultation
with the Commission, take the necessary measures to this end before
1 October 1962.

Article 15   Fines

1. The Commission may by decision impose on undertakings or
associations of undertakings fines of from 100 to 5000 units of account
where, intentionally or negligently:

(a) they supply incorrect or misleading information in an application
    pursuant to Article 2 or in a notification pursuant to Articles 4
    or 5; or

(b) they supply incorrect information in response to a request made
    pursuant to Article 11 (3) or (5) or to Article 12, or do not supply
    information within the time limit fixed by a decision taken
    under Article 11 (5); or

(c) they produce the required books or other business records in
    incomplete form during investigations under Article 13 or 14,
    or refuse to submit to an investigation ordered by decision
    issued in implementation of Article 14 (3).

2. The Commission may by decision impose on undertakings or
associations of undertakings fines of from 1000 to 1000000 units of
account, or a sum in excess thereof but not exceeding 10% of the
turnover in the preceding business year of each of the undertakings
participating in the infringement where, either intentionally or
negligently:

(a) they infringe Article 85 (1) or Article 86 of the Treaty; or
(b) they commit a breach of any obligation imposed pursuant to
    Article 8 (1).

In fixing the amount of the fine, regard shall be had both to the gravity and to the duration of the infringement.

3. Article 10 (3) to (6) shall apply.

4. Decisions taken pursuant to paragraphs 1 and 2 shall not be of a criminal law nature.

5. The fines provided for in paragraph 2 (a) shall not be imposed in respect of acts taking place:

(a) after notification to the Commission and before its decision in application of Article 85 (3) of the Treaty, provided they fall within the limits of the activity described in the notification;
(b) before notification and in the course of agreements, decisions or concerted practices in existence at the date of entry into force of this Regulation, provided that notification was effected within the time limits specified in Article 5 (1) and Article 7 (2).

6. Paragraph 5 shall not have effect where the Commission has informed the undertakings concerned that after preliminary examination it is of opinion that Article 85 (1) of the Treaty applies and that application of Article 85 (3) is not justified.

Article 16   Periodic penalty payments

1. The Commission may by decision impose on undertakings or associations of undertakings periodic penalty payments of from 50 to 1,000 units of account per day, calculated from the date appointed by the decision, in order to compel them:

(a) to put an end to an infringement of Article 85 or 86 of the Treaty, in accordance with a decision taken pursuant to Article 3 of this Regulation;
(b) to refrain from any act prohibited under Article 8 (3);
(c) to supply complete and correct information which it has requested by decision taken pursuant to Article 11 (5);
(d) to submit to an investigation which it has ordered by decision taken pursuant to Article 14 (3).

2. Where the undertakings or associations of undertakings have satisfied the obligation which it was the purpose of the periodic penalty payment to enforce, the Commission may fix the total amount of the periodic penalty payment at a lower figure than that which would arise under the original decision.

3. Article 10 (3) to (6) shall apply.

Article 17   Review by the Court of Justice

The Court of Justice shall have unlimited jurisdiction within the meaning of Article 172 of the Treaty to review decisions whereby the Commission has fixed a fine or periodic penalty payment; it may cancel, reduce or increase the fine or periodic penalty payment imposed.

Article 18   Unit of account

For the purposes of applying Articles 15 to 17 the unit of account shall be that adopted in drawing up the budget of the Community in accordance with Articles 207 and 209 of the Treaty.

Article 19   Hearing of the parties and of third persons

1. Before taking decisions as provided for in Articles 2, 3, 6, 7, 8, 15 and 16, the Commission shall give the undertakings or associations of undertakings concerned the opportunity of being heard on the matters to which the Commission has taken objection.

2. If the Commission or the competent authorities of the Member States consider it necessary, they may also hear other natural or legal persons. Applications to be heard on the part of such persons shall, where they show a sufficient interest, be granted.

3. Where the Commission intends to give negative clearance pursuant to Article 2 or take a decision in application of Article 85 (3) of the Treaty, it shall publish a summary of the relevant application or notification and invite all interested third parties to submit their observations within a time limit which it shall fix being not less than one month. Publication shall have regard to the legitimate interest of undertakings in the protection of their business secrets.

Article 20   Professional secrecy

1. Information acquired as a result of the application of Articles 11, 12, 13 and 14 shall be used only for the purpose of the relevant request or investigation.

2. Without prejudice to the provisions of Articles 19 and 21, the Commission and the competent authorities of the Member States, their officials and other servants shall not disclose information acquired by them as a result of the application of this Regulation and of the kind covered by the obligation of professional secrecy.

3. The provisions of paragraphs 1 and 2 shall not prevent publication of general information or surveys which do not contain information relating to particular undertakings or associations of undertakings.

Article 21   Publication of decisions

1. The Commission shall publish the decisions which it takes pursuant to Articles 2, 3, 6, 7 and 8.

2. The publication shall state the names of the parties and the main content of the decision; it shall have regard to the legitimate interests of undertakings in the protection of their business secrets.

Article 22   Special provisions

1. The Commission shall submit to the Council proposals for making certain categories of agreement, decision and concerted practice falling within Article 4 (2) or Article 5 (2) compulsorily notifiable under Article 4 or 5.

2. Within one year from the date of entry into force of this Regulation, the Council shall examine, on a proposal from the Commission, what special provisions might be made for exempting from the provisions of this Regulation agreements, decisions and concerted practices falling within Article 4 (2) or Article 5 (2).

Article 23   Transitional provisions applicable to decisions of authorities of the Member States

1. Agreements, decisions and concerted practices of the kind described in Article 85 (1) of the Treaty to which, before the entry into force of this Regulation, the competent authority of a Member State has declared Article 85 (1) to be inapplicable pursuant to Article 85 (3) shall not be subject to compulsory notification under Article 5. The decision of the competent authority of the Member State shall be deemed to be a decision within the meaning of Article 6; it shall cease to be valid upon expiration of the period fixed by such authority but in any event not more than three years after the entry into force of this Regulation. Article 8 (3) shall apply.

2. Applications for renewal of decisions of the kind described in paragraph 1 shall be decided upon by the Commission in accordance with Article 8 (2).

Article 24   Implementing provisions

The Commission shall have power to adopt implementing provisions concerning the form, content and other details of applications pursuant to Articles 2 and 3 and of notifications pursuant to Articles 4 and 5, and concerning hearings pursuant to Article 19 (1) and (2).

[Article 25

1. As regards agreements, decisions and concerted practices to which Article 85 of the Treaty applies by virtue of accession, the date of accession shall be substituted for the date of entry into force of this Regulation in every place where reference is made in this Regulation to this latter date.

2. Agreements, decisions and concerted practices existing at the date of accession to which Article 85 of the Treaty applies by virtue of accession shall be notified pursuant to Article 5 (1) or Article 7 (1) and (2) within six months from the date of accession.

3. Fines under Article 15 (2) (a) shall not be imposed in respect of any act prior to notification of the agreements, decisions and practices to which paragraph 2 applies and which have been notified within the period therein specified.

4. New Member States shall take the measures referred to in Article 14 (6) within six months from the date of accession after consulting the Commission.][1]

This Regulation shall be binding in its entirety and directly applicable in all Member States.

Done at Brussels, 6 February 1962.

For the Council
The President

M. COUVE DE MURVILLE

---

1 Added by Annex 1 to the Act of Accession annexed to the Treaty of Accession signed on 22 January 1972.

REGULATION No 26

applying certain rules of competition to production of and trade in agricultural products

THE COUNCIL OF THE EUROPEAN ECONOMIC COMMUNITY,

Having regard to the Treaty establishing the European Economic Community, and in particular Articles 42 and 43 thereof;

Having regard to the proposal from the Commission;

Having regard to the Opinion of the European Parliament;

Whereas by virtue of Article 42 of the Treaty one of the matters to be decided under the common agricultural policy is whether the rules on competition laid down in the Treaty are to apply to production of and trade in agricultural products, and accordingly the provisions hereinafter contained will have to be supplemented in the light of developments in that policy;

Whereas the proposals submitted by the Commission for the formulation and implementation of the common agricultural policy show that certain rules on competition must forthwith be made applicable to production of and trade in agricultural products in order to eliminate practices contrary to the principles of the common market and prejudicial to attainment of the objectives set out in Article 39 of the Treaty and in order to provide a basis for the future establishment of a system of competition adapted to the development of the common agricultural policy;

Whereas the rules on competition relating to the agreements, decisions and practices referred to in Article 85 of the Treaty and to the abuse of dominant positions must be applied to production of and trade in agricultural products, in so far as their application does not impede the functioning of national organisations of agricultural markets or jeopardise attainment of the objectives of the common agricultural policy;

Whereas special attention is warranted in the case of farmers' organisations which are particularly concerned with the joint production or marketing of agricultural products or the use of joint facilities, unless such joint action excludes competition or jeopardises attainment of the objectives of Article 39 of the Treaty;

Whereas, in order both to avoid compromising the development of a common agricultural policy and to ensure certainty in the law and non-discriminatory treatment of the undertakings concerned, the

Commission must have sole power, subject to review by the Court of Justice, to determine whether the conditions provided for in the two preceding recitals are fulfilled as regards the agreements, decisions and practices referred to in Article 85 of the Treaty;

Whereas, in order to enable the specific provisions of the Treaty regarding agriculture, and in particular those of Article 39 thereof, to be taken into consideration, the Commission must, in questions of dumping, assess all the causes of the practices complained of and in particular the price level at which products from other sources are imported into the market in question; whereas it must, in the light of its assessment, make recommendations and authorise protective measures as provided in Article 91 (1) of the Treaty;

Whereas, in order to implement, as part of the development of the common agricultural policy, the rules on aids for production of or trade in agricultural products, the Commission should be in a position to draw up a list of existing, new or proposed aids, to make appropriate observations to the Member States and to propose suitable measures to them;

HAS ADOPTED THIS REGULATION:

Article 1

From the entry into force of this Regulation, Articles 85 to 90 of the Treaty and provisions made in implementation thereof shall, subject to Article 2 below, apply to all agreements, decisions and practices referred to in Articles 85 (1) and 86 of the Treaty which relate to production of or trade in the products listed in Annex II to the Treaty;

Article 2

1. Article 85 (1) of the Treaty shall not apply to such of the agreements, decisions and practices referred to in the preceding Article as form an integral part of a national market organisation or are necessary for attainment of the objectives set out in Article 39 of the Treaty. In particular, it shall not apply to agreements, decisions and practices of farmers, farmers' associations, or associations of such associations belonging to a single Member State which concern the production or sale of agricultural products or the use of joint facilities for the storage, treatment or processing of agricultural products, and under which there is no obligation to charge identical prices, unless the Commission finds that competition is thereby excluded or that the objectives of Article 39 of the Treaty are jeopardised.

2. After consulting the Member States and hearing the undertakings or associations of undertakings concerned and any other natural or

legal person that it considers appropriate, the Commission shall have sole power, subject to review by the Court of Justice, to determine, by decision which shall be published, which agreements, decisions and practices fulfil the conditions specified in paragraph 1.

3. The Commission shall undertake such determination either on its own initiative or at the request of a competent authority of a Member State or of an interested undertaking or association of undertakings.

4. The publication shall state the names of the parties and the main content of the decision; it shall have regard to the legitimate interest of undertakings in the protection of their business secrets.

Article 3

1. Without prejudice to Article 46 of the Treaty, Article 91 (1) thereof shall apply to trade in the products listed in Annex II to the Treaty.

2. With due regard for the provisions of the Treaty relating to agriculture, and in particular those of Article 39, the Commission shall assess all the causes of the practices complained of, in particular the price level at which products from other sources are imported into the market in question.

In the light of its assessment, it shall make recommendations and authorise protective measures as provided in Article 91 (1) of the Treaty.

Article 4

The provisions of Article 93 (1) and of the first sentence of Article 93 (3) of the Treaty shall apply to aids granted for production of or trade in the products listed in Annex II to the Treaty.

Article 5

This Regulation shall enter into force on the day following its publication in the *Official Journal of the European Communities*, with the exception of Articles 1 to 3, which shall enter into force on [30][1] July 1962.

This Regulation shall be binding in its entirety and directly applicable in all Member States.

Done at Brussels, 4 April 1962.

For the Council
The President
M. COUVE de MURVILLE

---

1 As amended by Regulation 49, OJ 53/1571.

REGULATION No 27 OF THE COMMISSION

First Regulation implementing Council Regulation No 17 of 6 February 1962

(Form, content and other details concerning applications and notifications)

THE COMMISSION OF THE EUROPEAN ECONOMIC COMMUNITY,

Having regard to the provisions of the Treaty establishing the European Economic Community, and in particular Articles 87 and 155 thereof;

Having regard to Article 24 of Council Regulation No 17 of 6 February 1962 (First Regulation implementing Articles 85 and 86 of the Treaty);

Whereas under Article 24 of Council Regulation No 17 the Commission is authorised to adopt implementing provisions concerning the form, content and other details of applications under Articles 2 and 3 and of notifications under Articles 4 and 5 of that Regulation;

Whereas the submission of such applications and notifications may have important legal consequences for each of the undertakings which is party to an agreement, decision or concerted practice; whereas every undertaking should accordingly have the right to submit an application or a notification to the Commission; whereas, furthermore, an undertaking exercising this right must inform the other undertakings which are parties to the agreement, decision or concerted practice in order to enable them to protect their interests;

Whereas it is for the undertakings and associations of undertakings to transmit to the Commission information as to facts and circumstances in support of applications under Article 2 and of notifications under Articles 4 and 5;

Whereas it is desirable to prescribe forms for use in applications for negative clearance relating to implementation of Article 85 (1) and for notifications relating to implementation of Article 85 (3) of the Treaty, in order to simplify and accelerate consideration by the competent departments, in the interests of all concerned;

HAS ADOPTED THIS REGULATION:

Article 1 Persons entitled to submit applications and notifications

1. Any undertaking which is party to agreements, decisions or

practices of the kind described in Articles 85 and 86 of the Treaty may submit an application under Article 2 or a notification under Articles 4 and 5 of Regulation No 17. Where the application or notification is submitted by some, but not all, of the undertakings concerned, they shall give notice to the others.

2. Where applications and notifications under Articles 2, 3 (1), 3 (2) (b), 4 and 5 of Regulation No 17 are signed by representatives of undertakings, associations of undertakings, or natural or legal persons, such representatives shall produce written proof that they are authorised to act.

3. Where a joint application or notification is submitted, a joint representative should be appointed.

Article 2   Submission of applications and notifications

1. Seven copies of each application and notification and of the supporting documents shall be submitted to the Commission.

2. The supporting documents shall be either originals or copies. Copies must be certified as true copies of the original.

3. Applications and notifications shall be in one of the official languages of the Community. Supporting documents shall be submitted in their original language. Where the original language is not one of the official languages, a translation in one of the official languages shall be attached.

Article 3   Effective date of submission of applications and registrations

The date of submission of an application or notification shall be the date on which it is received by the Commission. Where, however, the application or notification is sent by registered post, it shall be deemed to have been received on the date shown on the postmark of the place of posting.

Article 4   Content of applications and notifications

[1. Applications under Article 2 of Regulation No 17 relating to the applicability of Article 85 (1) of the Treaty and notifications under Article 4 or Article 5 (2) of Regulation No 17 shall be submitted on Form A/B as shown in the Annex to this Regulation.

2. Applications and notifications shall contain the information asked for in Form A/B.

3. Several participating undertakings may submit an application or notification on a single form.

4. Applications under Article 2 of Regulation No 17 relating to the applicability of Article 86 of the Treaty shall contain a full statement

of the facts, specifying, in particular, the practice concerned and the position of the undertaking or undertakings within the common market or a substantial part thereof in regard to products or services to which the practice relates.][1]

Article 5 Transitional provisions

1. Applications and notifications submitted prior to the date of entry into force of this Regulation otherwise than on the prescribed forms shall be deemed to comply with Article 4 of this Regulation.

2. The Commission may require a duly completed form to be submitted to it within such time as it shall appoint. In that event, applications and notifications shall be treated as properly made only if the forms are submitted within the prescribed period and in accordance with the provisions of this Regulation.

Article 6

This Regulation shall enter into force on the day following its publication in the *Official Journal of the European Communities*.

This Regulation shall be binding in its entirety and directly applicable in all Member States.

Done at Brussels, 3 May 1962.

For the Commission
The President
W. HALLSTEIN

---

1 As amended by Regulation 1133/68, OJ 1968 L189/1, part of the preamble to which states:

Whereas it is advisable, in view of the general preference of undertakings to have the two alternatives open to them, to provide for the use of a single form for applications for negative clearance and for notification in order to simplify the procedure for all parties to an agreement and for the competent departments;

Whereas negative clearance and exemption pursuant to Article 85 (3) of the Treaty have different consequences and whereas the single form must leave it open to undertakings to apply either for negative clearance or for a declaration of non-applicability".

FORM A/B[1]

This form and the supporting documents should be forwarded in seven copies together with proof in duplicate of the representative's authority to act.

If the space opposite each question is insufficient, please use extra pages, specifying to which item on the form they relate.

TO THE COMMISSION OF THE EUROPEAN COMMUNITIES

Directorate General for Competition
rue de la Loi, 200,
1040, Brussels.

A. Application for negative clearance pursuant to Article 2 of Council Regulation No 17 of 6 February 1962 relating to implementation of Article 85 (1) of the Treaty

B. Notification of an agreement, decision or concerted practice under Articles 4 and 5 of Council Regulation No 17 of 6 February 1962.

I. *Information regarding parties*

1. Name, forenames and address of person submitting the application or notification. If such person is acting as representative, state also the name and address of the undertaking or association of undertakings represented and the name, forenames and address of the proprietors or partners or, in the case of legal persons, of their legal representatives.

Proof of representative's authority to act must be supplied.

If the application or notification is submitted by a number of persons or on behalf of a number of undertakings, the information must be given in respect of each person or undertaking.

2. Name and address of the undertakings which are parties to the agreement, decision or concerted practice and name, forenames and address of the proprietors or partners or, in the case of legal persons, of their legal representatives (unless this information has been given under I (1)).

---

1 As amended by Regulation 1133/68, OJ L189/1.

If the undertakings which are parties to the agreement are not all associated in submitting the application or notification, state what steps have been taken to inform the other undertakings.

This information is not necessary in respect of standard contracts (see Section II 1 (b) below).

3. If a firm or joint agency has been formed in pursuance of the agreement, state the name and address of such firm or agency and the names, forenames and addresses of its legal or other representatives.

4. If a firm or joint agency is responsible for operating the agreement, state the name and address of such firm or agency and the names, forenames and addresses of its legal or other representatives.

Attach a copy of the statutes.

5. In the case of a decision of an association of undertakings, state the name and address of the association and the names, forenames and addresses of its legal representatives.

Attach a copy of the statutes.

6. If the undertakings are established or have their seat outside the territory of the common market (Article 227 (1) and (2) of the Treaty), state the name and address of a representative or branch established in the territory of the common market.

II. *Information regarding contents of agreement, decision or concerted practice:*

1. If the contents were reduced to writing, attach a copy of the full text unless (a), (b) or (c) below provides otherwise.

(a) Is there only an outline agreement or outline decision?
    If so, attach also copy of the full text of the individual agreements and implementing provisions.

(b) Is there a standard contract, i.e., a contract which the undertaking submitting the notification regularly concludes with particular persons or groups of persons (e.g., a contract restricting the freedom of action of one of the contracting parties in respect of resale prices or terms of business for goods supplied by the other contracting party)?
    If so, only the text of the standard contract need be attached.

(c) If there is a licensing agreement of the type covered by Article 4 (2) (2b) of Regulation No 17, it is not necessary to submit those clauses of the contract which only describe a technical manufacturing process and have no connection with the restriction of competition; in such cases, however, an indication of the parts omitted from the text must be given.

2. If the contents were not, or were only partially, reduced to writing, state the contents in the space opposite.

3. In all cases give the following additional information:

(a) Date of agreement, decision or concerted practice.
(b) Date when it came into force and, where applicable, proposed period of validity.
(c) Subject: exact description of the goods or services involved.
(d) Aims of the agreement, decision or concerted practice.
(e) Terms of adherence, termination or withdrawal.
(f) Sanctions which may be taken against participating undertakings (penalty clause, expulsion, withholding of supplies, etc.).

III. *Means of achieving the aims of the agreement, decision or concerted practice:*

1. State whether and how far the agreement, decision or concerted practice relates to:

– adherence to certain buying or selling prices, discounts or other trading conditions
– restriction or control of production, technical development or investment
– sharing of markets or sources of supply
– restrictions on freedom to purchase from, or resell to, third parties (exclusive contracts)
– application of different terms for supply of equivalent goods or services

2. Is the agreement, decision or concerted practice concerned with supply of goods or services

(a) within one Member State only?
(b) between a Member State and third States?
(c) between Member States?

IV. *If you consider Article 85 (1) to be inapplicable and are notifying the agreement, decision or concerted practice as a precaution only:*

(a) Please attach a statement of the relevant facts and reasons as to why you consider Article 85 (1) to be inapplicable, e.g., that the agreement, decision or concerted practice
  1. does not have the object or effect or preventing, restricting or distorting competition; or
  2. is not one which may affect trade between Member States.
(b) Are you asking for a negative clearance pursuant to Article 2 of Regulation No 17?

V. *Are you notifying the agreement, decision or concerted practice, even if only as a precaution, in order to obtain a declaration of applicability under Article 85 (3)?*

If so, explain to what extent
1. the agreement, decision or concerted practice contributes towards

– improving production or distribution, or
– promoting technical or economic progress;

2. a proper share of the benefits arising from such improvement or progress accrues to the consumers;
3. the agreement, decision or concerted practice is essential for realising the aims set out under 1 above; and
4. the agreement, decision or concerted practice does not eliminate competition in respect of a substantial part of the goods concerned.

VI. *State whether you intend to produce further supporting arguments and, if so, on which points.*

The undersigned declare that the information given above and in the .... annexes attached hereto is correct. They are aware of the provisions of Article 15 (1) (a) of Regulation No 17.

.... (date) ....

Signatures:

....

....

....

EUROPEAN COMMUNITIES
COMMISSION   Brussels, (date).....................

Directorate General for Competition   200, rue de la Loi

```
┌─────────────────────────────────────────────────────────────────────┐
│                                                                       │
│    To                                                                 │
│                                                                       │
│                                                                       │
│                                                                       │
│                                                                       │
│                                                                       │
│                                                                       │
└─────────────────────────────────────────────────────────────────────┘
```

Acknowledgement of receipt

(This form will be returned to the address inserted above if completed
in a single copy by the person lodging it.)

Your application for negative clearance dated ....

Your notification dated ....

concerning:
(a) Parties:

1 ....

2 .... and others

(There is no need to name the other undertakings party to the
arrangement)

(b) Subject ....

....

....

(brief description of the restriction on competition)

was received on ....

and registered under No IV ....

Please quote the above number in all correspondence.

REGULATION No 141 OF THE COUNCIL
exempting transport from the application of Council Regulation No 17

THE COUNCIL OF THE EUROPEAN ECONOMIC COMMUNITY,

Having regard to the Treaty establishing the European Economic Community, and in particular Article 67 thereof;

Having regard to the first Regulation made in implementation of Articles 85 and 86 of the Treaty (Regulation No 17) of 6 February 1962, as amended by Regulation No 59 of 3 July 1962;

Having regard to the proposal from the Commission;

Having regard to the Opinion of the Economic and Social Committee;

Having regard to the Opinion of the Assembly;

Whereas, in pursuance of the common transport policy, account being taken of the distinctive features of the transport sector, it may prove necessary to lay down rules governing competition different from those laid down or to be laid down for other sectors of the economy, and whereas Regulation No 17 should not therefore apply to transport;

Whereas, in the light of work in hand on the formulation of a common transport policy, it is possible, as regards transport by rail, road and inland waterway, to envisage the introduction within a foreseeable period of rules of competition; whereas, on the other hand, as regards sea and air transport it is impossible to foresee whether and at what date the Council will adopt appropriate provisions; whereas accordingly a limit to the period during which Regulation No 17 shall not apply can be set only for transport by rail, road and inland waterway;

Whereas the distinctive features of transport make it justifiable to exempt from the application of Regulation No 17 only agreements, decisions and concerted practices directly relating to the provision of transport services;

HAS ADOPTED THIS REGULATION:

Article 1

Regulation No 17 shall not apply to agreements, decisions or concerted practices in the transport sector which have as their object or effect the fixing of transport rates and conditions, the limitation or control of the supply of transport or the sharing of transport markets; nor shall it apply to the abuse of a dominant position, within the meaning of Article 86 of the Treaty, within the transport market.

Article 2

The Council, taking account of any measures that may be taken in pursuance of the common transport policy, shall adopt appropriate provisions in order to apply rules of competition to transport by rail, road and inland waterway. To this end, the Commission shall, before 30 June 1964, submit proposals to the Council.

Article 3

Article 1 of this Regulation shall remain in force, as regards transport by rail, road and inland waterway, until 31 December 1965.

Article 4

This Regulation shall enter into force on 13 March 1962. This provision shall not be invoked against undertakings or associations of undertakings which, before the day following the date of publication of this Regulation in the *Official Journal of the European Communities*, shall have terminated any agreement, decision or concerted practice covered by Article 1.

This Regulation shall be binding in its entirety and directly applicable in all Member States.

Done at Paris, 26 November 1962.

For the Council
The President

B. MATTARELLA

REGULATION No 99/63/EEC OF THE COMMISSION
of 25 July 1963
on the hearings provided for in Article 19 (1) and (2) of Council Regulation No 17

THE COMMISSION OF THE EUROPEAN ECONOMIC COMMUNITY,

Having regard to the Treaty establishing the European Economic Community, and in particular Articles 87 and 155 thereof;

Having regard to Article 24 of Council Regulation No 17[1] of 6 February 1962 (First Regulation implementing Articles 85 and 86 of the Treaty),

Whereas the Commission has power under Article 24 of Council Regulation No 17 to lay down implementing provisions concerning the hearings provided for in Article 19 (1) and (2) of that Regulation;

Whereas in most cases the Commission will in the course of its inquiries already be in close touch with the undertakings or associations of undertakings which are the subject thereof and they will accordingly have the opportunity of making known their views regarding the objections raised against them;

Whereas, however, in accordance with Article 19 (1) of Regulation No 17 and with the rights of defence, the undertakings and associations of undertakings concerned must have the right on conclusion of the inquiry to submit their comments on the whole of the objections raised against them which the Commission proposes to deal with in its decisions;

Whereas persons other than the undertakings or associations of undertakings which are the subject of the inquiry may have an interest in being heard; whereas, by the second sentence of Article 19 (2) of Regulation No 17, such persons must have the opportunity of being heard if they apply and show that they have a sufficient interest;

Whereas it is desirable to enable persons who, pursuant to Article 3 (2) of Regulation No 17, have applied for an infringement to be terminated to submit their comments where the Commission considers that on the basis of the information in its possession there are insufficient grounds for granting the application;

Whereas the various persons entitled to submit comments must do so in writing, both in their own interest and in the interests of good administration, without prejudice to oral procedure where appropriate to supplement the written evidence;

---

1 Page, 318 above.

Whereas it is necessary to define the rights of persons who are to be heard, and in particular the conditions upon which they may be represented or assisted and the setting and calculation of time limits;

Whereas the Advisory Committee on Restrictive Practices and Monopolies delivers its Opinion on the basis of a preliminary draft decision; whereas it must therefore be consulted concerning a case after the inquiry in respect thereof has been completed; whereas such consultation does not prevent the Commission from re-opening an inquiry if need be;

HAS ADOPTED THIS REGULATION:

Article 1

Before consulting the Advisory Committee on Restrictive Practices and Monopolies, the Commission shall hold a hearing pursuant to Article 19 (1) of Regulation No 17.

Article 2

1. The Commission shall inform undertakings and associations of undertakings in writing of the objections raised against them. The communication shall be addressed to each of them or to a joint agent appointed by them.

2. The Commission may inform the parties by giving notice in the *Official Journal of the European Communities*, if from the circumstances of the case this appears appropriate, in particular where notice is to be given to a number of undertakings but no joint agent has been appointed. The notice shall have regard to the legitimate interest of the undertakings in the protection of their business secrets.

3. A fine or a periodic penalty payment may be imposed on an undertaking or association of undertakings only if the objections were notified in the manner provided for in paragraph 1.

4. The Commission shall when giving notice of objections fix a time limit up to which the undertakings and associations of undertakings may inform the Commission of their views.

Article 3

1. Undertakings and associations of undertakings shall, within the appointed time limit, make known in writing their views concerning the objections raised against them.

2. They may in their written comments set out all matters relevant to their defence.

3. They may attach any relevant documents in proof of the facts set out. They may also propose that the Commission hear persons who may corroborate those facts.

Article 4

The Commission shall in its decisions deal only with those objections raised against undertakings and associations of undertakings in respect of which they have been afforded the opportunity of making known their views.

Article 5

If natural or legal persons showing a sufficient interest apply to be heard pursuant to Article 19 (2) of Regulation No. 17, the Commission shall afford them the opportunity of making known their views in writing within such time limit as it shall fix.

Article 6

Where the Commission, having received an application pursuant to Article 3 (2) of Regulation No 17, considers that on the basis of the information in its possession there are insufficient grounds for granting the application, it shall inform the applicants of its reasons and fix a time limit for them to submit any further comments in writing.

Article 7

1. The Commission shall afford to persons who have so requested in their written comments the opportunity to put forward their arguments orally, if those persons show a sufficient interest or if the Commission proposes to impose on them a fine or periodic penalty payment.

2. The Commission may likewise afford to any other person the opportunity of orally expressing his views.

Article 8

1. The Commission shall summon the persons to be heard to attend on such date as it shall appoint.

2. It shall forthwith transmit a copy of the summons to the competent authorities of the Member States, who may appoint an official to take part in the hearing.

Article 9

1. Hearings shall be conducted by the persons appointed by the Commission for that purpose.

2. Persons summoned to attend shall appear either in person or be

represented by legal representatives or by representatives authorised by their constitution. Undertakings and associations of undertakings may moreover be represented by a duly authorised agent appointed from among their permanent staff.

Persons heard by the Commission may be assisted by lawyers or university teachers who are entitled to plead before the Court of Justice of the European Communities in accordance with Article 17 of the Protocol on the Statute of the Court, or by other qualified persons.

3. Hearings shall not be public. Persons shall be heard separately or in the presence of other persons summoned to attend. In the latter case, regard shall be had to the legitimate interest of the undertakings in the protection of their business secrets.

4. The essential content of the statements made by each person heard shall be recorded in minutes which shall be read and approved by him.

Article 10

Without prejudice to Article 2 (2), information and summonses from the Commission shall be sent to the addressees by registered letter with acknowledgement of receipt, or shall be delivered by hand against receipt.

Article 11

1. In fixing the time limits provided for in Articles 2, 5 and 6, the Commission shall have regard both to the time required for preparation of comments and to the urgency of the case. The time limit shall be not less than two weeks; it may be extended.

2. Time limits shall run from the day following receipt of a communication or delivery thereof by hand.

3. Written comments must reach the Commission or be dispatched by registered letter before expiry of the time limit. Where the time limit would expire on a Sunday or public holiday, it shall be extended up to the end of the next following working day. For the purpose of calculating this extension, public holidays shall, in cases where the relevant date is the date of receipt of written comments, be those set out in the Annex to this Regulation, and in cases where the relevant date is the date of dispatch, those appointed by law in the country of dispatch.

This Regulation shall be binding in its entirety and directly applicable in all Member States.

Done at Brussels, 25 July 1963.

For the Commission
The President
Walter HALLSTEIN

ANNEX

referred to in the third sentence of Article 11 (3)

(List of public holidays)

New Year	1 Jan
Good Friday	
Easter Saturday	
Easter Monday	
Labour Day	1 May
Schuman Plan Day	9 May
Ascension Day	
Whit Monday	
Belgian National Day	21 July
Assumption	15 Aug
All Saints	1 Nov
All Souls	2 Nov
Christmas Eve	24 Dec
Christmas Day	25 Dec
The day following Christmas Day	26 Dec
New Year's Eve	31 Dec

REGULATION No 19/65/EEC OF THE COUNCIL

of 2 March 1965

on application of Article 85 (3) of the Treaty to certain categories of agreements and concerted practices

THE COUNCIL OF THE EUROPEAN ECONOMIC COMMUNITY,

Having regard to the Treaty establishing the European Economic Community, and in particular Article 87 thereof;
Having regard to the proposal from the Commission;
Having regard to the Opinion of the European Parliament;[1]

---

1 OJ 1964, 81/1275.

Having regard to the Opinion of the Economic and Social Committee;[1]

Whereas Article 85 (1) of the Treaty may in accordance with Article 85 (3) be declared inapplicable to certain categories of agreements, decisions and concerted practices which fulfil the conditions contained in Article 85 (3);

Whereas the provisions for implementation of Article 85 (3) must be adopted by way of regulation pursuant to Article 87;

Whereas in view of the large number of notifications submitted in pursuance of Regulation No 17[2] it is desirable that in order to facilitate the task of the Commission it should be enabled to declare by way of regulation that the provisions of Article 85 (1) do not apply to certain categories of agreements and concerted practices;

Whereas it should be laid down under what conditions the Commission, in close and constant liaison with the competent authorities of the Member States, may exercise such powers after sufficient experience has been gained in the light of individual decisions and it becomes possible to define categories of agreements and concerted practices in respect of which the conditions of Article 85 (3) may be considered as being fulfilled;

Whereas the Commission has indicated by the action it has taken, in particular by Regulation No 153,[3] that there can be no easing of the procedures prescribed by Regulations No 17 in respect of certain types of agreements and concerted practices that are particularly liable to distort competition in the common market;

Whereas under Article 6 of Regulation No 17 the Commission may provide that a decision taken pursuant to Article 85 (3) of the Treaty shall apply with retroactive effect; whereas it is desirable that the Commission be also empowered to adopt, by regulation, provisions to the like effect;

Whereas under Article 7 of Regulation No 17 agreements, decisions and concerted practices may, by decision of the Commission, be exempted from prohibition in particular if they are modified in such manner that they satisfy the requirements of Article 85 (3); whereas it is desirable that the Commission be enabled to grant like exemption by regulation to such agreements and concerted practices if they are modified in such manner as to fall within a category defined in an exempting regulation;

---

1 OJ 1964, 197/3320.
2 Page 318, above.
3 OJ 1962, 139/2918.

Whereas, since there can be no exemption if the conditions set out in Article 85 (3) are not satisfied, the Commission must have power to lay down by decision the conditions that must be satisfied by an agreement or concerted practice which owing to special circumstances has certain effects incompatible with Article 85 (3);

HAS ADOPTED THIS REGULATION:

Article 1

1. Without prejudice to the application of Council Regulation No 17 and in accordance with Article 85 (3) of the Treaty the Commission may by regulation declare that Article 85 (1) shall not apply to categories of agreements to which only two undertakings are party and:

(a) – whereby one party agrees with the other to supply only to that other certain goods for resale within a defined area of the common market; or
   – whereby one party agrees with the other to purchase only from that other certain goods for resale; or
   – whereby the two undertakings have entered into obligations, as in the two preceding sub-paragraphs, with each other in respect of exclusive supply and purchase for resale;

(b) which include restrictions imposed in relation to the acquisition or use of industrial property rights—in particular of patents, utility models, designs or trade marks—or to the rights arising out of contracts for assignment of, or the right to use, a method of manufacture or knowledge relating to the use or to the application of industrial processes.

2. The regulation shall define the categories of agreements to which it applies and shall specify in particular:

(a) the restrictions of clauses which must not be contained in the agreements;

(b) the clauses which must be contained in the agreements, or the other conditions which must be satisfied.

3. Paragraphs 1 and 2 shall apply by analogy to categories of concerted practices to which only two undertakings are party.

Article 2

1. A regulation pursuant to Article 1 shall be made for a specified period.

2. It may be repealed or amended where circumstances have changed with respect to any factor which was basic to its being made; in such case, a period shall be fixed for modification of the agreements and concerted practices to which the earlier regulation applies.

Article 3

A regulation pursuant to Article 1 may stipulate that it shall apply with retroactive effect to agreements and concerted practices to which, at the date of entry into force of that regulation, a decision issued with retroactive effect in pursuance of Article 6 of Regulation No 17 would have applied.

Article 4

1. A regulation pursuant to Article 1 may stipulate that the prohibition contained in Article 85 (1) of the Treaty shall not apply, for such period as shall be fixed by that regulation, to agreements and concerted practices already in existence on 13 March 1962 which do not satisfy the conditions of Article 85 (3), [and a regulation pursuant to Article 1 may stipulate that the prohibition contained in Article 85 (1) of the Treaty shall not apply, for such period as shall be fixed by that regulation, to agreements and concerted practices already in existence at the date of accession to which Article 85 applies by virtue of accession and which do not satisfy the conditions of Article 85 (3), where:][1]

- within three months from the entry into force of the Regulation, they are so modified as to satisfy the said conditions in accordance with the provisions of the regulation; and
- the modifications are brought to the notice of the Commission within the time limit fixed by the regulation.

2. Paragraph 1 shall apply to agreements and concerted practices which had to be notified before 1 February 1963, in accordance with Article 5 of Regulation No 17, only where they have been so notified before that date.

[Paragraph 1 shall not apply to agreements and concerted practices to which Article 85 (1) of the Treaty applies by virtue of accession and which must be notified before 1 July 1973, in accordance with Articles 5 and 25 of Regulation No 17, unless they have been so notified before that date.][1]

3. The benefit of the provisions laid down pursuant to paragraph 1 may not be claimed in actions pending at the date of entry into force

---

1 Added by Annex I to the Act of Accession annexed to the Treaty of Accession signed on 22 January 1972.

of a regulation adopted pursuant to Article 1; neither may it be relied on as grounds for claims for damages against third parties.

Article 5

Before adopting a regulation, the Commission shall publish a draft thereof and invite all persons concerned to submit their comments within such time limit, being not less than one month, as the Commission shall fix.

Article 6

1. The Commission shall consult the Advisory Committee on Restrictive Practices and Monopolies:

(a) before publishing a draft regulation;
(b) before adopting a regulation.

2. Article 10 (5) and (6) of Regulation No 17, relating to consultation with the Advisory Committee, shall apply by analogy, it being understood that joint meetings with the Commission shall take place not earlier than one month after dispatch of the notice convening them.

Article 7

Where the Commission, either on its own initiative or at the request of a Member State or of natural or legal persons claiming a legitimate interest, finds that in any particular case agreements or concerted practices to which a regulation adopted pursuant to Article 1 of this Regulation applies have nevertheless certain effects which are incompatible with the conditions laid down in Article 85 (3) of the Treaty, it may withdraw the benefit of application of that regulation and issue a decision in accordance with Articles 6 and 8 of Regulation No 17, without any notification under Article 4 (1) of Regulation No 17 being required.

Article 8

The Commission shall, before 1 January 1970, submit to the Council a proposal for a Regulation for such amendment of this Regulation as may prove necessary in the light of experience.

This Regulation shall be binding in its entirety and directly applicable in all Member States.

Done at Brussels, 2 March 1965.

For the Council
The President
M. COUVE DE MURVILLE

REGULATION No 67/67/EEC OF THE COMMISSION
of 22 March 1967

on the application of Article 85 (3) of the Treaty to certain categories of exclusive dealing agreements

THE COMMISSION OF THE EUROPEAN ECONOMIC COMMUNITY,

Having regard to the Treaty establishing the European Economic Community, and in particular Articles 87 and 155 thereof;

Having regard to Article 24 of Regulation No 17 of 6 February 1962[1];

Having regard to Regulation No 19/65/EEC of 2 March 1965[2] on the application of Article 85 (3) of the Treaty to certain categories of agreements and concerted practices;

Having regard to the Opinions delivered by the Advisory Committee on Restrictive Practices and Monopolies in accordance with Article 6 of Regulation No 19/65/EEC;

Whereas under Regulation No 19/65/EEC the Commission has power to apply Article 85 (3) of the Treaty by regulation to certain categories of bilateral exclusive dealing agreements and concerted practices coming within Article 85;

Whereas the experience gained up to now, on the basis of individual decisions, makes it possible to define a first category of agreements and concerted practices which can be accepted as normally satisfying the conditions laid down in Article 85 (3);

Whereas, since adoption of such a regulation would not conflict with the application of Regulation No 17, the right of undertakings to request the Commission, on an individual basis, for a declaration under Article 85 (3) of the Treaty would not be affected;

Whereas exclusive dealing agreements of the category defined in Article 1 of this Regulation may fall within the prohibition contained in Article 85 (1) of the Treaty; whereas since it is only in exceptional cases that exclusive dealing agreements concluded within a Member State affect trade between Member States, there is no need to include them in this Regulation;

Whereas it is not necessary expressly to exclude from the category as defined those agreements which do not fulfil the conditions of Article 85 (1) of the Treaty;

Whereas in the present state of trade exclusive dealing agreements

---

1 Page 318, above.
2 Page 349, above.

relating to international trade lead in general to an improvement in distribution because the entrepreneur is able to consolidate his sales activities; whereas he is not obliged to maintain numerous business contacts with a large number of dealers, and whereas the fact of maintaining contacts with only one dealer makes it easier to overcome sales difficulties resulting from linguistic, legal, and other differences; whereas exclusive dealing agreements facilitate the promotion of the sale of a product and make it possible to carry out more intensive marketing and to ensure continuity of supplies, while at the same time rationalising distribution; whereas, moreover, the appointment of an exclusive distributor or of an exclusive purchaser who will take over, in place of the manufacturer, sales promotion, after-sales service and carrying of stocks, is often the sole means whereby small and medium-size undertakings can compete in the market; whereas it should be left to the contracting parties to decide whether and to what extent they consider it desirable to incorporate in the agreements terms designed to promote sales; whereas there can only be an improvement in distribution if dealing is not entrusted to a competitor;

Whereas as a rule such exclusive dealing agreements also help to give consumers a proper share of the resulting benefit as they gain directly from the improvement in distribution, and their economic or supply position is thereby improved as they can obtain products manufactured in other countries more quickly and more easily;

Whereas this Regulation must determine the obligations restricting competition which may be included in an exclusive dealing agreement; whereas it may be left to the contracting parties to decide which of those obligations they include in exclusive dealing agreements in order to draw the maximum advantages from exclusive dealing;

Whereas any exemptions must be subject to certain conditions; whereas it is in particular advisable to ensure through the possibility of parallel imports that consumers obtain a proper share of the advantages resulting from exclusive dealing; whereas it is therefore not possible to allow industrial property rights and other rights to be exercised in an abusive manner in order to create absolute territorial protection; whereas these considerations do not prejudice the relationship between the law of competition and industrial property rights, since the sole object here is to determine the conditions for exemption of certain categories of agreements under this Regulation;

Whereas competition at the distribution stage is ensured by the possibility of parallel imports, whereas, therefore, the exclusive dealing agreements covered by this Regulation will not normally afford any possibility of preventing competition in respect of a substantial part of the products in question;

Whereas it is desirable to allow contracting parties a limited period of time within which they may, in accordance with Article 4 of Regulation No 19/65/EEC, modify their agreements and practices so as to satisfy the conditions laid down in this Regulation, without it being possible, under Article 4 (3) of Regulation No 19/65/EEC, to rely thereon in actions which are pending at the time of entry into force of this Regulation, or as grounds for claims for damages against third parties;

Whereas agreements and concerted practices which satisfy the conditions set out in this Regulation need no longer be notified; whereas Article 4 (2) (a) of Regulation No 27, as amended by Regulation No 153, can be repealed, since agreements which it was possible to notify on Form B 1 would normally come within the scope of the exemption;

Whereas agreements notified on Form B 1 and not amended so as to satisfy the conditions of this Regulation should be made subject to the normal notification procedure, in order that they may be examined individually;

HAS ADOPTED THIS REGULATION:

Article 1

1. Pursuant to Article 85 (3) of the Treaty and subject to the provisions of this Regulation it is hereby declared that until 31 December [1982][1] Article 85 (1) of the Treaty shall not apply to agreements to which only two undertakings are party and whereby:

(a) one party agrees with the other to supply only to that other certain goods for resale within a defined area of the common market; or

(b) one party agrees with the other to purchase only from that other certain goods for resale; or

(c) the two undertakings have entered into obligations, as in (a) and (b) above, with each other in respect of exclusive supply and purchase for resale.

2. Paragraph 1 shall not apply to agreements to which undertakings from one Member State only are party and which concern the resale of goods within that Member State.

---

1 As amended by Regulation 2591/72, OJ 1972 L276/15.

Article 2

1. Apart from an obligation falling within Article 1, no restriction on competition shall be imposed on the exclusive dealer other than:

(a) the obligation not to manufacture or distribute, during the duration of the contract or until one year after its expiration, goods which compete with the goods to which the contract relates;

(b) the obligation to refrain, outside the territory covered by the contract, from seeking customers for the goods to which the contract relates, from establishing any branch, or from maintaining any distribution depot.

2. Article 1 (1) shall apply notwithstanding that the exclusive dealer undertakes all or any of the following obligations:

(a) to purchase complete ranges of goods or minimum quantities;
(b) to sell the goods to which the contract relates under trade marks or packed and presented as specified by the manufacturer;
(c) To take measures for promotion of sales, in particular:

    – to advertise;
    – to maintain a sales network or stock of goods;
    – to provide after-sale and guarantee services;
    – to employ staff having specialised or technical training.

Article 3

Article 1 (1) of this Regulation shall not apply where:

(a) manufacturers of competing goods entrust each other with exclusive dealing in those goods;
(b) the contracting parties make it difficult for intermediaries or consumers to obtain the goods to which the contract relates from other dealers within the common market, in particular where the contracting parties:

    (1) exercise industrial property rights to prevent dealers or consumers from obtaining from other parts of the common market or from selling in the territory covered by the contract goods to which the contract relates which are properly marked or otherwise properly placed on the market;

    (2) exercise other rights or take other measures to prevent dealers or consumers from obtaining from elsewhere goods to which the contract relates or from selling them in the territory covered by the contract.

Article 4

1. As regards agreements which were in existence on 13 March 1962 and were notified before 1 February 1963, the declaration contained in Article 1 (1) of inapplicability of Article 85 (1) of the Treaty shall have retroactive effect from the time when the conditions of application of this Regulation were fulfilled.

2. As regards all other agreements notified before the entry into force of this Regulation, the declaration contained in Article 1 (1) of inapplicability of Article 85 (1) of the Treaty shall have retroactive effect from the time when the conditions of application of this Regulation were fulfilled, but not earlier than the day of notification.

Article 5

As regards agreements which were in existence on 13 March 1962, notified before 1 February 1963 and amended before 2 August 1967 so as to fulfil the conditions of application of this Regulation, the prohibition in Article 85 (1) of the Treaty shall not apply in respect of the period prior to the amendment, where such amendment is notified to the Commission before 3 October 1967. [As regards agreements, decisions or concerted practices for exclusive dealing already in existence at the date of accession to which Article 85 (1) applies by virtue of accession, the prohibition in Article 85 (1) of the Treaty shall not apply where they are modified within six months from the date of accession so as to fulfil the conditions contained in this Regulation.][1] The notification shall take effect from the time of receipt thereof by the Commission. Where the notification is sent by registered post, it shall take effect from the date on the postmark of the place of dispatch.

Article 6

The Commission shall examine whether Article 7 of Regulation No 19/65/EEC applies in individual cases, in particular when there are grounds for believing that:

(a) the goods to which the contract relates are not subject, in the territory covered by the contract, to competition from goods considered by the consumer as similar goods in view of their properties, price and intended use;

(b) it is not possible for other manufacturers to sell, in the territory covered by the contract, similar goods at the same stage of distribution as that of the exclusive dealer;

---

1 Added by Annex 1 to the Act of Accession annexed to the Treaty of Accession signed on 22 January 1972.

(c) the exclusive dealer has abused the exemption:

    (1) by refusing, without objectively valid reasons, to supply in the territory covered by the contract categories of purchasers who cannot obtain supplies elsewhere, on suitable terms, of the goods to which the contract relates;

    (2) by selling the goods to which the contract relates at excessive prices.

Article 7

1. Article 4 (2) (a) of Regulation No 27 of 3 May 1962, as amended by Regulation No 153, is hereby repealed.

2. Notification, on Form B 1, on an exclusive dealing agreement which does not fulfil the conditions contained in Articles 1 to 3 of this Regulation shall, if such agreement is not amended so as to satisfy those conditions, be effected before 3 October 1967, by submission of Form B, with annexes, in accordance with the provisions of Regulation No 27.

Article 8

Articles 1 to 7 of this Regulation shall apply by analogy to the category of concerted practices defined in Article 1 (1).

Article 9

This Regulation shall enter into force on 1 May 1967.

This Regulation shall be binding in its entirety and directly applicable in all Member States.

Done at Brussels, 16 June 1967.

For the Commission
The President

Walter HALLSTEIN

REGULATION (EEC) No 1017/68 OF THE COUNCIL
of 19 July 1968
applying rules of competition to transport by rail, road and inland waterway

THE COUNCIL OF THE EUROPEAN COMMUNITIES,

Having regard to the Treaty establishing the European Economic Community, and in particular Articles 75 and 87 thereof;

Having regard to the proposal from the Commission;

Having regard to the Opinion of the European Parliament;[1]

Having regard to the Opinion of the Economic and Social Committee;[2]

Whereas Council Regulation No 141[3] exempting transport from the application of Regulation No 17 provides that the said Regulation No 17[4] shall not apply to agreements, decisions and concerted practices in the transport sector the effect of which is to fix transport rates and conditions, to limit or control the supply of transport or to share transport markets, nor to dominant positions, within the meaning of Article 86 of the Treaty, on the transport market;

Whereas, for transport by rail, road and inland waterway, Regulation No 1002/67/CEE[5] provides that such exemption shall not extend beyond 30 June 1968;

Whereas the establishing of rules of competition for transport by rail, road and inland waterway is part of the common transport policy and of general economic policy;

Whereas, when rules of competition for these sectors are being settled, account must be taken of the distinctive features of transport;

Whereas, since the rules of competition for transport derogate from the general rules of competition, it must be made possible for undertakings to ascertain what rules apply in any particular case;

Whereas, with the introduction of a system of rules on competition for transport, it is desirable that such rules should apply equally to the joint financing or acquisition of transport equipment for the joint operation of services by certain groupings of undertakings, and also to certain operations in connection with transport by rail, road or inland waterway of providers of services ancillary to transport;

---

1 OJ 1964, 205/3505.
2 OJ 1965 103/1792.
3 Page 343, above.
4 Page 318, above.
5 OJ 1971 306/1.

Whereas, in order to ensure that trade between Member States is not affected or competition within the common market distorted, it is necessary to prohibit in principle for the three modes of transport specified above all agreements between undertakings, decisions of associations of undertakings and concerted practices between undertakings and all instances of abuse of a dominant position within the common market which could have such effects;

Whereas certain types of agreement, decision and concerted practice in the transport sector the object and effect of which is merely to apply technical improvements or to achieve technical co-operation may be exempted from the prohibition on restrictive agreements since they contribute to improving productivity; whereas, in the light of experience following application of this Regulation, the Council may, on a proposal from the Commission, amend the list of such types of agreement;

Whereas, in order that an improvement may be fostered in the sometimes too dispersed structure of the industry in the road and inland waterway sectors, there should also be exempted from the prohibition on restrictive agreements those agreements, decisions and concerted practices providing for the creation and operation of groupings of undertakings in these two transport sectors whose object is the carrying on of transport operations, including the joint financing or acquisition of transport equipment for the joint operation of services; whereas such overall exemption can be granted only on condition that the total carrying capacity of a grouping does not exceed a fixed maximum, and that the individual capacity of undertakings belonging to the grouping does not exceed certain limits so fixed as to ensure that no one undertaking can hold a dominant position within the grouping; whereas the Commission must, however, have power to intervene if, in specific cases, such agreements should have effects incompatible with the conditions under which a restrictive agreement may be recognised as lawful, and should constitute an abuse of the exemption; whereas, nevertheless, the fact that a grouping has a total carrying capacity greater than the fixed maximum, or cannot claim the overall exemption because of the individual capacity of the undertakings belonging to the grouping, does not in itself prevent such a grouping from constituting a lawful agreement, decision or concerted practice if it satisfies the conditions therefor laid down in this Regulation;

Whereas, where an agreement, decision or concerted practice contributes towards improving the quality of transport services, or towards promoting greater continuity and stability in the satisfaction of transport needs on markets where supply and demand may be subject to considerable temporal fluctuation, or towards increasing the productivity of undertakings, or towards furthering technical or economic progress, it must be made possible for the prohibition to be declared not to apply, always provided, however, that the agreement, decision or concerted practice takes fair account of the interests of transport users, and neither imposes on the undertakings concerned any restriction not indispensable to the attainment of the above objectives nor makes it possible for such undertakings to eliminate competition in respect of a substantial part of the transport market concerned, having regard to competition from alternative modes of transport;

Whereas it is desirable until such time as the Council, acting in pursuance of the common transport policy, introduces appropriate measures to ensure a stable transport market, and subject to the condition that the Council shall have found that a state of crisis exists, to authorise, for the market in question, such agreements as are needed in order to reduce disturbance resulting from the structure of the transport market;

Whereas, in respect of transport by rail, road and inland waterway, it is desirable that Member States should neither enact nor maintain in force measures contrary to this Regulation concerning public undertakings or undertakings to which they grant special or exclusive rights; whereas it is also desirable that undertakings entrusted with the operation of services of general economic importance should be subject to the provisions of this Regulation in so far as the application thereof does not obstruct, in law or in fact, the accomplishment of the particular tasks assigned to them, always provided that the development of trade is not thereby affected to such an extent as would be contrary to the interests of the Community; whereas the Commission must have power to see that these principles are applied and to address the appropriate directives or decisions for this purpose to Member States;

Whereas the detailed rules for application of the basic principles of this Regulation must be so drawn that they not only ensure effective supervision while simplifying administration as far as possible but also meet the needs of undertakings for certainty in the law;

Whereas it is for the undertakings themselves, in the first instance, to judge whether the predominant effects of their agreements, decisions or concerted practices are the restriction of competition or the economic benefits acceptable as justification for such restriction and to decide accordingly, on their own responsibility, as to the illegality or legality of such agreements, decisions or concerted practices;

Whereas, therefore, undertakings should be allowed to conlude or operate agreements without declaring them; whereas this exposes such agreements to the risk of being declared void with retroactive effect should they be examined following a complaint or on the Commissions's own initiative, but does not prevent their being retroactively declared lawful in the event of such subsequent examination;

Whereas, however, undertakings may, in certain cases, desire the assistance of the competent authorities to ensure that their agreements, decisions or concerted practices are in conformity with the rules applicable; whereas for this purpose there should be made available to undertakings a procedure whereby they may submit applications to the Commission and a summary of each such application is published in the *Official Journal of the European Communities*, enabling any interested third parties to submit their comments on the agreement in question; whereas, in the absence of any complaint from Member States or interested third parties and unless the Commission notifies applicants within a fixed time limit, that there are serious doubts as to the legality of the agreement in question, that agreement should be deemed exempt from the prohibition for the time already elapsed and for a further period of three years;

Whereas, in view of the exceptional nature of agreements needed in order to reduce disturbances resulting from the structure of the transport market, once the Council has found that a state of crisis exists undertakings wishing to obtain authorisation for such an agreement should be required to notify it to the Commission; whereas authorisation by the Commission should have effect only from the date when it is decided to grant it; whereas the period of validity of such authorisation should not exceed three years from the finding of a state of crisis by the Council; whereas renewal of the decision should depend upon renewal of the finding of a state of crisis by the Council; whereas, in any event, the authorisation should cease to be valid not later than six months from the bringing into operation by the Council of appropriate measures to ensure the stability of the transport market to which the agreement relates;

Whereas, in order to secure uniform application within the common market of the rules of competition for transport, rules must be made under which the Commission, acting in close and constant liaison with the competent authorities of the Member States, may take the measures required for the application of such rules of competition;

Whereas for this purpose the Commission must have the co-operation of the competent authorities of the Member States and be empowered throughout the common market to request such information and to carry out such investigations as are necessary to bring to light any agreement, decision or concerted practice prohibited under this Regulation, or any abuse of a dominant position prohibited under this Regulation.

Whereas, if, on the application of the Regulation to a specific case, a Member State is of the opinion that a question of principle concerning the common transport policy is involved, it should be possible for such questions of principle to be examined by the Council; whereas it should be possible for any general questions raised by the implementation of the competition policy in the transport sector to be referred to the Council; whereas a procedure must be provided for which ensures that any decision to apply the Regulation in a specific case will be taken by the Commission only after the questions of principle have been examined by the Council, and in the light of the policy guidelines that emerge from that examination;

Whereas, in order to carry out its duty of ensuring that the provisions of this Regulation are applied, the Commission must be empowered to address to undertakings or associations of undertakings recommendations and decisions for the purpose of bringing to an end infringements of the provisions of this Regulation prohibiting certain agreements, decisions or practices;

Whereas compliance with the prohibitions laid down in this Regulation and the fulfilment of obligations imposed on undertakings and associations of undertakings under this Regulation must be enforceable by means of fines and periodic penalty payments;

Whereas undertakings concerned must be accorded the right to be heard by the Commission, third parties whose interests may be affected by a decision must be given the opportunity of submitting their comments beforehand, and it must be ensured that wide publicity is given to decisions taken;

Whereas it is desirable to confer upon the Court of Justice, pursuant to Article 172, unlimited jurisdiction in respect of decisions under which the Commission imposes fines or periodic penalty payments;

Whereas it is expedient to postpone for six months, as regards agreements, decisions and concerted practices in existence at the date of publication of this Regulation in the *Official Journal of the European Communities*, the entry into force of the prohibition laid down in the Regulation, in order to make it easier for undertakings to adjust their operations so as to conform to its provisions;

Whereas, following discussions with the third countries signatories to the Revised Convention for the Navigation of the Rhine, and within an appropriate period of time from the conclusion of those discussions, this Regulation as a whole should be amended as necessary in the light of the obligations arising out of the Revised Convention for the Navigation of the Rhine;

Whereas the Regulation should be amended as necessary in the light of the experience gained over a three-year period; whereas it will in particular be desirable to consider whether, in the light of the development of the common transport policy over that period, the scope of the Regulation should be extended to agreements, decisions and concerted practices, and to instances of abuse of a dominant position, not affecting trade between Member States;

HAS ADOPTED THIS REGULATION:

Article 1 Basic provision

The provisions of this Regulation shall, in the field of transport by rail, road and inland waterway, apply both to all agreements, decisions and concerted practices which have as their object or effect the fixing of transport rates and conditions, the limitation or control of the supply of transport, the sharing of transport markets, the application of technical improvements or technical co-operation, or the joint financing or acquisition of transport equipment or supplies where such operations are directly related to the provision of transport services and are necessary for the joint operation of services by a grouping within the meaning of Article 4 of road or inland waterway transport undertakings, and to the abuse of a dominant position on the transport market. These provisions shall apply also to operations of providers of services ancillary to transport which have any of the objects or effects listed above.

Article 2 Prohibition of restrictive practices

Subject to the provisions of Articles 3 to 6, the following shall be prohibited as incompatible with the common market, no prior decision to that effect being required: all agreements between undertakings, decisions by associations of undertakings and concerted practices liable to affect trade between Member States which have as their object or effect the prevention, restriction or distortion of completion within the common market, and in particular those which:

(a) directly or indirectly fix transport rates and conditions or any other trading conditions;

(b) limit or control the supply of transport, markets, technical development or investment;

(c) share transport markets;

(d) apply dissimilar conditions to equivalent transactions with other trading parties, thereby placing them at a competitive disadvantage;

(e) make the conclusion of contracts subject to acceptance by the other parties of additional obligations which, by their nature or according to commercial usage, have no connection with the provision of transport services.

Article 3   Exception for technical agreements

1. The prohibition laid down in Article 2 shall not apply to agreements, decisions or concerted practices the object and effect of which is to apply technical improvements or to achieve technical co-operation by means of:

- (a) the standardisation of equipment, transport supplies, vehicles or fixed installations;
- (b) the exchange or pooling, for the purpose of operating transport services, of staff, equipment, vehicles or fixed installations;
- (c) the organisation and execution of successive, complementary, substitute or combined transport operations, and the fixing and application of inclusive rates and conditions for such operations, including special competitive rates;
- (d) the use, for journeys by a single mode of transport, of the routes which are most rational from the operational point of view;
- (e) the co-ordination of transport timetables for connecting routes;
- (f) the grouping of single consignments;
- (g) the establishment of uniform rules as to the structure of tariffs and their conditions of application, provided such rules do not lay down transport rates and conditions.

2. The Commission shall, where appropriate, submit proposals to the Council with a view to extending or reducing the list in paragraph 1.

Article 4   Exemption for groups of small and medium-sized undertakings

1. The agreements, decisions and concerted practices referred to in Article 2 shall be exempt from the prohibition in that Article where their purpose is:

- the constitution and operation of groupings of road or inland waterway transport undertakings with a view to carrying on transport activities;
- the joint financing or acquisition of transport equipment or supplies, where these operations are directly related to the provision of transport services and are necessary for the joint operations of the aforesaid groupings;

always provided that the total carrying capacity of any grouping does not exceed:

– 10000 metric tons in the case of road transport,
– 500000 metric tons in the case of transport by inland waterway.

The individual capacity of each undertaking belonging to a grouping shall not exceed 1000 metric tons in the case of road transport or 50000 metric tons in the case of transport by inland waterway.

2. If the implementation of any agreement, decision or concerted practice covered by paragraph 1 has, in a given case, effects which are incompatible with the requirements of Article 5 and which constitute an abuse of the exemption from the provisions of Article 2, undertakings or associations of undertakings may be required to make such effects cease.

Article 5   Non-applicability of the prohibition

The prohibition in Article 2 may be declared inapplicable with retroactive effect to:

– any agreement or category of agreement between undertakings,
– any decision or category of decision of an association of undertakings, or
– any concerted practice or category of concerted practice which contributes towards:
– improving the quality of transport services; or
– promoting greater continuity and stability in the satisfaction of transport needs on markets where supply and demand are subject to considerable temporal fluctuation; or
– increasing the productivity of undertakings; or
– furthering technical or economic progress;

and at the same time takes fair account of the interests of transport users and neither:

(a) imposes on the transport undertakings concerned any restriction not essential to the attainment of the above objectives; nor
(b) makes it possible for such undertakings to eliminate competition in respect of a substantial part of the transport market concerned.

Article 6   Agreements intended to reduce disturbances resulting from the structure of the transport market

1. Until such time as the Council, acting in pursuance of the common transport policy, introduces appropriate measures to ensure a stable transport market, the prohibition laid down in Article 2 may be declared inapplicable to any agreement, decision or concerted practice which tends to reduce disturbances on the market in question.

2. A decision not to apply the prohibition laid down in Article 2, made in accordance with the procedure laid down in Article 14, may not be taken until the Council, either acting by a qualified majority or, where any Member State considers that the conditions set out in Article 75 (3) of the Treaty are satisfied, acting unanimously, has found, on the basis of a report by the Commission, that a state of crisis exists in all or part of a transport market.

3. Without prejudice to the provisions of paragraph 2, the prohibition in Article 2 may be declared inapplicable only where:

(a) the agreement, decision or concerted practice in question does not impose upon the undertakings concerned any restriction not indispensable to the reduction of disturbances; and

(b) does not make it possible for such undertakings to eliminate competition in respect of a substantial part of the transport market concerned.

Article 7   Invalidity of agreements and decisions

Any agreement or decision prohibited under the foregoing provisions shall be automatically void.

Article 8   Prohibition of abuse of dominant positions

Any abuse by one or more undertakings of a dominant position within the common market or in a substantial part of it shall be prohibited as incompatible with the common market in so far as trade between Member States may be affected thereby.

Such abuse may, in particular, consist in:

(a) directly or indirectly imposing unfair transport rates or conditions;

(b) limiting the supply of transport, markets or technical development to the prejudice of consumers;

(c) applying dissimilar conditions to equivalent transactions with other trading parties, thereby placing them at a competitive disadvantage;

(d) making the conclusion of contracts subject to acceptance by the other parties of supplementary obligations which, by their nature or according to commercial usage, have no connection with the provision of transport services.

Article 9 Public undertakings

1. In the case of public undertakings and undertakings to which Member States grant special or exclusive rights, Member States shall neither enact nor maintain in force any measure contrary to the provisions of the foregoing Articles.

2. Undertakings entrusted with the operation of services of general economic importance shall be subject to the provisions of the foregoing Articles, in so far as the application thereof does not obstruct, in law or in fact, the accomplishment of the particular tasks assigned to them. The development of trade must not be affected to such an extent as would be contrary to the interests of the Community.

3. The Commission shall see that the provisions of this Article are applied and shall, where necessary, address appropriate directives or decisions to Member States.

Article 10 Procedures on complaint or on the Commission's own initiative

Acting on receipt of a complaint or on its own initiative, the Commission shall initiate procedures to terminate any infringement of the provisions of Article 2 or of Article 8 or to enforce Article 4 (2).

Complaints may be submitted by:

(a) Member States;
(b) natural or legal persons who claim a legitimate interest.

Article 11 Result of procedures on complaint or on the Commission's own initiative

1. Where the Commission finds that there has been an infringement of Article 2 or Article 8, it may by decision require the undertakings or associations of undertakings concerned to bring such infringement to an end.

Without prejudice to the other provisions of this Regulation, the Commission may, before taking a decision under the preceding subparagraph, address to the undertakings or associations of undertakings concerned recommendations for termination of the infringement.

2. Paragraph 1 shall apply also to cases falling within Article 4 (2).

3. If the Commission, acting on a complaint received, concludes that on the evidence before it there are no grounds for intervention under Article 2, Article 4 (2) or Article 8 in respect of any agreement, decision or practice, it shall issue a decision rejecting the complaint as unfounded.

4. If the Commission, whether acting on a complaint received or on its own initiative, concludes that an agreement, decision or concerted

practice satisfies the provisions both of Article 2 and of Article 5, it shall issue a decision applying Article 5. Such decision shall indicate the date from which it is to take effect. This date may be prior to that of the decision.

Article 12   Application of Article 5—objections

1. Undertakings and associations of undertakings which seek application of Article 5 in respect of agreements, decisions and concerted practices falling within the provisions of Article 2 to which they are parties may submit applications to the Commission.

2. If the Commission judges an application admissible and is in possession of all the available evidence, and no action under Article 10 has been taken against the agreement, decision or concerted practice in question, then it shall publish as soon as possible in the *Official Journal of the European Communities* a summary of the application and invite all interested third parties to submit their comments to the Commission within thirty days. Such publication shall have regard to the legitimate interest of undertakings in the protection of their business secrets.

3. Unless the Commission notifies applicants, within ninety days from the date of such publication in the *Official Journal of the European Communities*, that there are serious doubts as to the applicability of Article 5, the agreement, decision or concerted practice shall be deemed exempt, in so far as it conforms with the description given in the application, from the prohibition for the time already elapsed and for a maximum of three years from the date of publication in the *Official Journal of the European Communities*.

If the Commission finds, after expiry of the ninety-day time limit, but before the expiry of the three-year period, that the conditions for applying Article 5 are not satisfied, it shall issue a decision declaring that the prohibition in Article 2 is applicable. Such decision may be retroactive where the parties concerned have given inaccurate information or where they abuse the exemption from the provisions of Article 2.

4. If, within the ninety-day time limit, the Commission notifies applicants as referred to in the first subparagraph of paragraph 3, it shall examine whether the provisions of Article 2 and of Article 5 are satisfied.

If it finds that the provisions of Article 2 and of Article 5 are satisfied it shall issue a decision applying Article 5. The decision shall indicate the date from which it is to take effect. This date may be prior to that of the application.

Article 13 Duration and revocation of decisions applying Article 5

1. Any decision applying Article 5 taken under Article 11 (4) or under the second subparagraph of Article 12 (4) shall indicate the period for which it is to be valid; normally such period shall not be less than six years. Conditions and obligations may be attached to the decision.

2. The decision may be renewed if the conditions for applying Article 5 continue to be satisfied.

3. The Commission may revoke or amend its decision or prohibit specified acts by the parties:

(a) where there has been a change in any of the facts which were basic to the making of the decision;

(b) where the parties commit a breach of any obligation attached to the decision;

(c) where the decision is based on incorrect information or was induced by deceit;

(d) where the parties abuse the exemption from the provisions of Article 2 granted to them by the decision.

In cases falling within (b), (c) or (d), the decision may be revoked with retroactive effect.

Article 14 Decisions applying Article 6

1. Any agreement, decision or concerted practice covered by Article 2 in respect of which the parties seek application of Article 6 shall be notified to the Commission.

2. Any decision by the Commission to apply Article 6 shall have effect only from the date of its adoption. It shall state the period for which it is to be valid. Such period shall not exceed three years from the finding of a state of crisis by the Council provided for in Article 6 (2).

3. Such decision may be renewed by the Commission if the Council again finds, acting under the procedure provided for in Article 6 (2), that there is a state of crisis and if the other conditions laid down in Article 6 continue to be satisfied.

4. Conditions and obligations may be attached to the decision.

5. The decision of the Commission shall cease to have effect not later than six months from the coming into operation of the measures referred to in Article 6 (1).

6. The provisions of Article 13 (3) shall apply.

Article 15   Powers

Subject to review of its decision by the Court of Justice, the Commission shall have sole power:

– to impose obligations pursuant to Article 4 (2);
– to issue decisions pursuant to Articles 5 and 6.

The authorities of the Member States shall retain the power to decide whether any case falls within the provisions of Article 2 or Article 8, until such time as the Commission has initiated a procedure with a view to formulating a decision in the case in question or has sent notification as provided for in the first subparagraph of Article 12 (3).

Article 16   Liaison with the authorities of the Member States

1. The Commission shall carry out the procedures provided for in this Regulation in close and constant liaison with the competent authorities of the Member States; these authorities shall have the right to express their views on such procedures.

2. The Commission shall immediately forward to the competent authorities of the Member States copies of the complaints and applications, and of the most important documents sent to it or which it sends out in the course of such procedures.

3. An Advisory Committee on Restrictive Practices and Monopolies in the Transport Industry shall be consulted prior to the taking of any decision following upon a procedure under Article 10 or of any decision under the second subparagraph of Article 12 (3), or under the second subparagraph of paragraph 4 of the same Article, or under paragraph 2 or paragraph 3 of Article 14. The Advisory Committee shall also be consulted prior to adoption of the implementing provisions provided for in Article 29.

4. The Advisory Committee shall be composed of officials competent in the matter of restrictive practices and monopolies in transport. Each Member State shall appoint two officials to represent it, each of whom, if prevented from attending, may be replaced by some other official.

5. Consultation shall take place at a joint meeting convened by the Commission; such meeting shall be held not earlier than fourteen days after dispatch of the notice convening it. This notice shall, in respect of each case to be examined, be accompanied by a summary of the case together with an indication of the most important documents, and a preliminary draft decision.

6. The Advisory Committee may deliver an opinion notwithstanding that some of its members or their alternates are not present.

A report of the outcome of the consultative proceedings shall be annexed to the draft decision. It shall not be made public.

Article 17 Consideration by the Council of questions of principle concerning the common transport policy raised in connection with specific cases

1. The Commission shall not give a decision in respect of which consultation as laid down in Article 16 is compulsory until after the expiry of twenty days from the date on which the Advisory Committee has delivered its Opinion.

2. Before the expiry of the period specified in paragraph 1, any Member State may request that the Council be convened to examine with the Commission any question of principle concerning the common transport policy which such Member State considers to be involved in the particular case for decision.

The Council shall meet within thirty days from the request by the Member State concerned for the sole purpose of considering such questions of principle.

The Commission shall not give its decision until after the Council meeting.

3. Further, the Council may at any time, at the request of a Member State or of the Commission, consider general questions raised by the implementation of the competition policy in the transport sector.

4. In all cases where the Council is asked to meet to consider under paragraph 2 questions of principle or under paragraph 3 general questions, the Commission shall, for the purposes of this Regulation, take into account the policy guidelines which emerge from that meeting.

Article 18 Inquiries into transport sectors

1. If trends in transport, fluctuations in or inflexibility of transport rates, or other circumstances, suggest that competition in transport is being restricted or distorted within the common market in a specific geographical area, or over one or more transport links, or in respect of the carriage of passengers or goods belonging to one or more specific categories, the Commission may decide to conduct a general inquiry into the sector concerned, in the course of which it may request transport undertakings in that sector to supply the information and documentation necessary for giving effect to the principles formulated in Articles 2 to 8.

2. When making inquiries pursuant to paragraph 1, the Commission shall also request undertakings or groups of undertakings whose size

suggests that they occupy a dominant position within the common market or a substantial part thereof to supply such particulars of the structure of the undertakings and of their behaviour as are requisite to an appraisal of their position in the light of the provisions of Article 8.

3. Article 16 (2) to (6) and Articles 17, 19, 20 and 21 shall apply.

Article 19 Requests for information

1. In carrying out the duties assigned to it by this Regulation, the Commission may obtain all necessary information from the Governments and competent authorities of the Member States and from undertakings and associations of undertakings.

2. When sending a request for information to an undertaking or association of undertakings, the Commission shall at the same time forward a copy of the request to the competent authority of the Member State in whose territory the seat of the undertakings is situated.

3. In its request, the Commission shall state the legal basis and the purpose of the request, and also the penalties provided for in Article 22 (1) (b) for supplying incorrect information.

4. The owners of the undertakings or their representatives and, in the case of legal persons, companies or firms, or of associations having no legal personality, the person authorised to represent them by law or by their constitution, shall be bound to supply the information requested.

5. Where an undertaking or association of undertakings does not supply the information requested within the time limit fixed by the Commission, or supplies incomplete information, the Commission shall by decision require the information to be supplied. The decision shall specify what information is required, fix an appropriate time limit within which it is to be supplied and indicate the penalties provided for in Article 22 (1) (b) and Article 23 (1) (c), and the right to have the decision reviewed by the Court of Justice.

6. The Commission shall at the same time forward a copy of its decision to the competent authority of the Member State in whose territory the seat of the undertaking or association of undertakings is situated.

Article 20 Investigations by the authorities of the Member States

1. At the request of the Commission, the competent authorities of the Member States shall undertake the investigations which the Commission considers to be necessary under Article 21 (1), or which it has

ordered by decision pursuant to Article 21 (3). The officials of the competent authorities of the Member States responsible for conducting these investigations shall exercise their powers upon production of an authorisation in writing issued by the competent authority of the Member State in whose territory the investigation is to be made. Such authorisation shall specify the subject matter and purpose of the investigation.

2. If so requested by the Commission or by the competent authority of the Member State in whose territory the investigation is to be made, the officials of the Commission may assist the officials of such authority in carrying out their duties.

Article 21   Investigating powers of the Commission

1. In carrying out the duties assigned to it by this Regulation, the Commission may undertake all necessary investigations into undertakings and associations of undertakings. To this end the officials authorised by the Commission are empowered:

(a) to examine the books and other business records;
(b) to take copies of or extracts from the books and business records;
(c) to ask for oral explanations on the spot;
(d) to enter any premises, land and vehicles of undertakings.

2. The officials of the Commission authorised for the purpose of these investigations shall exercise their powers upon production of an authorisation in writing specifying the subject matter and purpose of the investigation and the penalties provided for in Article 22 (1) (c) in cases where production of the required books or other business records is incomplete.

In good time before the investigation, the Commission shall inform the competent authority of the Member State in whose territory the same is to be made of the investigation and of the identity of the authorised officials.

3. Undertakings and associations of undertakings shall submit to investigations ordered by decision of the Commission. The decision shall specify the subject matter and purpose of the investigation, appoint the date on which it is to begin and indicate the penalties provided for in Article 22 (1) (c) and Article 23 (1) (d) and the right to have the decision reviewed by the Court of Justice.

4. The Commission shall take decisions referred to in paragraph 3 after consultation with the competent authority of the Member State in whose territory the investigation is to be made.

5. Officials of the competent authority of the Member State in whose territory the investigation is to be made, may at the request of such authority or of the Commission, assist the officials of the Commission in carrying out their duties.

6. Where an undertaking opposes an investigation ordered pursuant to this Article, the Member State concerned shall afford the necessary assistance to the officials authorised by the Commission to enable them to make their investigation. Member States shall, after consultation with the Commission, take the necessary measures to this end before 1 January 1970. [New Member States shall, after consulting the Commission, take the necessary measures to this end within six months from the date of accession.][1]

Article 22   Fines

1. The Commission may by decision impose on undertakings or associations of undertakings fines of from one hundred to five thousand units of account where, intentionally or negligently:

  (a) they supply incorrect or misleading information in an application pursuant to Article 12 or in a notification pursuant to Article 14; or
  (b) they supply incorrect information in response to a request made pursuant to Article 18 or to Article 19 (3) or (5), or do not supply information within the time limit fixed by a decision taken under Article 19 (5); or
  (c) they produce the required books or other business records in incomplete form during investigations under Article 20 or Article 21, or refuse to submit to an investigation ordered by decision issued in implementation of Article 21 (3).

2. The Commission may by decision impose on undertakings or associations of undertakings fines of from one thousand to one million units of account, or a sum in excess thereof but not exceeding 10% of the turnover in the preceding business year of each of the undertakings participating in the infringement, where either intentionally or negligently:

  (a) they infringe Article 2 or Article 8; or
  (b) they commit a breach of any obligation imposed pursuant to Article 13 (1) or Article 14 (4).

---

1 Added by Annex 1 to the Act of Accession annexed to the Treaty of Accession signed on 22 January 1972.

In fixing the amount of the fine, regard shall be had both to the gravity and to the duration of the infringement.

3. Article 16 (3) to (6) and Article 17 shall apply.

4. Decisions taken pursuant to paragraphs 1 and 2 shall not be of a criminal law nature.

Article 23   Periodic penalty payments

1. The Commission may by decision impose on undertakings or associations of undertakings periodic penalty payments of from fifty to one thousand units of account per day, calculated from the date appointed by the decision, in order to compel them:

- (a) to put an end to an infringement of Article 2 or Article 8 of this Regulation the termination of which it has ordered pursuant to Article 11 or to comply with an obligation imposed pursuant to Article 4 (2);
- (b) to refrain from any act prohibited under Article 13 (3);
- (c) to supply complete and correct information which it has requested by decision taken pursuant to Article 19 (5);
- (d) to submit to an investigation which it has ordered by decision taken pursuant to Article 21 (3).

2. Where the undertakings or associations of undertakings have satisfied the obligation which it was the purpose of the periodic penalty payment to enforce, the Commission may fix the total amount of the periodic penalty payment at a lower figure than that which would arise under the original decision.

3. Article 16 (3) to (6) and Article 17 shall apply.

Article 24   Review by the Court of Justice

The Court of Justice shall have unlimited jurisdiction within the meaning of Article 172 of the Treaty to review decisions whereby the Commission has fixed a fine or periodic penalty payment; it may cancel, reduce or increase the fine or periodic penalty payment imposed.

Article 25   Unit of account

For the purpose of applying Articles 23 to 24 the unit of account shall be that adopted in drawing up the budget of the Community in accordance with Articles 207 and 209 of the Treaty.

Article 26 Hearing of the parties and of third persons

1. Before taking decisions as provided for in Articles 11, 12 (3), second subparagraph, and 12 (4), 13 (3), 14 (2) and (3), 22 and 23, the Commission shall give the undertakings or associations of undertakings concerned the opportunity of being heard on the matters to which the Commission has taken objection.

2. If the Commission or the competent authorities of the Member States consider it necessary, they may also hear other natural or legal persons. Applications to be heard on the part of such persons where they show a sufficient interest shall be granted.

3. Where the Commission intends to give negative clearance pursuant to Article 5 or Article 6, it shall publish a summary of the relevant agreement, decision or concerted practice and invite all interested third parties to submit their observations within a time limit which it shall fix being not less than one month. Publication shall have regard to the legitimate interest of undertakings in the protection of their business secrets.

Article 27 Professional secrecy

1. Information acquired as a result of the application of Articles 18, 19, 20 and 21 shall be used only for the purpose of the relevant request or investigation.

2. Without prejudice to the provisions of Articles 26 and 28, the Commission and the competent authorities of the Member States, their officials and other servants shall not disclose information acquired by them as a result of the application of this Regulation and of the kind covered by the obligation of professional secrecy.

3. The provisions of paragraphs 1 and 2 shall not prevent publication of general information or surveys which do not contain information relating to particular undertakings or associations of undertakings.

Article 28 Publication of decisions

1. The Commission shall publish the decisions which it takes pursuant to Articles 11, 12 (3), second sub-paragraph, 12 (4), 13 (3) and 14 (2) and (3).

2. The publication shall state the names of the parties and the main content of the decision; it shall have regard to the legitimate interest of undertakings in the protection of their business secrets.

Article 29 Implementing provisions

The Commission shall have power to adopt implementing provisions concerning the form, content and other details of complaints pursuant to Article 10, applications pursuant to Article 12, notifications pursuant to Article 14 (1) and the hearings provided for in Article 26 (1) and (2).

Article 30 Entry into force, existing agreements

1. This Regulation shall enter into force on 1 July 1968.

2. Notwithstanding the provisions of paragraph 1, Article 8 shall enter into force on the day following the publication of this Regulation in the *Official Journal of the European Communities*.

3. The prohibition in Article 2 shall apply from 1 January 1969 to all agreements, decisions and concerted practices falling within Article 2 which were in existence at the date of entry into force of this Regulation or which came into being between that date and the date of publication of this Regulation in the *Official Journal of the European Communities*.

4. Paragraph 3 shall not be invoked against undertakings or associations of undertakings which, before the day following publication of this Regulation in the *Official Journal of the European Communities*, shall have terminated any agreements, decisions or concerted practices to which they are party.

Article 31 Review of the Regulation

1. Within six months of the conclusion of discussions with the third countries signatories to the Revised Convention for the Navigation of the Rhine; the Council, on a proposal from the Commission, shall make any amendments to this Regulation which may prove necessary in the light of the obligations arising out of the Revised Convention for the Navigation of the Rhine.

2. The Commission shall submit to the Council, before 1 January 1971, a general report on the operation of this Regulation and, before 1 July 1971, a proposal for a Regulation to make the necessary amendments to this Regulation.

This Regulation shall be binding in its entirety and directly applicable in all Member States.

Done at Brussels, 19 July 1968.

For the Council
The President
O. L. SCALFARO

REGULATION (EEC) No 2821/71 OF THE COUNCIL
of 20 December 1971
on application of Article 85 (3) of the Treaty to categories of agreements, decisions and concerted practices

THE COUNCIL OF THE EUROPEAN COMMUNITIES,

Having regard to the Treaty establishing the European Economic Community, and in particular Article 87 thereof;

Having regard to the proposal from the Commission;

Having regard to the Opinion of the European Parliament;

Having regard to the Opinion of the Economic and Social Committee;

Whereas Article 85 (1) of the Treaty may in accordance with Article 85 (3) be declared inapplicable to categories of agreements, decisions and concerted practices which fulfil the conditions contained in Article 85 (3);

Whereas the provisions for implementation of Article 85 (3) must be adopted by way of regulation pursuant to Article 87;

Whereas the creation of a common market requires that undertakings be adapted to the conditions of the enlarged market and whereas co-operation between undertakings can be a suitable means of achieving this;

Whereas agreements, decisions and concerted practices for co-operation between undertakings which enable the undertakings to work more rationally and adapt their productivity and competitiveness to the enlarged market may, in so far as they fall within the prohibition contained in Article 85 (1), be exempted therefrom under certain conditions; whereas this measure is necessary in particular as regards agreements, decisions and concerted practices relating to the application of standards and types, research and development of products or processes up to the stage of industrial application, exploitation of the results thereof and specialisation;

Whereas it is desirable that the Commission be enabled to declare by way of regulation that the provisions of Article 85 (1) do not apply to those categories of agreements, decisions and concerted practices, in order to make it easier for undertakings to co-operate in ways which are economically desirable and without adverse effect from the point of view of competition policy;

Whereas it should be laid down under what conditions the Commission, in close and constant liaison with the competent authorities of the Member States, may exercise such powers;

Whereas under Article 6 of Regulation No 17[1] the Commission may provide that a decision taken in accordance with Article 85 (3) of the Treaty shall apply with retroactive effect; whereas it is desirable that the Commission be empowered to issue regulations whose provisions are to the like effect;

Whereas under Article 7 of Regulation No 17 agreements, decisions and concerted practices may by decision of the Commission be exempted from prohibition, in particular if they are modified in such manner that Article 85 (3) applies to them; whereas it is desirable that the Commission be enabled to grant by regulation like exemption to such agreements, decisions and concerted practices if they are modified in such manner as to fall within a category defined in an exempting regulation;

Whereas the possibility cannot be excluded that, in a specific case, the conditions set out in Article 85 (3) may not be fulfilled; whereas the Commission must have power to regulate such a case in pursuance of Regulation No 17 by way of decision having effect for the future;

HAS ADOPTED THIS REGULATION:

Article 1

1. Without prejudice to the application of Regulation No 17 the Commission may, by regulation and in accordance with Article 85 (3) of the Treaty, declare that Article 85 (1) shall not apply to categories of agreements between undertakings, decisions of associations of undertakings and concerted practices which have as their object:

(a) the application of standards or types;
(b) the research and development of products or processes up to the stage of industrial application, and exploitation of the results, including provisions regarding industrial property rights and confidential technical knowledge;
(c) specialisation, including agreements necessary for achieving it.

2. Such regulation shall define the categories of agreements, decisions and concerted practices to which it applies and shall specify in particular:

(a) the restrictions or clauses which may, or may not, appear in the agreements, decisions and concerted practices;
(b) the clauses which must be contained in the agreements, decisions and concerted practices or the other conditions which must be satisfied.

---

1 Page 318, above.

Article 2

1. Any regulation pursuant to Article 1 shall be made for a specified period.

2. It may be repealed or amended where circumstances have changed with respect to any of the facts which were basic to its being made; in such case, a period shall be fixed for modification of the agreements, decisions and concerted practices to which the earlier regulation applies.

Article 3

A regulation pursuant to Article 1 may provide that it shall apply with retroactive effect to agreements, decisions and concerted practices to which, at the date of entry into force of that regulation, a decision issued with retroactive effect in pursuance of Article 6 of Regulation No 17 would have applied.

Article 4

1. A regulation pursuant to Article 1 may provide that the prohibition contained in Article 85 (1) of the Treaty shall not apply, for such period as shall be fixed by that regulation, to agreements, decisions and concerted practices already in existence on 13 March 1962 which do not satisfy the conditions of Article 85 (3), where:

- within six months from the entry into force of the regulation, they are so modified as to satisfy the said conditions in accordance with the provisions of the regulation; and
- the modifications are brought to the notice of the Commission within the time limit fixed by the regulation.

[A Regulation adopted pursuant to Article 1 may lay down that the prohibition referred to in Article 85 (1) of the Treaty shall not apply, for the period fixed in the same Regulation, to agreements and concerted practices which existed at the date of accession and which, by virtue of accession, come within the scope of Article 85 and do not fulfil the conditions set out in Article 85 (3).][1]

2. Paragraph 1 shall apply to agreements, decisions and concerted practices which had to be notified before 1 February 1963, in accordance with Article 5 of Regulation No 17, only where they have been so notified before that date.

[Paragraph 1 shall be applicable to those agreements and concerted practices which, by virtue of the accession, come within the scope of Article 85 (1) of the Treaty and for which notification before 1 July

---

1 Added by Regulation 2743/72, OJ 1972 L291/144.

1973 is mandatory, in accordance with Articles 5 and 25 of Regulation No 17, only if notification was given before that date.]¹

3. The benefit of the provisions laid down pursuant to paragraph 1 may not be claimed in actions pending at the date of entry into force of a regulation adopted pursuant to Article 1; neither may it be relied on as grounds for claims for damages against third parties.

Article 5

Before making a regulation, the Commission shall publish a draft thereof to enable all persons and organisations concerned to submit their comments within such time limit, being not less than one month, as the Commission shall fix.

Article 6

1. The Commission shall consult the Advisory Committee on Restrictive Practices and Monopolies:

(a) before publishing a draft regulation;
(b) before making a regulation.

2. Paragraphs 5 and 6 of Article 10 of Regulation No 17, relating to consultation with the Advisory Committee, shall apply by analogy, it being understood that joint meetings with the Commission shall take place not earlier than one month after dispatch of the notice convening them.

Article 7

Where the Commission, either on its own initiative or at the request of a Member State or of natural or legal persons claiming a legitimate interest, finds that in any particular case agreements, decisions or concerted practices to which a regulation made pursuant to Article 1 of this Regulation applies have nevertheless certain effects which are incompatible with the conditions laid down in Article 85 (3) of the Treaty, it may withdraw the benefit of application of that regulation and take a decision in accordance with Articles 6 and 8 of Regulation No 17, without any notification under Article 4 (1) of Regulation No 17 being required.

This Regulation shall be binding in its entirety and directly applicable in all Member States.

Done at Brussels, 20 December 1971.

For the Council
The President
M. PEDINI

---

1 Added by Regulation 2743/72, OJ 1972 L291/144.

REGULATION (EEC) No 2779/72 OF THE COMMISSION
of 21 December 1972
on the application of Article 85 (3) of the Treaty to categories of specialisation agreements

THE COMMISSION OF THE EUROPEAN COMMUNITIES,

Having regard to the Treaty establishing the European Economic Community, and in particular Articles 87 and 155 thereof;

Having regard to Council Regulation (EEC) No 2821/71 of 20 December 1971[1] on application of Article 85 (3) of the Treaty to categories of agreements, decisions and concerted practices;

Having regard to the Opinions of the Advisory Committee on Restrictive Practices and Monopolies delivered pursuant to Article 6 of Regulation (EEC) No 2821/71;

Whereas under Regulation (EEC) No 2821/71 the Commission has power to apply Article 85 (3) of the Treaty by regulation to certain categories of agreements, decisions and concerted practices relating to specialisation, including agreements necessary for achieving it, which fall within Article 85 (1);

Whereas, since the adoption of such a Regulation would not conflict with the application of Regulation No 17, the right of undertakings to apply in individual cases to the Commission for a declaration under Article 85 (3) of the Treaty would not thereby be affected;

Whereas agreements for the specialisation of production may fall within the prohibition contained in Article 85 (1);

Whereas agreements for the specialisation of production lead in general to an improvement in the production or distribution of goods, because the undertakings can concentrate on the manufacture of certain products, thus operate on a more rational basis and offer these products at more favourable prices; whereas it is to be anticipated that, with effective competition, consumers will receive a fair share of the profit resulting therefrom;

Whereas this Regulation must determine what restrictions on competition may be included in a specialisation agreement; whereas the restrictions on competition provided for in this Regulation are, in general, indispensable for the purpose of ensuring that the desired benefits accrue to undertakings and consumers; whereas it may be left to the contracting parties to decide which of these provisions they include in their agreements;

---

1 Page 318, above.

Whereas in order to ensure that competition is not eliminated in respect of a substantial part of the goods in question, this Regulation applies only if the share of the market held by the participating undertakings and the size of the undertakings themselves do not exceed a specified limit;

Whereas this Regulation should also apply to specialisation agreements made prior to its entry into force;

HAS ADOPTED THIS REGULATION:

Article 1

Pursuant to Article 85 (3) it is hereby declared that, subject as provided in this Regulation, until 31 December 1977 Article 85 (1) of the Treaty shall not apply to agreements whereby, with the object of specialisation, undertakings mutually bind themselves for the duration of the agreements not to manufacture certain products or cause them to be manufactured by other undertakings, and to leave it to the other contracting parties to manufacture such products or cause them to be manufactured by other undertakings.

Article 2

1. Apart from the obligation referred to in Article 1, no other restriction on competition shall be imposed on the contracting parties save the following:

(a) the obligation not to conclude with other undertakings specialisation agreements relating to identical products or to products considered by consumers to be similar by reason of their characteristics, price or use, except with the consent of the other contracting parties;

(b) the obligation to supply the other contracting parties with the products which are the subject of specialisation, and in so doing to observe minimum standards of quality;

(c) the obligation to purchase products which are the subject of specialisation solely from the other contracting parties, except where more favourable terms of purchase are available elsewhere and the other contracting parties are not prepared to offer the same terms;

(d) the obligation to grant to the other contracting parties the exclusive right to distribute the products which are the subject of specialisation so long as those parties do not—in particular by the exercise of industrial property rights or of other rights and measures—limit the opportunities, for intermediaries or consumers, of purchasing the products to which the agreement relates from other dealers within the common market.

2. Article 1 shall apply notwithstanding that the following obligations are imposed:

(a) the obligation to maintain minimum stocks of the products which are the subject of specialisation and of replacement parts for them;

(b) the obligation to provide after-sale and guarantee services for the products which are the subject of specialisation.

Article 3

1. Article 1 shall apply only:

(a) if the products which are the subject of specialisation represent in any member country not more than 10 per cent of the volume of business done in identical products or in products considered by consumers to be similar by reason of their characteristics, price or use; and

(b) if the aggregate annual turnover of the participating undertakings does not exceed 150 million units of account.

2. For purposes of applying paragraph 1 the unit of account shall be that adopted in drawing up the budget of the Community in accordance with Articles 207 and 209 of the Treaty.

3. Article 1 of this Regulation shall continue to apply notwithstanding that in any two consecutive financial years the share of the market or the turnover is greater than as specified in paragraph 1, provided the excess is not more than 10%.

Article 4

The aggregate turnover within the meaning of Article 3 (1) (b) shall be calculated by adding together the turnover achieved during the last financial year in respect of all products and services:

1. by the undertakings which are parties to the agreement;

2. by undertakings in respect of which the undertakings which are parties to the agreement hold:

   - at least 25% of the capital or of the working capital whether directly or indirectly; or
   - at least half the voting rights; or
   - the power to appoint at least half the members of the supervisory board, board of management or bodies legally representing the undertaking; or
   - the right to manage the affairs of the undertaking.

3. by undertaking which hold in an undertaking which is a party to the agreement:

   - at least 25% of the capital or of the working capital whether directly or indirectly; or
   - at least half the voting rights; or
   - the power to appoint at least half the members of the supervisory board, board of management or bodies legally representing the undertaking; or
   - the right to manage the affairs of the undertaking.

In calculating aggregate turnover no account shall be taken of dealings between the undertakings which are parties to the agreement.

Article 5

The Commission shall examine whether Article 7 of Regulation (EEC) No 2821/71 applies in any specific case, in particular where there is reason to believe that rationalisation is not yielding significant results or that consumers are not receiving a fair share of the resulting profit.

Article 6

The non-applicability of Article 85 (1) provided for in Article 1 of this Regulation shall have retroactive effect from the time when the conditions requisite for the application of this Regulation were satisfied. In the case of agreements which, prior to 18 January 1972, were compulsorily notifiable, the time aforesaid shall not be earlier than the day of notification.

Article 7

Articles 1 to 6 of this Regulation shall apply by analogy to decisions by associations of undertakings and to concerted practices.

Article 8

This Regulation shall enter into force on 1 January 1973.

This Regulation shall be binding in its entirety and directly applicable in all Member States.

Done at Brussels, 21 December 1972.

For the Commission
The President
S. L. MANSHOLT

REGULATION (EEC) No. 2988/74 OF THE COUNCIL
of 26 November 1974

concerning limitation periods in proceedings and the enforcement of sanctions under the rules of the European Economic Community relating to transport and competition

THE COUNCIL OF THE EUROPEAN COMMUNITIES,

Having regard to the Treaty establishing the European Economic Community, and in particular Articles 75, 79 and 87 thereof;

Having regard to the proposal from the Commission;

Having regard to the Opinion of the European Parliament;[1]

Having regard to the Opinion of the Economic and Social Committee;[2]

Whereas under the rules of the European Economic Community relating to transport and competition the Commission has the power to impose fines, penalties and periodic penalty payments on undertakings or associations of undertakings which infringe Community law relating to information or investigation, or to the prohibition on discrimination, restrictive practices and abuse of dominant position; whereas those rules make no provision for any limitation period;

Whereas it is necessary in the interests of legal certainty that the principle of limitation be introduced and that implementing rules be laid down; whereas, for the matter to be covered fully, it is necessary that provision for limitation be made not only as regards the power to impose fines or penalties, but also as regards the power to enforce decisions, imposing fines, penalties or periodic penalty payments; whereas such provisions should specify the length of limitation periods, the date on which time starts to run and the events which have the effect of interrupting or suspending the limitation period; whereas in this respect the interests of undertakings and associations of undertakings on the one hand, and the requirements imposed by administrative practice, on the other hand, should be taken into account;

Whereas this Regulation must apply to the relevant provisions of Regulation No 11 concerning the abolition of discrimination in transport rates and conditions, in implementation of Article 79 (3) of the Treaty[3] establishing the European Economic Community, of Regulation No 17:[4] first Regulation implementing Articles 85 and 86 of the Treaty, and of Council Regulation (EEC) No 1017/68[5] of 19 July

---

1 OJ 1972 C 129/10.
2 OJ 1972 C 89/21.
3 OJ 1960 52/1121.

4 OJ 1962 13/204.
5 OJ 1968 L175/1.

1968 applying rules of competition to transport by rail, road and inland waterway; whereas it must also apply to the relevant provisions of future regulations in the fields of European Economic Community law relating to transport and competition,

HAS ADOPTED THIS REGULATION:

Article 1   Limitation periods in proceedings

1. The power of the Commission to impose fines or penalties for infringements of the rules of the European Economic Community relating to transport or competition shall be subject to the following limitation periods:

   (a) three years in the case of infringements of provisions concerning applications or notifications of undertakings or associations of undertakings, requests for information, or the carrying out of investigations;

   (b) five years in the case of all other infringements.

2. Time shall begin to run upon the day on which the infringement is committed. However, in the case of continuing or repeated infringements, time shall begin to run on the day on which the infringement ceases.

Article 2   Interruption of the limitation period in proceedings

1. Any action taken by the Commission, or by any Member State, acting at the request of the Commission, for the purpose of the preliminary investigation or proceedings in respect of an infringement shall interrupt the limitation period in proceedings. The limitation period shall be interrupted with effect from the date on which the action is notified to at least one undertaking or association of undertakings which have participated in the infringement.

Actions which interrupt the running of the period shall include in particular the following:

   (a) written requests for information by the Commission, or by the competent authority of a Member State acting at the request of the Commission; or a Commission decision requiring the requested information;

   (b) written authorizations to carry out investigations issued to their officials by the Commission or by the competent authority of any Member State at the request of the Commission; or a Commission decision ordering an investigation;

   (c) the commencement of proceedings by the Commission;

   (d) notification of the Commission's statement of objections.

2. The interruption of the limitation period shall apply for all the undertakings or associations of undertakings which have participated in the infringement.

3. Each interruption shall start time running afresh. However, the limitation period shall expire at the latest on the day on which a period equal to twice the limitation period has elapsed without the Commission having imposed a fine or a penalty; that period shall be extended by the time during which limitation is suspended pursuant to Article 3.

Article 3   Suspension of the limitation period in proceedings

The limitation period in proceedings shall be suspended for as long as the decision of the Commission is the subject of proceedings pending before the Court of Justice of the European Communities.

Article 4   Limitation period for the enforcement of sanctions

1. The power of the Commission to enforce decisions imposing fines, penalties or periodic payments for infringements of the rules of the European Economic Community relating to transport or competition shall be subject to a limitation period of five years.

2. Time shall begin to run on the day on which the decision becomes final.

Article 5   Interruption of the limitation period for the enforcement of sanctions

1. The limitation period for the enforcement of sanctions shall be interrupted:

(a) by notification of a decision varying the original amount of the fine, penalty or periodic penalty payments or refusing an application for variation;

(b) by any action of the Commission, or of a Member State at the request of the Commission, for the purpose of enforcing payments of a fine, penalty or periodic penalty payment.

2. Each interruption shall start time running afresh.

Article 6   Suspension of the limitation period for the enforcement of sanctions

The limitation period for the enforcement of sanctions shall be suspended for so long as:

(a) time to pay is allowed; or
(b) enforcement of payment is suspended pursuant to a decision of
the Court of Justice of the European Communities.

Article 7   Application to transitional cases

This Regulation shall also apply in respect of infringements committed before it enters into force.

Article 8   Entry into force

This Regulation shall enter into force on 1 January 1975.

This Regulation shall be binding in its entirety and directly applicable in all Member States.

Done at Brussels, 26 November 1974.

For the Council
The President
J. LECANUET

Appendix III

Proposals for Regulations

DRAFT REGULATION (EEC) OF THE COUNCIL
on the control of concentrations between undertakings[1]

THE COUNCIL OF THE EUROPEAN COMMUNITIES,

Having regard to the Treaty establishing the European Economic Community and in particular to Articles 87 and 235 thereof;

Having regard to the proposal from the Commission;

Having regard to the Opinion of the European Parliament;

Having regard to the Opinion of the Economic and Social Committee;

Whereas, for the achievement of the objectives of the Treaty establishing the European Economic Community, Article 3 (f) requires the Community to institute 'a system ensuring that competition in the common market is not distorted';

Whereas analysis of market structures in the Community shows that the concentration process is becoming faster and that the degree of concentration is growing in such manner that the preservation of effective competition in the common market and the objective set out in Article 3 (f) could be jeopardised;

Whereas concentration must therefore be made subject to a systematic control arrangement;

Whereas the Treaty already provides some powers of action of the Community to this end;

Whereas Article 86 applies to concentrations effected by undertakings holding a dominant position in the common market or in a substantial part of it which strengthen such position to such an extent that the resulting degree of dominance would substantially restrict competition;

Whereas the power of action aforesaid extends only to such concentrations, as would result in only undertakings remaining in the market whose conduct depended on the undertaking which had effected the concentration; whereas it does not extend to the prevention of such concentrations;

---

1 OJ 1973 C92/1. *Submitted to the Council by the Commission on 20 July 1973.*

Whereas additional powers of action must be provided for to make it possible to act against other concentrations which may distort competition in the common market and to establish arrangements for controlling them before they are effected;

Whereas under Article 235 of the Treaty the Community may give itself the powers of action necessary for the attainment of its objectives;

Whereas, to institute a system ensuring that competition in the common market is not distorted, it is necessary, in so far as trade between Member States may be affected, to submit to control arrangements such concentrations which give undertakings the power to prevent effective competition in the common market or in a substantial part of it, or which strengthen such a power;

Whereas the power to prevent effective competition must be appraised by reference, in particular, to the scope for choice available to suppliers and consumers, the economic and financial power of the undertakings concerned, the structure of the markets affected and supply and demand trends for the relevant goods or services;

Whereas concentrations which, by reason of the small significance of turnover and market share of the undertakings concerned, are not likely to impede the preservation of effective competition in the common market may be excluded from this Regulation;

Whereas it may be found necessary, for the purpose of reconciling objectives to be attained in the common interest of the Community, especially within the frame of common policies, to exempt certain concentrations from incompatibility, under conditions and obligations to be determined case by case;

Whereas the Commission should be entitled to take decisions to prevent or terminate concentrations which are incompatible with the common market, decisions designed to re-establish conditions of effective competition and decisions declaring that a particular concentration may be considered to be compatible with the common market; whereas the Commission should be given exclusive jurisdiction in this matter, subject to review by the Court of Justice;

Whereas, to ensure effective supervision, prior notification of major concentrations and the suspension of concentrations by undertakings should be made obligatory;

Whereas a time limit within which the Commission must commence proceedings in respect of a concentration notified to it and a time-limit within which it must give a final decision on the incompatibility of a concentration with the common market should be laid down;

Whereas undertakings concerned must be accorded the right to be heard by the Commission as soon as proceedings have commenced, and third parties showing a sufficient interest must be given the opportunity of submitting their comments;

Whereas the Commission must have the assistance of the Member States and must also be empowered to require information to be given and to carry out the necessary investigations in order to examine concentrations in the light of provisions of this Regulation;

Whereas compliance with this Regulation must be enforceable by means of fines and periodic penalty payments; whereas it is desirable to confer upon the Court of Justice, pursuant to Article 172, unlimited jurisdiction to that extent;

Whereas this Regulation should extend both to concentrations which constitute abuses of dominant positions and to concentrations which give the undertakings concerned the power to prevent effective competition in the common market; whereas it should therefore be stipulated that Regulations (EEC) Nos 17 and 1017/68 no longer apply to concentrations from the date of entry into force of the present Regulation.

HAS ADOPTED THIS REGULATION:

Article 1 Basic provisions

1. Any transaction which has the direct or indirect effect of bringing about a concentration between undertakings or groups of undertakings, at least one of which is established in the common market, whereby they acquire or enhance the power to hinder effective competition in the common market or in a substantial part thereof, is incompatible with the common market in so far as the concentration may affect trade between Member States.

The power to hinder effective competition shall be appraised by reference in particular to the extent to which suppliers and consumers have a possibility of choice, to the economic and financial power of the undertakings concerned, to the structure of the markets affected, and to supply and demand trends for the relevant goods or services.

2. Paragraph 1 shall not apply where:

– the aggregate turnover of the undertakings participating in the concentration is less than 200 million units of account and
– the goods or services concerned by the concentration do not account in any Member State for more than 25% of the turnover in identical goods or services or in goods or services which, by reason of their characteristics, their price and the use for which they are intended, may be regarded as similar by the consumer.

3. Paragraph 1 may, however, be declared inapplicable to concentrations which are indispensable to the attainment of an objective which is given priority treatment in the common interest of the Community.

Article 2 Definition of concentration

1. The concentrations referred to in Article 1 are those whereby a person or an undertaking or a group of persons or undertakings, acquires control of one or several undertakings.

2. Control is constituted by rights or contracts which, either separately or jointly, and having regard to the considerations of fact or law involved, make it possible to determine how an undertaking shall operate, and particularly by:

(1) Ownership or the right to use all or part of the assets of an undertaking;

(2) Rights or contracts which confer power to influence the composition, voting or decisions of the organs of an undertaking;

(3) Rights or contracts which make it possible to manage the business of an undertaking;

(4) Contracts made with an undertaking concerning the computation or appropriation of its profits;

(5) Contracts made with an undertaking concerning the whole or an important part of supplies or outlets, where the duration of these contracts or the quantities to which they relate exceed what is usual in commercial contracts dealing with those matters.

3. Control is acquired by persons, undertakings or groups of persons or undertakings who:

(1) Are holders of the rights or entitled to rights under the contracts concerned;

(2) While not being holders of such rights or entitled to rights under such contracts, have power to exercise the rights deriving therefrom;

(3) In a fiduciary capacity own assets of an undertaking or shares in an undertaking, and have power to exercise the rights attaching thereto.

4. Control of an undertaking is not constituted where, upon formation of an undertaking or increase of its capital, banks or financial institutions acquire shares in that undertaking with a view to selling them on the market, provided that they do not exercise voting rights in respect of those shares.

Article 3 Powers of decision of the Commission

1. When the Commission finds that a concentration is caught by Article 1 (1) and that the conditions laid down in Article 1 (3) are not

satisfied, it shall issue a decision declaring the concentration to be incompatible with the common market.

2. The decision by which the Commission declares a concentration to be incompatible within the meaning of paragraph 1 shall not automatically render null and void the legal transactions relating to such operation.

3. Where a concentration has already been put into effect, the Commission may require, by decision taken under paragraph 1 or by a separate decision, the undertakings, or assets acquired or concentrated to be separated or the cessation of common control or any other action that may be appropriate in order to restore conditions of effective competition.

4. When the Commission finds that a concentration is caught by Article 1 (1) and that the conditions laid down in Article 1 (3) are satisfied, it shall issue a decision declaring Article 1 (1) to be inapplicable; conditions and obligations may be attached thereto.

5. Subject to review by the Court of Justice, the Commission shall have sole power to take the decisions provided for in this Article.

Article 4   Prior notifications of concentrations

1. Concentrations shall be notified to the Commission before they are put into effect, where the aggregate turnover of the undertakings concerned is not less than one thousand million units of account.

2. Where concentrations proposed by an undertaking or a group of undertakings have already reached or exceeded the amounts referred to in paragraph 1, they shall be exempted from the obligation of prior notification, if the turnover of the undertaking, the control of which they propose to acquire is less than 30 million units of account.

3. The obligation to notify shall be discharged by the person or undertaking or the group of persons or undertakings which proposes to acquire control within the meaning of Article 2.

4. Concentrations which are not caught by paragraph 1 may nevertheless be notified to the Commission before they are put into effect.

Article 5   Detailed rules for calculating turnover and market shares

1. (a) The aggregate turnover specified in Articles 1 (2) and 4 (1) shall be obtained by adding together the turnover for the last financial year for all goods and services of:

   (i) the undertakings participating in the concentration;

    (ii) the undertakings and groups of undertakings which control the undertakings participating in the concentration within the meaning of Article 2;

    (iii) the undertakings or groups of undertakings controlled within the meaning of Article 2 by the undertakings participating in the concentration.

(b) The market shares referred to in Article 1 (2) near those held in the last financial year by all the undertakings listed in subparagraph (a) above.

2. In place of turnover as specified in Articles 1 (2) and 4 (1) and in paragraph 1 of this Article, the following shall be used:

– for banking and financial institutions: one tenth of their assets;
– for insurance companies: the value of the premiums received by them.

Article 6   Commencement of proceedings

1. Where the Commission considers that a concentration is likely to become the subject of a decision under Article 1 (1) or (3), it shall commence proceedings and so inform the undertakings in question and the competent authorities in the Member States.

2, As regards concentrations notified to it, the Commission shall commence proceedings within a period not exceeding 3 months unless the relevant undertakings agree to extend that period. The period of 3 months shall commence on the day following receipt of the notification, or if the information to be supplied with the notification is incomplete, on the day following the receipt of the complete information.

3. The Commission may commence proceedings after the expiry of the 3 months period where the information supplied by the undertakings in the notification is false or misleading.

4. Without prejudice to paragraph 3 a concentration notified to the Commission shall be presumed to be compatible with the common market if the Commission does not commence proceedings before expiration of the period specified in paragraph 2.

Article 7   Suspension of the effecting of the concentration

1. Undertakings shall not put into effect a concentration notified to the Commission before the end of the time limit provided for in Article 6 (2) unless the Commission informs them before the end of the time limit that it is not necessary to commence proceedings.

2. Where the Commission commences proceedings it may by decision require the undertakings to suspend the concentration until it has decided whether the concentration is compatible with the common market or has closed the proceedings.

Article 8 Communications of objections and hearings

1. Before taking decisions as provided for in Articles 3, 7, 13 and 14, the Commission shall give the undertakings concerned the opportunity of being heard on the matters to which the Commission has taken objection. The same opportunity shall be given to associations of undertakings concerned before decisions before being taken as provided for in Articles 13 and 14.

2. If the Commission or the competent authorities of the Member States consider it necessary, the Commission may also hear other natural or legal persons. Applications to be heard on the part of such persons shall, where they show a sufficient interest, be granted.

3. Articles 2, 3, 4, 7, 8, 9, 10 and 11 of Regulation No. 99/63/ EEC shall be applied.

Article 9 Closure of proceedings

If, after having commenced proceedings, the Commission considers that there are no grounds for action against a concentration, it shall close the proceedings and so inform the undertakings concerned and the competent authorities of the Member States.

Article 10 Requests for information

1. In carrying out the duties assigned to it by this Regulation, the Commission may obtain all necessary information from the governments and competent authorities of the Member States and from undertakings and associations of undertakings.

2. When sending a request for information to an undertaking or association of undertakings, the Commission shall at the same time forward a copy of the request to the competent authority of the Member State in whose territory the seat of the undertaking or association of undertakings is situated.

3. In its request the Commission shall state the legal basis and the purpose of the request and also the penalties provided for in Article 13 (1) (b) for supplying incorrect information.

4. The owners of the undertakings or their representatives and, in the case of legal persons, companies or firms, or of associations having no legal personality, the persons authorized to represent them by law or by their constitution, shall supply the information requested.

5. Where an undertaking or association of undertakings does not supply the information requested within the time limit fixed by the Commission, or supplies incomplete information, the Commission shall by decision require the information to be supplied. The decision shall specify what information is required, fix an appropriate time limit within which it is to be supplied and mention the penalties provided for in Article 13 (1) (b) and Article 14 (1) (a) and the right to have the decision reviewed by the Court of Justice.

6. The Commission shall at the same time forward a copy of its decision to the competent authority of the Member State in whose territory the seat of the undertaking or association of undertakings is situated.

Article 11   Investigations by the authorities of the Member States

1. At the request of the Commission, the competent authorities of the Member States shall undertake the investigations which the Commission considers to be necessary under Article 12 (1), or which it has ordered by decision pursuant to Article 12 (3). The officials of the competent authorities of the Member States responsible for conducting these investigations shall exercise their powers upon production of an authorization in writing issued by the competent authority of the Member State in whose territory the investigation is to be made. Such authorization shall specify the subject matter and purpose of the investigation.

2. If so requested by the Commission or by the competent authority of the Member State in whose territory the investigation is to be made, officials of the Commission may assist the officials of such authority in carrying out their duties.

Article 12   Investigation powers of the Commission

1. In carrying out the duties assigned to it by this Regulation, the Commission may undertake all necessary investigations into undertakings and associations of undertakings.

To this end the officials authorized by the Commission are empowered:

(a) to examine the books and other business records;
(b) to take or demand copies of or extracts from the books and business records;
(c) to ask for oral explanations on the spot;
(d) to enter any premises, land and means of transport of undertakings.

2. The officials of the Commission authorized to carry out these investigations shall exercise their powers upon production of an authorization in writing specifying the subject matter and purpose of the investigation and the penalties provided for in Article 13 (1) (c) in cases where production of the required books or other business records is incomplete. In good time before the investigation, the Commission shall inform the competent authority of the Member State in whose territory the investigation is to be made of the investigation and of the identity of the authorized officials.

3. Undertakings and associations of undertakings shall submit to investigations ordered by decision of the Commission. The decision shall specify the subject matter and purpose of the investigation, appoint the date on which it is to begin and indicate the penalties provided for in Article 13 (1) (c) and Article 14 (1) (b) and the right to have the decision reviewed by the Court of Justice.

4. The Commission shall take decisions referred to in paragraph 3 after consultation with the competent authority of the Member State in whose territory the investigation is to be made.

5. Officials of the competent authority of the Member State in whose territory the investigation is to be made may, at the request of such authority or of the Commission, assist the officials of the Commission in carrying out their duties.

6. Where an undertaking opposes an investigation ordered pursuant to this Article, the Member State concerned shall afford the necessary assistance to the officials authorized by the Commission to enable them to make their investigation. Member States shall, after consultation with the Commission, take the necessary measures to this end before . . . .

Article 13   Fines

1. The Commission may by decision impose on undertakings and associations of undertakings fines of from 1 000 to 50 000 units of account where intentionally or negligently:

(a) they supply incorrect or misleading information in a notification pursuant to Article 4;

(b) they supply incorrect information in response to a request made pursuant to Article 10 or fail to supply information within the time limit fixed by a decision taken pursuant to Article 10,

(c) they produce the required books or other business records in incomplete form during investigations under Article 11 or 12, or refuse to submit to an investigation ordered by decision taken pursuant to Article 12.

2. The Commission may by decision impose on natural or legal persons fines of from 1 000 to 1 000 000 units of account where, either intentionally or negligently, they commit a breach of the obligation to notify under Article 4.

3. The Commission may by decision impose fines not exceeding 10% of the value of the reorganized assets where undertakings either intentionally or negligently, conclude an unlawful concentration before the end of the time limit provided for in Article 6 (2) or in spite of a decision taken by the Commission under Articles 3 (1) or 7 (2).

Article 14 Periodic penalty payments

1. The Commission may by decision impose on undertakings or associations of undertakings periodic penalty payments up to 25 000 units of account for each day of the delay calculated from the date appointed by the decision, in order to compel them:

(a) to supply complete and correct information which it has requested by decision taken pursuant to Article 10;
(b) to submit to an investigation which it has ordered by decision taken pursuant to Article 12.

2. The Commission may by decision impose on such undertakings periodic penalty payments up to 50 000 units of account for each day of the delay, calculated from the day appointed by the decision, in order to compel them to apply the measures resulting from a decision taken pursuant to Article 3 (3).

Article 15 Review by the Court of Justice

The Court of Justice shall have unlimited jurisdiction within the meaning of Article 17 of the Treaty to review decisions whereby the Commission has fixed a fine or periodic penalty payment; it may cancel, reduce or increase the fine or periodic penalty payment imposed.

Article 16 Professional secrecy

1. Information acquired as a result of the application of Articles 10, 11 and 12 shall be used only for the purpose of the relevant request or investigation.

2. The Commission and the competent authorities of the Member States, their officials and other servants shall not disclose information acquired by them as a result of the application of this Regulation and of the kind covered by the obligation of professional secrecy.

3. The provisions of paragraphs 1 and 2 shall not prevent publication of general information or surveys which do not contain information relating to particular undertakings or associations of undertakings.

Article 17 Time limits and publication of decisions

1. (a) Decisions under Article 3 (1) and (4) shall be taken within 9 months following the date of commencement of proceedings, save where there is agreement with the relevant undertakings to extend that period.

   (b) The period of 9 months shall not apply where the Commission is obliged to request information by decision taken pursuant to Article 10 or require an investigation by decision taken pursuant to Article 12.

2. The Commission shall publish the decisions which it takes pursuant to Article 3.

3. The publication shall state the names of the parties and the main content of the decision; it shall have regard to the legitimate interest of undertakings in the protection of their business secrets.

Article 18 Unit of account

For the purpose of this Regulation the unit of account shall be that used in drawing up the budget of the Community in accordance with Articles 207 and 209 of the Treaty.

Article 19 Liaison with the authorities of the Member States

1. The Commission shall forthwith transmit to the competent authorities of the Member States a copy of the notifications together with the most important documents lodged with the Commission pursuant to this Regulation.

2. The Commission shall carry out the procedure set out in this Regulation in close and constant cooperation with the competent authorities of the Member States; such authorities shall have the right to express their views upon that procedure, and in particular to request the Commission to commence proceedings under Article 6.

3. The Advisory Committee on Restrictive Practices and Monopolies shall be consulted prior to the taking of any decision under Articles 3, 13 and 14.

4. The Advisory Committee shall consist of officials having responsibility for restrictive practices and monopolies. Each Member State shall appoint an official to represent it; he may be replaced by another official where he is unable to act.

5. Consultation shall take place, at a meeting convened at the invitation of the Commission, not earlier than fourteen days following dispatch of the invitation. A summary of the facts together with the most important documents and a preliminary draft of the decision to be taken, shall be sent with the invitation.

6. The Committee may deliver an opinion even if certain members are absent and unrepresented. The outcome of the consultation shall be annexed to the draft decision. The minutes shall not be published.

Article 20　Exclusive application of this Regulation

Regulations (EEC) No 17 and 1017/68 shall not apply to the concentrations covered by this Regulation.

Article 21　Implementing provisions

The Commission shall have power to adopt implementing provisions concerning the form, content and other details of notifications pursuant to Article 4 of this Regulation.

Article 22

This Regulation shall enter into force . . . .

This Regulation shall be binding in its entirety and directly applicable in all Member States.

Communications of the Commission

COMMUNICATION[1]
(on exclusive dealing contracts with commercial agents)

I. The Commission considers that contracts made with commercial agents in which those agents undertake, for a specified part of the territory of the Common Market,

- to negotiate transactions on behalf of an enterprise,
  or
- to conclude transactions in the name and on behalf of an enterprise,
  or
- to conclude transactions in their own name and on behalf of this enterprise,

do not fall under the prohibition in Article 85 (1) of the Treaty.

It is essential in this case that the contracting party, described as a commercial agent, should, in fact, be such, by the nature of his functions, and that he should neither undertake nor engage in activities proper to an independent trader in the course of commercial operations. The Commission regards as the decisive criterion, which distinguishes the commercial agent from the independent trader, the agreement – express or implied – which deals with responsibility for the financial risks bound up with the sale or with the performance of the contract. Thus the Commission's assessment is not governed by the name used to describe the representative. Except for the usual *del credere* guarantee, a commercial agent must not by the nature of his functions assume any risk resulting from the transaction. If he does assume such risks, his function becomes economically akin to that of an independent trader and he must therefore be treated as such for the purposes of the rules of competition. In such a situation, the exclusive dealing contracts must be regarded as agreements made with independent traders.

The Commission considers that there is particular reason to assume

---

1 JO 1962 139/2921. Translation taken from "Competition Law in the EEC and the ECSC", published by the Office for Official Publications of the European Communities; available from HMSO.

that the function performed is that of an independent trader where the contracting party described as a commercial agent:

- is required to keep or does in fact keep, as his own property, a considerable stock of the products covered by the contract, or
- is required to organise maintain or ensure at his own expense a substantial service to customers free of charge, or does in fact organise, maintain or ensure such a service, or
- can determine or does in fact determine prices or terms of business.

II. Unlike the contracts with commercial agents covered here, exclusive dealing contracts with independent traders may well fall within Article 85 (1). In the case of such exclusive contracts the restriction of competition lies either in the limitation of supply, when the vendor undertakes to supply a given product to one purchaser only, or in the limitation of demand, when the purchaser undertakes to obtain a given product from only one vendor. Where there are reciprocal undertakings competition is being restricted by both parties. The question whether a restriction of competition of this nature may affect trade between Member States depends on the circumstances of the particular case.

On the other hand, the Commission takes the view that the test for prohibition under Article 85 (1) is not met by exclusive dealing contracts with commercial agents, since these contracts have neither the object nor the effect of preventing, restricting or distorting competition within the Common Market. The commercial agent only performs an auxiliary function in the market for goods. In that market he acts on the instructions and in the interest of the enterprise on whose behalf he is operating. Unlike the independent trader, he himself is neither a purchaser nor a vendor, but seeks purchasers or vendors in the interest of the other party to the contract, who is the person doing the buying or selling. In this type of exclusive dealing contract, the selling or buying enterprise does not cease to be a competitor; it merely uses an auxiliary, i.e. the commercial agent, to distribute or acquire products on the market.

The legal status of commercial agents is determined, more or less uniformly, by statute law in most of the Member States and by case law in others. The characteristic feature which all commercial agents have in common is their function as auxiliaries in the transaction of business. The powers of commercial agents are subject to the civil law provisions of agency. Within the limits of these provisions, the other party to the contract – who is the person selling or buying – is free to decide the product and the territory in respect of which he is willing to give these powers to his agent.

In addition to the competitive situation on the markets where the commercial agent functions as an auxiliary for the other party to the contract, the particular market on which the commercial agents offer their services for the negotiation or conclusion of transactions has to be considered. The obligation assumed by the agent – to work exclusively for one principal for a certain period of time – entails a limitation of supply on that market; the obligation assumed by the other party to the contract – to appoint him sole agent for a given territory – involves a limitation of demand on the market. Nevertheless, the Commission views these restrictions as a result of the special obligation between the commercial agent and his principal to protect each other's interests and therefore considers that they involve no restriction of competition.

The object of this Notice is to give enterprises some indication of the considerations by which the Commission will be guided when interpreting Article 85 (1) of the Treaty and applying it to exclusive dealing contracts with commercial agents. The situation having thus been clarified, it will as a general rule no longer be useful for enterprises to obtain negative clearance for the agreements mentioned, nor will it be necessary to have the legal position established through a Commission decision on an individual case; this also means that notification will no longer be necessary for agreements of this type. This Notice is without prejudice to any interpretation that may be given by other competent authorities and in particular by the courts.

COMMUNICATION[1]

(concerning agreements, decisions and concerted practices in the field of cooperation between enterprises)

Questions are frequently put to the Commission of the European Communities on the attitude it intends to take up, for purposes of implementation of the competition rules contained in the Treaties of Rome and Paris, with regard to cooperation between enterprises.

In this Notice, it endeavours to provide guidance which, though it cannot be exhaustive, may prove useful to enterprises in the correct interpretation, in particular, of Article 85 (1) of the EEC Treaty and Article 65 (1) of the ECSC Treaty.

I. The Commission welcomes cooperation among small and medium-sized enterprises where such cooperation enables them to

---

1 JO 1968 C75/3; translation taken from [1968] CMLR D5.

work more efficiently and increase their productivity and competitiveness on a larger market. While considering that its duty is to facilitate cooperation among small and medium-sized enterprises in particular, the Commission recognises that cooperation among large enterprises, too, can be economically desirable without presenting difficulties from the angle of competition policy.

Article 85 (1) of the Treaty establishing the European Economic Community (EEC Treaty) and Article 65 (1) of the Treaty establishing the European Coal and Steel Community (ECSC Treaty) provide that all agreements, decisions and concerted practices (hereafter referred to as "agreements") which have as their object or effect the prevention, restriction or distortion of competition within the Common Market (hereafter referred to as "restraints of competition") are prohibited as incompatible with the Common Market; under Article 85 (1) of the EEC Treaty this applies, however, only if such agreements may affect trade between Member States.

The Commission feels that, in the interests of the small and medium-sized enterprises in particular, it should give some indication of the considerations by which it will be guided when interpreting Article 85 (1) of the EEC Treaty and Article 65 (1) of the ECSC Treaty and applying them to certain cooperation arrangements between enterprises, and should indicate which of these arrangements in its opinion do not come under these provisions. This Notice applies to all enterprises, irrespective of their size.

There may also be forms of cooperation between enterprises other than those listed below which are not prohibited by Article 85 (1) of the EEC Treaty or Article 65 (1) of the ECSC Treaty. This applies in particular if the market position of the enterprises cooperating with each other is in the aggregate too weak for the cooperation agreement between them to lead to an appreciable restraint of competition in the Common Market and – where the agreements fall within the scope of Article 85 of the EEC Treaty – to affect trade between Member States.

It is also pointed out that other forms of cooperation between enterprises or agreements containing additional clauses, to which the rules of competition of the Treaties apply, can be exempted pursuant to Article 85 (3) of the EEC Treaty or be authorised pursuant to Article 65 (2) of the ECSC Treaty.

The Commission intends to clarify rapidly, by means of suitable decisions in individual cases or by general notices, the status of the various forms of cooperation in accordance with the provisions of the Treaties.

No general statement can be made at this stage on the application of

Article 86 of the EEC Treaty on the abuse of dominant positions within the Common Market or in a part of it. The same applies to Article 66 (7) of the ECSC Treaty.

As a result of this Notice, as a general rule, it should no longer be useful for enterprises to obtain negative clearance, as defined by Article 2 of Regulation No. 17[1], for the agreements listed, nor should it be necessary to have the legal position established through a Commission decision on an individual case. This also means that notification with this end in view will no longer be necessary for agreements of this type. However, if it is doubtful whether in an individual case an agreement between enterprises restricts competition or if other forms of cooperation between enterprises which, in the view of the enterprises, do not restrict competition are not listed here, the enterprises are free to apply, where the matter comes under Article 85 (1) of the EEC Treaty, for negative clearance, or to file as a precautionary measure, where Article 65 (1) of the ECSC Treaty is the relevant provision, an application on the basis of Article 65 (2) of that Treaty.

This Notice is without prejudice to any interpretation to be given by the Court of Justice of the European Communities.

II. The Commission takes the view that the following agreements do not restrict competition.

1. *Agreements having as their sole object:*

(a) *An exchange of opinion or experience,*
(b) *Joint market research,*
(c) *The joint carrying out of comparative studies of enterprises or industries,*
(d) *The joint preparation of statistics and calculation models.*

Agreements whose sole purpose is the joint procurement of information which the various enterprises need to determine their future market behaviour freely and independently, or the use by each of the enterprises of a joint advisory body, do not have as their object or effect the restriction of competition. But if the freedom of action of the enterprises is restricted or if their market behaviour is coordinated either expressly or through concerted practices, there may be restraint of competition.[2] This is in particular the case where concrete recom-

---

1 Page 318, above.
2 In the *S.C.P.A. – Kali und Salz* Decision, 11 May 1973, OJ 1973 L217/3; [1973] CMLR D219, the Commission held that the exchange of information between the French (SCPA) and German (Kali und Salz) trade associations of producers of potassium salts and their respective sales agents infringed art. 85 (1), both as being ancillary to or as a means of giving effect to a market sharing agreement which also limited production and contained other restrictions, and also as leading to a joint planning of production and to market sharing. See also the Commission's decision in *Re Agreements between Manufacturers of Glass Containers*, 15 May 1974, OJ 1974 L160/1; [1974] 2 CMLR D50.

mendations are made or where conclusions are given such a form that they induce at least some of the participating enterprises to behave in an identical manner on the market.

The exchange of information may take place between the enterprises themselves or through a body acting as an intermediary. It is, however, particularly difficult to distinguish between information which has no bearing on competition on the one hand and behaviour in restraint of competition on the other, if there are special bodies which have to register orders, turnover figures, investments and prices, so that it can as a rule not be automatically assumed that Articles 85 (1) of the EEC Treaty or Article 65 (1) of the ECSC Treaty do not apply to them. A restraint of competition may occur in particular on an oligopolistic market for homogeneous products.

In the absence of more far-reaching cooperation between the participating enterprises, joint market research and comparative studies of different enterprises and industries to collect information and ascertain facts and market conditions do not in themselves affect competition. Other arrangements of this type, as for instance the joint establishment of economic and structural analyses, so obviously do not affect competition that there is no need to mention them specifically.

Calculation models containing specified rates of calculation must be regarded as recommendations that may lead to restraints of competition.[1]

2. *Agreements having as their sole object:*

(a) *Cooperation in accounting matters,*
(b) *Joint provision of credit guarantees,*
(c) *Joint debt-collecting associations,*
(d) *Joint business or tax consultant agencies.*

In such cases, the cooperation involved covers fields that are not concerned with the supply of goods and services or the economic decisions of the enterprises taking part, and thus does not lead to restraints of competition.

Cooperation in accounting matters is neutral from the point of view of competition as it only assists in the technical handling of the accounting work. Nor is the creation of credit guarantee associations affected

---

1 In *Re Agreements between Manufacturers of Glass Containers,* 15 May 1974, OJ 1974 L160/1; [1974] 2 CMLR D50, the Commission considered a scheme consisting of a list and definition of various factors to be taken into account when calculating costs, which enabled competitors to reach similar if not identical cost curves. Paragraph II, 1 (d) of the Communication was held not to apply, however, on the basis that while the scheme might be a calculation model it was only one part of a series of agreements for restricting competition.

by the competition rules, since it does not modify the relationship between supply and demand.

Joint debt-collecting associations whose work is not confined to the collection of outstanding payments in line with the intentions and conditions of the participating enterprises, or which fix prices or exert in any other way an influence on price formation, may restrict competition. Application of uniform terms by all participating firms may constitute a concerted practice, and the making of joint price comparisons may have the same result. In this connection, no objection can be raised against the use of standardized printed forms; their use must, however, not be combined with an understanding or tacit agreement on uniform prices, rebates or conditions of sale.

3. *Agreements having as their sole object:*

(a) *The joint implementation of research and development projects,*
(b) *The joint placing of research and development contracts,*
(c) *The sharing out of research and development projects among participating enterprises.*

In the field of research, too, the mere exchange of experience and results serves for information only and does not restrict competition. It therefore need not be mentioned expressly.

Agreements on the joint execution of research work or the joint development of the results of research up to the stage of industrial application do not affect the competitive position of the parties. This also applies to the sharing of research fields and development work if the results are available to all participating enterprises.

However, if the enterprises enter into commitments which restrict their own research and development activity or the utilization of the results of joint work so that they do not have a free hand with regard to their own research and development outside the joint projects, this may constitute an infringement of the Treaties' rules of competition. Where firms do not carry out joint research work, any contractual obligations or concerted practices binding them to refrain from research work of their own either completely or in certain sectors may result in a restraint of competition.

The sharing out of sectors of research without an understanding providing for mutual access to the results is to be regarded as a case of specialization that may restrict competition.

There may also be a restraint of competition if agreements are concluded or corresponding concerted practices applied with regard to the practical exploitation of the results of research and development work carried out jointly, particularly if the participating enterprises undertake or agree to manufacture only the products or types of product developed jointly or to share out future production among themselves.

It is of the essence of joint research that the results should be exploited by the participating enterprises in proportion to their participation. If the participation of certain enterprises is confined to a specific sector of the joint research project or to the provision of only limited financial assistance, there is no restraint of competition – in so far as there has been any joint research at all – if the results of research are made available to these enterprises only in relation with the degree of their participation. There may, however, be a restraint of competition if certain participating enterprises are excluded from exploitation of the results, either entirely or to an extent not commensurate with their participation.

If the granting of licences to third parties is expressly or tacitly excluded, there may be a restraint of competition. However, the fact that research is carried out jointly warrants arrangements binding the enterprises to grant licences to third parties only by common agreement or by majority decision.

For the assessment of the compatibility of the agreement with the rules of competition, the legal status of the joint research and development work is immaterial.

4. *Agreements which have as their sole object the joint use of production facilities and storing and transport equipment*

These forms of cooperation do not restrict competition because they are confined to organization and technical arrangements for the use of the facilities. There may be a restraint of competition if the enterprises involved do not bear the cost of utilization of the installation or equipment themselves or if agreements are concluded or concerted practices applied regarding joint production or the sharing out of production or the establishment or running of a joint enterprise.

5. *Agreements having as their sole object the setting up of consortia for the joint execution of orders, where the participating enterprises do not compete with each other as regards the work to be done or where each of them by itself is unable to execute the orders*

Where enterprises do not compete with each other they cannot restrict competition between them by setting up consortia. This applies in particular to enterprises belonging to different industries but also to firms in the same industry to the extent that their contribution under the consortium consists only of goods or services which cannot be supplied by the other participating enterprises. It is not a question of whether the enterprises compete with each other in other sectors so much as whether in the light of the concrete circumstances of a particular case there is a possibility that in the foreseeable future they may compete with each other with regard to the products or services involved. If the absence of competition between the enterprises and the maintenance of this situation are based on agreements or concerted practices, there may be a restraint of competition.

But even in the case of consortia formed by enterprises which normally compete with each other there is no restraint of competition if the participating enterprises cannot execute a specific order by themselves. This applies in particular if, for lack of experience, specialized knowledge, capacity or financial resources, these enterprises, when working alone, have no chance of success or cannot finish the work within the required time-limit or cannot bear the financial risk.

Nor is there a restraint of competition if it is only by the setting up of a consortium that the enterprises are put in a position to make an attractive offer. There may, however, be a restraint of competition if the enterprises undertake to work solely in the framework of a consortium.

6. *Agreements having as their sole object:*

(a) *Joint selling arrangements,*
(b) *Joint after-sales and repairs service, provided the participating enterprises are not competitors with regard to the products or services covered by the agreement.*

As already explained in detail under heading 5, cooperation between enterprises cannot restrict competition if the firms are not in competition with each other.

Very often joint selling by small or medium-sized enterprises – even if they are competing with each other – does not entail an appreciable restraint of competition; it is, however, impossible to establish in this Notice any general criteria or to specify what enterprises may be deemed "small or medium-sized".

There is no joint after-sales and repair service if several manufacturers, without acting in concert with each other, arrange for an after-sales and repair service for their products to be provided by an enterprise which is independent of them. In such a case there is no restraint of competition even if the manufacturers are competitors.

7. *Agreements having joint advertising as their sole object*

Joint advertising is designed to draw the buyers' attention to the products of an industry or to a common brand; as such it does not restrict competition between the participating enterprises. However, if the participating enterprises are partly or wholly prevented, by agreements or concerted practices, from themselves advertising or if they are subjected to other restriction, there may be a restraint of competition.

8. *Agreements having as their sole object the use of a common label to designate a certain quality, where the label is available to all competitors on the same conditions*

Such associations for the joint use of a quality label do not restrict competition if other competitors, whose products objectively meet the stipulated quality requirements, can use the label on the same conditions as the members. Nor do the obligations to accept quality control of the products provided with the label, to issue uniform instructions for use, or to use the label for the products meeting the quality standards constitute restraints of competition. But there may be restraint of competition if the right to use the label is linked to obligations regarding production, marketing, price formation or obligations of any other type, as is for instance the case when the participating enterprises are obliged to manufacture or sell only products of guaranteed quality.

UK Legislation

THE REGISTRATION OF RESTRICTIVE TRADING AGREEMENTS (EEC DOCUMENTS) REGULATIONS 1973

(S.I. 1973 No. 950)

The Registrar of Restrictive Trading Agreements (in these regulations referred to as "the Registrar") in exercise of the powers conferred upon him by sections 11 and 19 of the Restrictive Trade Practices Act 1956 (hereinafter referred to as "the Act of 1956") and subsection (2) of section 10 of the European Communities Act 1972 hereby orders that the following regulations shall have effect:

1. – (1) These regulations may be cited as the Registration of Restrictive Trading Agreements (EEC Documents) Regulations 1973 and shall come into operation on the 25th June 1973.

(2) The Interpretation Act 1889 shall apply to the interpretation of these regulations as it applies to the interpretation of an Act of Parliament.

2. – (1) Where in relation to any agreement which is subject to registration under the Act of 1956 any such step or any such decision as is specified in paragraph (2) hereof is or has been taken or given under or for the purposes of any directly applicable Community provision affecting that agreement, there shall be delivered or sent to the Registrar by or on behalf of the parties to that agreement the information so specified in respect of that step or decision within 30 days of the taking or giving thereof or within 30 days of the coming into operation of these regulations, whichever is the later.

(2) The steps, decisions and information referred to are the following:

(a) applying for negative clearance for or notifying the agreement to the Commission of the European Communities—a copy of the application or notification submitted to the Commission;

415

(b) notification by the Commission to the parties to the agreement of the opportunity to be heard in relation to objections raised against them – a memorandum to that effect specifying the date of the notification;

(c) a decision of the Commission giving negative clearance in respect of the agreement – four copies of such part of the decision as sets out the effects thereof;

(d) a decision of the Commission pursuant to article 85 (3) of the EEC Treaty given in respect of the agreement – four copies of such part of the decision as sets out the effects thereof;

(e) a decision of the Commission finding infringement of article 85 of the EEC Treaty by the agreement – four copies of such part of the decision as sets out the effects thereof;

(f) a decision of the European Court relating to any decision of the Commission hereinbefore described – four copies of such part of the decision as sets out the effects thereof.

3. The particulars of an agreement subject to registration under the Act of 1956 to be entered or filed in the register shall include a copy of any such part of a decision of the Commission of the European Communities or the European Court affecting that agreement furnished in pursuance of regulation 2 hereof.

4. Anything required by these regulations to be delivered or sent to the Registrar shall be addressed to:

The Registrar of Restrictive Trading Agreements (Branch R)
    Chancery House
    Chancery Lane
    London WC2A 1SP.

Rupert Sich,
Registrar of Restrictive Trading Agreements.

22nd May 1973.

Index

BLOCK EXEMPTIONS. *See* CATEGORY EXEMPTIONS

BREACH OF STATUTORY DUTY
infringement of arts. 85 and 86. *See under* INFRINGEMENT OF ARTICLES 85 AND 86

BREWERY AGREEMENTS, 18, 259

BULLETIN OF THE EUROPEAN COMMUNITIES
recommendations published in, 288
source of information, 273

BUSINESS SECRETS. *See* SECRECY

BUYERS
dominant position of, 152, 164

C, FORM, 274, 304

CALCULATION MODELS
joint preparation of, Co-operation Communication, 80, 409

CANALS. *See* INLAND WATERWAYS

CATEGORY EXEMPTIONS
agreements for which exempting regulation may be made, 96–97
amended agreements, time-limits, 105–106
Commission's policy, 272
effect—
agreements registrable under RTPA, 139 *et seq.*
duration, 382
retroactive, 105–106, 114
exclusive dealing agreements, 97–108. *See also* EXCLUSIVE DISTRIBUTION AGREEMENTS
industrial property rights, bipartite, 96, 97
list of categories, 96–97
modified agreements, 105–106
notification unnecessary, 101
regulations exempting by category, 97
actions pending, effect on, 352–353
text, 354–359, 384–388
research agreements, 96
no exemption in force, 97
specialisation agreements. *See also* SPECIALISATION AGREEMENTS
regulation, 97, 108–115
standards application agreements, 96
no exemption in force, 97
two-party agreements—
exclusive dealings, 96–108
industrial property rights, 96–97
withdrawal of benefit—
Commission's powers, 107, 114
individual exemption possible, 107, 114

CEMENT INDUSTRY
examples of prohibited agreements, 38, 83, 86

CHANNEL ISLANDS, 29

CIRCULATION OF GOODS. *See* FREE MOVEMENT OF GOODS

CIVIL ACTIONS. *See also* DAMAGES AWARDS
appeals after referral to Court of Justice, 308
Commission's powers, in face of, 129
disadvantage of informal procedure, 273
third parties, by, 131–136

CIVIL CONSEQUENCES OF INFRINGEMENT. *See under* INFRINGEMENT OF ARTICLES 85 AND 86

COAL AND STEEL
competition rules, 27–28

COAL AND STEEL COMMUNITY TREATY
"control", notion of, 202
merger control, contrast with EEC, 12, 162, 196
products covered by, 27

COMMERCIAL AGENTS. *See* AGENTS, COMMERCIAL

COMMERCIAL UNDERTAKINGS
definition, 77

COMMISSION
actions against, in Court of Justice, 302–307
grounds, 303
time limit for, 304
actions by, time limit for, 301
administration of competition rules, 5, 250–251
attitude to agreements, informal expression, 273
consultations—
national authorities, 278
Restrictive Practices Committee, 285
transport, Restrictive Practices Committee, 372
decisions. *See* DECISIONS OF COMMISSION
departments—
co-operation between, 271
DG IV, 271
Legal Service, 271–272
documentary liaison with states, 274–275
exemption, individual, jurisdiction to grant, 81, 291. *See also* INDIVIDUAL EXEMPTION
failure to act, as appeal ground, 304

Printed in Great Britain
by Chapel River Press, Andover, Hants